D0570110

Excel® 2013
on**Demand**

WITHDRAWN

Steve Johnson

Perspection, Inc.

Que Publishing, 800 East 96th Street, Indianapolis, IN 46240 USA

Excel® 2013 on Demand

Copyright © 2013 by Perspection, Inc.

All rights reserved. No part of this book shall be reproduced, stored in a retrieval system, or transmitted by any means, electronic, mechanical, photocopying, recording, or otherwise, without written permission from the publisher. No patent liability is assumed with respect to the use of the information contained herein. Although every precaution has been taken in the preparation of this book, the publisher and author assume no responsibility for errors or omissions. Nor is any liability assumed for damages resulting from the use of the information contained herein.

Library of Congress Cataloging-in-Publication Data is on file

ISBN-13: 978-0-7897-5048-8
ISBN-10: 0-7897-5048-1

Printed and bound in the United States of America
First Printing: February 2013
16 15 14 13   4 3 2 1

Que Publishing offers excellent discounts on this book when ordered in quantity for bulk purchases or special sales.

For information, please contact: U.S. Corporate and Government Sales

   1-800-382-3419 or corpsales@pearsontechgroup.com

For sales outside the U.S., please contact: International Sales

   1-317-428-3341 or International@pearsontechgroup.com

Trademarks

All terms mentioned in this book that are known to be trademarks or service marks have been appropriately capitalized. Que cannot attest to the accuracy of this information. Use of a term in this book should not be regarded as affecting the validity of any trademark or service mark.

Microsoft and the Microsoft Office logo are registered trademarks of Microsoft Corporation in the United States and/or other countries.

Warning and Disclaimer

Every effort has been made to make this book as complete and as accurate as possible, but no warranty or fitness is implied. The authors and the publishers shall have neither liability nor responsibility to any person or entity with respect to any loss or damage arising from the information contained in this book.

Publisher
Paul Boger

Associate Publisher
Greg Wiegand

Executive Editor
Loretta Yates

Managing Editor
Steve Johnson

Author
Steve Johnson

Page Layout
James Teyler

Interior Designers
Steve Johnson
Marian Hartsough

Photographs
Tracy Teyler

Indexer
Katherine Stimson

Proofreader
Beth Teyler

Team Coordinator
Cindy Teeters

Acknowledgments

Perspection, Inc.

Excel 2013 on Demand has been created by the professional trainers and writers at Perspection, Inc. to the standards you've come to expect from Que publishing. Together, we are pleased to present this training book.

Perspection, Inc. is a software training company committed to providing information and training to help people use software more effectively in order to communicate, make decisions, and solve problems. Perspection writes and produces software training books, and develops multimedia and web-based training. Since 1991, we have written more than 130 computer books, with several bestsellers to our credit, and sold over 5 million books.

This book incorporates Perspection's training expertise to ensure that you'll receive the maximum return on your time. You'll focus on the tasks and skills that increase productivity while working at your own pace and convenience.

We invite you to visit the Perspection web site at:

www.perspection.com

Acknowledgments

The task of creating any book requires the talents of many hard-working people pulling together to meet impossible deadlines and untold stresses. We'd like to thank the outstanding team responsible for making this book possible: the writer, Steve Johnson; the production editor, James Teyler; the editor and proofreader, Beth Teyler; and the indexer, Katherine Stimson.

At Que publishing, we'd like to thank Greg Wiegand and Loretta Yates for the opportunity to undertake this project, Cindy Teeters for administrative support, and Lori Lyons for your production expertise and support.

Perspection

About the Author

Steve Johnson has written more than 80 books on a variety of computer software, including Adobe Edge Animate, Adobe Photoshop CS6, Adobe Dreamweaver CS6, Adobe InDesign CS6, Adobe Illustrator CS6, Adobe Flash Professional CS5, Microsoft Windows 8, Microsoft Office 2013 and 2010, Microsoft Office 2008 for the Macintosh, and Apple OS X Mountain Lion. In 1991, after working for Apple Computer and Microsoft, Steve founded Perspection, Inc., which writes and produces software training. When he is not staying up late writing, he enjoys coaching baseball, playing golf, gardening, and spending time with his wife, Holly, and three children, JP, Brett, and Hannah. Steve and his family live in Northern California, but can also be found visiting family all over the western United States.

We Want to Hear from You!

As the reader of this book, *you* are our most important critic and commentator. We value your opinion and want to know what we're doing right, what we could do better, what areas you'd like to see us publish in, and any other words of wisdom you're willing to pass our way.

As an associate publisher for Que, I welcome your comments. You can email or write me directly to let me know what you did or didn't like about this book—as well as what we can do to make our books better.

Please note that I cannot help you with technical problems related to the topic of this book. We do have a User Services group, however, where I will forward specific technical questions related to the book.

When you write, please be sure to include this book's title and author as well as your name, email address, and phone number. I will carefully review your comments and share them with the author and editors who worked on the book.

Email: feedback@quepublishing.com

Mail: Greg Wiegand
         Que Publishing
         800 East 96th Street
         Indianapolis, IN 46240 USA

For more information about this book or another Que title, visit our web site at *www.quepublishing.com*. Type the ISBN (excluding hyphens) or the title of a book in the Search field to find the page you're looking for.

Contents

4 Modifying Worksheets and Workbooks 115

5 Formatting a Worksheet 137

Introduction

Welcome to *Excel 2013 on Demand*, a visual quick reference book that shows you how to work efficiently with Microsoft Excel. This book provides complete coverage of basic to advanced Excel skills.

How This Book Works

You don't have to read this book in any particular order. We've designed the book so that you can jump in, get the information you need, and jump out. However, the book does follow a logical progression from simple tasks to more complex ones. Each task is presented on no more than two facing pages, which lets you focus on a single task without having to turn the page. To find the information that you need, just look up the task in the table of contents or index, and turn to the page listed. Read the task introduction, follow the step-by-step instructions in the left column along with screen illustrations in the right column, and you're done.

What's New

If you're searching for what's new in Excel 2013, just look for the icon: **New!**. The new icon appears in the table of contents and throughout this book so you can quickly and easily identify a new or improved feature in Excel 2013. A complete description of each new feature appears in the New Features guide in the back of this book.

Keyboard Shortcuts

Most menu commands have a keyboard equivalent, such as Ctrl+P, as a quicker alternative to using the mouse. A complete list of keyboard shortcuts is available on the web at *www.queondemand.com* or *www.perspection.com*.

How You'll Learn

How This Book Works

What's New

Keyboard Shortcuts

Step-by-Step Instructions

Real World Examples

Workshops

Microsoft Office Specialist

Get More on the Web

Step-by-Step Instructions

This book provides concise step-by-step instructions that show you "how" to accomplish a task. Each set of instructions includes illustrations that directly correspond to the easy-to-read steps. Also included in the text are time-savers, tables, and sidebars to help you work more efficiently or to teach you more in-depth information. A "Did You Know?" provides tips and techniques to help you work smarter, while a "See Also" leads you to other parts of the book containing related information about the task.

Easy-to-follow introductions focus on a single concept.

Illustrations match the numbered steps.

Numbered steps guide you through each task.

See Also points you to related information in the book.

Did You Know? alerts you to tips, techniques and related information.

Real World Examples

This book uses real world examples files to give you a context in which to use the task. By using the example files, you won't waste time looking for or creating sample files. You get a start file and a result file, so you can compare your work. Not every topic needs an example file, such as changing options, so we provide a complete list of the example files used through out the book. The example files that you need for project tasks along with a complete file list are available on the web at *www.queondemand.com* or *www.perspection.com.*

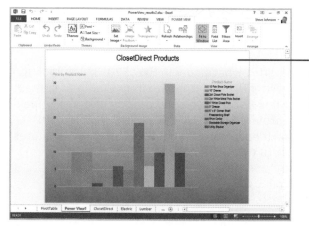

Real world examples help you apply what you've learned to other tasks.

Workshops

This book shows you how to put together the individual step-by-step tasks into in-depth projects with the Workshops. You start each project with a sample file, work through the steps, and then compare your results with a project results file at the end. The Workshop projects and associated files are available on the web at *www.queondemand.com* or *www.perspection.com.*

Workshops

Introduction

The Workshops are all about being creative and thinking outside of the box. These workshops will help your right-brain soar, while making your left-brain happy, by explaining why things work the way they do. Exploring possibilities is great fun; however, always stay grounded with knowledge of how things work.

Getting and Using the Project Files

Each project in the Workshops includes a start file to help you get started with the project, and a final file to provide you with the results of the project so you can see how well you accomplished the task.

Before you can use the project files, you need to download them from the web. You can access the files at *www.perspection.com* in the software downloads area. After you download the files from the web, uncompress the files into a folder on your hard drive to which you have easy access from your Microsoft Office program.

Project 1: Creating a Drop-Down List

Skills and Tools: Create a drop-down list

Entering data in a worksheet can be tedious and repetitive. To make the job easier and get consistent accurate data, you can create a drop-down list of entries you define. To create a drop-down list, you create a list of valid entries in a single column or row without blanks, define a name, and then use the List option in the Data Validation dialog box. To enter data using a drop-down list, click the cell with the defined drop-down list, click the list arrow, and then click the entry you want.

The Project

In this project, you'll learn how to create a drop-down list from a named range of cells for use in conditional formatting.

The Process

1. Open Excel 2013, open DropDown_start.xlsx, and then save it as DropDown.xlsx.

2. Click the Numbers tab.

1

The **Workshops** walks you through in-depth projects to help you put Microsoft Excel to work.

Microsoft Office Specialist

This book prepares you for the Microsoft Office Specialist (MOS) exam for Microsoft Excel 2013. Each MOS certification exam has a set of objectives, which are organized into broader skill sets. To prepare for the MOS certification exam, you should review and perform each task identified with a MOS objective to confirm that you can meet the requirements for the exam. Information about the MOS program is available in the back of this book. The MOS objectives and the specific pages that cover them are available on the web at *www.queondemand.com* or *www.perspection.com.*

Microsoft Office Specialist

About the MOS Program

The Microsoft Office Specialist (MOS) certification is the globally recognized standard for validating expertise with the Microsoft Office suite of business productivity programs. Earning an MOS certificate acknowledges you have the expertise to work with Microsoft Office programs. To earn the MOS certification, you must pass a certification exam for the Microsoft Office desktop applications of Microsoft Word, Excel, PowerPoint, Outlook, Access, OneNote, SharePoint, or Office 365. (The availability of Microsoft Office Specialist certification exams varies by program, program version, and language. Visit *www.microsoft.com* and search on *MOS* or *Microsoft Office Specialist* for exam availability and more information about the program.) The Microsoft Office Specialist program is the only Microsoft-approved program in the world for certifying proficiency with Microsoft Office programs.

What Does This Logo Mean?

It means that this book has been approved by the Microsoft Office Specialist program to be certified courseware for learning Microsoft Excel 2013 and preparing for the certification exam. This book will prepare you for the Microsoft Office Specialist exam for Microsoft Excel 2013. Each certification level, either Core or Expert, has a set of objectives, which are organized into broader skill sets. Content that pertains to a Microsoft Office Specialist objective is identified with the following objective number and the specific pages throughout this book:

EX13C-4.1
EX13C-2.2

521

Get More on the Web

In addition to the information in this book, you can also get more information on the web to help you get up to speed faster with Excel 2013. Some of the information includes:

Transition Helpers

◆ **Only New Features.** Download and print the new feature tasks as a quick and easy guide.

Productivity Tools

◆ **Keyboard Shortcuts.** Download a list of keyboard shortcuts to learn faster ways to get the job done.

More Content

◆ **Photographs.** Download photographs and other graphics to use in your Office documents.

◆ **More Content.** Download new content developed after publication. For example, you can download a chapter on SharePoint server and Office 365.

You can access these additional resources on the web at *www.perspection.com*.

Keyboard Shortcuts

k

Microsoft Excel 2013

If a command on the ribbon or a menu includes a keyboard reference, known as a **keyboard shortcut**, in a ScreenTip or next to the command name, you can perform the action by pressing and holding the first key, and then pressing the second key to perform the command quickly. In some cases, a keyboard shortcut uses three keys. Simply press and hold the first two keys, and then press the third key. For keyboard shortcuts in which you press one key immediately followed by another key, the keys to press are separated by a comma (,). Keyboard shortcuts provide an alternative to using the mouse and make it easy to perform repetitive commands.

Finding a Keyboard Shortcut

To help you find the keyboard shortcut you're looking for, the shortcuts are organized in categories and listed with page numbers.

Common Tasks

Cell Movement and Selection, 2	Format Cells, 5
Copy/Cut and Paste, 5	Help, 2
Dialog Boxes: Open and Save As, 4	Hide and Unhide, 4
File, 3	Insert, 4
Find and Replace, 4	Ribbon, 3
Font, 4	Work with SmartArt Graphics, 6
Format, 5	Undo and Redo, 6

Function Keys

Alt+Function, 7	Alt+Shift+Function, 8
Function, 6	Shift+Function, 7
Ctrl+Function, 7	Ctrl+Shift+Function, 7
Ctrl+Alt+Function, 8	

If you're searching for new keyboard shortcuts in Microsoft Excel 2013, just look for the letter: N. The N appears in the Keyboard Shortcuts table so you can quickly and easily identify new or changed shortcuts.

1

Additional content is available on the web. You can download keyboard shortcuts.

Getting Started with Excel

Introduction

Microsoft Excel 2013 is a spreadsheet program that you can use to track and analyze sales, create budgets, and organize finances—both business and personal. You can also use Excel to manage inventory, set up investment reports or create loan amortizations. Excel is a financial tool for performing calculations and other tasks automatically, which allows you to accomplish a variety of business or personal tasks in a fraction of the time it would take using pen and paper.

This chapter introduces you to the terminology and the basic Excel skills you can use in the program. In Excel, files are called **workbooks**. Each new workbook contains a default setting (which you can change) of three **worksheets**, which are similar to the pages in an accountant's ledger. You can format the worksheets for your specific project at hand, or you can download pre-made templates from Microsoft's Office Online web site.

With the results-oriented visual interface, you navigate through various tasks with a click of the mouse, or by using shortcut keys on your keyboard. Excel is set up with a tab-based Ribbon and dialog boxes that provide you with the tools you need when you need them to get tasks done. The customizable Quick Access Toolbar gives you easy access to commonly-used commands, such as Save and Print.

When you finish the design of your worksheet you can save it in a more efficient XML format or as a PDF or XPS document, send it through e-mail for review, or even collaborate and share it with co-workers using a SkyDrive or SharePoint site. Should something happen to your workbook or worksheets, Excel has a recovery feature designed to help recover your worksheet.

What You'll Do

Starting Excel

The two quickest ways to start Microsoft Excel are to select it on the Start screen (Win 8) (**New!**) or on the Start menu (Win 7). Excel lets you work the way you like and start programs with a click of a button. When you start Excel, a program window opens, displaying the Start screen (**New!**) where you can create or open a document in order to quickly get started.

Start Excel

1 Start Windows, if necessary, and then use the method for your Windows version.

◆ **Windows 8.** Display the Start screen; click or tap the **Start** button on the Charm bar.

◆ **Windows 7.** Click **Start** on the taskbar, point to **All Programs** (which changes to Back), and then point to **Microsoft Office**.

2 Click **Excel 2013**.

If Office asks you to activate the program, follow the instructions enter an account or product key. to complete the process.

TIMESAVER *To change the accounts, click the File tab, click Account, and then click the Switch Account link.*

Start screen   User name (account)

Did You Know?

You can create a program shortcut from the Start menu to the desktop. Right-click the Microsoft Excel 2013 program on the Start menu or screen. For Win 8, click the Pin To Taskbar button on the App bar. For Win 7, point to Send To, and then click Desktop (Create Shortcut).

You can start an Excel and open a workbook from an Explorer window. Double-clicking any Excel file icon in an Explorer window opens that file and Excel.

Excel 2013 System Requirements

Hardware/Software	Minimum (Recommended)
Computer Processor	1 gigahertz (Ghz) or faster x86 (32 bit) or x64 (64 bit) processor with SSE2
Operating System	Windows 7, Windows 8, Windows Server 2008 R2, or Windows Server 2012
Available RAM	1 GB (32 bit), 2 GB (64 bit)
Hard Drive	3 GB of available space
Monitor Resolution	1024 x 576
Video Card	Graphics hardware acceleration requires a DirectX10 graphics card
Browser	Microsoft IE 8, 9, or 10; Firefox 10.x or later; Apple Safari 5; or Google Chrome 17.x
.NET version	3.5, 4.0, or 4.5

Viewing the Excel Window

File tab
Click to access Excel file commands.

Quick Access Toolbar
Click to access commands on this customizable toolbar.

Tabs
Click to access tools and commands.

User Account
Click to access account options (**New!**).

Dialog Box Launcher
Click to open dialog boxes or task panes.

Ribbon
Commands and tools grouped by category onto different tabs.

Lists and Galleries
Click the down arrow to access lists and galleries.

Program window
Enter text and data here.

Status bar
Displays information about the active workbook.

View buttons
Use to switch between views.

Zoom controls
Use to zoom in or out using the slide, or the buttons.

Using the Ribbon

The **Ribbon** is a results oriented way of working in Excel 2013. The Ribbon is located at the top of the document window and is comprised of **tabs** that are organized by task or objects. The controls on each tab are organized into **groups**, or subtasks. The controls, or **command buttons**, in each group execute a command, or display a menu of commands or a drop-down gallery. Controls in each group provide a visual way to quickly make document changes. The File tab displays Backstage view, where you can access file-related commands.

If you prefer using the keyboard instead of the mouse to access commands on the Ribbon, Excel provides easy to use shortcuts. Simply press and release the [Alt] or [F10] key to display **KeyTips** over each feature in the current view, and then continue to press the letter shown in the KeyTip until you press the one that you want to use. To cancel an action and hide the KeyTips, press and release the [Alt] or [F10] key again. If you prefer using the keyboard shortcuts found in previous versions of Excel, such as Ctrl+P (for Print), all the keyboard shortcuts and keyboard accelerators work exactly the same in Excel 2013.

Tabs

Excel provides three types of tabs on the Ribbon. The first type is called a **standard** tab—such as File, Home, Insert, Page layout, Formulas, Data, Review, View, and Add-Ins—that you see whenever you start Excel. The second type is called a **contextual** tab—such as Picture Tools, Drawing, or Table—that appears only when they are needed based on the type of task you are doing. Excel recognizes what you're doing and provides the right set of tabs and tools to use when you need them. The third type is called a **program** tab that replaces the standard set of tabs when you switch to certain views or modes.

Live Preview

When you point to a gallery option, such as WordArt, on the Ribbon, Excel displays a **live preview** of the option change so that you can see what your change will look like before selecting it. The Paste Options button also displays a live preview for pasted content.

Display Options

If you want more display screen, you can collapse and expand the Ribbon as you need it. Click the Ribbon Display Options button (**New!**) to select an option: Auto-hide Ribbon, Show Tabs, or Show Tabs and Commands. Auto-hide Ribbon collapses the Ribbon until you click the top of the program. Show Tabs displays only tabs until you click a tab to show it. Show Tabs and Commands displays the Ribbon all the time.

> **TIMESAVER** *To collapse the Ribbon, click the Collapse the Ribbon button (Ctrl+F1) or double-click the current tab. Click a tab to auto display it (Ribbon remains collapsed). To expand the Ribbon, press Ctrl+F1 or double-click a tab.*

Key Tip   Standard tabs   Contextual tab   Ribbon Display Options

Collapse the Ribbon

Choosing Commands

Excel commands are organized in groups on the Ribbon, Quick Access Toolbar, and Mini-Toolbar. Commands are available as buttons or options on the Ribbon, or as menus on button or option arrows or the File tab. The Quick Access Toolbar and Mini-Toolbar display frequently used buttons that you may be already familiar with from previous versions of Excel, while the File tab on the Ribbon displays file related menu commands; to exit the File tab, click the Back button (**New!**). In addition to the File tab, you can also open a **shortcut menu** with a group of related commands by right-clicking a program element.

Choose a Menu Command Using the File Tab

1. Click the **File** tab on the Ribbon.

2. Click the command you want.

   TIMESAVER *You can use a shortcut key to choose a command. Press and hold down the first key and then press the second key. For example, press and hold the Ctrl key and then press S (or Ctrl+S) to select the Save command.*

3. To return to the program window, click the **Back** button (**New!**).

Choose a Menu Command from a Shortcut Menu

1. Right-click an object (a cell or graphic element).

   TIMESAVER *Press Shift+F10 to display the shortcut menu for a selected command.*

2. Click a command on the shortcut menu. If the command is followed by an arrow, point to the command to see a list of related options, and then click the option you want.

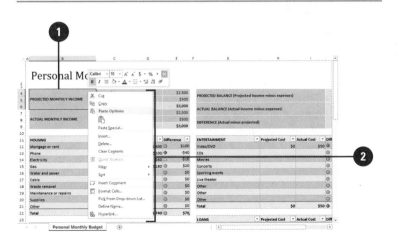

Working with the Ribbon and Toolbars

Excel includes its most common commands, such as Save and Undo, on the **Quick Access Toolbar**. Click a toolbar button to choose a command. If you are not sure what a toolbar button does, point to it to display a ScreenTip. When Excel starts, the Quick Access Toolbar appears at the top of the window, unless you've changed your settings. You can customize the Quick Access Toolbar or Ribbon by adding command buttons or groups to it. You can also move the toolbar below or above the Ribbon so it's right where you need it. In addition to the Quick Access Toolbar, Excel also displays the Mini-Toolbar when you point to selected text. The **Mini-Toolbar** appears above the selected text and provides quick access to formatting tools.

Choose a Command Using a Toolbar or Ribbon

◆ **Get command help**. If you're not sure what a button does, point to it to display a ScreenTip. If the ScreenTip includes *Press F1 for more help*, press F1.

◆ **Choose a command**. Click the button, or button arrow, and then click a command or option.

ScreenTip

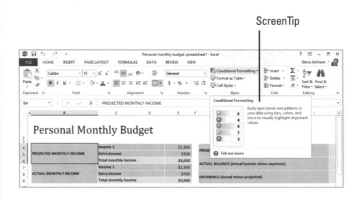

Add or Remove Items from the Quick Access Toolbar

◆ **Add or remove a common button**. Click the **Customize Quick Access Toolbar list arrow**, and then click a button name (checked item appears on the toolbar).

◆ **Add a Ribbon button or group**. Right-click the button or group name on the Ribbon, and then click **Add to Quick Access Toolbar**.

◆ **Remove a button or group**. Right-click the button or group name on the Quick Access Toolbar, and then click **Remove from Quick Access Toolbar**.

Customize Quick Access Toolbar list arrow

Click to add or remove frequently used buttons

Right-click to add a button or group

Customize the Ribbon or Quick Access Toolbar

1 Click the **File** tab, and then click **Options**.

2 Click the **Customize Ribbon** or **Quick Access Toolbar**.

3 Click the **Choose commands from** list arrow, and then click **All Commands** or a specific Ribbon.

4 Click the list arrow (right column), and then select the tabs or toolbar you want to change.

5 For the Ribbon, click **New Tab** to create a new tab, or click **New Group** to create a new group on the selected tab (right column), or click **Rename** to change the name.

6 To import or export a customized Ribbon or Quick Access Toolbar, click the **Import/Export** list arrow, select a command, and then select an import file or create an export file.

7 Click the command you want to add (left column) or remove (right column), and then click **Add** or **Remove**.

  ◆ To insert a separator line between buttons in the Quick Access Toolbar, click **<Separator>**, and then click **Add**.

8 Click the **Move Up** and **Move Down** arrow buttons to arrange the order.

9 To reset the Ribbon or Quick Access Toolbar, click the **Reset** list arrow, and then select a reset option.

10 Click **OK**.

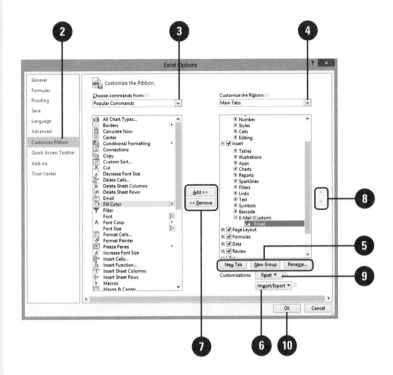

For Your Information

Moving Toolbars and the Ribbon

You can move the Quick Access Toolbar to another location. Click the Customize Quick Access Toolbar list arrow, and then click Show Below The Ribbon or Show Above The Ribbon. You can collapse and expand the Ribbon. To collapse the Ribbon, click the Collapse The Ribbon (Ctrl+F1) button on the right side of the Ribbon. To expand the Ribbon, press Ctrl+F1 or click the Ribbon Display Options, and then click Show Tabs and Commands. When the Ribbon is collapsed, you can click a tab to auto expand it. When you click an option or in the document, the Ribbon minimizes again, just like an auto-hide option.

Changing ScreenTips

You can turn off or change ScreenTips. Click the File tab, click Options, click General, click the ScreenTip Style list arrow, click Don't Show Feature Descriptions In ScreenTips or Don't Show ScreenTips, and then click OK.

Choosing Dialog Box Options

A **dialog box** is a window that opens when you click a Dialog Box Launcher or a link. **Dialog Box Launchers** are small arrow icons that appear at the bottom corner of some groups. When you point to a Dialog Box Launcher, a ScreenTip with a thumbnail of the dialog box appears to show you which dialog box opens. A dialog box allows you to supply more information before the program carries out the command you selected. After you enter information or make selections in a dialog box, click the OK button to complete the command. Click the Cancel button to close the dialog box without issuing the command. In many dialog boxes, you can also click an Apply button to apply your changes without closing the dialog box.

Choose Dialog Box Options

All dialog boxes contain the same types of options, including the following:

- **Tabs**. Each tab groups a related set of options. Click a tab to display its options.

- **Option buttons**. Click an option button to select it. You can usually select only one.

- **Up and down arrows**. Click the up or down arrow to increase or decrease the number, or type a number in the box.

- **Check box**. Click the box to turn on or off the option. A checked box means the option is selected; a cleared box means it's not.

- **List box**. Click the list arrow to display a list of options, and then click the option you want.

- **Text box**. Click in the box and type the requested information.

- **Button**. Click a button to perform a specific action or command. A button name followed by an ellipsis (...) opens another dialog box.

- **Preview box**. Many dialog boxes show an image that reflects the options you select.

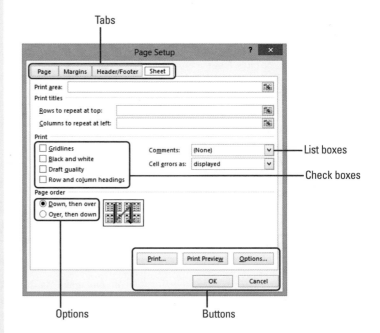

Tabs

List boxes

Check boxes

Options

Buttons

For Your Information

Navigating a Dialog Box

Rather than clicking to move around a dialog box, you can press the Tab key to move from one box or button to the next. You can also use Shift+Tab to move backward, or Ctrl+Tab and Ctrl+Shift+Tab to move between dialog box tabs.

Using the Status Bar

The **Status bar** appears across the bottom of your screen and displays workbook information—such as cell mode, theme name, and current display zoom percentage—and some Excel controls, such as view shortcut buttons, zoom slider, and Fit To Window button. With the click of the mouse, you can quickly customize exactly what you see on the Status bar. In addition to displaying information, the Status bar also allows you to check the on/off status of certain features, such as Signatures, Permissions, Selection Mode, Page Number, Caps Lock, Num Lock, Macro Recording and Playback, and much more.

Add or Remove Items from the Status Bar

◆ **Add Item**. Right-click the Status bar, and then click an unchecked item.

◆ **Remove Item**. Right-click the Status bar, and then click a checked item.

See Also

See "Adding a Digital Signature" on page 374 or "Recording a Macro" on page 471 for information on changing the status of items on the Status bar.

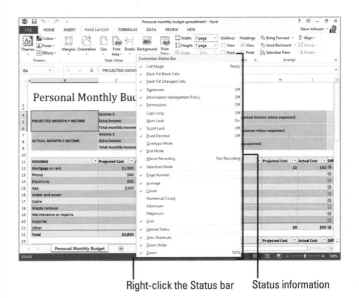

Right-click the Status bar   Status information

Creating a Blank Workbook

When you start Excel, the program opens by default with the Start screen (**New!**) on the Backstage, where you can open a new workbook so that you can begin working in it. If you're already working in Excel, you can use the New command (**New!**) on the File tab to create a new workbook. Each new workbook displays a default name("Book1," "Book2," and so on), numbered according to how many new workbooks you have started during the session until you save it with a more meaningful name. The workbook name appears on the title bar and taskbar buttons.

Start a Blank Workbook

1. Start a blank Excel workbook from either of the following:

   - **Start Screen.** Start Excel 2013 from Windows (**New!**).

   - **New Screen.** Click the **File** tab, and then click **New** (**New!**).

   TIMESAVER *To create a blank Excel workbook without the New screen, press Ctrl+N.*

2. Click **Blank Workbook**.

   A new blank workbook appears in the Excel program window.

Did You Know?

You can start Excel and not show the Start screen. Click the File tab, click Options, clear the Show The Start Screen When This Application Starts check box (**New!**), and then click OK.

See Also

See "Saving a Workbook" on page 22 or "Saving a Workbook to Online Services" on page 26 for information on saving a workbook.

Back button   **2** New screen

Use to open documents   **2** Start screen

Creating a Workbook Using a Template

Excel provides a collection of professionally designed templates that you can use to help you create workbooks. Start with a template when you have a good idea of your content but want to take advantage of a template's professional look. A **template** is an Excel workbook file that provides you with an unified design, which includes themes, so you only need to add text and graphics. In the Start or New screen (**New!**), you can choose a template from those already installed with Excel or from the library on the Microsoft Office Online web site. If you frequently use a template, you can pin it (**New!**) to the Start or New screen.

Start a Workbook with a Template

1. Start an Excel workbook from either of the following:
   - **Start Screen.** Start Excel 2013 from Windows (**New!**).
   - **New Screen.** Click the **File** tab, and then click **New** (**New!**).

2. Use one of the following (**New!**):
   - **Featured or Personal.** Click a template.
   - **Suggested searches.** Click a suggested search option, and then click a template.
   - **Search for online templates.** Type criteria in the Search box, click the **Search** button or press Enter, click a category, and then click a template.

3. To pin a template to the New screen, point to a template, and then click the **Pin to List** button (**New!**). To unpin a template, click the **Pin from List** (**New!**).

4. To navigate, click the **Home** button.

5. If prompted, click **Create**.

Did You Know?

You can download templates on the web. Go to *www.microsoft.com*, click the Office link, and then search for Office Templates.

New on the File tab

Opening an Existing Workbook

You can open an Excel workbook and start Excel simultaneously, or you can open an Excel workbook or file created in another spreadsheet program after you start Excel. You can open an existing workbook from within Excel by using the File tab. On the File tab, you can choose the Open command to choose a recently used document, locate and select the workbook on your SkyDrive or computer. SkyDrive (**New!**) is a cloud-based online storage system, which requires a Microsoft account to access. The Open screen allows you to pin recently used documents or folders (**New!**) that you want to remain accessible regardless of recent use. The Pin icon to the right of the file name on the File tab makes it easy to pin or unpin as needed.

Open an Existing Workbook

1. Click the **File** tab, and then click **Open**.

2. Click **Computer**.

3. Click **Browse** or a recent folder.

4. If you want to open a specific file type, click the **Files of type** list arrow, and then click a file type.

   ◆ **Strict Open XML**. You can also open workbooks in the Strict Open XML format (**New!**) to resolve leap year issues with 1900.

5. Navigate to the location where you want to open the file, and then select the file.

6. Click **Open**, or click the **Open** button arrow, and then click one of the following options:

   ◆ **Open Read-Only** to open the selected file with protection.

   ◆ **Open as Copy** to open a copy of the selected file.

   ◆ **Open in Browser** to open the selected web file in a browser.

   ◆ **Open in Protected View** to open the selected file in protected view.

   ◆ **Open and Repair** to open the damaged file.

Access SkyDrive   2   Recent folder locations

Excel 2013 Open File Formats

Opening Files with Different File Formats

Microsoft Excel can open a variety of different file formats using the Open dialog box. These include All Web Pages, XML Files, Text Files, All Data Sources, Access Databases, Query Files, dBASE Files, Microsoft Excel 4.0 Macros, Microsoft Excel 4.0 Workbooks, Worksheets, Workspaces, Templates, Add-Ins, Toolbars, SYLK Files, Data Interchange Format (DIF), and Backup Files. See "Saving a Workbook with Different Formats" on page 24 for a list and description of many of these formats.

Open a Recently Opened Workbook or Folder

1. Click the **File** tab, and then click **Open**.

   TIMESAVER *In the Start screen (**New!**), click a recent workbook.*

2. Click **Recent Workbooks** or **Computer (New!)**.

3. To pin or unpin a document or folder, point to a document or folder (displays the pin):

   - **Pin a document or folder**. Click the Pin icon on the Recent Workbooks or Recent Folders list.

   - **Unpin a document or folder**. Click the Pin icon to display a pin on the Recent Workbooks or Recent Folders list.

4. Click the workbook you want to open.

Did You Know?

You can add recently used documents to the File tab. Click the File tab, click Options, click Advanced, select the Quickly Access This Number Of Recent Workbooks check box, specify the number of workbooks you want to display, and then click OK.

You can change the number of recently opened files that appear on the File tab. Click the File tab, click Options, click Advanced, change the Show This Number Of Recent Workbooks list, and then click OK.

You can change the default file location of the Open dialog box. Click the File tab, click Options, click Save, enter a new location in the Default File Location box, and then click OK.

Pinned item

Access local files

Unpinned item

Open recent workbooks on the Start screen

Click to open a workbook

Converting an Existing Workbook

When you open a workbook from 97-2003, Excel 2013 goes into compatibility mode—indicated on the title bar—where it disables new features that cannot be displayed or converted well by previous versions. When you save a workbook, Excel 2013 saves Excel 97-2003 files in their older format using compatibility mode. The workbook stays in compatibility mode until you convert it to the Excel 2007-2013 file format. Excel 2007, Excel 2010, and Excel 2013 use the same file format, so you don't need to convert files between them.

Convert an Excel 97-2003 to Excel 2013

1. Open the Excel 97-2003 workbook you want to convert to the Excel 2007-2013 file format.

   The Excel 97-2003 workbook opens in compatibility mode.

2. Click the **File** tab, and then click **Info**.

3. Click **Convert**.

4. Click **OK** to convert the file to the Excel 2007-2013 format.

   Excel exits compatibility mode, which is only turned on when a previous version is in use.

Compatibility mode

Upgrade to new file format in Word

Did You Know?

You can display extensions in the Save and Open dialog boxes and Recent Documents list. Changing the Windows option also changes Excel. In the Folder Options dialog box on the View tab, clear the Hide Extensions For Known File Types check box.

Using Task and Window Panes

Task panes are separate windows that appear when you need them, such as Signatures, or when you click a Dialog Box Launcher icon, such as Clipboard. A task pane displays various options that relate to the current task. **Window panes** are sections of a window, such as a split window. If you need a larger work area, you can use the Close button in the upper-right corner of the pane to close a task or window pane, or move a border edge (for task panes) or **splitter** (for window panes) to resize it.

Work with Task and Window Panes

◆ **Open a Task Pane**. It appears when you need it or when you click a Dialog Box Launcher icon.

◆ **Close a Task or Window Pane**. Click the Close button in upper-right corner of the pane.

◆ **Resize a Task Pane**. Point to the Task Pane border edge until the pointer changes to double arrows, then drag the edge to resize it.

◆ **Resize a Window Pane**. Point to the window pane border bar until the pointer changes to a double bar with arrows, then drag the edge to resize it.

Did You Know?

You can insert window panes. Click the View tab, click the Split button in the Window group.

See Also

See "Splitting a Worksheet into Panes" on page 129 for more information on using the Split button.

Click to open task pane

Task pane options

Close

Moving Around the Workbook

You can move around a worksheet using your mouse or the keyboard, or your finger (**New!**) on a tablet or touch screen. You might find that using your mouse or finger to move from cell to cell is most convenient, while using various keyboard combinations is easier for quickly covering large areas of a worksheet. Or, you might find that entering numbers on the keypad and pressing Enter is a better method. Certain keys on the keyboard—Home, End, Delete, Page Up, and Page Down to name a few—are best used as shortcuts to navigate in the worksheet. If you have a table or touch screen (**New!**), a tap is like a click and a tap-hold is like a right-click. However, there is no right way; whichever method feels the most comfortable is the one you should use.

Use the Mouse or Finger to Navigate

Using the mouse or finger (**New!**), you can navigate to:

◆ Another cell

◆ Another part of the worksheet

◆ Another worksheet

Did You Know?

Microsoft IntelliMouse users can roll from cell to cell with IntelliMouse. If you have the new Microsoft IntelliMouse—with the wheel button between the left and right buttons—you can click the wheel button and move the mouse in any direction to move quickly around the worksheet.

You can quickly zoom in or out using IntelliMouse. Instead of scrolling when you roll with the IntelliMouse, you can zoom in or out. To turn on this feature, click the File tab, click Options, click Advanced, select the Zoom On Roll With IntelliMouse check box, and then click OK.

Excel stores a lot of data. Excel supports over 1 million rows and 16 thousand columns in each worksheet, dual-processors and multi-threaded chips, memory management up to 2 GB, and up to 16 million colors.

To move from one cell to another, point to the cell you what to move to, and then click.

When you click the wheel button on the IntelliMouse, the pointer changes shape. Drag the pointer in any direction to move to a new location quickly.

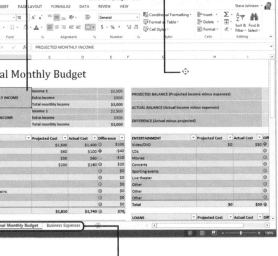

To see more sheet tabs without changing the location of the active cell, click a sheet scroll button.

To move from one worksheet to another, click the tab of the sheet you want to move to.

Use the Keyboard to Navigate

Using the keyboard, you can navigate in a worksheet to:

◆ Another cell

◆ Another part of the worksheet

Refer to the table for keyboard shortcuts for navigating around a worksheet.

Did You Know?

You can change or move cell selections after pressing Enter. When you press Enter, the active cell moves down one cell. To change the direction, click the File tab, click Options, click Advanced, select the After Pressing Enter, Move Selection check box, click the Direction list arrow, select a direction, and then click OK.

Keys For Navigating in a Worksheet

Press This Key	To Move
Left or Right arrow	One cell to the left or right
Up or Down arrow	One cell up or down
Enter	One cell down
Tab	One cell to the right
Shift+Tab	One cell to the left
Page Up	One screen up
Page Down	One screen down
End+arrow key	In the direction of the arrow key to the next cell containing data or to the last empty cell in current row or column
Home	To column A in the current row
Ctrl+Home	To cell A1
Ctrl+End	To the last cell in the worksheet containing data
Ctrl+Page Up or Ctrl+Page Down	Between worksheet tabs from left-to-right or right-to-left

Go To a Specific Location

1 Click the **Home** tab.

2 Click the **Find & Select** button, and then click **Go To**.

3 Select a location or type a cell address to where you want to go.

4 To go to other locations (such as comments, blanks, last cell, objects, formulas, etc.), click **Special**, select an option, and then click **OK**.

> **TIMESAVER** *To open the Special dialog box directly, click the Find & Select button, and then click Go To Special.*

5 Click **OK**.

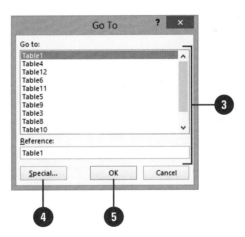

Arranging Windows

Every Office program and workbook opens inside a **window**, which contains a title bar, Ribbon, and work area to create and edit your data. Most often, you'll probably fill the entire screen with one window. But when you want to move or copy information between programs or documents or use two monitors, it's easier to display several windows at once, where one document appears in one window (**New!**). You can arrange two or more windows on the screen at the same time. However, you must make the window active to work in it. You can also click the document buttons on the taskbar to switch between open documents.

Resize and Move a Window

- **Maximize button**. Click to make a window fill the entire screen.

- **Restore Down button**. Click to reduce a maximized window to a reduced size.

- **Minimize button**. Click to shrink a window to a taskbar button. To restore the window to its previous size, click the taskbar button.

- **Close button**. Click to shut a window.

Restore Down button
Minimize button
Close button
Maximize button

Resize and Move a Window Using a Mouse

1. If the window is maximized, click the **Restore Down** button.

2. Use the following methods:

   - **Move**. Move the mouse over the title bar.

   - **Resize**. Move the mouse over one of the borders of the window until the mouse pointer changes into a two-headed arrow. The directions of the arrowheads show you the directions in which you can resize the window.

3. Drag to move or resize the window.

Arrange or Switch Between Windows

1. Open the workbooks you want to arrange or switch between.

2. Click the **View** tab.

3. In the Window group, perform any of the following:

   ◆ Click **Switch Windows**, and then click the document name you want.

   ◆ Click **Arrange All**, click an arrange window option (Tiled, Horizontal, Vertical, or Cascade), and then click OK.

   ◆ Click **New Window** to open a new window containing a view of the current document.

Compare Windows Side By Side

1. Open the workbooks you want to arrange or switch between.

2. Click the **View** tab.

3. In the Window group, perform any of the following:

   ◆ Click **View Side By Side** to compare two worksheets vertically.

   ◆ Click **Synchronous Scrolling** to synchronize the scrolling of two documents so that they scroll together. To enable this feature turn on View Side By Side.

   ◆ Click **Reset Window** to reset the window position of the documents being compared side-by-side so that they share the screen equally. To enable this feature turn on View Side By Side.

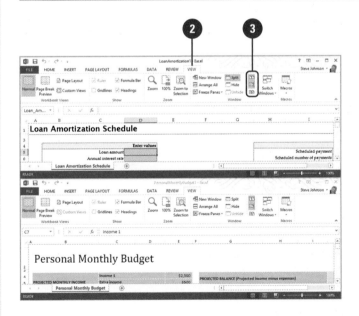

Getting Help While You Work

At some time, everyone has a question or two about the program they are using. The Office Help Viewer provides the answers and resources you need, including feature help, articles, tips, templates, training, and downloads. By connecting to Office.com on the Microsoft web site, you not only have access to standard product help information, but you also have access to updated information over the web without leaving the Help Viewer. The web browser-like Help Viewer allows you to browse a catalog of topics to locate information (**New!**), use popular searches (**New!**), or enter your own phrases to search for information. When you use any of these help options, a list of possible answers is shown to you with the most likely answer or most frequently-used at the top of the list.

Use the Help Viewer to Get Answers

1 Click the **Help** button on the Ribbon.

   TIMESAVER *Press F1.*

2 Locate the Help topic you want.

   ◆ **Popular searches.** Click a popular search (**New!**).

   ◆ **Help topic.** Click a topic tile on the home page (**New!**).

3 Read the topic, and then click any links to get Help information.

4 Click the **Back**, **Forward**, and **Home** buttons on the toolbar to move around in the Help Viewer.

5 If you want to print the topic, click the **Print** button on the toolbar.

6 To keep the Help Viewer window (not maximized) on top or behind, click to toggle the **Keep Help On Top** button (pin pushed in) and **Don't Keep Help On Top** button (pin not pushed in) on the toolbar.

   TIMESAVER *Press Ctrl+T to toggle Help On Top (**New!**).*

7 When you're done, click the **Close** button.

Click to change the topic font size

Topic

Search for Help

1 Click the **Help** button on the Ribbon.

2 To use a popular search, click one of the popular searches (**New!**).

3 Type one or more keywords in the Search For box, and then click the **Search** button to display results.

  ◆ **Prev or Next.** Scroll to the bottom, and then click **Prev** or **Next** to view more results.

4 Click a topic.

5 Read the topic, and then click any links to get information on related topics or definitions.

6 When you're done, click the **Close** button.

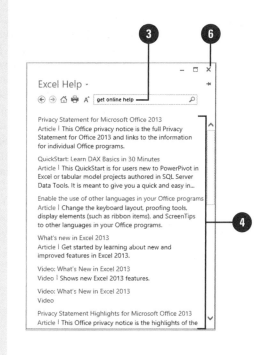

Use Local or Online Help

1 Click the **Help** button on the Ribbon.

2 Click the **Help** list arrow at the top of the Help Viewer.

3 Click the option where you want to get help information:

  ◆ **Help from Office.com** to get product help from this computer and the internet (online).

  ◆ **Help from your computer** to get product help from this computer only (offline).

4 When you're done, click the **Close** button.

Saving a Workbook

When you create an Excel workbook, you can save it to your computer, SkyDrive (**New!**) cloud-based online storage system, or Office 365 SharePoint service (**New!**). When you save a workbook for the first time or if you want to save a copy of a file, use the Save As command. When you want to save an open workbook, use the Save button on the Quick Access Toolbar. When you save a workbook, Excel 2013 saves 97-2003 files in an older format using compatibility mode and 2007-2013 files in an XML (Extensible Markup Language) based file format. The XML format significantly reduces file sizes, provides enhanced file recovery, and allows for increased compatibility, sharing, reuse, and transportability. If you have issues with leap year for 1900, you can use the Strict Open XML format (**New!**) with ISO8601. An Excel 97-2003 workbook stays in compatibility mode—indicated on the title bar—until you convert it to the 2007-2013 file format. Compatibility mode disables new features that cannot be displayed or converted well by previous versions.

Save a Workbook for Excel 2013

1. Click the **File** tab, and then click **Save As**.

2. Click **Computer**.

3. Click **Browse** or a recent folder.

4. Click the **Save in** list arrow, and then select the location where you want to save the file.

5. Type a workbook file name.

6. Click the **Save as type** list arrow, and then click **Excel Workbook**.

7. To enter Document properties, click the **Authors** or **Tags** box, and then enter the text you want.

8. Click **Save**.

9. If prompted to upgrade, click **OK**.

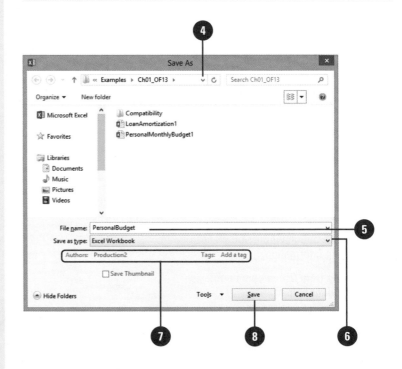

Did You Know?

You can access options from the Save dialog box. In the Save dialog box, click Tools, and then click the option you want, either General Options, Web Options, or Compress Pictures.

Microsoft Word

Save an Excel 97-2003 Workbook

1. Open the Excel 97-2003 workbook you want to continue to save in the Excel 97-2003 format.

   The Excel 97-2003 workbook opens in compatibility mode.

2. Click the **Save** button on the Quick Access Toolbar, or click the **File** tab, and then click **Save**.

   Excel stays in compatibility mode.

Set Save Options

1. Click the **File** tab, and then click **Options**.

2. In the left pane, click **Save**.

3. Set the save options you want:

   ◆ **Default Save Format.** Click the **Save files in this format** list arrow, and then click the default format you want.

   ◆ **Don't show the Backstage when opening or saving files.** Select to enable (**New!**).

   ◆ **Show additional places for saving, even if sign-in may be required.** Select to enable (**New!**).

   ◆ **Save to Computer by default.** Select to enable (**New!**).

   ◆ **Default local file location.** Specify the complete path to the folder location where you want to save your workbooks.

4. Click **OK**.

Saving a Workbook with Different Formats

Excel is a versatile spreadsheet program that allows you to save your workbook in a variety of different formats—see the table on the following page for a complete list and description. For example, you might want to save your workbook as a web page that you can view in a web browser. Or you can save a workbook in an earlier version of Excel (97-2003) in case the people you work with have not upgraded to Excel 2013. If you save a workbook to Excel 97-2003, some new features and formatting are converted to uneditable pictures or not retained. The 2007-2013 format is compatible with Office 2003, Office XP, and Office 2000 with a software patch. However, for best results, if you're creating a workbook for someone with Excel 97 to Excel 2003, it's better to save it with the .xls file format. In addition to the new XML-based file format, Excel also allows you to save a workbook in a binary file format (or BIFF12), which is based on the segmented compressed file format. This file format is most useful for large or complex workbooks, and optimized for performance and backward compatibility.

Save a Workbook with Another Format

1. Click the **File** tab, and then click **Export**.

2. Click **Change File Type**.

3. Click the file type you want.

4. Click the **Save As** button.

   The Save As dialog box opens with the selected file type.

   ◆ You can also click the **File** tab, click **Save As**, and then select a file format.

5. Navigate to the location where you want to save the file.

6. Type a workbook file name.

7. Click **Save**.

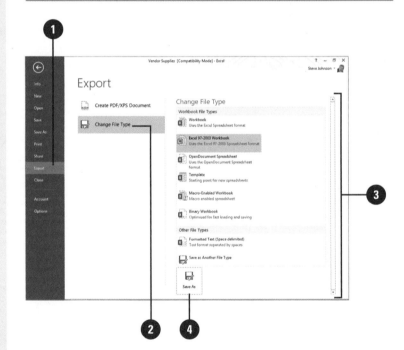

See Also

See "Creating a PDF Document" on page 192 or "Creating an XPS Document" on page 192 for information on using and saving a workbook with different formats.

Excel 2013 Save File Formats

Save As file type	Extension	Used to save
Excel Workbook	.xlsx	Excel 2007-2013 workbook
Excel Macro-Enabled Workbook	.xlsm	Excel 2007-2013 workbook that contains Visual Basic for Applications (VBA) code
Excel Binary Workbook	.xlsb	Excel 2007-2013 workbook with a binary format (compressed) for large or complex workbooks
Excel 97-2003 Workbook	.xls	Excel 97 to Excel 2003 workbook
XML Data	.xml	XML document
Single File Web Page	.mht; .mhtml	Web page as a single file with an .htm file
Web Page	.htm; .html	Web page as a folder with an .htm file
Excel Template	.xltx	Excel 2007-2013 template
Excel Macro-Enabled Template	.xltm	Excel 2007-2013 template that includes macros
Excel 97-2003 Template	.xlt	Excel 97-2003 template
Text (Tab delimited)	.txt	Text file with tabs between the data
Unicode Text	.txt	Character format; useful for complex languages, such as Greek, Chinese and Japanese.
XML Spreadsheet 2003	.xml	Excel workbook 2003 with the XML format
Microsoft Excel 5.0/95	.xls	Excel workbook in the Excel 5.0/95 version
CSV (Comma delimited)	.csv	Text file with commas separating data
Formatted Text (Space delimited)	.prn	Text file with spaces separating data
Text (Macintosh) or Text (MS-DOS)	.txt	Text file with the Macintosh or MS-DOS
CSV (Macintosh) or CSV (MS-DOS)	.csv	Text file with commas separating data
DIF (Data Interchange Format)	.dif	Text file with a header and body
SYLK (Symbolic Link)	.slk	File divided into records by a return or Enter key
Excel Add-in	.xlam	Excel 2007-2013 add-in that stores specialized functionality, such as VBA code
Excel 97-2003 Add-in	.xla	Excel 97-2003 add-in that stores specialized functionality, such as VBA code
PDF Workbook	.pdf	Fixed-layout file format that preserves document formatting developed by Adobe
XPS Document Format	.xps	Fixed-layout file format that preserves document formatting developed by Microsoft
Strict Open XML Spreadsheet (**New!**)	.xlsx	Excel workbook 2013 format to resolve leap year issues with 1900
OpenDocument Spreadsheet (**New!**)	.ods	XML-based file for spreadsheets in the Open Document Format for Office Applications (ODF)

Saving a Workbook to Online Services

Excel 2013 is integrated to work with online services (**New!**) to make it easier to save and open workbooks on other devices and share them with others. With a Microsoft or SharePoint account, you can save workbooks directly to a SkyDrive (**New!**), a personal cloud-based online storage system, or Office 365 SharePoint (**New!**), a customized Microsoft web site with SharePoint services. With your workbooks on a SkyDrive or SharePoint site, you can do a lot of things. You can sync the files from the SkyDrive or SharePoint site to other desktops or devices, such as a tablet or mobile phone for easy access from anywhere. You can view or edit workbooks online from the desktop Excel program or browser-based Excel Web App. You can share a workbook with other people using e-mail or social networks (**New!**) and even work on the same workbook at the same time with more than one person (**New!**).

Save a Workbook to Online Storage

1 Click the **File** tab, and then click **Save As**.

2 To add a shortcut place for easy access later, click **Add a Place**, click **Office 365 SharePoint** or **SkyDrive**, and then follow the on-screen connection instructions.

3 Click the SkyDrive or SharePoint name.

4 Click **Browse** or a recent folder.

5 Navigate to the location where you want to save the file.

6 Type a workbook file name.

7 Click the **Save as type** list arrow, and then click **Excel Workbook**.

8 To change browser view options, click **Browser View Options**, select options to view workbooks, and then click **OK**.

9 Click **Save**.

Add a Place

Working with Accounts

When you set up Excel 2013 or Office 2013, it requests a Microsoft account to work with online services, such as SkyDrive or SharePoint. You can add, switch, or modify accounts or sign out entirely. You can also use to other online services (**New!**), such as Flickr and YouTube for images and video, and Facebook, LinkedIn, and Twitter for sharing. Before you can use the services, you need to add them to Excel, which requires an established account with a user name and password.

Work with Online Accounts

1. Click the **File** tab, and then click **Account** (**New!**).

   TIMESAVER *Click the User Account list arrow, and then click an account option.*

2. Click any of the following links:

   - **Change photo.** Click to open your account profile.

   - **About me.** Click to open your account profile.

   - **Sign out.** Click to sign out of your account.

   - **Switch Account.** Click to switch or add accounts.

3. Click the **Back** button to exit the File tab.

User Account list arrow

Switch accounts

Add an account

Add Online Services

1. Click the **File** tab, and then click **Account** (**New!**).

2. Click **Add a service** (**New!**), point to a service type (options vary):

   - **Images & Videos**, and then click **Flickr** or **YouTube**.

   - **Storage**, and then click **Office 365 SharePoint** or **SkyDrive**.

   - **Sharing**, and then click **Facebook**, **LinkedIn**, or **Twitter**.

3. Follow the on-screen instructions to add the service.

4. Click the **Back** button to exit the File tab.

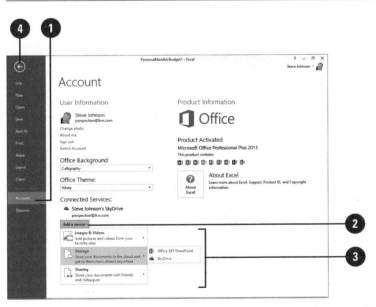

Checking Compatibility

The Compatibility Checker identifies the potential loss of functionality when you save an Excel workbook in the Excel 97-2003 Workbook file format. The Compatibility Checker generates a report that provides a summary of the potential losses and the number of occurrences in the workbook. You can also specify what versions to show compatibility issues. Use the report information to determine what caused each message and for suggestions on how to change it. If the loss is due to a new feature in Excel 2013—such as new functions, custom layouts or Quick Styles applied to shapes, pictures, and WordArt—you might be able to simply remove the effect or feature. In other cases, you might not be able to do anything about it. To maintain a visual appearance, SmartArt graphics and other objects with new effects are converted to bitmaps to preserve their overall look and cannot be edited.

Check Workbook Compatibility

1. Click the **File** tab, and then click **Info**.

2. Click the **Check For Issues** button, and then click **Check Compatibility**.

   Excel checks compatibility of the workbook for non supported features in earlier versions of Excel.

3. Click the **Select versions to show** list arrow, and then select one or more versions to check.

4. View the compatibility summary information, so you can make changes, as necessary.

5. To have the compatibility checker check the workbook when Excel saves the file, select the **Check compatibility when saving this workbook** check box.

6. Click **OK**.

Checking Accessibility

The Accessibility Checker identifies potential difficulties that people with disabilities might have reading or interactive with an Excel workbook. The Accessibility Checker generates a list of errors and warning and possible fixes in the Accessibility Checker panel. Use the information to determine what caused each issue and for suggestions on how to fix it. In addition to the Accessibility Checker, you can also add alternative text (also known as alt text) to objects and other items to provide information for people with visual impairments who may be unable to easily or fully see it. Alternative text also helps people with screen readers understand the content in a workbook. You can create alternative text for shapes, pictures, charts, tables, SmartArt graphics, or other objects. When you point to an object with alternative text in a screen reader or DAISY (digital Accessible Information System) or in most browsers, the alternative text appears.

Check Accessibility and Add Alternative Text

1 Click the **File** tab, and then click **Info**.

2 Click the **Check For Issues** button, and then click **Check Accessibility**.

Excel checks compatibility for content that people with disabilities might find difficult to read.

3 View the compatibility summary information of errors and warnings in the Accessibility Checker pane.

4 Select an issue under Inspection Results to find out how to fix it under Additional Information.

5 To add alternative text, right-click the object or item, point to a command (varies depending on the object or item), such as Format, click **Alternative Text** or **Alt Text**, enter a title and description, and then click **OK**.

6 When you're done with the Accessibility Checker pane, click the **Close** button on the pane.

Documenting Workbook Properties

Excel automatically documents workbook properties while you work, such as file size, save dates, and various statistics, and allows you to document other properties, such as title, author, subject, keywords, category, and status. You can view or edit standard document properties or create advanced custom properties by using the **Document Information Panel**, which is actually an XML-based Microsoft InfoPath 2013 form hosted in Excel. You can use document properties—also known as metadata—to help you manage and track files; search tools can use the metadata to find a workbook based-on your search criteria. If you associate a document property to an item in the document, the document property updates when you change the item.

View and Edit Document Properties

1. Click the **File** tab, and then click **Info**.

2. To display other properties, click the **Properties** button, and then select an option:

   ◆ **Show Document Panel.** Shows Document panel in the workbook.

   ◆ **Advanced Properties.** Displays the Properties dialog box.

3. Enter the standard properties, such as author, title, subject, keywords, category, status, and comments.

   ◆ **Show All Properties.** Click the link to displays more options.

Did You Know?

You can view or change document properties when you open or save a file. In the Open or Save As dialog box, select the document you want, click the arrow next to the Views, and then click Details to view file size and last changed date, or click Properties to view all information. If you want to insert or change author names or keywords, click the Authors box or Tags box, and then type what you want.

Document Panel

Switching Views

Excel includes a view selector in the lower-right of the workbook window, where you can use buttons to quickly switch between Excel views: Normal, Page Layout, and Page Break Preview. **Normal view** is the main view in Excel. It lets you focus on entering, modifying, and managing your data. **Page Layout view** is the printout related view. It lets you focus on how your worksheet is going to look when you print it. You can work with page setup, headers, footers, margins, and shapes in this view to make sure pages look the way you want. You use Page Break Preview view along with Page Layout view. **Page Break Preview view** lets you see how your worksheet data appears on pages. In addition to the view selector, you can also use the View tab to switch between views. On the View tab, you can also switch to Full Screen view, which allows you to see the maximum amount of worksheet data your screen can display without the Ribbon, tabs, or Status bar.

Switch Between Views

◆ **Use the View Selector.** On the right-side of the Status bar, click any of the following view buttons: **Normal View**, **Page Layout View**, or **Page Break Preview View**.

◆ **Use the View tab.** Click the **View** tab, and then click any of the following view buttons: **Normal View**, **Page Layout View**, **Page Break Preview View**, or **Full Screen**.

To exit Full Screen View, press Esc.

View tab buttons

View Selector buttons

Recovering a Workbook

If Excel encounters a problem and stops responding, the program automatically tries to recover the file. The recovered files are stored and managed by Excel. You can use the Manage Versions button on the Info screen under the File tab to open any available recovered unsaved files. If you have a lot of recovered files, you can also delete all file versions to save disk space. To use the AutoRecover option, you need to enable it in the Save category of the Options dialog box. You can set AutoRecover options to periodically save a temporary copy of your current file, which ensures proper recovery of the file and allows you to revert to an earlier version of a file. In addition, if you didn't save your changes when you closed a document, you can select an AutoRecover option to save your work as a safe guard.

Recover a Workbook

1. Click the **File** tab, and then click **Info**.

2. To open a recovered or previous version, click a file from the available list.

3. Click the **Manage Versions** button, and then click **Recover Unsaved Workbooks**.

   TIMESAVER *Click the File tab, click Open, and then click Recover Unsaved Workbooks folder icon.*

4. Select the file version you want to recover.

5. Click **Open**.

Did You Know?

You can delete all draft versions of unsaved files. Click the File tab, click Info, click the Manage Versions button, click Delete All Unsaved Workbooks, and then click Yes to confirm the deletions.

Use AutoRecover

1 Click the **File** tab, and then click **Options**.

2 In the left pane, click **Save**.

3 Select the **Save AutoRecover information every *x* minutes** check box.

4 Enter the number of minutes, or click the **Up** and **Down** arrows to adjust the minutes.

5 Select the **Keep the last autosaved version if I close without saving** check box as a safe guard to save your work if you don't save it.

6 Specify the complete path to the folder location where you want to save your AutoRecover file.

7 To disable AutoRecover for a specific document, perform the following:

◆ Click the **File** list arrow, and then select the document you want to disable.

◆ Select the **Disable AutoRecover for this workbook only** check box.

8 Click **OK**.

Closing a Workbook and Exiting Excel

After you finish working on a workbook, you can close it. Closing a workbook frees up more computer memory for other activities. Closing a workbook is different from exiting, or quitting, Excel; after you close a workbook, Excel is still running. You close a workbook by using the Close command on the File tab (**New!**), which keeps the Excel program window open. Since each workbook opens in its own program window, you don't need an Exit command, so you exit Excel by using the Close button (**New!**) on the program window. To protect your files, always save your documents and exit before turning off the computer.

Close a Workbook

1. Click the **File** tab, and then click **Close**.

   TIMESAVER *Press Ctrl+W.*

2. If you have made changes to any open files since last saving them, a dialog box opens, asking if you want to save changes. Click **Save** to save any changes, or click **Don't Save** to ignore your changes.

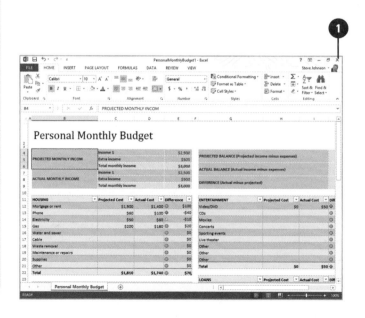

Exit Excel

1. Click the **Close** button on the Excel program window.

   ◆ **Close All.** Right-click the Excel icon on the Taskbar, and then click **Close all windows**.

   TIMESAVER *To create an Exit button, add the Exit command to the Quick Access Toolbar.*

2. If you have made changes to any open files since last saving them, a dialog box opens asking if you want to save changes. Click **Save** to save any changes, or click **Don't Save** to ignore your changes.

Basic Workbook Skills

Introduction

Creating a Microsoft Excel workbook is as easy as entering data in the cells of an Excel worksheet. Each cell has a **cell address** which is made up of its column and row intersection. Cells on a worksheet contain either labels or values, a formula or remain blank. Cell entries can be modified using the keyboard or mouse. You can select cells in ranges that are **contiguous** (selected cells are adjacent to each other) or **noncontiguous** (selected cells are in different parts of the worksheet). Selected cells are used in formulas, to copy and paste data, to AutoFill, to apply date and time and other formatting functions.

In addition, Excel offers a Find and Replace feature that allows you to look for labels and values and make changes as necessary. When you need to spell check your worksheet, Excel can check and suggest spelling corrections. You can even customize the spelling dictionary by adding company specific words into AutoCorrect so that the spell checker doesn't think it's a misspelled word. The Actions feature works with other Microsoft Office programs to enhance your worksheets. Contact information can be pulled from your address book in Outlook, to your worksheet in Excel. Stock symbols can trigger a Smart Tag choice to import data on a publicly traded company. Additional research and language tools area available to build up the content of your workbooks.

If you accidentally make a change to a cell, you can use the Undo feature to remove, or "undo," your last change. Excel remembers your recent changes to the worksheet, and gives you the opportunity to undo them. If you decide to Redo the Undo, you can erase the previous change. This is useful when moving, copying, inserting and deleting cell contents.

What You'll Do

Make Label Entries

Select Cells, Rows, Columns, and Special Ranges

Enter Labels and Values on a Worksheet

Enter Values Quickly with AutoFill

Insert Content with Flash Fill

Edit and Clear Cell Contents

Understand How Excel Pastes Data

Store and Copy Cell Contents

Move Cell Contents

Insert and Delete Cell Contents

Find and Replace Cell Contents

Correct Cell Contents with AutoCorrect

Insert Information the Smart Way

Check Spelling

Change Proofing Options

Use Custom Dictionaries

Insert Symbols

Find the Right Words

Insert Research Material

Translate Text to Another Language

Use Multiple Languages

Work with Touch Screens

Undo and Redo an Action

Making Label Entries

There are three basic types of cell entries: labels, values, and formulas. A **label** is text in a cell that identifies the data on the worksheet so readers can interpret the information. Excel does not use labels in its calculations. For example, the label *price* is used as a column header to identify the price of each item in the column. A **value** is a number you enter in a cell. Excel knows to include values in its calculations. To quickly and easily enter values, you can format a cell, a range of cells, or a column with a specific number-related format. Then, as you type, the cells are automatically formatted.

To perform a calculation in a worksheet, you enter a formula in a cell. A **formula** is a calculation that contains cell references, values, and arithmetic operators. The result of a formula appears in the worksheet cell where you entered the formula. The contents of the cell appears on the formula bar. Entering cell references rather than actual values in a formula has distinct advantages. When you change the data in the worksheet or copy the formula to other cells (copying this formula to the cell below), Excel automatically adjusts the cell references in the formula and returns the correct results.

The formula entered in cell C6 appears here

Active cell address

The result of the formula

Label

Value

Selecting Cells

In order to work with a cell—to enter data in it, edit or move it, or perform an action—you **select** the cell so it becomes the active cell. When you want to work with more than one cell at a time—to move or copy them, use them in a **formula**, or perform any group action—you must first select the cells as a **range**. A range can be **contiguous** (where selected cells are adjacent to each other) or **non-contiguous** (where the cells may be in different parts of the worksheet and are not adjacent to each other). As you select a range, you can see the range reference in the Name box. A **range reference** contains the cell address of the top-left cell in the range, a colon (:), and the cell address of the bottom-right cell in the range.

Select a Contiguous Range

1. Click the first cell that you want to include in the range.

2. Drag the mouse to the last cell you want to include in the range.

    TIMESAVER *Instead of dragging, hold down the Shift key, and then click the lower-right cell in the range.*

    When a range is selected, the top-left cell is surrounded by the cell pointer, while the additional cells are selected.

Select a Non-contiguous Range

1. Click the first cell you want to include in the range.

2. Drag the mouse to the last contiguous cell, and then release the mouse button.

3. Press and hold Ctrl, and then click the next cell or drag the pointer over the next group of cells you want in the range.

    To select more, repeat step 3 until all non-contiguous ranges are selected.

Selecting Rows, Columns, and Special Ranges

In addition to selecting a range of contiguous and non-contiguous cells in a single worksheet, you may need to select entire rows and columns, or even a range of cells across multiple worksheets. Cells can contain many different types of data, such as comments, constants, formulas, or conditional formats. Excel provides an easy way to locate these and many other special types of cells with the Go To Special dialog box. For example, you can select the Row Differences or Column Differences option to select cells that are different from other cells in a row or column, or select the Dependents option to select cells with formulas that refer to the active cell.

Select Entire Rows or Columns

◆ To select a single row or column, click in the row or column heading, or select any cell in the row or column, and press Shift+Spacebar.

◆ To select multiple adjacent rows or columns, drag in the row or column headings.

◆ To select multiple nonadjacent rows or columns, press Ctrl while you click the borders for the rows or columns you want to include.

Did You Know?

You can select the entire worksheet quickly. Click the Select All button located above the row number 1 and the left of column A.

Column headings

Multiple columns selected

Row headings

Select Multi-sheet Ranges

1. Select the range in one sheet.

2. Select the worksheets to include in the range.

   To select contiguous worksheets, press Shift and click the last sheet tab you want to include. To select non-contiguous worksheets, press Ctrl and click the sheets you want.

   When you make a worksheet selection, Excel enters Group mode.

3. To exit Group mode, click any sheet tab.

Group selection

Make Special Range Selections

1. If you want to make a selection from within a range, select the range you want.

2. Click the **Home** tab.

3. Click the **Find & Select** button, and then click **Go To Special**.

   TIMESAVER *Press F5 to open the Go To Special dialog box.*

4. Click the option in which you want to make a selection. When you click the Formulas option, select or clear the formula related check boxes.

5. Click **OK**.

   If no cells are found, Excel displays a message.

Entering Labels on a Worksheet

Labels turn a worksheet full of numbers into a meaningful report by identifying the different types of information it contains. You use labels to describe the data in worksheet cells, columns, and rows. You can enter a number as a label (for example, the year 2013), so that Excel does not use the number in its calculations. To help keep your labels consistent, you can use Excel's **AutoComplete** feature, which automatically completes your entries (excluding numbers, dates, or times) based on previously entered labels.

Enter a Text Label

1. Click the cell where you want to enter a label.

2. Type a label. A label can include uppercase and lowercase letters, spaces, punctuation, and numbers.

3. Press Enter, or click the **Enter** button on the formula bar.

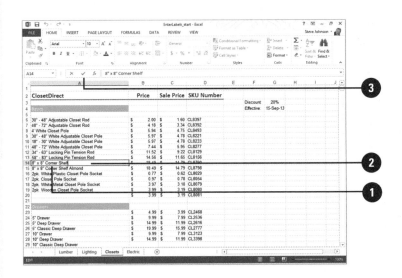

Enter a Number as a Label

1. Click the cell where you want to enter a number as a label.

2. Type ' (an apostrophe). The apostrophe is a label prefix and does not appear on the worksheet.

3. Type a number value.

4. Press Enter, or click the **Enter** button on the formula bar.

Enter a Label Using AutoComplete

1. Type the first few characters of a label.

   If Excel recognizes the entry, AutoComplete completes it.

2. To accept the suggested entry, press Enter or click the **Enter** button on the formula bar.

3. To reject the suggested completion, simply continue typing.

Did You Know?

Excel doesn't recognize the entry.
The AutoComplete option may not be turned on. To turn on the feature, click the File tab, click Options, click Advanced, select the Enable AutoComplete For Cell Values check box, and then click OK.

Long labels might appear truncated.
When you enter a label that is wider than the cell it occupies, the excess text appears to spill into the next cell to the right—unless there is data in the adjacent cell. If that cell contains data, the label will appear truncated—you'll only see the portion of the label that fits in the cell's current width. Click the cell to see its entire contents displayed on the formula bar.

AutoComplete label

Entering Values on a Worksheet

You can enter values as whole numbers, decimals, percentages, or dates using the numbers on the top row of your keyboard, or by pressing your Num Lock key, the numeric keypad on the right. When you enter a date or the time of day, Excel automatically recognizes these entries (if entered in an acceptable format) as numeric values and changes the cell's format to a default date or time format. You can also change the way values, dates or times of day are shown.

Enter a Value

1. Click the cell where you want to enter a value.

2. Type a value.

3. Press Enter, or click the **Enter** button on the formula bar.

Did You Know?

You can use the numeric keypad to enter numbers. Make sure NUM appears in the lower-right corner of the status bar before you begin using the numbers.

Enter a Date or Time

1. To enter a date, type the date using a slash (/) or a hyphen (-) between the month, day, and year in a cell or on the formula bar.

   To enter a time, type the hour based on a 12-hour clock, followed by a colon (:), followed by the minute, followed by a space, and ending with an "a" or a "p" to denote A.M. or P.M.

2. Press Enter, or click the **Enter** button on the formula bar.

Format Values Quickly

1. Click the cell that contains the date format you want to change.

2. Click the **Home** tab.

3. Click the **Number Format** list arrow.

4. Click the number format you want, which includes:

   ◆ **General.** No specific format.

   ◆ **Number.** 38873.00

   ◆ **Currency.** $38,873.00

   ◆ **Accounting.** $ 38,873.00

   ◆ **Short Date.** 9/15/2013

   ◆ **Long Date.** Wednesday, September 15, 2013

   ◆ **Time.** 12:00:00 AM

   ◆ **Percentage.** 38873.00%

   ◆ **Fraction.** 38873

   ◆ **Scientific.** 3.89E+04

   ◆ **More Number Formats.** Opens the Format Cell dialog box, where you can format cells with multiple options at one time.

More Number Formats command

Did You Know?

You can simplify data entry. Enter values as simply as possible to make data entry quicker. For example, to enter the value "10.00" simply type "10". Use the Number Format list arrow to format your cell entries with decimal places, commas, dollar signs, and other formatting attributes.

Entering Values Quickly with AutoFill

AutoFill is a feature that automatically fills in data based on the data in adjacent cells. Using the **fill handle**, you can enter data in a series, or you can copy values or formulas to adjacent cells. A single cell entry can result in a repeating value or label, or the results can be a more complex series. You can enter your value or label, and then complete entries such as days of the week, weeks of the year, months of the year, or consecutive numbering.

Enter Repeating Data or Series Using AutoFill

1. Select the first cell in the range you want to fill.

2. Enter the starting value to be repeated, or in a series.

3. Position the pointer on the lower-right corner of the selected cell. The pointer changes to the fill handle (a black plus sign).

4. Drag the fill handle over the range you want the value repeated.

5. To choose how to fill the selection, click the **AutoFill Options** button, and then click the option you want.

Create a Complex Series Using AutoFill

1. Enter the starting value for the series, and then press Enter.

2. Select the first cell in the range you want to fill.

3. Position the pointer on the lower-right corner of the selected cell. The pointer changes to the fill handle (a black plus sign).

4. Drag the fill handle over the range you want the value repeated.

5. To choose how to fill the selection, click the **AutoFill Options** button, and then click the option you want.

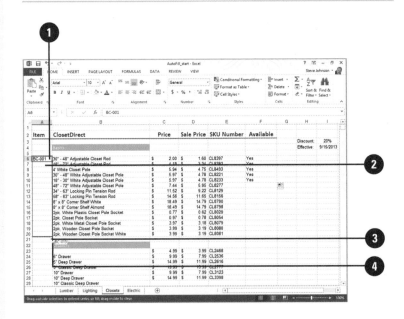

Fill with Contents of Adjacent Cells

1. Select the cell below, to the right, above, or to the left of the cell that contains the data you want to fill.

2. Click the **Home** tab.

3. Click the **Fill** button, and then click **Down**, **Right**, **Up** or **Left**.

   TIMESAVER *To quickly fill a cell with the contents of the cell above or to the left of it, press Ctrl+D or Ctrl+R.*

Did You Know?

You can suppress AutoFill. Hold down Ctrl while you drag the fill handle of a selection of two or more cells. The values are copied to the adjacent cells, and Excel does not extend a series.

Create a Custom Fill

1. If you want to use an existing list, select the list of items.

2. Click the **File** tab, and then click **Options**.

3. In the left pane, click **Advanced**.

4. Click **Edit Custom Lists**.

5. Click the option you want.

   ◆ **New list.** Click **NEW LIST**, type the entries you want, press Enter after each. Click **Add**.

   ◆ **Existing list.** Verify the cell reference of the selected list that appears in the Import list, and then click **Import**.

6. Click **OK**, and then click **OK** again.

Inserting Content with Flash Fill

Flash Fill (**New!**) is a feature that automatically fills in data based on the content it recognizes in other cells. Excel uses pattern recognition to help you fill in the content. For example, if you have a cell with a first name and last name, you can split the information into two cells with Flash Fill. In an adjacent cell, when you type the first name in a couple of cells to create a pattern, Excel recognizes it, and then allows you to auto fill in the rest of the column. After the auto fill, you can click the Flash Fill Options button (**New!**) to undo the Flash Fill, Accept Suggestions, or select all blank or changed cells.

Insert Data Using Flash Fill

1. Select the first cell in the range you want to flash fill.

2. Enter the value that you want recognized, and then press Enter.

3. Select the range you want to flash fill.

4. Click the **Data** tab.

5. Click the **Flash Fill** button on the Data tab to have Excel try to recognize the data pattern.

   Excel auto fills in the cells with the recognized data pattern.

6. To choose how to fill the selection, click the **Flash Fill Options** button, and then click the option you want:

   ◆ **Undo Flash Fill.** Performs an undo of the flash fill.

   ◆ **Accept suggestions.** Accepts the flash fill.

   ◆ **Select all X blank cells.** Selects all the blank cells from the flash fill.

   ◆ **Select all X changed cells.** Selects all the changed cells from the flash fill.

Excel recognizes the content and flash fills the selection

Insert Data Using Flash Fill Automatic Recognition

1 Select the first cell in the range you want to flash fill.

2 Enter the value that you want recognized, and then press Enter.

3 In the cell below it, enter the value that you want recognized.

After creating a pattern, Excel recognized it, and then auto fills in the cells.

4 Press Enter to accept the flash fill.

5 To choose how to fill the selection, click the **Flash Fill Options** button, and then click the option you want:

◆ **Undo Flash Fill.** Performs an undo of the flash fill.

◆ **Accept suggestions.** Accepts the flash fill.

◆ **Select all X blank cells.** Selects all the blank cells from the flash fill.

◆ **Select all X changed cells.** Selects all the changed cells from the flash fill.

Excel recognizes content from A and flash fills in B and C.

Editing Cell Contents

Even if you plan ahead, you can count on having to make changes on a worksheet. Sometimes it's because you want to correct an error. Other times it's because you want to see how your worksheet results would be affected by different conditions, such as higher sales, fewer units produced, or other variables. You can edit data just as easily as you enter it, using the formula bar or directly editing the active cell.

Edit Cell Contents

① Double-click the cell you want to edit. The insertion point appears in the cell.

   The Status bar now displays Edit instead of Ready.

② If necessary, use the Home, End, and arrow keys to position the insertion point within the cell contents.

③ Use any combination of the Backspace and Delete keys to erase unwanted characters, and then type new characters as needed.

④ Click the **Enter** button on the formula bar or press Enter to accept the edit, or click the Esc button to cancel the edit.

   The Status bar now displays Ready instead of Edit.

Edit mode

Did You Know?

You can change editing options. Click the File tab, click Options, click Advanced, change the editing options you want, and then click OK.

You can edit cell contents using the formula bar. Click the cell you want to edit, click to place the insertion point on the formula bar, and then edit the cell contents.

Ready mode

Clearing Cell Contents

You can clear a cell to remove its contents. Clearing a cell does not remove the cell from the worksheet; it just removes from the cell whatever elements you specify: data, comments (also called **cell notes**), or formatting instructions. When clearing a cell, you must specify whether to remove one, two, or all three of these elements from the selected cell or range.

Clear Cell Contents, Formatting, and Comments

1. Select the cell or range you want to clear.

2. Click the **Home** tab.

3. Click the **Clear** button, and then click any of the following options:

   ◆ **Clear All.** Clears contents and formatting.

   ◆ **Clear Formats.** Clears formatting and leaves contents.

   ◆ **Clear Contents.** Clears contents and leaves formatting.

   ◆ **Clear Comments.** Clears comments; removes purple triangle indicator.

   TIMESAVER *To quickly clear contents, select the cell or range you want to clear, right-click the cell or range, and then click Clear Contents, or press Delete.*

Did You Know?

You can find or replace cell contents. Click the cell or cells containing content you want to replace. Click the Home tab, click the Find & Select button, and then click Find. You can click the Replace tab for additional options.

Understanding How Excel Pastes Data

If you want to use data that has already been entered on your worksheet, you can cut or copy it, and then paste it in another location. When you cut or copy data, the data is stored in an area of memory called the Clipboard. When pasting a range of cells from the Clipboard, you only need to specify the first cell in the new location. After you select the first cell in the new location and then click the Paste button, Excel automatically places all the selected cells in the correct order. Depending on the number of cells you select before you cut or copy, Excel pastes data in one of the following ways:

◆ **One to one**. A single cell in the Clipboard is pasted to one cell location.

◆ **One to many**. A single cell in the Clipboard is pasted into a selected range of cells.

◆ **Many to one**. Many cells are pasted into a range of cells, but only the first cell is identified. The entire contents of the Clipboard will be pasted starting with the selected cell. Make sure there is enough room for the selection; if not, the selection will copy over any previously occupied cells.

◆ **Many to many**. Many cells are pasted into a range of cells. The entire contents of the Clipboard will be pasted into the selected cells. If the selected range is larger than the selection, the data will be repeated in the extra cells. To turn off the selection marquee and cancel your action, press the Esc key.

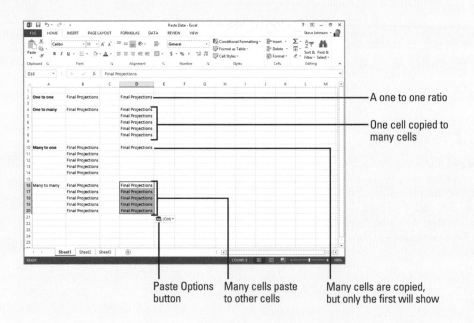

A one to one ratio

One cell copied to many cells

Many cells are copied, but only the first will show

Paste Options button

Many cells paste to other cells

Storing Cell Contents

With Microsoft Office, you can use the Office Clipboard to store multiple pieces of information from several different sources in one storage area shared by all Office programs. Unlike the Clipboard, which only stores a single piece of information at a time, the Office Clipboard allows you to copy text or pictures from one or more files. When you copy multiple items, you see the Office Clipboard, showing all the items you stored there. You can paste these pieces of information into any Office program, either individually or all at once.

Copy and Paste Data to the Office Clipboard

1. Click the **Home** tab.

2. Click the **Clipboard Dialog Box Launcher**.

3. Select the data you want to copy.

4. Click the **Copy** button.

   The data is copied into the first empty position on the Clipboard task pane.

5. Click the first cell or range where you want to paste data.

6. Click the Office Clipboard item you want to paste, or point to the item, click the list arrow, and then click **Paste**.

7. Click the **Close** button in the task pane.

Did You Know?

You can change Office Clipboard options. At the bottom of the Office Clipboard, you can click the Options button to turn on and off any of the following options: Show Office Clipboard Automatically, Show Office Clipboard When Ctrl+C Pressed Twice, Collect Without Showing Office Clipboard, Show Office Clipboard Icon on Taskbar, or Show Status Near Taskbar When Copying.

Copying Cell Contents

You can **copy** and move data on a worksheet from one cell or range to another location on any worksheet in your workbook. When you copy data, a duplicate of the selected cells is placed on the Clipboard. To complete the copy or move, you must **paste** the data stored on the Clipboard in another location. The Paste live preview allows you to view your paste results before you actually paste it. With the Paste Special command, you can control what you want to paste and even perform mathematical operations. To copy or move data without using the Clipboard, you can use a technique called **drag-and-drop**. Drag-and-drop makes it easy to copy or move data short distances on your worksheet.

Copy Data Using the Clipboard

1. Select the cell or range that contains the data you want to copy.

2. Click the **Home** tab.

3. Click the **Copy** button.

   The data in the cells remains in its original location and an outline of the selected cells, called a **marquee**, shows the size of the selection. If you don't want to paste this selection, press Esc to remove the marquee.

4. Click the first cell or range where you want to paste the data.

5. Click the **Paste** button or click the **Paste** button arrow, point to an option to display a live preview of the paste, and then click to paste the item.

   When you point to a paste option for the live preview, use the ScreenTip to determine the option.

   If you don't want to paste this selection anywhere else, press Esc to remove the marquee.

6. If you want to change the way the data pastes into the document, click the **Paste Options** button, point to an option for the live preview, and then select the option you want.

Paste button arrow

Live Preview options

Copy Data Using Drag-and-Drop

1. Select the cell or range that contains the data you want to copy.

2. Move the mouse pointer to an edge of the selected cell or range until the pointer changes to an arrowhead.

3. Press and hold the mouse button and Ctrl.

4. Drag the selection to the new location, and then release the mouse button and Ctrl.

Paste Data with Special Results

1. Select the cell or range that contains the data you want to copy.

2. Click the **Home** tab.

3. Click the **Copy** button.

4. Click the first cell or range where you want to paste the data.

5. Click the **Paste** button, and then click **Paste Special**.

6. Click the option buttons with the paste results and mathematical operations you want.

7. Click **OK**.

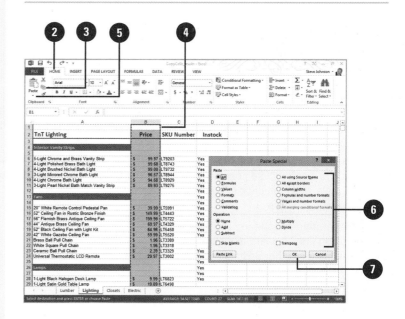

Did You Know?

You can use the Alt key to drag and drop to a different worksheet. Once cells are selected, press and hold Alt, and then drag the selection to the appropriate sheet tab. Release Alt, and then drag the selection to the desired location on the new worksheet.

Moving Cell Contents

Unlike copied data, moved data no longer remains in its original location. Perhaps you typed data in a range of cells near the top of a worksheet, but later realized it should appear near the bottom of the sheet. **Moving** data lets you change its location without having to retype it. When you move data, you are cutting the data from its current location and pasting it elsewhere. **Cutting** removes the selected cell or range content from the worksheet and places it on the Clipboard. The Paste live preview allows you to view your paste results before you actually paste it.

Move Data Using the Clipboard

1. Select the cell or range that contains the data you want to move.

2. Click the **Home** tab.

3. Click the **Cut** button.

   An outline of the selected cells, called a marquee, shows the size of the selection. If you don't want to paste this selection, press Esc to remove the marquee.

4. Click the top-left cell of the range where you want to paste the data.

5. Click the **Paste** button or click the **Paste** button arrow, point to an option to display a live preview of the paste, and then click to paste the item.

   The marquee disappears. The data is still on the Clipboard and still available for further pasting until you replace it with another selection.

Did You Know?

You can use the Office Clipboard to cut multiple items. When the Office Clipboard task pane is displayed, selections you cut can be placed on this clipboard. You can move data to the Clipboard, and then paste it at a later time.

Move Data Using Drag-and-Drop

1. Select the cell or range that contains the data you want to move.

2. Move the mouse pointer to an edge of the cell until the pointer changes to an arrowhead.

3. Press and hold the mouse button while dragging the selection to its new location, and then release the mouse button.

Did You Know?

You can reposition the mouse pointer to use drag-and-drop. If the mouse pointer changes to a thick plus sign, reposition the pointer on the edge of the selected range until the pointer changes to an arrowhead.

Paste Cells from Rows to Columns or Columns to Rows

1. Select the cells that you want to switch.

2. Click the **Home** tab.

3. Click the **Copy** button.

4. Click the top-left cell of where you want to paste the data.

5. Click the **Paste** button arrow, point to the **Transpose** icon to display a live preview of the paste, and then click the **Transpose** icon.

6. If you want to change the way the data pastes into the document, click the **Paste Options** button, point to an option for the live preview, and then select the option you want.

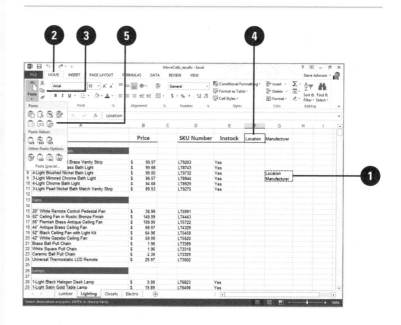

Inserting and Deleting Cell Contents

You can **insert** new, blank cells anywhere on the worksheet in order to enter new data or data you forgot to enter earlier. Inserting cells moves the remaining cells in the column or row in the direction of your choice, and Excel adjusts any formulas so they refer to the correct cells. You can also **delete** cells if you find you don't need them; deleting cells shifts the remaining cells to the left or up—just the opposite of inserting cells. When you delete a cell, Excel removes the actual cell from the worksheet.

Insert a Cell

1. Select the cell or cells where you want to insert the new cell(s).

2. Click the **Home** tab.

3. Click the **Insert Cells** button arrow, and then click **Insert Cells**.

    TIMESAVER *Click the Insert Cells button to quickly insert cells and shift to the right.*

4. Click the option you want:

    ◆ **Shift Cells Right** to move cells to the right one column.

    ◆ **Shift Cells Down** to move cells down one row.

    ◆ **Entire Row** to move the entire row down one row.

    ◆ **Entire Column** to move entire column over one column.

5. Click **OK**.

See Also

See "Finding and Replacing Cell Contents" on page 58 for information on substituting replacement text in a cell.

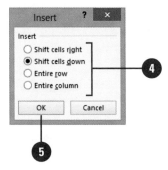

Delete a Cell

1. Select the cell or range you want to delete.

2. Click the **Home** tab.

3. Click the **Delete Cells** button arrow, and then click **Delete Cells**.

   TIMESAVER *Click the Delete Cells button to quickly delete cells and shift to the left.*

4. Click the option you want.

   - **Shift Cells Left** to move the remaining cells to the left.

   - **Shift Cells Up** to move the remaining cells up.

   - **Entire Row** to delete the entire row.

   - **Entire Column** to delete the entire column.

5. Click **OK**.

Did You Know?

There is a difference between deleting a cell and clearing a cell. Deleting a cell is different from clearing a cell: deleting removes the cells from the worksheet; clearing removes only the cell contents, or format, or both.

Finding and Replacing Cell Contents

The Find and Replace commands make it easy to locate or replace specific text or formulas in a document. For example, you might want to find each figure reference in a long report to verify that the proper graphic appears. Or you might want to replace all references to cell A3 in your Excel formulas with cell G3. The Find and Replace dialog boxes vary slightly from one Office program to the next, but the commands work essentially in the same way.

Find Cell Contents

1. Click at the beginning of the worksheet.

2. Click the **Home** tab.

3. Click the **Find & Select** button, and then click **Find**.

4. Type the text you want to find.

5. Click **Find Next** until the text you want to locate is highlighted.

   You can click **Find Next** repeatedly to locate each instance of the cell content.

6. To find all cells with the contents you want, click **Find All**.

7. If a message box opens when you reach the end of the worksheet, click **OK**.

8. Click **Close**.

Find All results

Replace Cell Contents

1. Click at the beginning of the worksheet.

2. Click the **Home** tab.

3. Click the **Find & Select** button, and then click **Replace**.

4. Type the text you want to search for.

5. Type the text you want to substitute.

6. Click **Find Next** to begin the search, and then select the next instance of the search text.

7. Click **Replace** to substitute the replacement text, or click **Replace All** to substitute text throughout the entire worksheet.

   You can click **Find Next** to locate the next instance of the cell content without making a replacement.

8. If a message box appears when you reach the end of the worksheet, click **OK**.

9. Click **Close**.

Correcting Cell Contents with AutoCorrect

Excel's **AutoCorrect** feature automatically corrects common capitalization and spelling errors as you type. AutoCorrect comes with hundreds of text and symbol entries you can edit or remove. You can add words and phrases to the AutoCorrect dictionary that you misspell, or add often-typed words and save time by just typing their initials. You could use AutoCorrect to automatically change the initials EPA to Environmental Protection Agency, for example. You can also use AutoCorrect to quickly insert symbols. For example, you can type (c) to insert ©. Use the AutoCorrect Exceptions dialog box to control how Excel handles capital letters. If you use math symbols in your work, you can use Math AutoCorrect to make it easier to insert them. It works just like AutoCorrect. When you point to a word that AutoCorrect changed, a small blue box appears under the first letter. When you point to the small blue box, the AutoCorrect Options button appears, which gives you control over whether you want the text to be corrected.

Turn On AutoCorrect

1. Click the **File** tab, and then click **Options**.

2. Click **Proofing**, and then click **AutoCorrect Options**.

3. Click the **AutoCorrect** tab.

4. Select the **Show AutoCorrect Options buttons** check box to display the button to change AutoCorrect options when corrections arise.

5. Select the **Replace Text As You Type** check box.

6. Select the capitalization related check boxes you want AutoCorrect to change for you.

7. To change AutoCorrect exceptions, click **Exceptions**, click the **First Letter** or **INitial CAps** tab, make the changes you want, and then click **OK**.

8. To use Math AutoCorrect, click the **Math AutoCorrect** tab, and then select the **Use Math AutoCorrect rules outside of math regions** check box.

9. Click **OK**, and then click **OK** again.

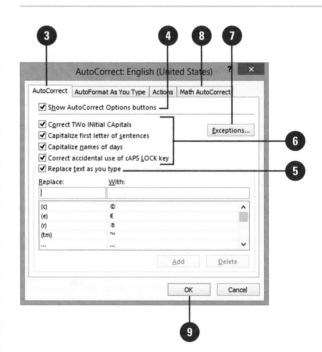

Add or Edit an AutoCorrect Entry

1. Click the **File** tab, and then click **Options**.

2. Click **Proofing**, and then click **AutoCorrect Options**.

3. Click the **AutoCorrect** tab.

4. Do one of the following:

    ◆ **Add.** Type a misspelled word or an abbreviation.

    ◆ **Edit.** Select the one you want to change. You can either type the first few letters of the entry to be changed in the Replace box, or scroll to the entry, and then click to select it.

5. Type the replacement entry.

6. Click **Add** or **Replace**. If necessary, click Yes to redefine entry.

7. Click **OK**, and then click **OK** again.

Did You Know?

You can correct text as you type. If Excel recognizes text to correct, it will correct the text and display the AutoCorrect button. Point to the small blue box under the corrected text, and then click the AutoCorrect Options button list arrow to view your options. Click an option, or click a blank area of the worksheet to deselect the AutoCorrect Options menu.

Examples of AutoCorrect Changes

Type of Correction	If You Type	AutoCorrect Inserts
Capitalization	cAP LOCK	Cap Lock
Capitalization	TWo INitial CAps	Two Initial Caps
Capitalization	thursday	Thursday
Common typos	can;t	can't
Common typos	windoes	windows
Superscript ordinals	2nd	2nd
Stacked fractions	1/2	½
Smart quotes	" "	" "
Em dashes	Madison--a small city in Wisconsin--is a nice place to live.	Madison—a small city in Wisconsin— is a nice place to live.
Symbols	(c)	©
Symbols	(r)	®

Inserting Information the Smart Way

Actions, a replacement for smart tags, help you integrate actions typically performed in other programs directly in Excel. For example, you can insert a financial symbol to get a stock quote, add a person's name and address in a document to the contacts list in Microsoft Outlook, or copy and paste information with added control. Excel analyzes what you type and recognizes certain types that it marks with actions. The types of actions you can take depend on the type of data in the cell with the action. To use an action, you right-click an item to view any custom actions associated with it.

Change Options for Actions

1. Click the **File** tab, and then click **Options**.

2. In the left pane, click **Proofing**, and then click **AutoCorrect Options**.

3. Click the **Actions** tab.

4. Select the **Enable additional actions in the right-click menu** check box.

5. Select the check boxes with the actions you want.

6. To add more actions, click **More Actions**, and then follow the online instructions.

7. Click **OK**.

8. Click **OK** again.

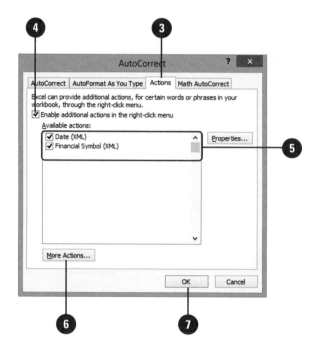

Insert Information Using an Action

1. Click an item, such as a cell, where you want to insert an action.

2. Type the information needed for the action, such as the date, a recognized financial symbol in capital letters, or a person's name from you contacts list, and then press Spacebar.

3. Right-click the item, and then point to **Additional Options** (name varies depending on item).

4. Click the action option you want; options vary depending on the action. For example, click Insert Refreshable Stock Price to insert a stock quote.

5. Click the **On a new sheet** option or the **Starting at cell** option, and then click **OK**.

Did You Know?

You can remove an action from text or item. Select text or item, and then press Delete to remove it.

Checking Spelling

A worksheet's textual inaccuracies can distract the reader, so it's important that your text be error-free. Excel provides a spelling checker —common for all Office programs—so that you can check the spelling in an entire worksheet for words not listed in Excel's dictionary (such as misspellings, names, technical terms, or acronyms) or duplicate words (such as *the the*). You can correct these errors as they arise or after you finish the entire workbook. You can use the Spelling button on the Review tab to check the entire workbook using the Spelling dialog box, or you can avoid spelling errors on a worksheet by enabling the AutoCorrect feature to automatically correct words as you type.

Check Spelling All at Once

① Click the **Review** tab.

② Click the **Spelling** button.

③ If the Spelling dialog box opens, choose an option:

- ◆ Click **Ignore Once** to skip the word, or click **Ignore All** to skip every instance of the word.

- ◆ Click **Add to Dictionary** to add a word to your dictionary, so it doesn't show up as a misspelled word in the future.

- ◆ Click a suggestion, and then click **Change** or **Change All**.

- ◆ Select the correct word, and then click **AutoCorrect** to add it to the AutoCorrect list.

- ◆ If no suggestion is appropriate, click in the workbook and edit the text yourself. Click **Resume** to continue.

④ Excel will prompt you when the spelling check is complete, or you can click **Close** to end the spelling check.

Word not recognized   Suggested corrections

Current dictionary

Changing Proofing Options

You can customize the way Microsoft Office spell checks a document by selecting proofing settings in Options. Some spelling options apply to specific Office programs, such as Check spelling as you type, while other options apply to all Microsoft Office programs, such as Ignore Internet and file addresses, and Flag repeated words. If you have ever mistakenly used their instead of *there*, you can use contextual spelling to fix it. While you work in a document, you can set options to have the spelling checker search for mistakes in the background.

Change Spelling Options

1. Click the **File** tab, and then click **Options**.

2. In the left pane, click **Proofing**.

3. Select or clear the Microsoft Office spelling options you want.

   ◆ **Ignore words in UPPERCASE**.

   ◆ **Ignore words that contain numbers**.

   ◆ **Ignore Internet and file addresses**.

   ◆ **Flag repeated words**.

   ◆ **Enforce accented uppercase in French**.

   ◆ **Suggest from main dictionary only**. Select to exclude your custom dictionary.

4. Click **OK**.

Using Custom Dictionaries

Before you can use a custom dictionary, you need to enable it first. You can enable and manage custom dictionaries by using the Custom Dictionaries dialog box. In the dialog box, you can change the language associated with a custom dictionary, create a new custom dictionary, or add or remove an existing custom dictionary. If you need to manage dictionary content, you can also change the default custom dictionary to which the spelling checker adds words, as well as add, delete, or edit words. All the modifications you make to your custom dictionaries are shared with all your Microsoft Office programs, so you only need to make changes once. If you mistakenly type an obscene or embarrassing word, such as *ass* instead of *ask*, the spelling checker will not catch it because both words are spelled correctly. You can avoid this problem by using an exclusion dictionary. When you use a language for the first time, Office automatically creates an exclusion dictionary. This dictionary forces the spelling checker to flag words you don't want to use.

Use a Custom Dictionary

1. Click the **File** tab, and then click **Options**.

2. In the left pane, click **Proofing**.

3. Click **Custom Dictionaries**.

4. Select the check box next to **CUSTOM.DIC (Default)**.

5. Click the **Dictionary language** list arrow, and then select a language for a dictionary.

6. Click the options you want:

   ◆ Click **Edit Word List** to add, delete, or edit words.

   ◆ Click **Change Default** to select a new default dictionary.

   ◆ Click **New** to create a new dictionary.

   ◆ Click **Add** to insert an existing dictionary.

   ◆ Click **Remove** to delete a dictionary.

7. Click **OK** to close the Custom Dictionaries dialog box.

8. Click **OK**.

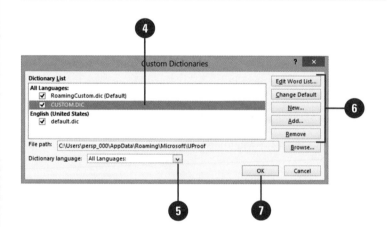

Find and Modify the Exclusion Dictionary

1. In Windows File Explorer, go to the folder location where the custom dictionaries are stored.

   ◆ **Windows 8 or 7.**
   C:\Users*user name* \AppData\ Roaming\Microsoft\UProof

   TROUBLE? *If you can't find the folder, change folder settings to show hidden files and folders.*

2. Locate the exclusion dictionary for the language you want to change.

   ◆ The file name you want is ExcludeDictionary *Language CodeLanguage LCID*.lex.

   For example, ExcludeDictionary EN0409.lex, where EN is for English.

   Check Excel Help for an updated list of LCID (Local Identification Number) number for each language.

3. Open the file using Microsoft Notepad or WordPad.

4. Add each word you want the spelling check to flag as misspelled. Type the words in all lowercase and then press Enter after each word.

5. Save and close the file.

Inserting Symbols

Excel comes with a host of symbols for every need. Insert just the right one to keep from compromising a workbook's professional appearance with a missing accent or mathematical symbol (å). In the Symbol dialog box, you use the Recently used symbols list to quickly insert a symbol that you want to insert again. If you don't see the symbol you want, use the Font list to look at the available symbols for other fonts installed on your computer.

Insert Symbols and Special Characters

1. Click the cell and then place the insertion point where you want to insert a symbol or character.

2. Click the **Insert** tab, and then click the **Symbol** button.

3. To see other symbols, click the **Font** list arrow, and then click a new font.

4. Click a symbol or character.

   You can use the Recently used symbols list to use a symbol you've already used.

5. Click **Insert**.

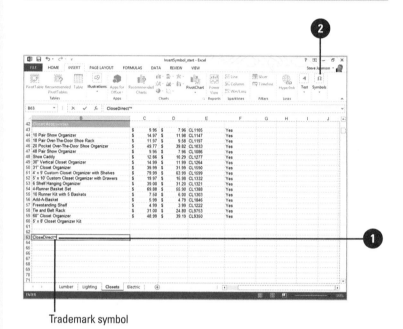

Trademark symbol

Did You Know?

You can insert a symbol using a character code. When the From box displays ASCII (decimal), you can use the number shown in the Character Code box to insert a character or symbol. Place your insertion point where you want the character on the slide, make sure Num Lock is on, hold down the Alt key, and then use the numeric keypad to type 0 (zero) followed by the character code. Then release the Alt key. The code applies to the current code page only, so some characters may not be available this way.

Finding the Right Words

Repeating the same word in a workbook can reduce a message's effectiveness. Instead, replace some words with synonyms or find antonyms. If you need help finding exactly the right words, use the shortcut menu to look up synonyms quickly or search a Thesaurus for more options. This feature can save you time and improve the quality and readability of your workbook. You can also install a Thesaurus for another language. Foreign language thesauruses can be accessed under Research Options on the Research task pane.

Use the Thesaurus

1. Select the text you want to translate.

2. Click the **Review** tab.

3. Click the **Thesaurus** button.

4. Click the list arrow, and then select a **Thesaurus**, if necessary.

5. Point to the word in the Research task pane.

6. Click the list arrow, and then click one of the following:

    ◆ **Insert** to replace the word you looked up with the new word.

    ◆ **Copy** to copy the new word and then paste it within the workbook.

    ◆ **Look Up** to look up the word for other options.

7. When you're done, click the **Close** button on the task pane.

Inserting Research Material

With the Research task pane, you can access data sources and insert research material right into your text without leaving your Excel workbook. The Research task pane can help you access electronic dictionaries, thesauruses, research sites, and proprietary company information. You can select one reference source or search in all reference books. The pane allows you to find information and easily incorporate it into your work. If you have a hard time finding research information on a topic, you can use Research Options to enable and update additional reference books and research web sites from which to search.

Research a Topic

1. Click the **Review** tab.

2. Click the **Research** button.

3. Type the topic you would like to research.

4. Click the list arrow, and then select a reference source, or click **All Reference Books**.

5. To customize which resources are used for translation, click **Research options**, select the reference books and research sites you want, and then click **OK**.

6. Click the **Start Searching** button (green arrow).

7. Select the information in the Research task pane that you want to copy.

   To search for more information, click one of the words in the list or click a link to an online site, such as Wikipedia.

8. Select the information you want, and then copy it.

   In the Research task pane, you can point to the item you want, click the list arrow, and then click **Copy**.

9. Paste the information into your workbook.

10. When you're done, click the **Close** button on the task pane.

Research options

Translating Text to Another Language

With the Research task pane, you can translate single words or short phrases into different languages by using bilingual dictionaries. The Research task pane provides you with different translations and allows you to incorporate it into your work. If you need to translate an entire document for basic subject matter understanding, web-based machine translations services are available. A machine translation is helpful for general meaning, but may not preserve the full meaning of the content.

Translate Text

1. Select the text you want to translate.

2. Click the **Review** tab.

3. Click the **Translate** button.

4. If necessary, click **Translate Selected Text**.

   ◆ To show a machine translation in a web browser, click the **Translate** button, and then click **Translate Document**.

5. Click the **From** list arrow, and then select the language of the selected text.

6. Click the **To** list arrow, and then select the language you want to translate into.

7. To customize which resources are used for translation, click **Translation options**, select the look-up options you want, and then click **OK**.

8. Right-click the translated text in the Research task pane that you want to copy, and then click **Copy**.

9. Paste the information into your workbook.

10. When you're done, click the **Close** button on the task pane.

Using Multiple Languages

International Microsoft Excel and Office users can change the language that appears on their screens by changing the default language settings. Users around the world can enter, display, and edit text in all supported languages—including European languages, Japanese, Chinese, Korean, Hebrew, and Arabic—to name a few. You'll probably be able to use Excel and Office programs in your native language. If the text in your document is written in more than one language, you can automatically detect languages or designate the language of selected text so the spelling checker uses the right dictionary. You can set preferences for editing, display, ScreenTip, and Help languages. If you don't have the keyboard layout or related software installed, you can click links to add or enable them.

Add a Language to Office Programs

1. Click the **File** tab, click **Options**, and then click **Language**.

   ◆ You can also click **Microsoft Office 2013 Language Preferences** on the All Apps screen (Win 8) or on the Start menu under Microsoft Office and Microsoft Office Tools (Win 7).

2. Click the **Language** list arrow, and then select the language you want to enable.

3. Click **Add**.

4. To enable the correct keyboard layout for the installed language, click the **Not enabled** link to open the Text Services and Input Language dialog box, where you can select a keyboard layout, and then click **OK**.

5. Set the language priority order for the buttons, tabs, and Help for the Display and Help languages.

6. Set your ScreenTip language to Match Display Language or a specific language.

7. Click **OK**, and then click **Yes** (if necessary) to quit and restart Office.

Working with Touch Screens

If you're working with Excel on a touch screen device, all you need is your finger to make gestures (**New!**). A gesture is the movement of one or more fingers on a touch screen or pad. For example, touching the screen is called tapping or dragging your finger with a flicking motion at the end of the movement is called swiping. In Excel, you can double-tap a cell to edit it, or tap and drag to select a range. To make Excel easier to use with touch, each program provides Touch/Mouse Mode (**New!**), which adds or removes more space between commands on the Ribbon.

Use Touch/Mouse Mode

1 Click the **Quick Access Toolbar** list arrow, and then click **Touch/Mouse Mode**.

This adds the button to the Quick Access Toolbar.

2 Click **Touch/Mouse Mode** button on the Quick Access Toolbar.

3 Click **Mouse** or **Touch**.

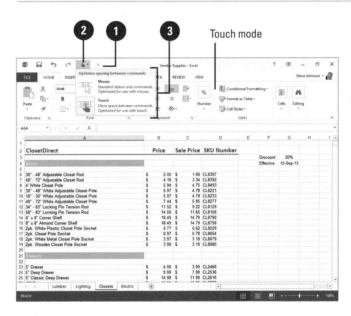
Touch mode

Did You Know?

You can use touch commands. In Office, you can use the following touch commands:

Click - Tap in the file.

Double-click - Double-tap in the file.

Drag - Tap and slide.

Zoom - Pinch or stretch two fingers.

Scroll - Touch and slide up or down.

Select - Tap an object. For multiple objects, select one, and then tap and hold the others. For text, tap and drag.

You can make text and objects bigger. In Windows, open the Control Panel, tap Appearance & Personalization, tap Display, and tap Medium - 125% or Larger - 150%, and then tap Apply.

Finger gestures

Swiping gestures

Undoing and Redoing an Action

You may realize you've made a mistake shortly after completing an action or a task. The Undo feature lets you "take back" one or more previous actions, including data you entered, edits you made, or commands you selected. For example, if you were to enter a number in a cell, and then decide the number was incorrect, you could undo the entry instead of selecting the data and deleting it. A few moments later, if you decide the number you deleted was correct after all, you could use the Redo feature to restore it to the cell.

Undo an Action

1. Click the **Undo** button on the Quick Access Toolbar to undo the last action you completed.

2. Click the **Undo** button arrow on the Quick Access Toolbar to see recent actions that can be undone.

3. Click an action. Office reverses the selected action and all actions above it.

Redo an Action

1. Click the **Redo** button on the Quick Access Toolbar to restore your last undone action.

   TROUBLE? *If the Redo button is not available on the Quick Access Toolbar, click the Customize Quick Access Toolbar list arrow, and then click Redo.*

2. Click the **Redo** button arrow on the Quick Access Toolbar to see actions that can be restored.

3. Click the action you want to restore. All actions above it will be restored as well.

Working with Formulas and Functions

Introduction

Once you enter data in a worksheet, you'll want to add formulas to perform calculations. Microsoft Excel can help you get the results you need. Formulas can be very basic entries to more complex ones. The difficulty of the formula depends on the complexity of the result you want from your data. For instance, if you are simply looking to total this months sales, then the formula would add your sales number and provide the result. However, if you were looking to show this months sales, greater than $100.00 with repeat customers, you would take a bit more time to design the formula.

Because Excel automatically recalculates formulas, your worksheets remain accurate and up-to-date no matter how often you change the data. Using absolute cell references anchors formulas to a specific cell. Excel provides numerous built-in functions to add to your worksheet calculations. Functions, such as AVERAGE or SUM, allow you to perform a quick formula calculation.

Another way to make your formulas easier to understand is by using name ranges in them. Name ranges—a group of selected cells named as a range—can help you understand your more complicated formulas. It is a lot easier to read a formula that uses name ranges, then to look at the formula and try to decipher it. Excel offers a tool to audit your worksheet. Looking at the "flow" of your formula greatly reduces errors in the calculation. You can see how your formula is built, one level at a time through a series of arrows that point out where the formula is pulling data from. As you develop your formula, you can make corrections to it.

What You'll Do

Understand Formulas

Create and Edit Formulas

Understand Cell Referencing

Use Absolute Cell References

Use Mixed and 3-D Cell References

Name Cells and Ranges

Enter and Manage Names

Simplify a Formula with Ranges

Display Calculations with the Status Bar

Calculate Totals with AutoSum

Perform One Time Calculations

Convert Formulas and Values

Correct Calculation Errors

Correct Formulas

Audit a Worksheet

Locate Circular References

Perform Calculations Using Functions

Create Functions and Nested Functions

Calculate Multiple Results

Use Constants and Functions in Names

Understanding Formulas

Introduction

A formula calculates values to return a result. On an Excel worksheet, you can create a formula using constant values (such as 147 or $10.00), operators (shown in the table), references, and functions. An Excel formula always begins with the equal sign (=).

A **constant** is a number or text value that is not calculated, such as the number 147, the text "Total Profits", and the date 7/22/2013. On the other hand, an **expression** is a value that is not a constant. Constants remain the same until you or the system change them. An **operator** performs a calculation, such as + (plus sign) or - (minus sign). A cell **reference** is a cell address that returns the value in a cell. For example, A1 (column A and row 1) returns the value in cell A1 (see table below).

Cell Reference Examples

Reference	Meaning
A1	Cell in column A and row 1
A1:A10	Range of cells in column A and rows 1 through 10
A1:F1	Range of cells in row 1 and columns A through F
1:1	All cells in row 1
1:5	All cells in rows 1 through 5
A:A	All cells in column A
A:F	All cells in columns A through F
Profits!A1:A10	Range of cells in column A and rows 1 through 10 in worksheet named Profits

A **function** performs predefined calculations using specific values, called arguments. For example, the function SUM(B1:B10) returns the sum of cells B1 through B10. An argument can be numbers, text, logical values such as TRUE or FALSE, arrays, error values such as #NA, or cell references. Arguments can also be constants, formulas, or other functions, known as **nested functions**. A function starts with the equal sign (=), followed by the function name, an opening parenthesis, the arguments for the function separated by commas, and a closing parenthesis. For example, the function, AVERAGE(A1:A10, B1:B10), returns a number with the average for the contents of cells A1 through A10 and B1 through B10. As you type a function, a ToolTip appears with the structure and arguments needed to complete the function. You can also use the Insert Function dialog box to help you add a function to a formula.

Perform Calculations

By default, every time you make a change to a value, formula, or name, Excel performs a calculation. To change the way Excel performs calculations, click the Formulas tab, click the Calculation Options button, and then click the option you want: Automatic, Automatic Except Data Tables, or Manual. To manually recalculate all open workbooks, click the Calculate Now button (or press F9). To recalculate the active worksheet, click the Calculate Sheet button (or press Shift+F9).

Precedence Order

Formulas perform calculations from left to right, according to a specific order for each operator. Formulas containing more than one operator follow precedence order: exponentiation, multiplication and division, and then addition and subtraction. So, in the formula 2 + 5 * 7, Excel performs multiplication first and addition next for a result of 37. Excel calculates operations within parentheses first. The result of the formula (2 + 5) * 7 is 49.

Types of Operators

Operator	Meaning	Example
Arithmetic		
= (plus sign)	Addition	2+7
- (minus sign)	Subtraction	7-2
	Negative	-2
* (asterisk)	Multiplication	2*7
/ (forward slash)	Division	7/2
% (percent)	Percent	70%
^ (caret)	Exponentiation	2^7
Comparison		
= (equal sign)	Equal to	A2=B7
> (greater than sign)	Greater than	A2>B7
< (less than sign)	Less than	A2<B7
>= (greater than or equal to sign)	Greater than or equal to	A2>=B7
<= (less than or equal to sign)	Less than or equal to	A2<=B7
<> (not equal to sign)	Not equal to	A2<>B7
Text concatenation		
& (ampersand)	Connects, or concatenates, two values to produce one continuous text value	"Total"&"Profit"
Reference		
: (colon)	Range operator, which produces one reference to all the cells between two references	A1:A10
, (comma)	Union operator, which combines multiple references into one reference	SUM(A1:A10,B1:B10)
(space)	Intersection operator, which produces on reference to cells common to the two references	A1:A10 B1:B10

Creating a Simple Formula

A **formula** calculates values to return a result. On an Excel worksheet, you can create a formula using values (such as 147 or $10.00), arithmetic operators (shown in the table), and cell references. An Excel formula always begins with the equal sign (=). The equal sign, when entered, automatically formats the cell as a formula entry. The best way to start a formula is to have an argument. An **argument** is the cell references or values in a formula that contribute to the result. Each function uses function-specific arguments, which may include numeric values, text values, cell references, ranges of cells, and so on. To accommodate long, complex formulas, you can resize the formula bar to prevent formulas from covering other data in your worksheet. By default, only formula results are displayed in a cell, but you can change the view of the worksheet to display formulas instead of results.

Enter a Formula

1. Click the cell where you want to enter a formula.

2. Type = (an equal sign). If you do not begin with an equal sign, Excel will display, not calculate, the information you type.

3. Enter the first argument. An argument can be a number or a cell reference.

   TIMESAVER *To avoid typing mistakes, click a cell to insert its cell reference in a formula rather than typing its address.*

4. Enter an arithmetic operator.

5. Enter the next argument.

6. Repeat steps 4 and 5 as needed to complete the formula.

7. Click the **Enter** button on the formula bar, or press Enter.

   Notice that the result of the formula appears in the cell (if you select the cell, the formula itself appears on the formula bar).

   TIMESAVER *To wrap text in a cell, press Alt+Enter, which manually inserts a line break.*

For Your Information

Understanding Order of Precedence

Formulas containing more than one operator follow the order of precedence: exponentiation, multiplication and division, and then addition and subtraction. So, in the formula 5 + 2 * 3, Excel performs multiplication first and addition next for a result of 11. Excel calculates operations within parentheses first. The result of the formula (5 + 2) * 3 is 21.

Resize the Formula Bar

◆ To switch between expanding the formula box to three or more lines or collapsing it to one line, click the down/up arrow at the end of the formula bar. You can also press Ctrl+Shift+U.

◆ To precisely adjust the height of the formula box, point to the bottom of the formula box until the pointer changes to a vertical double arrow, and then drag up or down, and then click the vertical double arrow or press Enter.

◆ To automatically fit the formula box to the number of lines of text in the active cell, point to the formula box until the pointer changes to a vertical double arrow, and then double-click the vertical arrow.

Display Formulas in Cells

1 Click the **Formulas** tab.

2 Click the **Show Formulas** button.

TIMESAVER *Press Ctrl+'.*

3 To turn off formula display, click the **Show Formulas** button again.

Did You Know?

Pointing to cells reduces errors. When building formulas, pointing to a cell rather than typing its address ensures that the correct cell is referenced.

You can print formulas. Click the Formulas tab, click the Show Formulas button to show formulas, click the File tab, click Print, and then click Print.

Down/Up arrow

Creating a Formula Using Formula AutoComplete

To minimize typing and syntax errors, you can create and edit formulas with Formula AutoComplete. After you type an = (equal sign) and begin typing to start a formula, Excel displays a dynamic drop-down list of valid functions, arguments, defined names, table names, special item specifiers—including [(open bracket), , (comma), : (colon)—and text string that match the letters you type. An argument is the cell references or values in a formula that contribute to the result. Each function uses function-specific arguments, which may include numeric values, text values, cell references, ranges of cells, and so on.

Enter Items in a Formula Using Formula AutoComplete

① Click the cell where you want to enter a formula.

② Type = (an equal sign), and beginning letters or a display trigger to start Formula AutoComplete.

For example, type *su* to display all value items, such as SUBTOTAL and SUM.

The text before the insertion point is used to display the values in the drop-down list.

③ As you type, a drop-down scrollable list of valid items is displayed.

Icons represent the type of entry, such as a function or table reference, and a ScreenTip appears next to a selected item.

④ To insert the selected item in the drop-down list into the formula, press Tab or double-click the item.

Did You Know?

You can turn on Formula AutoComplete. Click the File tab, click Options, click Formulas in the left pane, select the Formula AutoComplete check box, and then click OK.

Use the Keyboard to Navigate

Using the keyboard, you can navigate the Formula AutoComplete drop-down list to quickly find the entry you want.

◆ Refer to the table for keyboard shortcuts for navigating the Formula AutoComplete drop-down list.

Keys For Navigating AutoComplete List

Press This Key	To Move
Left arrow	Move the insertion point to the left
Right arrow	Move the insertion point to the right
Up arrow	Move the selection up one item
Down arrow	Move the selection down one item
End	Select the last item
Home	Select the first item
Page Down	Move down one page and select a new item
Page Up	Move up one page and select a new item
Esc	Close the drop-down list
Alt+Down arrow	Turn on or off Formula AutoComplete

Turn on Formula AutoComplete

1. Click the **File** tab, and then click **Options**.

2. In the left pane, click **Formulas**.

3. Select the **Formula AutoComplete** check box.

4. Click **OK**.

Did You Know?

Some items don't appear on the Formula AutoComplete drop-down list. Defined names that you create for enumerated constants, such as the ones used in the SUBTOTAL function, and Cube function connections do not appear in the Formula AutoComplete drop-down list, but you can still type them.

Editing a Formula

You can edit formulas just as you do other cell contents, using the formula bar or working in the cell. You can select, cut, copy, paste, delete, and format cells containing formulas just as you do cells containing labels or values. Using **AutoFill**, you can quickly copy formulas to adjacent cells. If you need to copy formulas to different parts of a worksheet, use the Paste command or Paste Options button.

Edit a Formula Using the Formula Bar

1. Select the cell that contains the formula you want to edit.

2. Press F2 to change to Edit mode.

3. If necessary, use the Home, End, and arrow keys to position the insertion point within the cell contents.

4. Use any combination of Backspace and Delete to erase unwanted characters, and then type new characters as needed.

5. Click the **Enter** button on the formula bar, or press Enter.

2 Edit mode

Copy a Formula Using AutoFill

1. Select the cell that contains the formula you want to copy.

2. Position the pointer (fill handle) on the lower-right corner of the selected cell.

3. Drag the mouse down until the adjacent cells where you want the formula pasted are selected, and then release the mouse button.

Fill handle

Copy and Paste a Formula

1. Select the cell that contains the formula you want to copy.

2. Click the **Home** tab.

3. Click the **Copy** button.

4. Select one or more cells where you want to paste the formula.

5. Click the **Paste** button or click the **Paste** button arrow, point to an option to display a live preview of the paste, and then click to paste the item.

6. Click the **Paste Options** button, point to an option for the live preview, and then select the option you want.

   If you don't want to paste this selection anywhere else, press Esc to remove the marquee.

Did You Know?

You can use Paste Special to copy only formulas. Select the cells containing the formulas you want to copy, click the Copy button on the Home tab, click where you want to paste the data, click the Paste button arrow, click Paste Special, click the Formulas button, and then click OK.

You can use keyboard commands to recalculate formulas. Press F9 to recalculate formulas that have changed since the last calculation in all open workbooks. Press Shift+F9 to recalculate formulas in the active workbook. Press Ctrl+Alt+F9 to recalculate all formulas in all open workbooks, regardless of whether formulas have changed. Press Ctrl+Shift+Alt+F9 to recheck dependent formulas in all open workbooks, regardless of whether formulas have changed.

Understanding Cell Referencing

Each cell, the intersection of a column and row on a worksheet, has a unique address, or **cell reference**, based on its column letter and row number. For example, the cell reference for the intersection of column D and row 4 is D4.

Cell References in Formulas

The simplest formula refers to a cell. If you want one cell to contain the same value as another cell, type an equal sign followed by the cell reference, such as =D4. The cell that contains the formula is known as a **dependent cell** because its value depends on the value in another cell. Whenever the cell that the formula refers to changes, the cell that contains the formula also changes.

Depending on your task, you can use **relative cell references**, which are references to cells relative to the position of the formula, **absolute cell references**, which are cell references that always refer to cells in a specific location, or **mixed cell references**, which use a combination of relative and absolute column and row references. If you use macros, the R1C1 cell references make it easy to compute row and column positions.

Relative Cell References

When you copy and paste or move a formula that uses relative references, the references in the formula change to reflect cells that are in the same relative position to the formula. The formula is the same, but it uses the new cells in its calculation. Relative addressing eliminates the tedium of creating new formulas for each row or column in a worksheet filled with repetitive information.

Absolute Cell References

If you don't want a cell reference to change when you copy a formula, make it an absolute reference by typing a dollar sign ($) before each part of the reference that you don't want to change. For example, A1 always refers to cell A1. If you copy or fill the formula down columns or across rows, the absolute reference doesn't change. You can add a $ before the column letter and the row number. To ensure accuracy and simplify updates, enter constant values (such as tax rates, hourly rates, and so on) in a cell, and then use absolute references to them in formulas.

Mixed Cell References

A mixed reference is either an absolute row and relative column or absolute column and relative row. You add the $ before the column letter to create an absolute column or before the row number to create an absolute row. For example, $A1 is absolute for column A and relative for row 1, and A$1 is absolute for row 1 and relative for column A. If you copy or fill the formula across rows or down columns, the relative references adjust, and the absolute ones don't adjust.

3-D References

3-D references allow you to analyze data in the same cell or range of cells on multiple worksheets within a workbook. A 3-D reference includes the cell or range reference, preceded by a range of worksheet names. For example, =AVERAGE(Sheet1:Sheet4!A1) returns the average for all the values contained in cell A1 on all the worksheets between and including Sheet 1 and Sheet 4.

Using Absolute Cell References

When you want a formula to consistently refer to a particular cell, even if you copy or move the formula elsewhere on the worksheet, you need to use an absolute cell reference. An absolute cell reference is a cell address that contains a dollar sign ($) in the row or column coordinate, or both. When you enter a cell reference in a formula, Excel assumes it is a relative reference unless you change it to an absolute reference. If you want part of a formula to remain a relative reference, remove the dollar sign that appears before the column letter or row number.

Create an Absolute Reference

1. Click a cell where you want to enter a formula.

2. Type = (an equal sign) to begin the formula.

3. Select a cell, and then type an arithmetic operator (+, -, *, or /).

4. Select another cell, and then press the F4 key to make that cell reference absolute.

   You can continue to press F4 to have Excel cycle through the different reference types.

5. If necessary, continue entering the formula.

6. Click the **Enter** button on the formula bar, or press Enter.

Did You Know?

You can change an absolute reference back to a relative reference. In the cell with the absolute formula, repeatedly press F4 until all the dollar signs are removed from the reference. You press F4 to cycle through all the reference types. For example, if you enter A1 to start a formula, press F4 to display A1. Press again to display A$1. Press again to display $A1. Press it again to display A1.

Price		Quantity	Total Price	
$	19.96	5	=D6*E6	
$	32.48	3	$	97.44
$	19.97	7	$	139.79
$	4.99	10	$	49.90
$	29.97	9	$	269.73

Absolute reference

Using Mixed Cell References

A mixed cell reference is either an absolute column and relative row or absolute row and relative column. When you add the $ before the column letter you create an absolute column or before the row number you create an absolute row. For example, $A1 is absolute for column A and relative for row 1, and A$1 is absolute for row 1 and relative for column A. If you copy or fill the formula across rows or down columns, the relative references adjust, and the absolute ones don't adjust.

Create a Mixed Reference

1. Click a cell where you want to enter a formula.

2. Type = (an equal sign) to begin the formula.

3. Select the cells you want to use and then complete the formula.

4. Click the insertion point in the formula bar, and then type $ before the column or row you want to make absolute.

5. Click the **Enter** button on the formula bar, or press Enter.

Price	Quantity	Total Price	
$ 19.96	5	$ 99.80	
$ 32.48	3	=D7*E$7	
$ 19.97	7	$ 139.79	
$ 4.99	10	$ 49.90	
$ 29.97	9	$ 269.73	
$ 21.00	25	$ 525.00	

Mixed reference

Using 3-D Cell References

If you want to analyze data in the same cell or range of cells on multiple worksheets within a workbook, use a mixed 3-D reference. For example, =SUM(Sheet3:Sheet6!A1:A10) returns the sum for all the values contained in the range of cells A1 through A10 on all the worksheets between and including Sheet 3 and Sheet 6. 3-D references work with the following functions: AVERAGE, AVERAGEA, COUNT, COUNTA, MAX, MAXA, MIN, MINA, PRODUCT, STDEV, STDEVA, STDE-VPA, VAR, VARA, VARP, and VARPA. However, 3-D references cannot be used with array formulas, the intersection operator (a single space), or the implicit intersection. If you move, insert, or copy sheets between the ones included in the range, Excel adds the values from the sheets in the calculations. If you move or remove sheets between the ones included in the range, Excel removes the values from the calculation.

Create a 3-D Cell Reference

1. Click a cell where you want to enter a formula.

2. Type = (an equal sign) to begin the formula.

3. Type the function you want to use followed by a ((left bracket).

4. Type the first worksheet name, followed by a : (colon), and then the last worksheet name in the range.

5. Type ! (exclamation).

6. Type or select the cell or cell range you want to use in the function.

7. Type) (right bracket).

8. Click the **Enter** button on the formula bar, or press Enter.

See Also

See "Performing Calculations Using Functions" on page 108 and "Creating Functions" on page 109 for information on creating and using functions.

Naming Cells and Ranges

To make working with ranges easier, Excel allows you to name them. The name BookTitle, for example, is easier to remember than the range reference B6:B21. Named ranges can be used to navigate large worksheets. Named ranges can also be used in formulas instead of typing or pointing to specific cells. When you name a cell or range, Excel uses an absolute reference for the name by default, which is almost always what you want. You can see the absolute reference in the Refers to box in the New Name dialog box. There are two types of names you can create and use: defined name and table name. A **defined name** represents a cell, a range of cells, formula or constant, while a **table name** represents an Excel table, which is a collection of data stored in records (rows) and fields (columns). You can define a name for use in a worksheet or an entire workbook, also known as **scope**. To accommodate long names, you can resize the name box in the formula bar. The worksheet and formula bar work together to avoid overlapping content.

Name a Cell or Range Using the Name Box

1. Select the cell or range, or nonadjacent selections you want to name.

2. Click the Name box on the formula bar.

3. Type a name for the range.

   A range name can include up to 255 characters, uppercase or lowercase letters (not case sensitive), numbers, and punctuation, but no spaces or cell references.

   By default, names use absolute cell references.

4. To adjust the width of the Name box, point between the Name box and the Formula box until the pointer changes to a horizontal double arrow, and then drag left or right.

5. Press Enter. The range name will appear in the Name box whenever you select the range in the workbook.

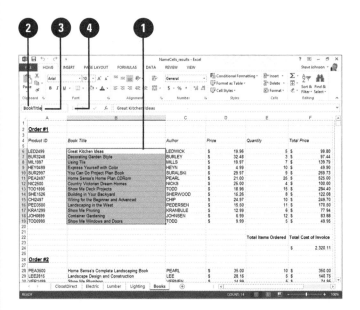

Let Excel Name a Cell or Range

1. Select the cells, including the column or row header, you want to name.

2. Click the **Formulas** tab.

3. Click the **Create from Selection** button.

4. Select the check box with the position of the labels in relation to the cells.

   Excel automatically tries to determine the position of the labels, so you might not have to change any options.

5. Click **OK**.

Name a Cell or Range Using the New Name Dialog Box

1. Select the cell or range, or nonadjacent selections you want to name.

2. Click the **Formulas** tab.

3. Click the **Define Name** button.

4. Type a name for the reference.

5. Click the **Scope** list arrow, and then click **Workbook** or a specific worksheet.

6. If you want, type a description of the name.

   The current selection appears in the Refer to box.

7. Click the **Collapse Dialog** button, select different cells and click the **Expand Dialog** button, or type = (equal sign) followed by a constant value or a formula.

8. Click **OK**.

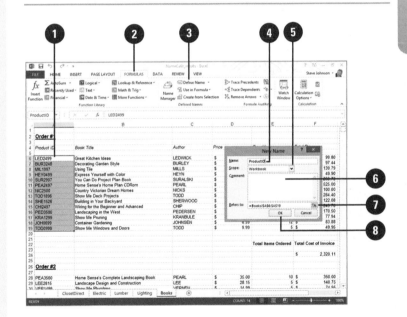

Entering Named Cells and Ranges

After you define a named cell or range, you can enter a name by typing, using the Name box, using Formula AutoComplete, or selecting from the Use in Formula command. As you begin to type a name in a formula, Formula AutoComplete displays valid matches in a drop-down list, which you can select and insert into a formula. You can also select a name from a list of available from the Use in Formula command. If you have already entered a cell or range address in a formula or function, you can apply a name to the address instead of re-creating it.

Enter a Named Cell or Range Using the Name Box

1. Click the **Name box** list arrow on the formula bar.

2. Click the name of the cell or range you want to use.

   The range name appears in the Name box, and all cells included in the range are highlighted on the worksheet.

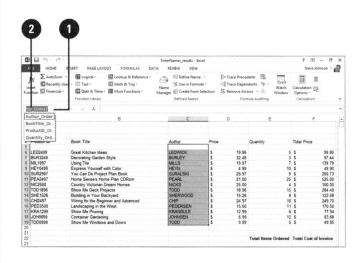

Enter a Named Cell or Range Using Formula AutoComplete

1. Type = (equal sign) to start a formula, and then type the first letter of the name.

2. To insert a name, type the first letter of the name to display it in the Formula AutoComplete drop-down list.

3. Scroll down the list, if necessary, to select the name you want, and then press Tab or double-click the name to insert it.

Enter a Named Cell or Range from the Use in Formula Command

1. Type = (equal sign) to start a formula.

2. Click the **Formulas** tab.

3. When you want to insert a name, click the **Use in Formula** button.

4. Use one of the following menu options:

   ◆ Click the name you want to use.

   ◆ Click **Paste Names**, select a name, and then click **OK**.

Apply a Name to a Cell or Range Address

1. Select the cells in which you want to apply a name.

2. Click the **Formulas** tab.

3. Click the **Define Name** button arrow, and then click **Apply Names**.

4. Click the name you want to apply.

5. Click **OK**.

Did You Know?

Should I select the Use row and column names option? When you select this option, Excel uses the range row and column headings to refer to the range you've selected (if a cell does not have its own name, but is part of a named range).

Managing Names

The Name Manager makes it easy to work with all the defined names and table names in a workbook from one location. You can display the value and reference of a name, specify the scope—either worksheet or workbook level—of a name, find names with errors, and view or edit name descriptions. In addition, you can add, change, or delete names, and sort and filter the names list. You can also use table column header names in formulas instead of cell references.

Organize and View Names

1. Click the **Formulas** tab.

2. Click the **Name Manager** button.

   TROUBLE? *You cannot use the Name Manager dialog box while you're editing a cell. The Name Manager doesn't display names defined in VBA or hidden names.*

3. Use one of the following menu options:

   ◆ **Resize columns.** Double-click the right side of the column header to automatically size the column to fit the largest value in that column.

   ◆ **Sort names.** Click the column header to sort the list of names in ascending or descending order.

   ◆ **Filter names.** Click the Filter button, and then select the filter command you want. See table for filter option details.

4. Click **Close**.

Column header

Did You Know?

What happens when you zoom in on a name range? When you zoom the view of the worksheet to 39 percent or less, Excel adds a blue border around the labels you have created. The blue border does not print.

Name Manager Filter Options

Option	Result
Names Scoped to Worksheet	Displays names local to a worksheet
Names Scoped to Workbook	Displays names global to a workbook
Names with Errors	Displays names with values that contain errors (such as #NAME, #VALUE, etc.)
Names without Errors	Displays names without errors
Defined Names	Displays names defined by you or by Excel
Table Names	Displays table names

Change a Name

1. Click the **Formulas** tab.

2. Click the **Name Manager** button.

3. Click the name you want to change.

4. Click **Edit**.

5. Type a new name for the reference in the Name box.

6. Change the reference. Enter a range or use the **Collapse** button to select one.

7. Click **OK**.

8. In the Refers to area, make any changes you want to the cell, formula, or constant represented by the name.

   To cancel unwanted changes, click the **Cancel** button or press Esc, or to save changes, click the **Commit** button or press Enter.

9. Click **Close**.

Did You Know?

You can delete a name range. Click the Formulas tab, click the Name Manager button, select the names you want to delete, click Delete or press Delete, click OK to confirm, and then click Close.

What happens when you change a label reference? If you change the name of a reference label, Excel automatically makes the change to every formula in which the name is used.

You can label names that are relative. When you use a label name in a formula or function, Excel sees it as a relative reference. You can copy the formula to other cells, or use AutoFill to copy it and the reference changes.

Simplifying a Formula with Ranges

You can simplify formulas by using ranges and range names. For example, if 12 cells on your worksheet contain monthly budget amounts, and you want to multiply each amount by 10%, you can insert one range address in a formula instead of inserting 12 different cell addresses, or you can insert a range name. Using a range name in a formula helps to identify what the formula does; the formula =TotalOrder*0.10, for example, is more meaningful than =SUM(F6:F19)*0.10.

Use a Range in a Formula

1. Put your cursor where you would like the formula. Type an equal sign (=) followed by the start of a formula, such as =SUM(.

2. Click the first cell of the range, and then drag to select the last cell in the range. Excel enters the range address for you.

3. Complete the formula by entering a close parentheses, or another function, and then click the **Enter** button.

Use a Range Name in a Formula

1. Put your cursor where you would like the formula. Type an equal sign (=) followed by the start of a formula, such as =SUM(.

2. Press F3 to display a list of named ranges.

   ◆ You can also click the **Use in Formula** button on the Formulas tab, and then click **Paste**.

3. Click the name of the range you want to insert.

4. Click **OK**.

5. Complete the formula by entering a close parentheses, or another function, and then click the **Enter** button.

Displaying Calculations with the Status Bar

You can simplify your work using the Status bar calculations when you don't want to insert a formula, but you want to quickly see the results of a simple calculation. The Status bar automatically displays the sum, average, maximum, minimum, or count of the selected values. The Status bar results do not appear on the worksheet when printed but are useful for giving you quick answers while you work. If a cell contains text, it's ignored, except when you select the Count option.

Calculate a Range Automatically

1 Select the range of cells you want to calculate.

The sum, average, and count of the selected cells appears on the status bar by default.

2 If you want to change the type of calculations that appear on the Status bar, right-click anywhere on the Status bar to display a shortcut menu.

The shortcut menu displays all the available status information you can track. The right side of the menu displays the current values for the different calculations.

3 Click to toggle (on or off) the available types of calculations.

- ◆ Average
- ◆ Count
- ◆ Numerical Count
- ◆ Minimum
- ◆ Maximum
- ◆ Sum

Calculating Totals with AutoSum

A range of cells can easily be added using the **AutoSum** button on the Formulas tab. AutoSum suggests the range to sum, although this range can be changed if it's incorrect. AutoSum looks at all of the data that is consecutively entered, and when it sees an empty cell, that is where the AutoSum stops. You can also use AutoSum to perform other calculations, such as AVERAGE, COUNT, MAX, and MIN. Subtotals can be calculated for data ranges using the Subtotals dialog box. This dialog box lets you select where the subtotals occur, as well as the function type.

Calculate Totals with AutoSum

1. Click the cell where you want to display the calculation.

   ◆ To sum with a range of numbers, select the range of cells you want.

   ◆ To sum with only some of the numbers in a range, select the cells or range you want using the Ctrl key. Excel inserts the sum in the first empty cell below the selected range.

   ◆ To sum both across and down a table of number, select the range of cells with an additional column to the right and a row at the bottom.

2. Click the **Formulas** tab.

3. Click the **AutoSum** button.

   TIMESAVER *Press Alt+= to access the AutoSum command.*

4. Click the **Enter** button on the formula bar, or press Enter.

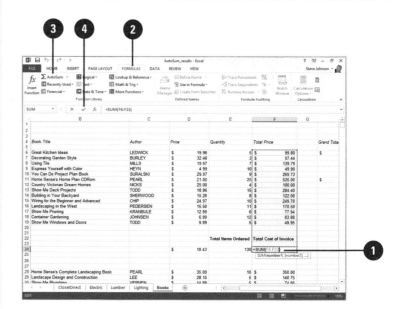

Did You Know?

You can select additional AutoFill commands. Click the Home tab, and then click the Fill button to select additional commands such as Up, Down, Left, Right, Series, or Justify.

Calculate with Extended AutoSum

1. Click the cell where you want to display the calculation.

2. Click the **Formulas** tab.

3. Click the **AutoSum** button arrow.

4. Click the function you want to use, such as AVERAGE, COUNT, MAX, and MIN.

5. Press Enter to accept the range selected.

Calculate Subtotals and Totals

1. Click anywhere within the data to be subtotaled.

2. Click the **Data** tab.

3. Click the **Subtotal** button.

   If a message box appears, read the message, and then click the appropriate button.

4. Select the appropriate check boxes to specify how the data is subtotaled.

5. Click **OK**.

Did You Know?

You can use AutoSum to calculate a subtotal. If you're working with a table, you can use the AutoSum button to insert the Subtotal function rather than the SUM function. The function only sums the visible cells in a filtered list.

Calculating Totals with Quick Analysis

When you select a range of cells, you can use the Quick Analysis tool (**New!**) to calculate totals for the data. The tool allows you to calculate totals for Sum, Average, Count, % Total, and Running Total. The result of the totals can appear below the selected range or to the right of the selected range. You can point to a button option to display a live preview of the results before you commit to it. In addition to calculating totals, you can also use the Quick Analysis tool (**New!**) to format data and create charts and tables.

Calculate Totals with Quick Analysis Below Selection

① Select the range of cells you want to total.

A Quick Analysis button appears in the lower right corner of the selection.

② Click the **Quick Analysis** button.

A menu appears, displaying heading tabs along the top, and buttons below it.

③ Click **Totals**.

④ To preview the totals result, point to the button (select an icon with blue row) with the type of total calculation you want.

◆ **Scroll Arrows.** Click a left or right scroll arrow to display buttons.

⑤ To set the totals results result, click the button (select an icon with blue row) with the type of total calculation you want.

Preview of the result below selection

Calculate Totals with Quick Analysis Next to Selection

① Select the range of cells you want to total; make sure the column to the right is available to place the results.

A Quick Analysis button appears in the lower right corner of the selection.

② Click the **Quick Analysis** button.

A menu appears, displaying heading tabs along the top, and buttons below it.

③ Click **Totals**.

④ To preview the totals result, point to the button (select an icon with gold column) with the type of total calculation you want.

◆ **Scroll Arrows.** Click a left or right scroll arrow to display buttons.

⑤ To set the totals results result, click the button (select an icon with gold column) with the type of total calculation you want.

Preview of the result to the right of the selection

Performing One Time Calculations

Sometimes you may want to perform simple calculations, such as dividing each value in a range by 4, without having to take the time to use a formula. You can use the Paste Special command to perform simple mathematical operations, such as Add, Subtract, Multiply, and Divide. If you want to perform a more complex function, you can create a temporary formula to accomplish a one-time task. For example, if you want to display a list of names in proper case with only the first letter of each name in uppercase, you can use the Proper function.

Perform One Time Simple Calculations without Using a Formula

1. Select an empty cell, and then enter the number you want to use in a calculation.

2. Click the **Home** tab.

3. Click the **Copy** button.

4. Select the range you want to use in the calculation.

5. Click the **Paste** button arrow, and then click **Paste Special**.

6. Click the operation option you want to use: **Add**, **Subtract**, **Multiply**, or **Divide**.

7. Click **OK**.

8. Press Esc to cancel Copy mode.

The operation is applied to the contents of each cell in the range. The formula in each cell is changed to include the new operation.

Perform One Time Calculations Using a Formula

1 Create a temporary formula in an unused cell, typically a column out of the way. Select an empty cell at the top, type = (equal sign), and then type a function, such as Proper().

2 Click the **Home** tab.

3 If you want to change a range of data, use the fill down handle to copy the formula to unused cells.

4 Select the cell or range with the formula.

5 Click the **Copy** button.

6 Select the cell you want to change the contents with the formula.

7 Click the **Paste** button arrow, and then click **Paste Special**.

8 Click the **Values** option.

9 Click **OK**.

The original data is replaced with the changed data.

10 When you're done with the temporary formulas, select the cells, and delete them.

Converting Formulas and Values

If you have a range of cells that contain formulas, you can convert the cells to values only. This is useful when you have a range of cells that you don't want to change anymore. You use the Paste Special command to paste the contents of the selected range back into place as a value instead of a formula. If you're working with an input form in Excel, you probably need to delete values, but keep the formulas. You can do it with the help of the Go To Special dialog box.

Convert a Formula to a Value

1. Select the range of cells with formulas you want to convert to values.

2. Click the **Home** tab.

3. Click the **Copy** button.

4. Click the **Paste** button arrow, and then click **Paste Special**.

5. Click the **Values** option.

6. Click **OK**.

7. Press Esc to cancel Copy mode.

Delete Values and Keep Formulas

1. Click the **Home** tab.

2. Click the **Find & Select** button, and then click **Go To Special.**

3. Click the **Constants** option.

4. Select the **Numbers** check box, and then clear the other check boxes under Formula.

5. Click **OK**.

6. Press Delete to remove the selected values.

Number Constants selected

Correcting Calculation Errors

When Excel finds a possible error in a calculation, it displays a green triangle in the upper left corner of the cell. If Excel can't complete a calculation it displays an error message, such as "#DIV/0!" or "#NAME?. You can use the Error Options button to help you fix the problem. In a complex worksheet, it can be difficult to understand the relationships between cells and formulas. Auditing tools enable you to clearly determine these relationships. When the Auditing feature is turned on, it uses a series of arrows to show you which cells are part of which formulas. When you use the auditing tools, tracer arrows point out cells that provide data to formulas and the cells that contain formulas that refer to the cells. A box is drawn around the range of cells that provide data to formulas.

Review and Correct Errors

1. Select a cell that contains a green triangle in the upper left corner.

2. Click the **Error Options** button.

3. Click one of the troubleshooting options (menu options vary depending on the error).

   ◆ To have Excel fix the error, click one of the available options specific to the error.

   ◆ To find out more about an error, click **Help on this Error**.

   ◆ To evaluate the formula, click **Show Calculation Steps**.

   ◆ To remove the error alert, click **Ignore Error**.

   ◆ To fix the error manually, click **Edit in Formula Bar**.

   ◆ To enable background error checking, specify an error color, or reset ignored errors, click **Error Checking Options**.

For Your Information

Avoiding Error Displays in Formulas

If you include empty cells in a formula, an error message, such as #DIV/0! might appear in the formula cell. You can avoid this message by adding a function to check for errors. If the formula generating an error message for empty cells is =*Formula*, then change it to =IF(ISERROR(*Formula*),"",*Formula*). If the ISERROR function is true, the IF function returns an empty string, instead of an error message.

Correcting Formulas

Excel has several tools to help you find and correct problems with formulas. One tool is the **Watch window** and another is the **Error checker**. The Watch window keeps track of cells and their formulas as you make changes to a worksheet. Excel uses an error checker in the same way Microsoft Word uses a grammar checker. The Error checker uses certain rules, such as using the wrong argument type, a number stored as text or an empty cell reference, to check for problems in formulas.

Watch Cells and Formulas

1. Select the cells you want to watch.

2. Click the **Formulas** tab.

3. Click the **Watch Window** button.

4. Click the **Add Watch** button on the Watch Window dialog box.

5. Click **Add**.

6. Click **Close**.

Remove Cells from the Watch Window

1. Click the **Formulas** tab.

2. Click the **Watch Window** button.

3. Select the cells you want to delete. Use the Ctrl key to select multiple cells.

4. Click **Delete Watch**.

5. Click **Close**.

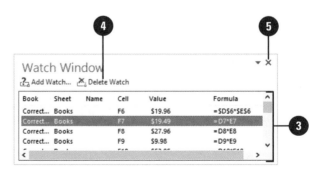

Set Error Checking Options

1. Click the **File** tab, and then click **Options**.

2. In the left pane, click **Formulas**.

3. Select the **Enable background error checking** check box.

4. Point to the help icons at the end of the error checking rule options to display a ScreenTip describing the rule.

5. Select the error checking rules check boxes you want to use.

6. Click **OK**.

Correct Errors

1. Open the worksheet where you want to check for errors.

2. Click the **Formulas** tab.

3. Click the **Error Checking** button.

    The error checker scans the worksheet for errors, generating the Error Checking dialog box every time it encounters an error.

4. If necessary, click **Resume**.

5. Choose a button to correct or ignore the problem.

    ◆ **Help on this error.**

    ◆ **Show Calculation Steps.** Click Evaluate to see results.

    ◆ **Ignore Error.**

    ◆ **Edit in Formula Bar.**

    ◆ **Previous** or **Next.**

6. If necessary, click **Close**.

Auditing a Worksheet

In a complex worksheet, it can be difficult to understand the relationships between cells and formulas. Auditing tools enable you to clearly determine these relationships. When the **Auditing** feature is turned on, it uses a series of arrows to show you which cells are part of which formulas. When you use the auditing tools, **tracer arrows** point out cells that provide data to formulas and the cells that contain formulas that refer to the cells. A box is drawn around the range of cells that provide data to formulas.

Trace Worksheet Relationships

1. Click the **Formulas** tab.

2. Use any of the following options:

   ◆ Click the **Trace Precedents** button to find cells that provide data to a formula.

   ◆ Click the **Trace Dependents** button to find out which formulas refer to a cell.

   ◆ Click the **Error Checking** button arrow, and then click **Trace Error** to locate the problem if a formula displays an error value, such as #DIV/0!.

   ◆ Click the **Remove Arrows** button arrow, and then click **Remove Precedent Arrows**, **Remove Dependent Arrows**, or **Remove All Arrows** to remove precedent and dependent arrows.

3. If necessary, click **OK** to locate the problem.

Trace arrow

Locating Circular References

A **circular reference** occurs when a formula directly or indirectly refers to its own cell. This causes the formula to use its result in the calculation, which can create errors. When a workbook contains a circular reference, Excel cannot automatically perform calculations. You can use error checking in Excel to locate circular references in a formula, and then remove them. If you leave them in, Excel calculates each cell involved in the circular reference by using the results of the previous iteration. An iteration is a repeated recalculation until a specific numeric condition is met. By default, Excel stops calculating after 100 iterations or after all values in the circular reference change by less than 0.001 between iterations, unless you change the Excel option.

Locate a Circular Reference

1. Click the **Formulas** tab.

2. Click the **Error Checking** button arrow, point to **Circular References**, and then click the first cell listed in the submenu.

3. Review the formula cell.

4. If you cannot figure out if the cell is the cause of the circular reference, click the next cell in the Circular References submenu, if available.

5. Continue to review and correct the circular reference until the status bar no longer displays the word "Circular."

Did You Know?

You can enable and increase formula iterations to make a circular reference work. Click the File tab, click Options, click Formulas, select the Enable iterative calculation check box, enter the maximum number of iterations you want (higher the number, the more time Excel needs to calculate a worksheet), and set the maximum amount of change you want to accept between calculation results (smaller the number, the more accurate the results).

Performing Calculations Using Functions

Functions are predesigned formulas that save you the time and trouble of creating commonly used or complex equations. Excel includes hundreds of functions that you can use alone or in combination with other formulas or functions. Functions perform a variety of calculations, from adding, averaging, and counting to more complicated tasks, such as calculating the monthly payment amount of a loan. You can enter a function manually if you know its name and all the required arguments, or you can easily insert a function using AutoComplete, which helps you select a function and enter arguments with the correct format.

Enter a Function

1. Click the cell where you want to enter the function.

2. Type = (an equal sign), type the name of the function, and then type ((an opening parenthesis).

   As you type, you can scroll down the Formula AutoComplete list, select the function you want, and then press Tab.

3. Type the argument or select the cell or range you want to insert in the function, and then type) (a closed parenthesis) to complete the function.

4. Click the **Enter** button on the formula bar, or press Enter.

   Excel will automatically add the closing parenthesis to complete the function.

See Also

See "Creating a Formula Using Formula AutoComplete" on page 80 for information on using Formula AutoComplete.

Commonly Used Excel Functions

Function	Description	Sample
SUM	Displays the sum of the argument	=SUM(argument)
AVERAGE	Displays the average value in the argument	=AVERAGE(argument)
COUNT	Calculates the number of values in the argument	=COUNT(argument)
PMT	Determines the monthly payment of a loan	=PMT(argument)

Creating Functions

Functions are predesigned formulas that save you the time and trouble of creating commonly used or complex equations. Trying to write a formula that calculates various pieces of data, such as calculating payments for an investment over a period of time at a certain rate, can be difficult and time-consuming. The **Insert Function** feature simplifies the process by organizing Excel's built-in formulas, called functions, into categories so they are easy to find and use. A function defines all the necessary components (also called arguments) you need to produce a specific result; all you have to do is supply the values, cell references, and other variables. You can even combine one or more functions.

Enter a Function Using Insert Function

1. Click the cell where you want to enter the function.

2. Click the **Insert Function** button on the Formula bar or click the **Function Wizard** button on the Formulas tab.

3. Type a brief description that describes what you want to do in the Search for a function box, and then click **Go**.

4. If necessary, click a function category you want to use.

5. Click the function you want to use.

6. Click **OK**.

7. Enter the cell addresses in the text boxes. Type them or click the **Collapse Dialog** button to the right of the text box, select the cell or range using your mouse, and then click the **Expand Dialog** button.

8. Click **OK**.

For Your Information

Inserting Placeholder Arguments

If you don't know the cell references you want to use for a function, you can insert argument names as placeholders, and then fill in the actual argument later. Press Ctrl+Shift+A after you type the functions name. Excel uses the arguments names as arguments. For example, =VLOOKUP(lookup_value, table_array, col_index_num, range_lookup).

Creating Functions Using the Library

To make it easier to find the function you need for a specific use, Excel has organized functions into categories—such as Financial, Logical, Text, Date & Time, Lookup & Reference, Math & Trig, and other functions—on the Formulas tab. Functions—such as beta and chi-squared distributions—for the academic, engineering, and scientific community have been improved for more accuracy and includes new ones in all categories (**New!**) and web services (**New!**). Some statistical functions have been renamed for consistency with the real world. After you use a function, Excel places it on the recently used list. When you insert a function from the Function Library, Excel inserts the function in the formula bar and opens a Function Argument dialog box, where you can enter or select the cells you want to use in the function.

Enter a Function Using the Function Library

1. Click the cell where you want to enter the function.

2. Click the **Formulas** tab.

3. Type = (an equal sign).

4. Click the button (**Financial, Logical, Text, Date & Time, Lookup & Reference, Math & Trig, More Functions**, or **Recently Used**) from the Function Library with the type of function you want to use, click a submenu if necessary, and then click the function you want to insert into a formula.

   Excel inserts the function you selected into the formula bar with a set of parenthesis, and opens the Function Arguments dialog box.

5. Type the argument or select the cell or range you want to insert in the function.

   You can click the Collapse Dialog button to the right of the text box, select the cell or range using your mouse, and then click the Expand Dialog button.

6. Click **OK**.

Calculating Multiple Results

An array formula can perform multiple calculations and then return either a single or multiple result. For example, when you want to count the number of distinct entries in a range, you can use an array formula, such as {=SUM(1/COUNTIF(range,range))}. You can also use an array formula to perform a two column lookup using the LOOKUP function. An array formula works on two or more sets of values, known as **array arguments**. Each argument must have the same number of rows and columns. You can create array formulas in the same way that you create other formulas, except you press Ctrl+Shift+Enter to enter the formula. When you enter an array formula, Excel inserts the formula between { } (brackets).

Create an Array Formula

1. Click the cell where you want to enter the array formula.

2. Click the **Formulas** tab.

3. Type = (an equal sign).

4. Use any of the following methods to enter the formula you want.

   ◆ Type the function.

   ◆ Type and use Formula AutoComplete.

   ◆ Use the Function Wizard.

   ◆ Use button in the Function Library.

5. Press Ctrl+Shift+Enter.

   { } (brackets) appear around the function to indicate it's an array formula.

Using Nested Functions

A nested function uses a function as one of the arguments. Excel allows you to nest up to 64 levels of functions. Users typically create nested functions as part of a conditional formula. For example, IF(AVERAGE(B2:B10)>100,SUM(C2:G10),0). The AVERAGE and SUM functions are nested within the IF function. The structure of the IF function is IF(condition_test, if_true, if_false). You can use the AND, OR, NOT, and IF functions to create conditional formulas. When you create a nested formula, it can be difficult to understand how Excel performs the calculations. You can use the Evaluate Formula dialog box to help you evaluate parts of a nested formula one step at a time.

Create a Conditional Formula Using a Nested Function

1. Click the cell where you want to enter the function.

2. Click the **Formulas** tab.

3. Type = (an equal sign).

4. Click a button from the Function Library with the type of function you want to use, click a submenu if necessary, and then click the function you want to insert into a formula.

   For example, click the Logical & Reference button, and then click COUNTIF.

   Excel inserts the function you selected into the formula bar with a set of parenthesis, and opens the Function Arguments dialog box.

5. Type a function as an argument to create a nested function, or a regular argument.

   For example, =COUNTIF(E6:E19), ">"&AVERAGE(E6:E19)).

6. Click **OK**.

Conditional Formula Examples

Formula	Result
=AND(A2>A3, A2<A4)	If A2 is greater than A3 and less than A4, then return TRUE, otherwise return FALSE
=OR(A2>A3, A2<A4)	If A2 is greater than A3 or A2 is less than A4, then return TRUE, otherwise return FALSE
=NOT(A2+A3=24)	If A2 plus A3 is not equal to 24, then return TRUE, otherwise return FALSE
IF(A2<>15, "OK", "Not OK")	If the value in cell A2 is not equal to 15, then return "OK", otherwise return "Not OK"

Evaluate a Nested Formula One Step at a Time

1 Select the cell with the nested formula you want to evaluate. You can only evaluate one cell at a time.

2 Click the **Formulas** tab.

3 Click the **Evaluate Formula** button.

4 Click **Evaluate** to examine the value of the underlined reference.

The result of the evaluation appears in italics.

5 If the underlined part of the formula is a reference to another formula, click **Step In** to display the other formula in the Evaluation box.

The Step In button is not available for a reference the second time the reference appears in the formula, or if the formula refers to a cell in a separate workbook.

6 Continue until each part of the formula has been evaluated, and then click **Close**.

7 To see the evaluation again, click **Restart**.

Some parts of formulas that use IF and CHOOSE functions are not evaluated, and #NA is displayed. If a reference is blank, a zero value (0) is displayed.

IMPORTANT *Some functions recalculate each time the worksheet changes, and can cause the Evaluate Formula to display different results. These functions include RAND, AREAS, INDEX, OFFSET, CELL, INDIRECT, ROWS, COLUMNS, NOW, TODAY, AND RANDBETWEEN.*

Using Constants and Functions in Names

Instead of using a cell to store a constant value or function for use in a formula, you can create a name to store it and then use the name in a formula. If you wanted to calculate sales tax, for example, you could create a name called Sales Tax and assign it a constant value. You can also store text in a name. Instead of typing a long name, such as Environmental Protection Agency, you could create a name called EPA and then use the easy-to-type three letter abbreviation in a formula. When you use EPA in a formula as a text string, Excel replaces it with Environmental Protection Agency. It also works for functions and nested functions.

Use a Constant or Function in a Name

1. Click the **Formulas** tab.

2. Click the **Define Name** button.

3. Type a name for the reference.

4. Click the **Scope** list arrow, and then click **Workbook** or a specific worksheet.

5. If you want, type a description of the name.

   The current selection appears in the Refers to box.

6. In the Refers to box, type = (equal sign) followed by the constant, text, or function you want to use.

   =.0875, or ="Environmental Protection Agency"

7. Click **OK**.

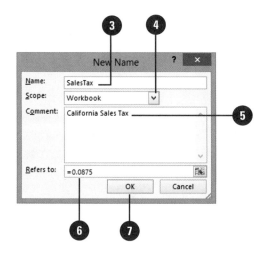

Did You Know?

You can edit the contents of the Refers to box in the New Names dialog box. Since the contents of the Refer to box is in point mode, you can not use the insertion point and arrow keys to edit it. Press F2 to switch to edit mode, where you can use the insertion point and arrow keys to edit it.

Constant name used in formula   Define Name button

Modifying Worksheets and Workbooks

Introduction

At times, you'll need to reorganize a workbook by adding additional worksheets, moving their appearance order within the workbook, or even deleting an unused or outdated worksheet. You can rename worksheets to better show the theme of your workbook. When using your workbook, there may be times when you'll want to hide certain worksheets due to sensitive or confidential information. You can also freeze the column and row headings to ease viewing a long list of data.

On any worksheet, you can insert and delete cells, rows, and columns. You can adjust column width and row height so that you can structure the worksheet exactly the way you want. It's easy to make changes because Microsoft Excel updates cell references in existing formulas as necessary whenever you modify a worksheet and automatically recalculates formulas to ensure that the results are always up-to-date.

Perhaps each month you create an inventory worksheet in which you enter repetitive information; all that changes is the actual data. By creating your own template, you can have a custom form that is ready for completion each time you take inventory. Formatting, formulas and other settings are already set up, so that you can begin working on the task at hand. A template file saves all the customization you made to reuse in other workbooks. Excel and Office comes with a variety of pre-made templates that you can use for your own business and personal needs.

What You'll Do

Select and Name a Worksheet

Insert and Delete a Worksheet

Move and Copy a Worksheet

Hide and Unhide Worksheets and Workbooks

Select a Column or Row

Hide and Unhide a Column or Row

Insert a Column or Row

Delete a Column or Row

Adjust Column Width and Row Height

Freeze and Unfreeze a Column or Row

Split a Worksheet into Panes

Show and Hide Workbook Elements

Zoom the View In and Out

Create Custom Views

Set Up for Personal Templates

Create a Personal Template

Open and Change a Template

Selecting and Naming a Worksheet

Each new workbook opens with three worksheets (or sheets), in which you store and analyze values. You can work in the active, or selected, worksheet. The default worksheet names are Sheet1, Sheet2, and Sheet3, which appear on the sheet tab, like file folder labels. As you create a worksheet, give it a meaningful name to help you remember its contents. The sheet tab size adjusts to fit the name's length, so using short names means more sheet tabs will be visible. If you work on a project that requires more than three worksheets, add additional sheets to the workbook so all related information is stored in one file.

Select a Worksheet

1. If necessary, click a sheet tab scroll button to display other tabs.

2. Click a sheet tab to make it the active worksheet.

3. To select multiple worksheets, press and hold Ctrl as you click other sheet tabs. When multiple worksheets are selected, [Group] appears in the title bar.

Name or Rename a Worksheet

1. Double-click the sheet tab you want to name.

   ◆ You can also click the **Home** tab, click the **Format** button, and then click **Rename**.

2. Type a new name.

3. Press Enter.

Did You Know?

You can select all worksheets. Right-click any sheet tab, and then click Select All Sheets.

Inserting and Deleting a Worksheet

You can add or delete sheets in a workbook. If, for example, you are working on a project that requires more than three worksheets, you can insert additional sheets in one workbook rather than open multiple workbooks. You can insert as many sheets in a workbook as you want. On the other hand, if you are using only one or two sheets in a workbook, you can delete the unused sheets to save disk space. Before you delete a sheet from a workbook, make sure you don't need the data. You cannot undo the deletion.

Insert a Worksheet

1 Click the sheet tab to the right of where you want to insert the new sheet.

2 Click the **Insert Worksheet** icon at the end of the sheet tabs.

TIMESAVER *Press Shift+F11.*

◆ You can also click the **Home** tab, click the **Insert Cells** button, and then click **Insert Sheet**.

A new worksheet is inserted to the left of the selected worksheet.

New sheet

Delete a Worksheet

1 Click the sheet tab of the worksheet you want to delete.

2 Click the **Home** tab.

3 Click the **Delete** button arrow, and then click **Delete Sheet**.

4 Click **Delete** to confirm the deletion.

Moving and Copying a Worksheet

After adding several sheets to a workbook, you might want to reorganize them. You can arrange sheets in chronological order or in order of importance. You can easily move or copy a sheet within a workbook or to a different open workbook. Copying a worksheet is easier and often more convenient then re-entering similar information on a new sheet. If you are moving or copying a worksheet a short distance, you should use the mouse. For longer distances, you should use the Move or Copy command.

Move a Worksheet Within a Workbook

1. Click the sheet tab of the worksheet you want to move, and then hold down the mouse button.

2. When the mouse pointer changes to a sheet of paper, drag it to the right of the sheet tab where you want to move the worksheet.

3. Release the mouse button.

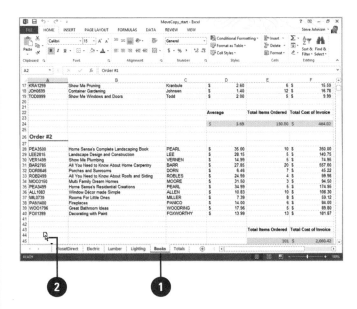

Did You Know?

You can give your worksheet a different background. Click the tab of the sheet on which you want to insert a background, click the Page Layout tab, and then click the Background button. Select the picture you want to use as a background, and then click Open.

You can use groups to affect multiple worksheets. Click a sheet tab, press and hold Shift, and then click another sheet tab to group worksheets. Right-click a grouped sheet tab, and then click Ungroup Sheet on the shortcut menu.

Copy a Worksheet

1 Click the sheet tab of the worksheet you want to copy.

TIMESAVER *Press and hold the Ctrl key while you drag a sheet name to copy a worksheet.*

2 Click the **Home** tab.

3 Click the **Format** button arrow, and then click **Move or Copy Sheet**.

4 If you want to copy the sheet to another open workbook, click the **To book** list arrow, and then select the name of that workbook. The sheets of the selected workbook appear in the Before Sheet list.

TROUBLE? *If the workbook you want to copy to does not show up in the To Book drop-down list, you must first open the workbook.*

5 Click a sheet name in the Before Sheet list. Excel inserts the copy to the left of this sheet.

6 Select the **Create a copy** check box.

7 Click **OK**.

Did You Know?

You can copy or move a sheet to a different workbook. You must first open the other workbook, and then switch back to the workbook of the sheet you want to copy or move.

You can use the Create A Copy check box to move a worksheet. Clear the Create A Copy check box in the Move or Copy dialog box to move a worksheet rather than copy it.

Hiding and Unhiding Worksheets and Workbooks

Not all worksheets and workbooks should be available to everyone. You can hide sensitive information without deleting it by hiding selected worksheets or workbooks. For example, if you want to share a workbook with others, but it includes confidential employee salaries, you can simply hide a worksheet. Hiding worksheets does not affect calculations in the other worksheets; all data in hidden worksheets is still referenced by formulas as necessary. Hidden worksheets do not appear in a printout either. When you need the data, you can unhide the sensitive information.

Hide a Worksheet

1. Click the sheet tab you want to hide.

2. Click the **Home** tab.

3. Click the **Format** button, point to **Hide & Unhide**, and then click **Hide Sheet**.

   TIMESAVER *Right-click the sheet you want to hide, and then click Hide.*

Unhide a Worksheet

1. Click the **Home** tab.

2. Click the **Format** button, point to **Hide & Unhide**, and then click **Unhide Sheet**.

3. Select the worksheet you want to unhide.

4. Click **OK**.

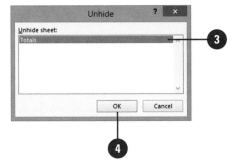

Hide a Workbook

1. Open the workbook you want to hide.

2. Click the **View** tab.

3. Click the **Hide** button.

Did You Know?

You can change the color of the sheet tab names. By right-clicking the sheet tab of the worksheet you want, and point to Tab Color, and then select a color. Click No Color to remove a color.

Unhide a Workbook

1. Click the **View** tab.

2. Click the **Unhide** button.

3. Select the workbook you want to unhide.

4. Click **OK**.

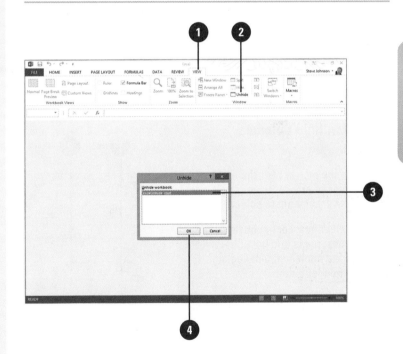

Selecting a Column or Row

You can select one or more columns or rows in a worksheet in order to apply formatting attributes, insert or delete columns or rows, or perform other group actions. The header buttons above each column and to the left of each row indicate the letter or number of the column or row. You can select multiple columns or rows even if they are non-contiguous—that is, not next to one another in the worksheet.

Select a Column or Row

① Click the column or row header button of the column or row you want to select.

An arrow appears when you point to a header button.

Did You Know?

You can select the entire worksheet quickly. Click the Select All button located above the row number 1 and the left of column A.

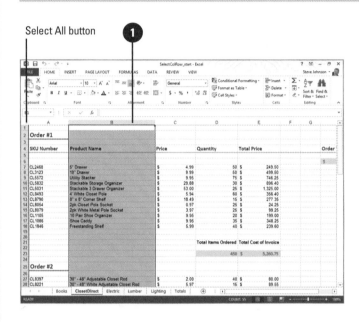

Select All button ①

Select Multiple Columns or Rows

① Drag the mouse over the header buttons of any contiguous columns or rows you want to select.

② To select non-contiguous columns or rows, press and hold Ctrl while clicking each additional column or row header button.

An arrow appears when you point to a header button.

Hiding and Unhiding a Column or Row

Not all the data on a worksheet should be available to everyone. You can hide sensitive information without deleting it by hiding selected columns or rows. For example, if you want to share a worksheet with others, but it includes confidential employee salaries, you can simply hide the salary column. Hiding columns and rows does not affect calculations in a worksheet; all data in hidden columns and rows is still referenced by formulas as necessary. Hidden columns and rows do not appear in a printout either. When you need the data, you can unhide the sensitive information.

Hide a Column or Row

1. Click the column or row header button of the column or row you want to hide. (Drag to select multiple header buttons to hide more than one column or row.)

2. Click the **Home** tab.

3. Click the **Format** button, point to **Hide & Unhide**, and then click **Hide Columns** or **Hide Rows**.

Unhide a Column or Row

1. Drag to select the column or row header buttons on either side of the hidden column or row.

2. Click the **Home** tab.

3. Click the **Format** button, point to **Hide & Unhide**, and then click **Unhide Columns** or **Unhide Rows**.

Inserting a Column or Row

You can insert blank columns and rows between existing data, without disturbing your worksheet. Excel repositions existing cells to accommodate the new columns and rows and adjusts any existing formulas so that they refer to the correct cells. Formulas containing absolute cell references will need to be adjusted to the new columns or rows. When you insert one or more columns, they insert to the left. When you add one or more rows, they are inserted above the selected row.

Insert a Column or Row

1. Click to the right of the location of the new column you want to insert.

   To insert a row, click the row immediately below the location of the row you want to insert.

2. Click the **Home** tab.

3. Click the **Insert** button arrow, and then click **Insert Sheet Columns** or **Insert Sheet Rows**.

4. To adjust formatting, click the **Insert Options** button, and then click a formatting option.

Insert Multiple Columns or Rows

1. Drag to select the column header buttons for the number of columns you want to insert.

   To insert multiple rows, drag to select the row header buttons for the number of rows you want to insert.

2. Click the **Home** tab.

3. Click the **Insert** button arrow, and then click **Insert Sheet Columns** or **Insert Sheet Rows**.

4. To adjust formatting, click the **Insert Options** button, and then click a formatting option.

Deleting a Column or Row

At some point in time, you may want to remove an entire column or row of data from a worksheet rather than deleting or editing individual cells. You can delete columns and rows just as easily as you insert them. Formulas will need to be checked in your worksheet prior to deleting a row or column, especially when referencing absolute cell addresses. Remaining columns and rows move to the left or up to join the other remaining data.

Delete a Column or Row

1. Select the column header button or row header button that you want to delete.

2. Click the **Home** tab.

3. Click the **Delete** button arrow, and then click **Delete Sheet Columns** or **Delete Sheet Rows**.

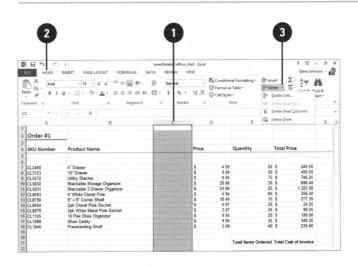

Delete Multiple Columns or Rows

1. Select the columns header buttons or rows header buttons that you want to delete.

2. Click the **Home** tab.

3. Click the **Delete** button arrow, and then click **Delete Sheet Columns** or **Delete Sheet Rows**.

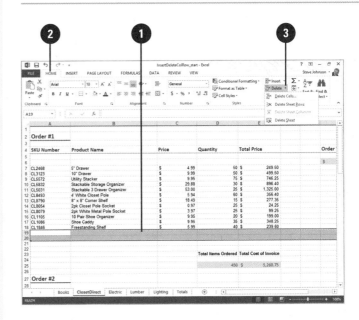

Did You Know?

You can re-check your formulas. When deleting columns or rows that are referenced in a formula, it is important to adjust your formula for recalculations.

Adjusting Column Width and Row Height

You've entered labels and values, constructed formulas, and even formatted the cells, but now some of your data isn't visible; the value displays as ##### in the cell. Also, some larger-sized labels are cut off. You can narrow or widen each column width to fit its contents and adjust your row heights as needed. As you build your worksheet, you can change the default width of some columns or the default height of some rows to accommodate long strings of data or larger font sizes. You can manually adjust column or row size to fit data you have entered, or you can use AutoFit to resize a column or row to the width or height of its largest entry.

Adjust Column Width or Row Height

1. Click the column or row header button for the first column or row you want to adjust.

2. If you want, drag to select more columns or rows.

3. Click the **Home** tab.

4. Click the **Format** button, and then click **Column Width** or **Row Height**.

   TIMESAVER *Right-click the selected column(s) or row(s), and then click Column Width or Row Height.*

5. Type a new column width or row height in points.

6. Click **OK**.

Did You Know?

What is a point? A point is a measurement unit used to size text and space on a worksheet. One inch equals 72 points.

You can change the default column width. Click the Home tab, click the Format button, click Default Width, type a column width in points, and then click OK.

Adjust Column Width or Row Height Using the Mouse

1. Position the mouse pointer on the right edge of the column header button or the bottom edge of the row header button for the column or row you want to change.

2. When the mouse pointer changes to a double-headed arrow, click and drag the pointer to a new width or height.

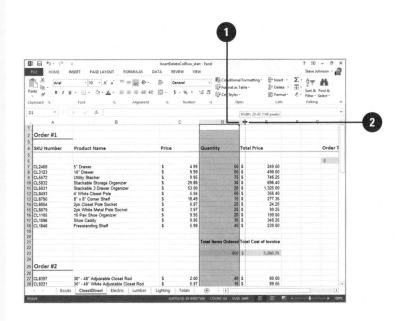

Change Column Width or Row Height Using AutoFit

1. Position the mouse pointer on the right edge of the column header button or the bottom edge of the row header button for the column or row you want to change.

2. When the mouse pointer changes to a double-headed arrow, double-click the mouse.

   ◆ You can also click the **Home** tab, click the **Format** button, and then click **AutoFit Column Width** or **AutoFit Row Height**.

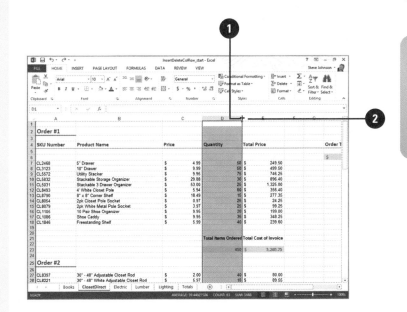

Freezing and Unfreezing a Column or Row

Large worksheets can be difficult to work with, especially on low-resolution or small screens. If you scroll down to see the bottom of the list, you can no longer see the column names at the top of the list. Instead of repeatedly scrolling up and down, you can temporarily set, or **freeze**, those column or row headings so that you can see them no matter where you scroll in the list. When you freeze a row or column, you are actually splitting the screen into one or more panes (window sections) and freezing one of the panes. You can split the screen into up to four panes and can freeze up to two of these panes. You can edit the data in a frozen pane just as you do any Excel data, but the cells remain stationary even when you use the scroll bars; only the unfrozen part of the screen scrolls. When you freeze a pane, it has no effect on how a worksheet looks when printed.

Freeze and Unfreeze a Column or Row

1. Select the column to the right of the columns you want to freeze, or select the row below the rows you want to freeze.

   To freeze both, click the cell to the right and below of the column and row you want to freeze.

2. Click the **View** tab.

3. Click the **Freeze Panes** button, and then click the option you want.

   - **Freeze Panes.** Keeps rows and columns visible based on the current selection.

   - **Freeze Top Row.** Keeps top row visible.

   - **Freeze First Column.** Keeps first column visible.

   When you freeze a pane horizontally, all the rows **above** the active cell freeze. When you freeze a pane vertically, all the columns to the **left** of the active cell freeze.

4. To unfreeze a column or row, click the **Freeze Panes** button, and then click **Unfreeze Panes**.

Splitting a Worksheet into Panes

If you are working on a large worksheet, it can be time consuming and tiring to scroll back and forth between two parts of the worksheet. You can split the worksheet into four panes and two scrollable windows that you can view simultaneously but edit and scroll independently using the Split button. As you work in two parts of the same worksheet, you can resize the window panes to fit your task. Drag the split bar between the panes to resize the windows. No matter how you display worksheets, Excel's commands and buttons work the same as usual.

Split a Worksheet into Panes

1 Select the row, column, or cell location where you want to split a worksheet into panes.

A column or row selection creates two panes, while a cell selection creates four panes.

2 Click the **View** tab.

3 Click the **Split** button.

The button appears highlighted.

4 To remove the split, click the **Split** button again.

The button doesn't appear highlighted.

Did You Know?

You can search for a value or data in a cell, and then replace it with different content. Click the cell or cells containing content you want to replace. Click the Home tab, click the Find & Select button, click Replace, specify the values or data you want to find and replace, and then click the appropriate Find or Replace buttons.

You can no longer use the Split box control. The Split box control (**New!**) on the worksheet window has been removed in Excel 2013.

Worksheet split into four panes

Scroll panes separately

Showing and Hiding Workbook Elements

When you open a new or existing workbook, Excel displays a standard set of elements, such as the Formula Bar, Headings (columns and rows), Gridlines, and Ruler, which is available in Page Layout view. If you need a little more display room to see your data or you want to see how your data looks without the gridlines, you can quickly select or clear view settings on the Data tab in Excel to show or hide these elements.

Show or Hide Workbook Elements

1. Click the **View** tab.

2. Select or clear the check box for the element you want to show or hide.

- ◆ **Ruler**. In Page Layout view, the horizontal and vertical rulers.

- ◆ **Gridlines**. The gray outline around cells.

- ◆ **Formula Bar**. The bar below the Ribbon.

- ◆ **Headings**. The column (letters) and row (numbers) headings.

No gridlines or headings

Did You Know?

You can view a workbook in full screen without the Ribbon, tabs, and toolbars. Click the View tab, and then click the Full Screen button. To exit Full Screen view, right-click anywhere on the worksheet, and then click Close Full Screen.

Zooming the View In and Out

Working with the Zoom tools gives you one more way to control exactly what you see in an Excel worksheet. The Zoom tools are located in the bottom-right corner of the window. Large worksheet are difficult to work with and difficult to view. Many worksheets, when viewed at 100%, are larger than the maximized size of the window. When this happens, viewing the entire worksheet requires reducing the zoom.

Change the View

1. Use any of the following zoom options available on the Status bar:

   ◆ **Zoom Out**. Click to zoom out (percentage gets smaller).

   ◆ **Zoom In**. Click to zoom in (percentage gets larger).

   ◆ **Slider**. Drag to zoom out or in to the percentage you want.

   ◆ **Zoom Level**. Click to display the Zoom dialog box, where you can select the magnification you want.

2. For additional zoom options, click the **View** tab, and then use any of the following options:

   ◆ **Zoom**. Click to display the Zoom dialog box, where you can select the magnification you want.

   This is the same as Zoom Level above.

   ◆ **100%**. Click to display the view at 100%.

   ◆ **Zoom to Selection**. Click to zoom the current selection in view.

Zoom dialog box

Creating Custom Views

A **view** is a set of display and print settings that you can name and apply to a workbook. In Excel, you can create multiple custom views—such as one for developing a worksheet and another for entering data—in the same workbook without having to save separate copies. If you include print settings in a view, the view includes the defined print area. If the sheet has no defined print area, the view displays the entire worksheet. If one or more worksheets contain an Excel list, the Custom Views command is disabled for the entire workbook.

Create a Custom View

1. Set up the workbook to appear the way you want to view and print it.

2. Click the **View** tab.

3. Click the **Custom Views** button.

4. Click **Add**.

5. Type a name for the custom view.

   To make it easier to identify, use the sheet name in the view name.

6. Select or clear the **Print settings** check box and the **Hidden rows, columns and filter settings** check box.

7. Click **OK**.

Show or Delete a Custom View

1. Click the **View** tab.

2. Click the **Custom Views** button.

3. Click the view you want to display.

4. Click **Show**.

   Excel switches to the sheet that was active when you created the view and displays the custom view.

5. To delete a view, click **Delete**, and then click **Yes** to confirm.

6. If you deleted a view, click **Close**.

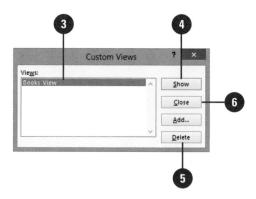

Setting Up for Personal Templates

If you want to create your own custom personal templates and access them from the Start or New screen, you should create a My Templates folder (**New!**)—such as C:\Users*user name*\My Templates—and then specify the folder as the default for your personal templates (**New!**). If you don't create a folder, Microsoft creates one named Custom Office Templates in the C:\Users*user name*\Documents folder. You can specify your default personal templates folder in the Options dialog box under Save. After you set up your personal templates folder, you can access them from the Start or New screen under Personal (**New!**).

Set Up for Personal Templates

1. In Windows Explorer, navigate to the location where you want to store your personal templates, and then create a folder named My Templates.

   ◆ **Personal Templates Folder.** C:\Users*user name*\My Templates; typical location, yours can differ.

2. In Excel, click the **File** tab, and then click **Options**.

3. In the left pane, click **Save**.

4. In the Default personal templates location box, enter the path to a personal templates folder.

   My Templates Folder. C:\Users*user name*\My Templates; typical location, yours can differ.

   Custom Office Templates Folder. C:\Users*user name*\Documents\ Custom Office Templates.

5. Click **OK**.

See Also

See "Creating a Personal Template" on page 134 for more information on creating a custom template for use in the My Templates folder.

Creating a Personal Template

You can create your own personal template as easily as you create a worksheet. Like those that come with Excel, custom templates can save you time. Perhaps each month you create an inventory worksheet in which you enter repetitive information; all that changes is the actual data. By creating your own template, you can have a custom form that is ready for completion each time you take inventory. A template file (.xltx) saves all the customization you made to reuse in other workbooks. You can store your template anywhere you want; you may find it handy to store it in a My Templates folder (**New!**), or the default Custom Office Templates folder (**New!**). When you set up the default personal templates folder in the Options dialog box under Save, your personal templates appear under Personal c in the Start or New screen.

Create a Personal Template

1. Enter all the necessary information in a new workbook—including formulas, labels, graphics, and formatting.

2. Click the **File** tab, and then click **Save As**.

3. Click **Computer**, and then click **Browse**.

4. Click the **Save as type** list arrow, and then select a template format.

   ◆ **Excel Template**. Creates a template for Excel 2007-2013.

   ◆ **Excel Macro-Enabled Template**. Creates a template for Excel 2007-2013 with macros.

   ◆ **Excel 97-2003 Template**. Creates a template for Excel 97-2003.

5. Navigate to your personal templates folder.

   My Templates. C:\Users\ *user name*\My Templates; your location might differ.

   Custom Office Templates. C:\Users*user name*\Documents\ Custom Office Templates.

6. Type a name for your template.

7. Click **Save**.

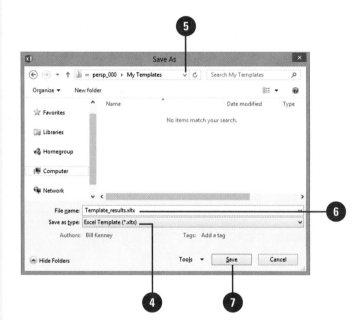

Opening a Template

You may not realize it, but every workbook you create is based on a template. When you start a new workbook without specifying a template, Excel creates a new workbook based on the default template file (Book.xltx), which includes three worksheets and no special formulas, labels, or formatting. When you specify a particular template in the Start or New screen (**New!**), whether it's one supplied by Excel or one you created yourself, Excel starts a new workbook that contains the formulas, labels, graphics, and formatting contained in that template. The template itself does not change when you enter data in the new workbook, because you are working on a new file, not with the template file.

Open a Template

① Click the **File** tab, and then click **Open**.

② Click **Computer**, and then click **Browse**.

③ Click the **Files of type** list arrow, and then click **Templates**.

④ Click the **Look in** list arrow, and then select the folder that contain the template you want to open.

   Personal Templates. C:\Users\ *user name*\My Templates; your location might differ, or C:\Users\ *user name*\Documents\Custom Office Templates (default).

   Office Templates. C:\Program Files\Microsoft Office\ Templates\1033

⑤ Click the file name of the template you want to open.

⑥ Click **Open**.

See Also

See "Set Up for Personal Templates" on page 133 for more information on creating a My Templates folder and setting the default personal templates folder.

For Your Information

Customizing the Excel Blank Template

In previous versions of Excel, when you saved workbook settings you used in the blank workbook template called Book.xltx that is stored in the XLStart folder (typically C:\Users*user name*\AppData\Local\ Microsoft\ Excel\XLStart), the template automatically opened when you created a blank template. In Excel 2013, the blank workbook is not automatically created with Book.xltx when you start. If you want to still use Book.xltx as a custom blank workbook, click the File tab, click Options, click General, deselect the Show the Start screen when this application starts check box (**New!**), and then click OK.

Changing a Template

Office has a selection of premade Excel templates designed for you to use. These templates are available in the Start or New screen under Featured (**New!**). If you like one of these templates, you can use it as the basis of your own template. To customize one, open the template, make the changes you want, and then save it. If you save the original template back in the same location with the same name as the original, you create a new default template. The original one is replaced by the newly saved template. If you don't want to change the original, save the template in your My Templates or Custom Office Templates folder.

Change an Excel Template

1. Click the **File** tab, and then click **New**.

2. Open the template you want to change using the following:
   - ◆ **Featured Templates.** Click **Featured**, and then click the template you want, and then click **Create**.
   - ◆ **Personal Templates.** Click **Personal**, and then click the custom template you want.

3. Make the changes you want to the template.

4. Click the **File** tab, and then click **Save As**.

5. Click **Computer**, and then click **Browse**.

6. Click the **Save as type** list arrow, and then click **Excel Template**.

7. Navigate to a templates folder.

   Office Templates. C:\Program Files\Microsoft Office\Templates\1033

   Personal Templates. C:\Users\ *user name*/My Templates; your location might differ, or C:\Users\ *user name*\Documents\Custom Office Templates (default).

8. Type a new file name or the same as the existing name to replace it.

9. Click **Save**, and then click **Yes**, if necessary, to replace the file.

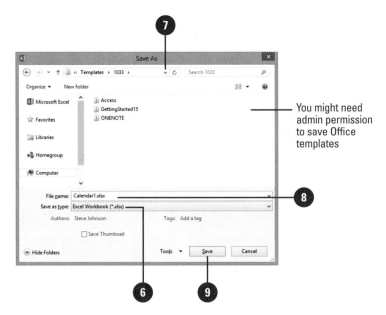

You might need admin permission to save Office templates

Formatting a Worksheet

Introduction

Microsoft Excel offers several tools for making your worksheets look more attractive and professional. Without formatting, a worksheet can look like a sea of meaningless data. To highlight important information, you can change the appearance of selected numbers and text by adding dollar signs, commas, and other numerical formats, or by applying attributes, such as boldface, italics, and underline.

Once you've set up your worksheet, additional changes are available to customize your worksheet's look. You can change the default font and font size, or maybe you'd like to adjust the alignment of data in cells. In addition to column, row, or font changes, you can add colors to cells or fonts, and include patterns to cells. You can also add borders around columns of data to help visually group them, or even add some clip art, a company logo, or some pictures.

Not everyone has an eye for color, and pulling it all together can be daunting, so Excel provides you with professionally designed themes, which you can apply to any workbook. A **theme** is a set of unified design elements that provides a consistent look for a workbook by using color themes, fonts, and effects, such as shadows, shading, and animations. However, if you simply want to format a range of cells in a worksheet you can quickly apply a cell style. A **cell style** is a defined collection of formats—font, font size, attributes, numeric formats, and so on—that you can store as a set and later apply to other cells. You can use one of Excel's built-in cell styles, or create one of your own.

If you need to find the various formatting attributes and change them, you can use the Find and Replace Formatting feature to change them all at once instead of making individual changes.

What You'll Do

Format Numbers and Text

AutoFormat Text While You Type

Apply Conditional Formatting

Create and Manage Conditional Formatting

Create Sparkline Formatting

Change Data Alignment

Control Text Flow

Change Data Color

Add Color and Patterns to Cells

Add Custom Colors

Add Borders to Cells

Format Tabs and Background

Copy Cell Formats

Understand, Apply, and Create Themes

Choose Theme Colors, Fonts, and Effects

Create, Apply, and Modify a Cell Style

Find and Replace Cell Formatting

Formatting Numbers

You can change the appearance of the data in the cells of a worksheet without changing the actual value in the cell. You can apply **numeric formats** to numbers to better reflect the type of information they represent—dollar amounts, dates, decimals, and so on. For example, you can format a number to display up to 15 decimal places or none at all. If you don't see the number format you need, you can create a custom one.

Format Numbers Quickly

1. Select a cell or range that contains the number(s) you want to format.

2. Click the **Home** tab.

3. Click the **Number Format** list arrow, and then click any of the following formats:

   ◆ **General.** No specific format.

   ◆ **Number.** 0.75

   ◆ **Currency.** $0.75

   ◆ **Accounting.** $ 0.75

   ◆ **Short Date.** 3/17/2013

   ◆ **Long Date.** Wednesday, March 17, 2013

   ◆ **Time.** 6:00:00 PM

   ◆ **Percentage.** 75.00%

   ◆ **Fraction.** 3/4

   ◆ **Scientific.** 7.50E-01

4. To fine-tune the format, click any of the following format buttons:

   ◆ **Currency Style.** Click the button arrow to select a currency symbol.

   ◆ **Percent Style.**

   ◆ **Comma Style.**

   ◆ **Increase Decimal.**

   ◆ **Decrease Decimal.**

   You can apply multiple attributes to the range.

Format a Number Using the Format Cells Dialog Box

1. Select a cell or range that contains the number(s) you want to format.

2. Click the **Home** tab.

3. Click the **Number Dialog Box Launcher**.

   The dialog box opens, displaying the Number tab.

4. Click to select a category.

5. Select the options you want to apply.

   To create a custom format, click Custom, type the number format code, and then use one of the existing codes as a starting point.

6. Preview your selections in the Sample box.

7. Click **OK**.

Did You Know?

You can format numbers in international currencies. In the Format Cells dialog box, click the Number tab, click Currency in the Category list, click the Symbol list arrow, and then click an international currency symbol.

You can quickly remove a numeric format or font attribute. The buttons on the Home tab Ribbon and the Mini-Toolbar are toggle buttons, which means you simply click to turn them on and off. To add or remove a numeric format or a font attribute, select the cell, range, or text, and then click the appropriate button on the Home tab or the Mini-Toolbar to turn the format or attribute off.

Formatting Text

A **font** is a collection of alphanumeric characters that share the same typeface, or design, and have similar characteristics. Most fonts are available in a number of styles (such as bold and italic) and sizes. You can format text and numbers with font attributes, such as bolding, italics, or underlining, to enhance data to catch the reader's attention. The basic formats you apply to text are available on the Home tab in the Font group or in the Font dialog box. Some of the formats available in the Font dialog box include strikethrough, and single or double normal and accounting underline. When you point to selected text, Excel displays the Mini-Toolbar above it. The **Mini-Toolbar** provides easy access to common formatting toolbar buttons, such as font, font size, increase and decrease font size, bold, italic, font color, and increase and decrease list level. If you don't want to display the Mini-Toolbar, you can use Excel Options to turn it off.

Format Text Quickly

1 Select the text you want to format.

2 Click the **Home** tab.

3 To change fonts, click the **Font** list arrow on the Ribbon or Mini-Toolbar, and then point for a live preview, or click the font you want, either a theme font or any available fonts.

The font name appears in the font style.

To change the font size, click one or more of the font size buttons on the Ribbon or Mini-Toolbar:

◆ Click the **Font Size** list arrow, and then click the font size you want.

◆ Click the **Increase Font Size** button or **Decrease Font Size** button.

To apply other formatting, click one or more of the formatting buttons on the Ribbon or Mini-Toolbar: **Bold**, **Italic**, **Underline**, **Shadow**, **Strikethrough**, or **Font Color**.

◆ The Font Color button displays the last font color you used. To apply this color, simply click the button, not the list arrow.

Mini-Toolbar

Format Text Using the Format Cells Dialog Box

1. Select the text you want to format.

2. Click the **Home** tab.

3. Click the **Font Dialog Box Launcher**.

   The dialog box opens, displaying the Font tab.

4. Select the font, font style, and font size you want.

5. Select or clear the effects you want or don't want: **Strikethrough**, **Superscript**, and **Subscript**.

6. If you want, click **Font Color**, and then click a color.

7. If you want, click the **Underline** list arrow, and then click a style.

8. Click **OK**.

Did You Know?

You can tell the difference between a TrueType and printer font. A TrueType (outline) font is a font that uses special software capabilities to print exactly what is seen on the screen. A printer (screen) font is a font that comes only in specified sizes. If you are creating a worksheet for publication, you need to use printer fonts.

What is a point? The size of each font character is measured in points (a point is approximately 1/72 of an inch). You can use any font that is installed on your computer on a worksheet, but the default is 10-point Arial.

Each computer has different fonts installed. Users with whom you share files may not have all the fonts you've used in a workbook installed on their computers.

Applying Conditional Formatting

You can make your worksheets more powerful by setting up **conditional formatting**, which lets the value of a cell determine its formatting. For example, you might want this year's sales total to be displayed in red and italics if it's less than last year's total, but in green and bold if it's more. The formatting is applied to the cell values only if the values meet the condition that you specify. Otherwise, no conditional formatting is applied to the cell values. With Excel, you can apply conditional formatting only to cells that contain text, number, or date or time values. You can quickly format only top or bottom ranked values, values above or below average, unique or duplicate values, or use a formula to determine which cells to format. You can also apply multiple formatting to the same data in order to achieve the results you want. In addition, you can refer to values in other worksheets. You can apply a preset format using the Quick Analysis tool (**New!**) or apply a format with specific criteria.

Format Cell Contents Based on Comparison

1. Select a cell or range you want to conditionally format.

2. Click the **Home** tab.

3. To format with a preset, click the **Quick Analysis** button (**New!**), click **Formatting**, and then click the **Greater Than** button.

4. To format with specified criteria, click the **Conditional Formatting** button, and then point to **Highlight Cells Rules**.

5. Click the comparison rule you want to apply to conditionally format the selected data.

   ◆ **Greater Than.**

   ◆ **Less Than.**

   ◆ **Between.**

   ◆ **Equal To.**

   ◆ **Text that Contains.**

   ◆ **A Date Occurring.**

   ◆ **Duplicate Values.**

6. Specify the criteria you want. Each rule supplies different criteria.

7. Click **OK**.

Format Cell Contents Based on Ranking and Average

1. Select a cell or range you want to conditionally format.

2. Click the **Home** tab.

3. To format with a preset, click the **Quick Analysis** button (**New!**), click **Formatting**, and then click the **Top 10%** button.

4. To format with specified criteria, click the **Conditional Formatting** button, and then point to **Top/Bottom Rules**.

5. Click the comparison rule you want to apply to conditionally format the selected data.

   ◆ **Top 10 Items.**

   ◆ **Top 10 %.**

   ◆ **Bottom 10 Items.**

   ◆ **Bottom 10 %.**

   ◆ **Above Average.**

   ◆ **Below Average.**

6. Specify the criteria you want. Each rule supplies different criteria.

7. Click **OK**.

Applying Specialized Conditional Formatting

With Excel, you can apply specialized conditional formatting by using data bars, color scales, and icon sets. A colored **data bar** helps you see the value of a cell relative to other cells. The length of the data bar represents the value in the cell. A longer bar represents a higher value. A negative value displays a bar on the opposite side of an axis from positive values. A **color scale** is a visual guide that helps you represent data distribution and variation using two or three color gradients. The color shade represents the value in the cell. A two-color scale represents higher and lower values, while a three-color scale represents higher, middle, and lower values. An **icon set** helps you annotate and classify data into three to five categories separated by a threshold value. Each icon represents a value in the cell. You can apply multiple formatting to the same data in order to display the results you want. In addition, you can refer to values in other worksheets. You can apply a preset format using the Quick Analysis tool (**New!**) or apply other conditional formats.

Format Using Data Bars

1. Select a cell or range you want to conditionally format.

2. Click the **Home** tab.

3. To format with a preset, click the **Quick Analysis** button (**New!**), click **Formatting**, and then click the **Data Bars** button.

4. To format with an expanded menu, click the **Conditional Formatting** button, and then point to **Data Bars**.

5. Click the colored data bar you want, either gradient or solid fills.

6. To create a custom data bar, click **More Rules**, specify the description you want (including bar direction), and then click **OK**.

Format Using Color Scales

1. Select a cell or range you want to conditionally format.

2. Click the **Home** tab.

3. To format with a preset, click the **Quick Analysis** button (**New!**), click **Formatting**, and then click the **Color Scale** button.

4. To format with an expanded menu, click the **Conditional Formatting** button, and then point to **Color Scales**.

5. Click the two or three colored scale you want (top is higher values, center is middle values, and bottom is lower values).

6. To create a custom color scale, click **More Rules**, specify the description you want, and then click **OK**.

Format Using Icon Sets

1. Select a cell or range you want to conditionally format.

2. Click the **Home** tab.

3. To format with a preset, click the **Quick Analysis** button (**New!**), click **Formatting**, and then click the **Icon Set** button.

4. To format with an expanded menu, click the **Conditional Formatting** button, and then point to **Icon Sets**.

5. Click the colored icon sets you want.

6. To create a custom icon set, click **More Rules**, specify the description you want, and then click **OK**.

Icons

Creating Conditional Formatting

Instead of using one of the built-in conditional formatting rules, you can create your own rules. The New Formatting Rule dialog box allows you to create rules based on different rule types, such as format all cells based on their values, or use a formula to determine which cells to format. After you select a rule type, you specify the rule criteria to trigger conditional formatting. Many of the rule types include the Format button, which opens the familiar Format Cells dialog box. You can specify number, font, border, and fill formatting options. For icon sets, you can mix and match icons for a custom look as well as hide them based on your criteria. For data bars, you can set the bar direction, and specify custom formatting for negative values.

Create Conditional Formatting Rules

1. Click the **Home** tab.

2. Click the **Conditional Formatting** button, and then click **New Rules**.

3. Click the rule type you want.

   - Format all cells based on their values.

   - Format only cells that contain.

   - Format only top or bottom ranked values.

   - Format only values that are above or below average.

   - Format only unique or duplicate values.

   - Use a formula to determine which cells to format.

4. Specify the rule criteria you want to create a conditional format. Each rule type provides a different set of options you can set.

   If available, click **Format** to specify number, font, border, and fill formatting options in the Format Cells dialog box.

5. Click **OK**.

Data bar conditional formatting

Clearing Conditional Formatting

If you no longer need the conditional formatting applied to a cell, range, table, or PivotTable, you can quickly clear the formatting using any of the Clear Rules commands on the Conditional Formatting menu. You can clear rules from selected cells, entire sheet, table, or PivotTable. When you clear conditional formatting rules, the contents of the cell, range, table or PivotTable remain intact. Only the cell formatting is removed.

Clear Conditional Formatting Rules

1. Select the cell or range with the conditional formatting rules you want to clear.

2. Click the **Home** tab.

3. Click the **Conditional Formatting** button, and then point to **Clear Rules**.

4. Click the clear rule option you want:

   ◆ **Clear Rules from Selected Cells.**

   ◆ **Clear Rules from Entire Sheet.**

   ◆ **Clear Rules from This Table.**

   ◆ **Clear Rules from This PivotTable.**

Managing Conditional Formatting

When you apply conditional formatting to a cell or range of cells, Excel stores the rules associated with the conditional formatting in the Conditional Formatting Rules Manager. You can use the Conditional Formatting Rules Manager to create, edit, delete, and view all conditional formatting rules in a workbook. When two or more conditional formatting rules apply to the same cells (that conflict or not), the rules are evaluated in order of precedence as they appear in the dialog box. You can move a rule up or down in the precedence list. Conditional formatting takes precedence over a manual format, which doesn't appear in the Conditional Formatting Rules Manager.

Edit Conditional Formatting Rule Precedence

1. If you want, select the cell or range with the conditional formatting rules you want to edit.

2. Click the **Home** tab.

3. Click the **Conditional Formatting** button, and then click **Manage Rules**.

4. Click the **Show formatting rules for** list arrow, and then select an option to show the rules you want.

5. Select the rule you want to change.

6. To move the selected rule up or down in precedence, click **Move Up** or **Move Down**.

7. To stop rule evaluation at a specific rule, select the **Stop If True** check box.

   Select this option for backwards compatibility with previous versions of Excel that don't support multiple conditional formatting rules.

8. To delete a rule, click **Delete Rule**.

9. To edit a rule, click **Edit Rule**, make the changes you want, and then click **OK**.

10. Click **OK**.

Edit a rule

Finding Conditional Formatting

If you have cells in your workbook that contain conditional formatting, you can quickly find them using the Find & Select button in order to change, copy or delete the formatting. You can use the Conditional Formatting command to find all cells that have a conditional format, or use the Go To Special command to find only cells that have the same conditional format.

Find Cells with Conditional Formatting

1. Select any cell with or without a conditional format.

2. Click the **Home** tab.

3. Click the **Find & Select** button arrow, and then click **Conditional Formatting**.

Find Cells with the Same Conditional Format

1. Select a cell with the conditional format you want to find.

2. Click the **Home** tab.

3. Click the **Find & Select** button arrow, and then click **Go To Special**.

4. Click the **Conditional formats** option.

5. Click the **Same** option.

6. Click **OK**.

Creating Sparkline Formatting

A sparkline is a tiny chart in the background of a cell that provides a visual for a data range. Sparklines are useful for showing trends in a series of data, which you can print in a worksheet. You can display line, column, and win/loss charts. After you create a sparkline chart, you can format it using the Design tab under Sparkline Tools. You can quickly select a Quick Style layout or set individual options, such as chart type, sparkline color, marker color, axis display, and control points (high, low, first, last, or any negative values). If you have several sparkline cells, you can group them together. If you no longer want to use a sparkline, you can clear it. Since a sparkline is embedded, you can still enter text in the cell. You can create a sparkline format using the Quick Analysis tool (**New!**) for a data range or the Insert tab for a destination cell.

Create Sparkline Formatting

① Select a range of data (Quick Analysis tool) or the destination cell (Insert tab) for the sparkline formatting chart.

② Use either of the following:

◆ **Quick Analysis Tool.** Click the **Quick Analysis** button (**New!**), click **Sparkline**, and then click the **Line**, **Column**, or **Win/Loss** button.

◆ **Insert Tab.** Click the **Insert** tab, click the button (**Line, Column, or Win/Loss**), click the **Collapse Dialog** button, select the data range, click the **Expand Dialog** button, and then click **OK**.

Did You Know?

You can apply conditional formatting. Select a range of data, click the Quick Analysis button, click Formatting, and then click a conditional formatting rule.

See Also

See "Creating a Chart" on page 268 for more information on using the Quick Analysis button for charting data.

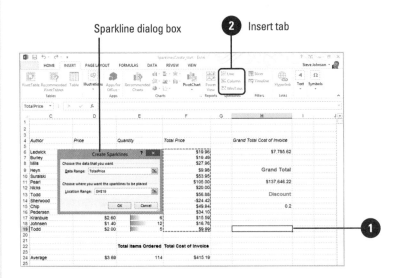

Sparkline dialog box — Insert tab

Quick Analysis tool

Change Sparkline Formatting

1. Select the cell with the sparkline you want to change.

2. Click the **Design** tab under Sparkline Tools.

3. To edit the data or handle empty cells or zero values, click the **Edit Data** button arrow, and then click the data option you want:

   ◆ **Edit Group Location & Data.**

   ◆ **Edit Single Sparkline's Data.**

   ◆ **Hidden & Empty Cells.**

4. To format a sparkline, select options on the Design tab in any of the following sections:

   ◆ **Type.** Select a type button (**Line**, **Column**, or **Win/Loss**) to change the type.

   ◆ **Show.** Select or clear check boxes to show or hide points or markers on the chart.

   ◆ **Style.** Select a built-in style or click the **Sparkline Color** or **Marker Color** buttons to select your own colors.

   ◆ **Group.** Click the **Axis** button to change the scaling and visibility of each sparkline axis, or click the **Group** or **Ungroup** buttons to group or ungroup sparklines to share formatting.

5. To clear a sparkline, click the **Clear** button arrow, and then click **Clear Selected Sparklines**, or **Clear Selected Sparkline Groups**.

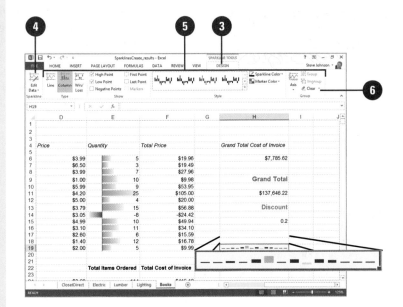

Changing Data Alignment

When you enter data in a cell, Excel aligns labels on the left edge of the cell and aligns values and formulas on the right edge of the cell. **Horizontal alignment** is the way in which Excel aligns the contents of a cell relative to the left or right edge of the cell; **vertical alignment** is the way in which Excel aligns cell contents relative to the top and bottom of the cell. Excel also provides an option for changing the flow and angle of characters within a cell. The **orientation** of the contents of a cell is expressed in degrees. The default orientation is 0 degrees, in which characters are horizontally aligned within a cell.

Change Alignment Using the Ribbon

1. Select a cell or range containing the data to be realigned.

2. Click the **Home** tab.

3. Click any of the alignment buttons on the Ribbon:

   ◆ Click **Align Left**, **Center**, or **Align Right** to align cell contents left to right.

   ◆ Click **Top Align**, **Middle Align**, or **Bottom Align** to align cell contents from top to bottom.

   ◆ Click **Decrease Indent** or **Increase Indent** to shift cell contents to the left or right.

   ◆ Click **Orientation**, and then click **Angle Counterclockwise**, **Angle Clockwise**, **Vertical Text**, **Rotate Text Up**, or **Rotate Text Down** to rotate cell contents.

Change Alignment Using the Format Dialog Box

1 Select a cell or range containing the data to be realigned.

2 Click the **Home** tab.

3 Click the **Alignment** or **Paragraph Dialog Box Launcher**.

The Format Cells dialog box opens, displaying the Alignment tab.

4 Click the **Horizontal** list arrow or the **Vertical** list arrow, and then select an alignment.

5 Select an orientation. Click a point on the map, or click the **Degrees** up or down arrow.

6 If you want, select one or more of the Text control check boxes.

7 Click the **Text Direction** list arrow, and then select a direction: **Context**, **Left-to-Right**, or **Right-to-Left**.

8 Click **OK**.

Did You Know?

You can use the Format Cells dialog box to select other alignment options. Many more alignment options are available from the Format Cells dialog box, but for centering across columns and simple left, right, and center alignment, it's easier to use the Home or Format tab buttons.

Controlling Text Flow

The length of a label might not always fit within the width you've chosen for a column. If the cell to the right is empty, text spills over into it, but if that cell contains data, the text will be truncated (that is, cut off). A cell can be formatted so its text automatically wraps to multiple lines or cell contents can also be shrunk to fit within the available space; that way, you don't have to widen the column to achieve an attractive effect. If the cell to the right is empty, cell contents can be combined, or merged, with the contents of other cells.

Control the Flow of Text in a Cell

1. Select a cell or range whose text flow you want to change.

2. Click the **Home** tab.

3. To center cell contents across selected columns, click the **Merge & Center** button arrow, and then click one of the options:

   ◆ **Merge & Center.**

   ◆ **Merge Across.**

   ◆ **Merge Cells.**

   ◆ **Unmerge Cells.**

4. To wrap text in a cell, click the **Wrap Text** button.

5. To set multiple alignment options at the same time or shrink text to fit in a cell, click the **Alignment Dialog Box Launcher**.

   The Format Cells dialog box opens, displaying the Alignment tab.

6. Select one or more Text Control check boxes.

   ◆ **Wrap text** moves the text to multiple lines within a cell.

   ◆ **Shrink to fit** reduces character size to fit within a cell.

   ◆ **Merge cells** combines selected cells into a single cell.

7. Click **OK**.

Selected cells to merge

Selected cell to wrap text

Changing Data Color

You can change the color of the numbers and text on a worksheet. Strategic use of **font color** can be an effective way of tying similar values together. For instance, on a sales worksheet you might want to display sales in green and returns in red. Or, you may want to highlight column or row headers with colored labels. Either way, using color to highlight numbers and texts makes deciphering your worksheet data easier.

Change Font Color

1 Select a cell or range that contains the text you want to change.

2 Click the **Home** tab.

3 Click the **Font Color** button arrow.

4 Click a color.

Did You Know?

The Font Color button on the Ribbon displays the last font color you used. To apply this color to another selection, simply click the button, not the list arrow.

Adding Color and Patterns to Cells

You can **fill** the background of a cell with a color and a pattern to make its data stand out. Fill colors and patterns can also lend consistency to related information on a worksheet. On a sales worksheet, for example, formatting all fourth-quarter sales figures with a blue background and all second-quarter sales with a yellow background would make each group of figures easy to identify. You can use fill colors and patterns in conjunction with text attributes, fonts, and font colors to further enhance the appearance of your worksheet. If you no longer need cell shading, you can remove it by using No Fill.

Apply Solid Colors to Cells

1. Select a cell or range you want to apply cell color.

2. Click the **Home** tab.

3. Click the **Fill Color** button arrow, and then click the color on the palette you want.

   TIMESAVER *To apply the most recently selected color, click the Fill Color button.*

4. To remove the cell shading, click the **Fill Color** button arrow, and then click **No Fill**.

Apply Color and Pattern to Cells

1. Select a cell or range you want to apply cell shading.

2. Click the **Home** tab.

3. Click the **Font Dialog Box Launcher**.

4. Click the **Fill** tab.

5. Click the **Pattern Color** list arrow, and then click a pattern color.

6. Click the **Pattern Style** list arrow, and then click a pattern.

7. Click **OK**.

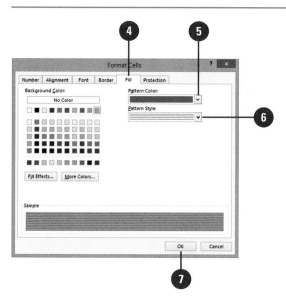

Adding Custom Colors

In addition to the standard and theme colors, Excel allows you to add more colors to your workbook. These additional colors are available on each color button palette on the Ribbon or in a dialog box, such as the Fill Color or Font Color button. These colors are useful when you want to use a specific color, but the workbook color theme does not have that color. Colors that you add to a workbook appear in all color palettes and remain in the palette even if the color theme changes.

Add a Color to the Menus

1. Click the **Font Color** button on the Home tab, and then click **More Colors**.

   This is one method. You can also use other color menus to access the Colors dialog box.

2. Click the **Custom** tab.

3. Click the **Color model** list arrow, and then click **RGB** or **HSL**.

4. Select a custom color using one of the following methods:

   ◆ If you know the color values, enter them, either Hue, Sat, Lum, or Red, Green, and Blue.

   ◆ Drag across the palette until the pointer is over the color you want. Drag the black arrow to adjust the amount of black and white in the color.

   The new color appears above the current color at the bottom right.

5. Click **OK**.

   The current selection is changed to the new color, plus the new color is added to the Recent Colors section of all document color menus.

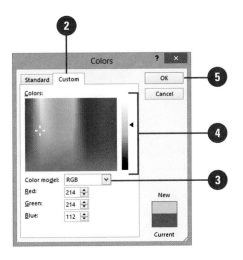

> ## See Also
>
> See "Creating Theme Colors" on page 164 for information on using color.

Added custom color

Adding Borders to Cells

The light gray grid that appears on the worksheet helps your eyes move from cell to cell. Although you can print these gridlines, sometimes a different grid pattern better emphasizes your data. For example, you might put a decorative line border around the title or a double-line bottom border below cells with totals. You can add borders of varying colors and widths to any or all sides of a single cell or range. If you prefer, you can draw a border outline or grid directly on a worksheet.

Apply or Remove a Border Using the Ribbon

1. Select a cell or range to which you want to apply a border.

2. Click the **Home** tab.

3. Click the **Borders** button arrow.

   TIMESAVER *To apply the most recently selected border, click the Borders button.*

4. Select a border from the menu.

5. To remove cell borders, click **No Border**.

Draw a Border

1. Click the **Home** tab.

2. Click the **Borders** button arrow.

3. Select a draw borders option from the menu.

   ◆ Point to **Line Color**, and then click the color you want.

   ◆ Point to **Line Style**, and then click the style you want.

   ◆ Click **Draw Border**, and then drag a border.

   ◆ Click **Draw Border Grid**, and then drag a border.

   ◆ Click **Erase Border**, and then drag a border.

4. Press Esc to exit.

Use to draw a border

Apply a Border Using the Format Cells Dialog Box

1. Select a cell or range to which you want to apply borders.

2. Click the **Home** tab.

3. Click the **Borders** button arrow, and then click **More Borders**.

   The Format Cells dialog box opens, displaying the Border tab.

4. Select a line style.

5. Click the **Color** list arrow, and then click a color for the border.

6. If you want a border on the outside of a cell or range, click **Outline**. If you want a border between cells, click **Inside**. If you want to remove a border, click **None**.

7. To set a custom border, click a Border button, or click the Preview Border box where you want to add a border.

   Use these buttons to create a diagonal border.

8. Click **OK**.

Did You Know?

You can quickly switch between Draw Border and Draw Border Grid. Click the Borders button arrow on the Home tab, click Draw Border or Draw Border Grid. Hold down the Ctrl key to switch to the other border drawing cursor.

You can use the Select All button. To place a border around the entire worksheet, click the Select All button, and then apply the border.

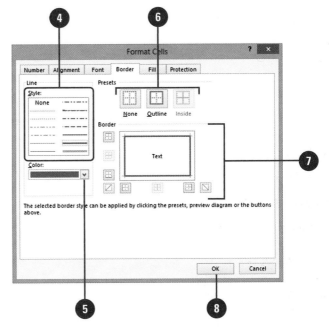

Formatting Tabs and Background

Depending on your screen size, the sheet tabs at the bottom of your workbook can be hard to view. You can add color to the sheet tabs to make them more distinguishable. If you want to add artistic style to your workbook or you are creating a web page from your workbook, you can add a background picture. When you add a background to a worksheet, the background does not print, and it's not included when you save an individual worksheet as a web page. You need to publish the entire workbook as a web page to include the background.

Add or Remove Color to Worksheet Tabs

1. Click the sheet tab you want to color.

2. Click the **Home** tab.

3. Click the **Format** button, point to **Tab Color**, and then do any of the following:

   ◆ **Add.** Click a color.

   ◆ **Remove.** Click **No Color**.

Add or Remove a Background

1. Click the sheet tab to which you want to add a background.

2. Click the **Page Layout** tab.

3. Click the **Background** button.

4. Browse your computer or SkyDrive or search Office.com or Bing Image Search for a background graphic (**New!**).

5. Select the graphic you want.

6. Click **Insert**.

7. To remove the background, click **Delete Background** on the Page Layout tab.

Changes to Delete Background

Copying Cell Formats

After formatting a cell on a worksheet, you might want to apply those same formatting changes to other cells on the worksheet. For example, you might want each subtotal on your worksheet to be formatted in italic, bold, 12-point Times New Roman, with a dollar sign, commas, and two decimal places. Rather than selecting each subtotal and applying the individual formatting to each cell, you can **paint** (that is, copy) the formatting from one cell to others. The Format Painter lets you "pick up" the style of one section and apply, or "paint," it to another. To apply a format style to more than one item, double-click the Format Painter button on the Home tab instead of a single-click. The double-click keeps the Format Painter active until you want to press Esc to disable it, so you can apply formatting styles to multiple elements in your workbook.

Apply a Format Style Using the Format Painter

1. Select a cell, range, or object containing the formatting you want to copy.

2. Click the **Home** tab.

3. Click the **Format Painter** button.

   If you want to apply the format to more than one item, double-click the Format Painter button.

4. Drag to select the cell or click the object to which you want to apply the format.

5. If you double-clicked the Format Painter button, drag to select the cell or click the object to which you want to apply the format, and then press Esc when you're done.

Did You Know?

You can use the Esc key to cancel format painting. If you change your mind about painting a format, cancel the marquee by pressing Esc.

Understanding Color Themes

A theme helps you create professional-looking workbooks that use an appropriate balance of color for your workbook content. You can use a default color theme or create a custom one.

Themes in Excel are made up of a palette of twelve colors. These colors appear on color palettes when you click a color-related button, such as Fill Color or Font Color button on the Home tab or in a dialog box. These twelve colors correspond to the following elements in a workbook:

Four Text and Background. The two background colors (light and dark combinations) are the canvas, or drawing area, color of the worksheet. The two text colors (light and dark combinations) are for typing text and drawing lines, and contrast with the background colors.

Six Accent. These colors are designed to work as a complementary color palette for objects, such as shadows and fills. These colors contrast with both the background and text colors.

One hyperlink. This color is designed to work as a complementary color for objects and hyperlinks.

One followed hyperlink. This color is designed to work as a complementary color for objects and visited hyperlinks.

The first four colors in the Theme Colors list represent the workbook text and background colors (light and dark for each). The remaining colors represent the six accent and two hyperlink colors for the theme. When you apply another theme or change any of these colors to create a new theme, the colors shown in the Theme Colors dialog box and color palettes change to match the current colors.

Accent 5   Accent 4   Accent 6   Accent 1   Accent 3

Twelve theme colors   **Sample color themes:** Dark and Light

Text/Background - Light 1   Text/Background - Light 2   Accent 2

Viewing and Applying a Theme

A theme consists of theme colors, fonts, and effects. You can quickly format an entire workbook with a professional look by applying a theme. Office comes with more themes and styles. To quickly see if you like a theme, point to one on the themes gallery to display a ScreenTip with name and information about it, and a live preview of it on the current workbook. If you like the theme, you can apply it. When you apply a theme, the background, text, graphics, charts, and tables all change to reflect the theme. You can choose from one or more standard themes. When you add new content, the workbook elements change to match the theme ensuring all of your material will look consistent. You can even use the same theme in other Microsoft Office programs, such as Word and PowerPoint, so all your work matches. Can't find a theme you like? Search Microsoft Office.com on the web.

View and Apply a Theme

1. Open the workbook you want to apply a theme.

2. Click the **Page Layout** tab.

3. Click the **Themes** button to display the themes gallery.

4. Point to a theme.

    A live preview of the theme appears in the workbook, along with a ScreenTip.

5. Click the theme you want to apply to the active workbook.

Did You Know?

You can apply themes from Office.com. In your browser, go to *Office.com*, download the online theme you want. Click the Page Layout tab, click the Themes button or the More list arrow, click Browse for Themes, and then choose the theme file.

Creating Theme Colors

You may like a certain color theme except for one or two colors. You can change an existing color theme and apply your changes to the entire workbook. You can add other custom colors to your theme by using RGB (Red, Green, and Blue) or HSL (Hues, Saturation, and Luminosity) color modes. The RGB color mode is probably the most widely used of all the color modes. You can accomplish this by using sliders, dragging on a color-space, or entering a numeric value that corresponds to a specific color. Once you create this new color theme, you can add it to your collection of color themes so that you can make it available to any workbook.

Apply or Create Theme Colors

1. Open the workbook you want to apply a color theme.

2. Click the **Page Layout** tab.

3. To apply theme colors to a document, click the **Theme Colors** button, and then click a color theme.

   ◆ To apply individual theme colors, click an element, click a color button, such as Font Color, and then click a theme color.

4. To create theme colors, click the **Theme Colors** button, and then click **Customize Colors**.

5. Click the Theme Colors buttons (Text/Background, Accent, or Hyperlink, etc.) for the colors you want to change.

6. Click a new color, or click **More Colors** to select a color from the **Standard** or **Custom** tab, and then click **OK**.

7. If you don't like your color choices, click the **Reset** button to return all color changes to their original colors.

8. Type a new name for the color theme.

9. Click **Save**.

Select Custom Colors

1 Select a cell or range you want to apply a custom color.

2 Click the **Font Color** button on the Home tab, and then click **More Colors**.

This is one method. You can also use other color menus to access the Colors dialog box.

3 Click the **Custom** tab.

4 Click the **Color model** list arrow, and then click **RGB** or **HSL**.

5 Select a custom color using one of the following methods:

◆ If you know the color values, enter them, either Hue, Sat, Lum, or Red, Green, and Blue.

◆ Drag across the palette until the pointer is over the color you want. Drag the black arrow to adjust the amount of black and white in the color.

The new color appears above the current color at the bottom right.

6 Click **OK**.

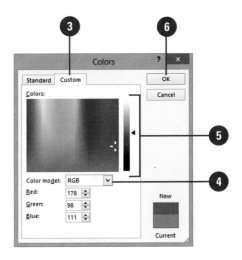

Did You Know?

You can edit a custom color theme.
On the Page Layout tab, click the Theme Colors button, right-click the theme color you want to edit, click Edit, make changes, and then click Save.

You can delete a custom color theme.
On the Page Layout tab, click the Theme Colors button, right-click the theme color you want to edit, click Edit, click Delete, and then click Yes.

The Properties of Color

Characteristic	Description
Hue	The color itself; every color is identified by a number, determined by the number of colors available on your monitor.
Saturation	The intensity of the color. The higher the number, the more vivid the color.
Luminosity	The brightness of the color, or how close the color is to black or white. The larger the number, the lighter the color.
Red, Green, Blue	Primary colors of the visible light spectrum. RGB generates color using three 8-bit channels: 1 red, 1 green, and 1 blue. RGB is an additive color system, which means that color is added to a black background. The additive process mixes various amounts of red, green and blue light to produce other colors.

Choosing Theme Fonts

A workbook theme consists of theme colors, fonts, and effects. Theme fonts include heading and body text fonts. Each workbook uses a set of theme fonts. When you click the Theme Fonts button on the Page Layout tab, the name of the current heading and body text font appear highlighted in the gallery menu. To quickly see if you like a theme font, point to one on the menu, and a live preview of it appears on the current worksheet. If you want to apply the theme, click it on the menu. You can apply a set of theme fonts to another theme or create your own set of theme fonts.

Apply and Choose Theme Fonts

1. Open the document you want to apply theme fonts.

2. Click the **Home** tab.

3. Select the cell or range you want to change, click the **Font** list arrow, and then click the theme font you want.

   TIMESAVER *To select the entire worksheet, press Ctrl+A.*

4. Click the **Page Layout** tab.

5. Click the **Theme Fonts** button.

   The current theme fonts appear highlighted on the menu.

   TIMESAVER *Point to the Fonts button to display a ScreenTip with the current theme fonts.*

6. Click the theme fonts you want from the gallery menu.

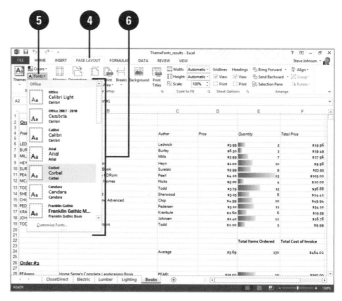

Create Theme Fonts

1. Click the **Page Layout** tab.

2. Click the **Theme Fonts** button, and then click **Customize Fonts**.

3. Click the **Heading font** list arrow, and then select a font.

4. Click the **Body font** list arrow, and then select a font.

5. Type a name for the custom theme fonts.

6. Click **Save**.

Did You Know?

The Font Color button on the Ribbon displays the last font color you used. To apply this color to another selection, simply click the button, not the list arrow.

Choosing Theme Effects

A workbook theme consists of theme colors, fonts, and effects. Theme effects are sets of lines, fills, and special effects styles for shapes, graphics, charts, SmartArt, and other design elements. By combining the lines, fills, and special effects styles with different formatting levels (subtle, moderate, and intense), Excel provides a variety of visual theme effects. Each workbook uses a set of theme effects. Some are more basic while others are more elaborate. When you click the Theme Effects button on the Page Layout tab, the name of the current theme effects appears highlighted in the gallery menu. While you can apply a set of theme effects to another theme, you cannot create your own set of theme effects at this time.

View and Apply Theme Effects

1. Open the document you want to apply a theme effect.

2. Click the **Page Layout** tab.

3. Click the **Theme Effects** button.

   The current theme effects appear highlighted on the menu.

   TIMESAVER *Point to the Effects button to display a ScreenTip with the current theme effects name.*

4. Click the theme effects you want from the menu.

Did You Know?

You can delete a custom theme effects or fonts. On the Page Layout tab, click the Theme Effects or Theme Fonts button or the More list arrow, right-click the theme you want to edit, click Edit, click Delete, and then click Yes.

See Also

See "Viewing and Applying a Theme" on page 163 for information on applying a theme from the Themes gallery.

Creating a Custom Theme

If you have special needs for specific colors, fonts, and effects, such as a company sales or marketing document, you can create your own theme by customizing theme colors, theme fonts, and theme effects, and saving them as a theme file (.thmx), which you can reuse. You can apply the saved theme to other workbooks. When you save a custom theme, the file is automatically saved in the Document Themes folder and added to the list of custom themes used by Office 2007-2013 and other Office programs. When you no longer need a custom theme, you can delete it.

Create a Custom Theme

1. Click the **Page Layout** tab, and then create a theme by customizing theme colors, theme fonts, and theme effects.

2. Click the **Themes** button, and then click **Save Current Theme**.

3. Type a name for the theme file.

4. Click **Save**.

Did You Know?

You can remove a custom theme from the gallery menu. Simply move or delete the theme file from the Document Themes folder into another folder.

Custom theme

Choosing a Custom Theme

When you can create your own theme by customizing theme colors, theme fonts, and theme effects, and saving them as a theme file (.thmx), you can apply the saved theme to other workbooks. When you save a custom theme file in the Document Themes folder, you can choose the custom theme from the Themes gallery, available on the Page Layout tab. If you save a custom theme file in another folder location, you can use the Browse for Themes command to locate and select the custom theme file you want to reuse. When you no longer need a custom theme, you can delete it from the Browse dialog box.

Choose and Apply a Custom Theme

1. Open the workbook you want to apply a custom theme.

2. Click the **Page Layout** tab.

3. Click the **Themes** button to see additional themes.

   Custom themes are at the top of the gallery and Office themes are below it.

4. Point to gallery to display the theme name, and then click the one you want.

See Also

See "Viewing and Applying a Theme" on page 163 for information on applying a theme from the Themes gallery.

Select and Apply a Custom Theme From a File

1 Open the workbook you want to apply a custom theme.

2 Click the **Page Layout** tab.

3 Click the **Themes** button, and then click **Browse for Themes**.

4 If you want to open a specific file type, click the **Files of type** list arrow, and then click a file type.

- ◆ **Office Themes and Themed Documents.**

- ◆ **Office Themes.**

- ◆ **Office Themes and Excel Templates.**

5 If the file is located in another folder, click the **Look in** list arrow, and then navigate to the file.

6 Click the theme file you want.

7 Click **Open**.

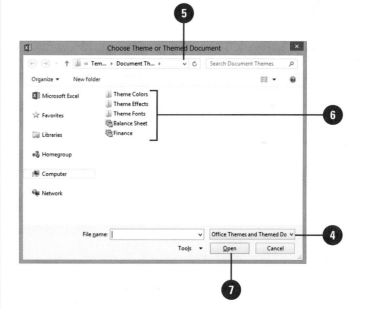

Applying and Creating Cell Styles

A **cell style** is a defined collection of formats—font, font size, attributes, numeric formats, and so on—that you can store as a set and later apply to other cells. For example if you always want subtotals to display in blue 14-point Times New Roman, bold, italic, with two decimal places and commas, you can create a style that includes all these formats. A cell style can help you quickly create a consistent look for your workbook. If you plan to enter repetitive information, such as a list of dollar amounts in a row or column, it's often easier to apply the desired style to the range before you enter the data. That way you can simply enter each number, and Excel formats it as soon as you press Enter. You can use one of Excel's built-in cell styles, or create one of your own. Once you create a style, it is available to you in every workbook. If you need to prevent users from making changes to specific cells, you can use a cell style that locks cells.

Apply a Cell Style

1 Select a cell or range you want to apply cell shading.

2 Click the **Home** tab.

3 Click the **Cell Styles** button, and then click the cell style you want to apply.

Did You Know?

You can add a cell styles gallery to the Quick Access Toolbar. Click the Home tab, click the Cell Styles button, right-click any cell style, and then click Add Gallery to Quick Access Toolbar.

See Also

See "Modifying a Cell Style" on page 174 for information on merging a style from another workbook.

Create a Custom Cell Style

1. Select a cell or range you want to apply cell shading.

2. Click the **Home** tab.

3. Click the **Cell Styles** button, and then click **New Cell Style**.

4. Type a name for the cell style.

5. Click **Format**.

   The Format Cells dialog box opens.

6. Select the formatting you want on the Number, Alignment, Font, Border, Fill, and Protection tabs, and then click **OK**.

7. Clear the check boxes for any formatting you don't want to use.

   ◆ **Number.**

   ◆ **Alignment.**

   ◆ **Font.**

   ◆ **Border.**

   ◆ **Fill.**

   ◆ **Protection.**

8. Click **OK**.

   The new cell style is available on the Cell Styles gallery.

Modifying a Cell Style

Any style—whether it was supplied by Excel or created by you or someone else—can be modified. Suppose you created a style containing fonts and colors your company uses. If those specifications changed, you could modify the style to include the new attributes. If you want to use styles created or modified in another workbook, you can merge the styles into the open workbook. If you no longer use a style, you can delete it from the workbook.

Modify a Custom Cell Style

1. Click the **Home** tab.

2. Click the **Cell Styles** button.

3. Right-click the custom cell style you want to change, and then click **Modify**.

4. To create a new style based on an existing style, type a name for the cell style.

5. Click **Format**.

   The Format Cells dialog box opens.

6. Select the formatting you want on the Number, Alignment, Font, Border, Fill, and Protection tabs, and then click **OK**.

7. Clear the check boxes for any formatting you don't want to use.

   ◆ **Number.**

   ◆ **Alignment.**

   ◆ **Font.**

   ◆ **Border.**

   ◆ **Fill.**

   ◆ **Protection.**

8. Click **OK**.

Merge Cell Styles

1. Open the workbook that contains the styles you want to merge first, and then open the workbook to which you want to merge styles.

2. Click the **Home** tab.

3. Click the **Cell Styles** button, and then click **Merge Styles**.

4. Click the workbook that contains the styles you want to merge with the current workbook.

5. Click **OK**.

6. Click **Yes or No** to merge or not merge styles with the same name.

Delete a Cell Style

1. Click the **Home** tab.

2. Click the **Cell Styles** button.

3. To delete the cell style and remove it from all cells using it, right-click the cell style, and then click **Delete**.

Did You Know?

You can remove a custom cell style from a cell. Select the cell or range with the custom style you want to remove, click the Home tab, click the Cell Styles button, and then click Normal.

Finding and Replacing Cell Formatting

The Find and Replace commands make it easy to locate or replace specific text, numbers, and formatting in a workbook. For example, you might want to replace all the references to cell A6 in your formulas with data contained in cell H2, or you might want to replace bold text with italic text. Or, you may want to change a client name or contact on all of your financial reports. You can be specific in your replacing, by replacing one at a time, or all matches found.

Find or Replace Cell Formatting

1. Click the **Home** tab.

2. Click the **Find & Select** button, and then click **Find** or **Replace**.

3. If you want, enter the word or words you want to find.

4. Click **Options** to display formatting options. If necessary, click **Format**, and then click **Clear Formatting From Cell** to clear previous criteria.

5. Click **Format**.

6. Specify the formatting you want to locate, and then click **OK**.

   TIMESAVER *To quickly specify formatting, click Choose Format From Cell, and then click the cell with the format you want to find.*

7. To replace text and formatting, click the **Replace** tab, and then enter the word or words you want to replace in the Replace With text box.

8. Click the **Format** button next to Replace with, specify the formatting you want to replace, and then click **OK**.

9. Click **Find Next** or **Find All** to select the next instance of the formatted text or click **Replace** or **Replace All** to substitute formatting.

Click to select a cell with the format you want to find.

Viewing and Printing Worksheets and Workbooks

6

Introduction

When your Microsoft Excel worksheet is completed, you can preview and print its contents. While previewing the worksheet, you might find that rows of data might flow better on one page or the other. You can add page breaks to segment what you want to appear on a page. You can insert page breaks to control what you print on each page. You can change the orientation of the page from the default of portrait (vertical) to landscape (horizontal). This is helpful when you have wide or multiple columns that would look better on one page. You can also adjust your margins to better fit the worksheet on the page. Previewing a worksheet before printing saves you time and money by not printing unnecessary copies.

After you make layout adjustments you can add headers and footers on the page in Page Layout view, which lets you focus on how your worksheet is going to look when you print it. Headers are typically a descriptive title about your worksheet or workbook. Footers can include date printed, page numbers, or other company related information. You can add additional elements to your printout by showing gridlines or column letters and row numbers.

When you're ready to print your work, you can quickly print the entire worksheet, or print only part of the worksheet. Excel provides options to set the print area and customize what you want to print. For example, you might want to print a different range in a worksheet for different people. After you set the print area, you can choose to print your worksheet. The Print dialog box allows you to customize all the options and more, and then you can send your worksheet or entire workbook to the printer.

If you need to send a workbook to others, which cannot be changed, Excel provides the option to save a workbook as an XPS or PDF file, which are secure fixed-layout formats.

What You'll Do

Set Up the Page

Adjust Page Margins

Add Headers and Footers

Insert Page Breaks

Customize Worksheet Printing

Set the Print Area

Preview a Worksheet

Print a Worksheet and Workbook

Create a PDF Document

Create an XPS Document

Setting Up the Page

You can set up the worksheet page to print just the way you want. In Page Layout view, you can choose **page orientation**, which determines whether Excel prints the worksheet portrait (vertically) or landscape (horizontally), and paper size (to match the size of paper in your printer). With the Page Setup dialog box, you can also adjust the **print scaling** (to reduce or enlarge the size of printed characters). Changes made in the Page Setup dialog box are not reflected in the worksheet window. You can see them only when you preview or print the worksheet.

Change Page Orientation

1. Click the **Page Layout** tab.

2. Click the **Orientation** button.

   The current orientation is highlighted on the menu.

3. Click **Portrait** or **Landscape** from the menu.

Did You Know?

You can print comments. Display the comments you want to print. Click the Page Layout tab, click the Page Setup Dialog Box Launcher, click the Sheet tab, click the Comments list arrow, click the As Displayed On Sheet or At End Of Sheet option, and then click Print.

Change the Page Size

① Click the **Page Layout** tab.

② Click the **Size** button from the submenu.

The current margin setting is highlighted on the submenu.

③ Click **Letter** (8.5 x 11), **Letter Small** (8.5 x 11), **Tabloid** (11 x 17), **Ledger** (17 x 11, **Legal** (8.5 x 14), **Statement** (5.5 x 8.5), **Executive** (7.25 x 10.5), **A3** (11.69 x 16.54), **A4** (8.27 x 11.69), **A4 Small** (8.27 x 11.69) from the submenu.

Customize the Page Size

① Click the **Page Layout** tab.

② Click the **Size** button, and then click **More Paper Sizes**.

The Page Setup dialog box opens, displaying the Page tab.

③ To scale the page, click the **Adjust to** or **Fit to** option, and then specify the adjust to percentage, or fit to the option you want.

④ Click the **Paper size** list arrow, and then select a paper size.

⑤ Click the **Print quality** list arrow, and then select a quality option; higher the number, the better the quality.

⑥ To start the first page on a specific number, enter the number you want.

⑦ Click **OK**.

Adjusting Page Margins

A page margin is the blank areas along each edge of the paper. You can set up page margins to print your worksheets just the way you want. If you need to quickly set margins, you can use the Margins button on the Page Layout tab. Otherwise, you can use the mouse pointer to adjust margins visually for the entire workbook in Page Layout view, or you can use the Page Setup dialog box to set precise measurements for an entire workbook or a specific section. You can resize or realign the left, right, top, and bottom margins (the blank areas along each edge of the paper). Changes made in the Page Setup dialog box are not reflected in the worksheet window. You can see them only when you preview or print the worksheet.

Change the Margin Settings

1. Click the **Page Layout** tab.

2. Click the **Margins** button.

   The current margin setting is highlighted on the menu.

3. Click the option you want from the menu.

   ◆ **Last Custom Setting.** Only available if you previously changed margin settings.

   ◆ **Normal.**

   ◆ **Wide.**

   ◆ **Narrow.**

Change the Margin Using the Mouse in Page Layout View

1. Click the **View** tab.

2. Click the **Page Layout View** button.

3. Select the **Ruler** check box.

4. Position the cursor over the left, right, top, or bottom edge of the ruler until the cursor changes to a double arrow.

   A ScreenTip appears indicating the margin name and current position.

5. Drag to change the margin.

6. To exit Page Layout view, click the **Normal** button.

Customize Margin Settings

1. Click the **Page Layout** tab.

2. Click the **Margins** button, and then click **Custom Margins**.

   The Page Setup dialog box opens, displaying the Margins tab.

3. Click the **Top**, **Bottom**, **Left**, and **Right** up or down arrows to adjust the margins.

4. To automatically center your data, select the **Horizontally** and **Vertically** check boxes under Center on page.

5. Click **OK**.

   ◆ Or click **Print Preview** to see how the margin changes look.

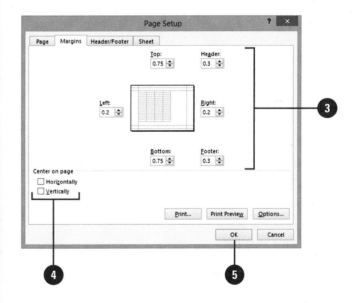

Adding Headers and Footers

Adding a header or footer to a workbook is a convenient way to make your printout easier for readers to follow. Using the Design tab under Header & Footer Tools, you can add predefined header or footer information—such as a page number and worksheet title—at the top and bottom of each page or section of a worksheet or workbook. If a predefined header or footer doesn't work, you can insert individual elements such as your computer system's date and time, the name of the workbook and sheet, a picture, or other custom information. When you insert elements in a header or footer, Excel inserts an ampersand followed by brackets with the name of the element, such as &[Page] for Page Number. Excel changes the code to the actual element when you exit headers or footers. Instead of having the same header or footer on every page, you can select options on the Design tab to create a different first page, or different odd and even pages.

Add a Predefined Header or Footer in Page Layout View

1. Click the **Insert** tab.

2. Click the **Header & Footer** button.

   The worksheet appears in Page Layout view.

3. To insert predefined header and footer information, click the **Header** or **Footer** button, and then click the information you want.

   A sample of the information appears on the menu. After you make a selection, Excel exits the Design tab.

4. To add more header or footer text, click the left, center, or right header or footer boxes at the top or at the bottom of the worksheet page where you want to add text to place the insertion point.

   To change a header or footer, select the current text.

5. Type the text you want.

   To start a new line in a header or footer text box, press Enter.

6. To close the headers or footers, click anywhere in the worksheet, or press Esc.

Insert Elements in a Header or Footer in Page Layout View

1. Click the **Insert** tab.

2. Click the **Header & Footer** button.

   The worksheet appears in Page Layout view.

3. Click the left, center, or right header or footer text at the top or at the bottom of the worksheet page where you want to insert an element.

4. Click the **Design** tab under Header & Footer Tools.

5. To insert individual elements, click the button in the Header & Footer Elements group you want.

6. Select or clear the options you want:

   ◆ **Different First Page.** Removes headers and footer from the first page.

   ◆ **Different Odd & Even Pages.** Different header or footer for odd and even pages.

   ◆ **Scale with Document.** Use the same font size and scaling as the worksheet.

   ◆ **Align with Page Margins.** Align header or footer margin with page margins.

7. To close the headers or footers, click anywhere in the worksheet, or press Esc.

Did You Know?

You can enter an "&" in a header or footer. To include a single ampersand (&) within the text of a header or footer, use two ampersands (&&).

For Your Information

Inserting a Watermark

The watermark feature is not available in Excel. However, you can still perform the same function by inserting a picture in a header or footer. The picture appears behind the text and on every printed page. Click the Insert tab, click the Header & Footer button, click in the header or footer box where you want to insert a picture, click the Picture button, and then double-click the picture you want. To resize or scale the picture, click Format Picture, select the options you want on the Size tab, and then click OK. To add space above or below the picture, use the Enter key. To replace a picture, select &[Picture], click the Picture button, and then click Replace. You might need to adjust the margins so the picture and any text fit on the page the way you want.

Inserting Page Breaks

If you want to print a worksheet that is larger than one page, Excel divides it into pages by inserting **automatic page breaks**. These page breaks are based on paper size, margin settings, and scaling options you set. You can change which rows or columns are printed on the page by inserting **horizontal** or **vertical page breaks**. In page break preview, you can view the page breaks and move them by dragging them to a different location on the worksheet.

Insert a Page Break

1. Select the location where you want to insert a page break:

    ◆ **Horizontal.** To insert a horizontal page break, click the row where you want to insert a page break.

    ◆ **Vertical.** To insert a vertical page break, click the column where you want to insert a page break.

    ◆ **Cell.** To insert a horizontal and vertical page break, click the cell below and to the right from where you want to insert a page break.

2. Click the **Page Layout** tab.

3. Click the **Breaks** button, and then click **Insert Page Break**.

    A dotted line appears on the worksheet indicating the location of the page break.

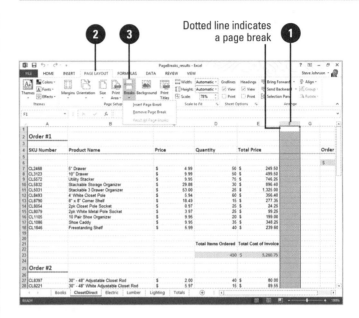

Dotted line indicates a page break

Preview and Move a Page Break

1. Click the **View** tab.

2. Click the **Page Break Preview** button.

   If the Welcome to Page Break Preview dialog box appears, select the **Do not show this dialog box again** check box, and then click **OK**.

3. Drag a page break (a thick solid or dashed blue line) to a new location.

4. When you're done, click the **Normal View** button.

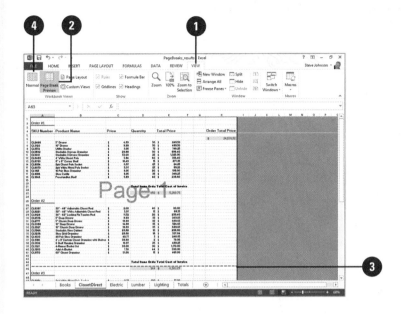

Remove a Page Break

1. Select the column or row next to the page break you want to remove.

2. Click the **Page Layout** tab.

3. Click the **Breaks** button, and then click **Remove Page Break**.

Did You Know?

You can reset page breaks back to the default. Click the Page Layout tab, click the Breaks button, and then click Reset All Page Breaks.

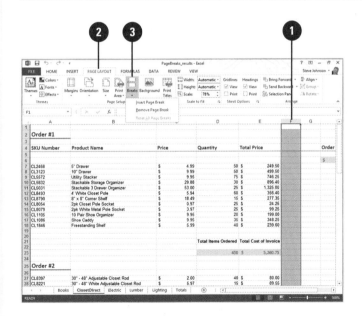

Customizing Worksheet Printing

At some point you'll want to print your worksheet so you can distribute it to others or use it for other purposes. You can print all or part of any worksheet, and you can control the appearance of many features, such as whether gridlines are displayed, whether column letters and row numbers are displayed, or whether to include print titles, columns and rows that are repeated on each page. If you have already set a print area, it will appear in the Print Area box on the Sheet tab of the Page Setup dialog box. You don't need to re-select it.

Print Part of a Worksheet

1. Click the **Page Layout** tab.

2. Click the **Page Setup Dialog Box Launcher.**

3. Click the **Sheet** tab.

4. Type the range you want to print. Or click the **Collapse Dialog** button, select the cells you want to print, and then click the **Expand Dialog** button to restore the dialog box.

5. Click **OK**.

Print Row and Column Titles on Each Page

1. Click the **Page Layout** tab.

2. Click the **Print Titles** button.

   The Page Setup dialog box opens, displaying the Sheet tab.

3. Enter the number of the row or the letter of the column that contains the titles. Or click the **Collapse Dialog** button, select the row or column with the mouse, and then click the **Expand Dialog** button to restore the dialog box.

4. Click **OK**.

Print Gridlines, Column Letters, and Row Numbers

① Click the **Page Layout** tab.

② Select the **Print** check box under Gridlines.

③ Select the **Print** check box under Headings.

◆ You can also click the **Sheet Options Dialog Box Launcher** to select these print options.

Fit a Worksheet on a Specific Number of Pages

① Click the **Page Layout** tab.

② Select a scaling option.

◆ Click the **Height** list arrow and the **Width** list arrow, and then select the number of pages you want to force a worksheet to print.

◆ Click the **Scale** up and down arrows to scale the worksheet using a percentage.

◆ You can also click the **Scale to Fit Dialog Box Launcher** to select these options.

Setting the Print Area

When you're ready to print your worksheet, you can choose several printing options. The **print area** is the section of your worksheet that Excel prints. You can set the print area when you customize worksheet printing or any time when you are working on a worksheet. For example, you might want to print a different range in a worksheet for different people. In order to use headers and footers, you must first establish, or set, the print area. You can set a single cell or a contiguous or non-contiguous range.

Set the Print Area

1. Select the range of cells you want to print.

2. Click the **Page Layout** tab.

3. Click the **Print Area** button, and then click **Set Print Area**.

Did You Know?

You can add to a print area. Click the cell where you want to extend the print area, click the Page Layout tab, click the Print Area button, and then click Add To Print Area.

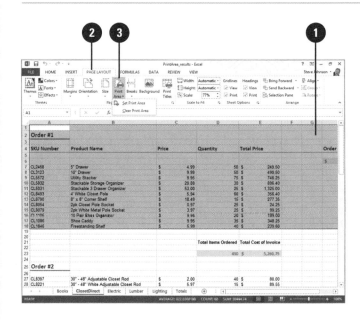

Clear the Print Area

1. Click the **Page Layout** tab.

2. Click the **Print Area** button, and then click **Clear Print Area**.

Did You Know?

You can avoid repeating rows and columns. For best results when printing a multipage worksheet, you'll want to coordinate the print area with specified print titles so that columns or rows are not repeated on a single page.

Adds the current selection to the print area

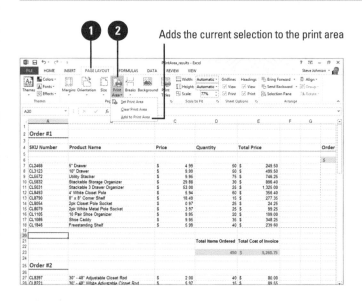

Previewing a Worksheet

Before printing, you should verify that the page looks the way you want. You save time, money, and paper by avoiding duplicate printing. Print Preview shows you the exact placement of your data on each printed page. You can view all or part of your workbook as it will appear when you print it. Print Preview shows you the pages based on the properties of the selected printer. For example, if the selected printer is setup to print color, Print Preview displays in color. The Print screen on the File tab makes it easy to zoom in and out to view data more comfortably, set margins and other page options, preview page breaks, and print.

Preview a Worksheet

1. Click the **File** tab, and then click **Print**.

2. Click the **Zoom to Page** button to toggle the zoom in and out to the page.

3. To adjust margins visually, click the **Show Margins** button, and then drag the margin lines where you want.

4. To switch pages, click the **Next Page** or **Previous Page** button, or enter a specific page in the Current Page box.

5. If you want to print, click the **Print** button.

Print Preview

Printing a Worksheet and Workbook

When you're ready to print your workbook, you can choose several printing options on the Print screen on the File tab, such as choosing a new printer, selecting the number of pages you want printed and the number of copies, specifying the page size, margins, and orientation, and selecting any scaling or pages to fit on a printed page. You can also use the Page Setup dialog box to control the appearance of pages, such as whether gridlines are displayed, whether column letters and row numbers are displayed, and whether to include print titles. You can quickly print a copy of your workbook without using the Print screen by clicking the Quick Print button on the Quick Access Toolbar.

Print All or Part of a Worksheet

1. Click the **File** tab, and then click **Print**.

   TIMESAVER *To print without the Print screen, press Ctrl+P, or click the Quick Print button on the Quick Access Toolbar.*

2. Click the **Printer** list arrow, and then click the printer you want to use.

3. To change printer properties, click the **Printer Properties** link, select the options you want, and then click **OK**.

4. Select whether you want to print the entire workbook or only the worksheets you specify.

5. Select what you want to print.

6. To change page options, click the **Page Setup** link, select the options you want, and then click **OK**.

7. Click **Print**.

Print Preview

Creating a PDF Document

Portable Document Format (PDF) is a fixed-layout format developed by Adobe Systems that retains the form you intended on a computer monitor or printer. A PDF is useful when you want to create a document primarily intended to be read and printed, not modified. Excel allows you to save a workbook as a PDF file, which you can send to others for review in an e-mail. To view a PDF file, you need to have Acrobat Reader—free downloadable software from Adobe Systems—installed on your computer.

Save a Workbook as a PDF Document

1. Click the **File** tab, click **Export**, and then click **Create PDF/XPS Document**.

2. Click the **Create PDF/XPS** button.

3. Click the **Save as type** list arrow, and then click **PDF**.

4. Click the **Save in** list arrow, and then click the drive or folder where you want to save the file.

5. Type a PDF file name.

6. To open the file in Adobe Reader after saving, select the **Open file after publishing** check box.

7. Click the **Standard** or **Minimum size** option to specify how you want to optimize the file.

8. Click **Options**.

9. Select the publishing options you want, such as what to publish, range to publish, whether to include non-printing information, or PDF options.

10. Click **OK**.

11. Click **Publish**.

12. If necessary, install Adobe Acrobat Reader and related software as directed.

Creating a XPS Document

XML Paper Specification (XPS) is a secure fixed-layout format developed by Microsoft that retains the form you intended on a monitor or printer. An XPS is useful when you want to create a document primarily intended to be read and printed, not modified. Excel allows you to save a workbook as an XPS file, which you can send to others for review in an e-mail. XPS includes support for digital signatures and is compatible with Windows Rights Management for additional protection. The XPS format also preserves live links with documents, making files fully functional. To view an XPS file, you need to have a viewer—free downloadable software from Microsoft Office Online—installed on your computer.

Save a Workbook as a XPS Document

1. Click the **File** tab, click **Export**, and then click **Create PDF/XPS Document**.

2. Click the **Create PDF/XPS** button.

3. Click the **Save as type** list arrow, and then click **XPS Document**.

4. Click the **Save in** list arrow, and then click the drive or folder where you want to save the file.

5. Type an XPS file name.

6. To open the file in viewer after saving, select the **Open file after publishing** check box.

7. Click the **Standard** or **Minimum size** option to specify how you want to optimize the file.

8. Click **Options**.

9. Select the publishing options you want, such as what to publish, range to publish, whether to include non-printing information, or XPS options.

10. Click **OK**.

11. Click **Publish**.

Inserting and Modifying Graphics

Introduction

Although well-illustrated worksheets can't make up for a lack of content, you can capture your audiences' attention if your worksheets are vibrant and visually interesting. You can easily enhance a worksheet by adding a picture—one of your own or one of the hundreds that come with Microsoft Excel. If you have the appropriate hardware, such as a sound card and speakers, you can also include sound files and video clips in your workbook.

Microsoft Office comes with a vast array of online Clip Art, and there are endless amounts available through other software packages or on the web. When going online to look at clips, you can categorize them so that it's easier to find the best choice for your workbook. You can use the Microsoft Office.com web site to search for and download clip art images or use Bing image search on the web.

If you need to modify your pictures, you can resize them, compress them for storage, change their brightness or contrast, recolor them, or change their shape by cropping them.

WordArt is another feature that adds detail to your workbook. Available in other Office applications, WordArt can bring together your worksheets—you can change its color, shape, shadow, or size. Because WordArt comes with so many style choices, time spent customizing your worksheets is minimal.

In Excel and other Microsoft Office programs, you can insert SmartArt graphics to create diagrams that convey processes or relationships. Excel offers a wide-variety of built-in SmartArt graphic types from which to choose, including graphical lists, process, cycle, hierarchy, relationship, matrix, and pyramid. Using built-in SmartArt graphics makes it easy to create and modify charts without having to create them from scratch.

What You'll Do

Locate and Insert Online Pictures

Insert a Picture from an Online Service

Insert a Picture from a SkyDrive or SharePoint

Insert a Picture from a File

Insert a Picture Screen Shot

Add an Artistic Style to a Picture

Add a Quick Style to a Picture

Apply a Shape and Border to a Picture

Apply Picture Effects

Modify Picture Size

Compress and Correct a Picture

Crop, Rotate and Recolor a Picture

Create and Format WordArt Text

Apply and Modify WordArt Text Effects

Create SmartArt Graphics

Use the Text Pane with SmartArt Graphics

Modify, Resize, and Format a SmartArt Graphic

Format a Shape in a SmartArt Graphic

Create and Modify an Organization Chart

Locating and Inserting Online Pictures

If you need a picture to insert into a workbook and don't have one, you can search for and insert clip art from Office.com (**New!**) or a picture from the web using Bing Image Search (**New!**). Office.com is a clip gallery that Microsoft maintains on its web site. Clip art includes photos and illustrations, such as vector images, which are mathematically defined to make them easy to resize and manipulate. To add an online picture to a workbook, you click the Online Pictures button on the Insert tab, and then locate, select, and insert the picture you want.

Locate and Insert Online Clip Art from Office.com

1. Click the **Insert** tab.

2. Click the **Online Pictures** button.

3. In the Search Office.com box, enter search criteria to locate the online picture you want.

   ◆ To cancel the search, click the **Close** button in the Search box.

4. Click the **Search** button or press Enter.

5. Select the picture(s) you want.

   ◆ To preview a larger picture, point to a picture, and then click the **View Larger** button.

6. Click **Insert**.

7. Select the picture, and then move and resize it, as desired.

View Larger button

Locate and Insert Online Pictures from Bing Image Search

1 Click the **Insert** tab.

2 Click the **Online Pictures** button.

3 In the Search Office.com box, enter search criteria to locate the online picture you want.

◆ To cancel the search, click the Close button in the Search box.

4 Click the **Search** button or press Enter.

5 If prompted, click **Show all web results**. If a message bar appears, read it, then click the **Close** button to dismiss it.

6 Select the picture(s) you want.

◆ To preview a larger picture, point to a picture, and then click the **View Larger** button.

7 Click **Insert**.

8 Select the picture, and then move and resize it, as desired.

Did You Know?

You can select multiple pictures from within a search. To select multiple pictures in consecutive order, press Shift, click first image, and then click the last image. To select multiple pictures in non-consecutive order, press Ctrl, and then click images.

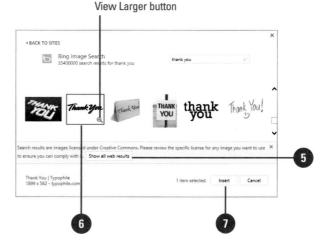

View Larger button

Inserting Pictures from an Online Service

If you have an account for an online service (**New!**) for images and video, such as Flickr or YouTube, you can insert pictures into a workbook directly from the service. Before you can use an online service, you need to add them (establishing a connection to your Microsoft account) to Excel, which requires an established account with a user name and password. In addition to the image and video online services, you can also establish connections to access pictures stored on other online services, such as a SkyDrive (**New!**) or Office 365 SharePoint (**New!**). To add an online picture from an online service to a workbook, you click the Online Pictures button on the Insert tab, click the service icon, and then locate, select, and insert the picture you want.

Add Online Services

1. Click the **File** tab, and then click **Account** (**New!**).

2. Click **Add a service** (**New!**), point to a service type (options vary):

   ◆ **Images & Videos**, and then click **Flickr** or **YouTube**.

   ◆ **Storage**, and then click **Office 365 SharePoint** or **SkyDrive**.

3. Follow the on-screen instructions to sign-in and connect to the service.

   After the service is connected to your Microsoft account, it appears in the list of connected services.

4. To manage or remove a connected service, click the **Manage** or **Remove** link; options vary depending on the service.

   When you manage a connected service, your web browser opens, displaying options for the account.

5. Click the **Back** button to exit the File tab.

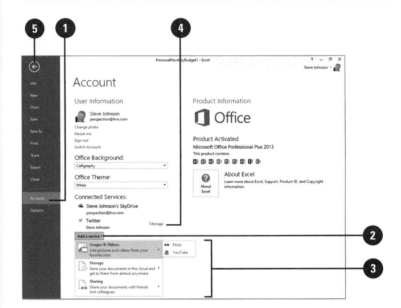

Insert Pictures from an Image Online Service

1. Click the **Insert** tab.

2. Click the **Online Pictures** button.

3. If the online service isn't connected, click the online service icon, such as Flickr, click **Connect**, and then enter your user name and password to establish a connection to the online service.

   The online service appears in the Insert Pictures window.

4. To manage the account, click the **Manage** link, make any option changes, click **Save**, and then close your web browser.

5. Click the **See more** link for more pictures.

   ◆ To quickly insert a recent picture, click one from the Recently Used list in the Insert Pictures window.

6. Select the picture(s) you want.

   ◆ To preview a larger picture, point to a picture, and then click the **View Larger** button.

7. Click **Insert**.

8. Select the picture, and then move and resize it, as desired.

3 Flickr

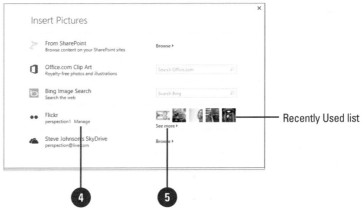

Recently Used list

4   5

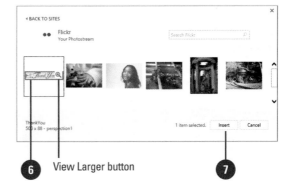

6 View Larger button   7

Inserting a Picture from a SkyDrive or SharePoint

If you have pictures stored on a SkyDrive (**New!**) or Office 365 SharePoint (**New!**), you can access them from Online Pictures on the Insert tab. Before you can use an online service, you need to add them (establishing a connection to your Microsoft account) to Excel, which requires an established account with a user name and password. After you establish a connection, you can browse for pictures directly on the SkyDrive or Office 365 SharePoint sites.

Insert a Picture from SkyDrive or SharePoint

1. Click the **Insert** tab.

2. Click the **Online Pictures** button.

3. Click **Browse** for SharePoint or SkyDrive.

   The main folder for your SkyDrive or SharePoint site appears.

4. Navigate to the folder that contains the picture files you want to insert.

5. Click the file you want to insert.

6. Click **Insert**.

See Also

See "Inserting Pictures from an Online Service" on page 196 for information on adding an online service to connect to a SkyDrive or Office 365 SharePoint site.

Inserting a Picture from a File

Excel makes it possible for you to insert pictures, graphics, scanned photographs, art, photos, or artwork from a collection of stock images or other program into a document. When you use the Pictures button on the Insert tab, you specify the source of the picture. When you insert pictures from files on your hard disk drive, scanner, digital camera, or web camera, Excel allows you to select multiple pictures, view thumbnails of them, and insert them all at once, which speeds up the process.

Insert a Picture from a File

1. Click the **Insert** tab.

2. Click the **Pictures** button.

3. Navigate to the folder that contains the picture files you want to insert.

4. Click the file you want to insert.

5. Click **Insert**.

   ◆ To link a picture file, click the **Insert** button arrow, and then click **Link to File**.

   ◆ To insert and link a picture file, click the **Insert** button arrow, and then click **Insert and Link**.

   TROUBLE? *If you see a red "x" instead of a picture or motion clip in your document, then you don't have a graphics filter installed on your computer for that clip.*

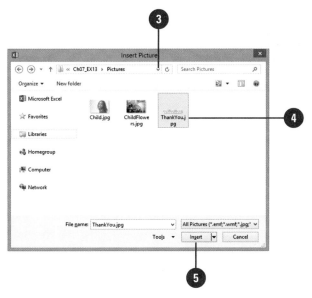

Did You Know?

You can change a picture. Select the picture, click the Change Picture button on the Format tab, select a picture, and then click Insert.

You can add graphic formats. If the graphic format you want to insert is not in the list, you can use Office Setup's Add or Remove Features option to install additional graphic formats.

Inserting a Picture Screen Shot

If you're working on a training manual, presentation, or document that requires a picture of your computer screen, then the Screenshot button on the Insert tab just made your life a lot easier. You use the Screen Clipping tool to drag a selection around the screen area that you want to capture, and then select the picture from the Screenshot gallery. The Screenshot gallery holds multiple screen shots, so you can capture several screens before you insert them into your document. After you insert the screen shot into a document, you can use the tools on the Picture Tools tab to edit and improve it.

Insert a Picture Screen Shot

1. Click the **Insert** tab.

2. Click the **Screenshot** button.

3. Click **Screen Clipping**.

4. Display the screen you want to capture, and then drag the large plus cursor to select the screen area to capture.

5. Click the **Screenshot** button, and then click the thumbnail of the screen shot you want to insert.

6. Use the tools on the Picture Tools tab to edit and improve the screen shot.

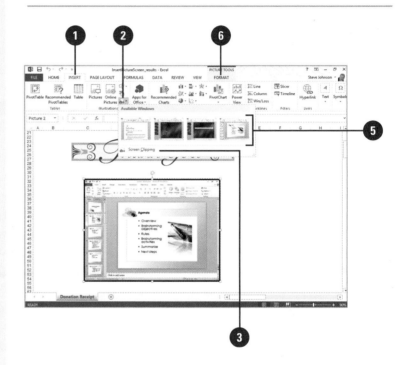

Did You Know?

You can copy the window or screen contents. To make a copy of the active window, press Alt+Print Scrn. To copy the entire screen as it appears on your monitor, press Print Scrn.

Adding an Artistic Style to a Picture

With the Artistic Quick Style gallery, you can transform a picture into a piece of artwork. The Artistic Quick Style gallery makes it easy to change the look of a picture to a sketch, drawing, or painting. The Picture Quick Style gallery provides a variety of different formatting options—such as Pencil Sketch, Line Drawing, Watercolor Sponge, Mosaic Bubble, Glass, Pastels Smooth, Plastic Wrap, Photocopy, and Paint Strokes—to create a professional look. To quickly see if you like an Artistic Quick Style, point to a thumbnail in the gallery to display a live preview of it in the selected shape. If you like it, you can apply it.

Add an Artistic Style to a Picture

1. Click the picture you want to change.

2. Click the **Format** tab under Picture Tools.

3. Click the **Artistic Effects** button.

   The current style appears highlighted in the gallery.

4. Point to a style.

   A live preview of the style appears in the picture.

5. Click the style you want from the gallery to apply it to the selected picture.

Adding a Quick Style to a Picture

Instead of changing individual attributes of a picture—such as shape, border, and effects—you can quickly add them all at once with the Picture Quick Style gallery. The Picture Quick Style gallery provides a variety of different formatting combinations to create a professional look. To quickly see if you like a Picture Quick Style, point to a thumbnail in the gallery to display a live preview of it in the selected shape. If you like it, you can apply it.

Add a Quick Style to a Picture

1. Click the picture you want to change.

2. Click the **Format** tab under Picture Tools.

3. Click the scroll up or down arrow, or click the **More** list arrow in the Picture Styles group to see additional styles.

   The current style appears highlighted in the gallery.

4. Point to a style.

   A live preview of the style appears in the current shape.

5. Click the style you want from the gallery to apply it to the selected picture.

Did You Know?

You can save a shape as a picture in the PNG format. Right-click the shape, click Save As Picture, type a name, and then click Save.

Applying a Shape to a Picture

After you insert a picture into your document, you can select it and apply one of Excel's shapes to it. The picture appears in the shape just like it has been cropped. The Crop to Shape gallery makes it easy to choose the shape you want to use. Live preview is not available with the Crop to Shape gallery. You can try different shapes to find the one you want. If you don't find the one you want, you can use the Reset Picture button to return the picture back to its original state.

Apply a Shape to a Picture

1. Click the picture you want to change.

2. Click the **Format** tab under Picture Tools.

3. Click the **Crop** button arrow, and then point to **Crop to Shape**.

4. Select the shape you want to apply to the selected picture.

Did You Know?

You can quickly return a picture back to its original form. Select the picture, click the Format tab, and then click the Reset Picture button.

Applying a Border to a Picture

After you insert a picture, you can add and modify the picture border by changing individual outline formatting using the Picture Border button on the Format tab under Picture Tools. The Picture Border button works just like the Shape Outline button and provides similar options to add a border, select a border color, and change border width and style. You can try different border combinations to find the one you want. If you don't find one that works for you, you can use the No Outline command on the Picture Border gallery to remove it.

Apply a Border to a Picture

1. Click the picture you want to change.

2. Click the **Format** tab under Picture Tools.

3. Click the **Picture Border** button.

4. Click a color, or point to **Weight**, or **Dashes**, and then select a style, or click **More Lines** to select multiple options.

5. Drag a sizing handle to change the size or angle of the line or arrow.

Did You Know?

You can remove a border. Select the picture, click the Format tab, click the Picture Border button, and then click No Outline.

Applying Picture Effects

You can change the look of a picture by applying effects, such as shadows, reflections, glow, soft edges, bevels, and 3-D rotations. You can also apply effects to a shape by using the Picture Effects gallery for quick results, or by using the Format Shape pane (**New!**) for custom results. From the Picture Effects gallery, you can apply a built-in combination of 3-D effects or individual effects to a picture. To quickly see if you like a picture effect, point to a thumbnail in the Picture Effects gallery to display a live preview of it. If you like it, you can apply it. If you no longer want to apply a picture effect to an object, you can remove it. Simply select the picture, point to the effect type on the Picture Effects gallery, and then select the No effect type option.

Add an Effect to a Picture

1. Click the picture you want to change.

2. Click the **Format** tab under Picture Tools.

3. Click the **Picture Effects** button, and then point to the following:

   ◆ **Preset** to select No 3-D, one of the preset types, or 3-D Options.

   ◆ **Shadow** to select No Shadow, one of the shadow types, or Shadow Options.

   ◆ **Reflection** to select No Reflection, one of the Reflection Variations, or Reflection Options.

   ◆ **Glow** to select No Glow, one of the Glow Variations, More Glow Colors, or Glow Options.

   ◆ **Soft Edges** to select No Soft Edges or a point size to determine the soft edge amount, or Soft Edges Options.

   ◆ **Bevel** to select No Bevel, one of the bevels, or 3-D Options.

   ◆ **3-D Rotation** to select No Rotation, one of the rotation types, or 3-D Options.

   When you point to an effect, a live preview of the style appears in the current shape.

4. Click the effect you want from the gallery to apply it to the selected shape.

Modifying Picture Size

Once you have inserted a picture, clip art and other objects into your document, you can adapt them to meet your needs. Like any object, you can resize a picture. You can use the sizing handles to quickly resize a picture or use height and width options in the Size group on the Format tab to resize a picture more precisely. If you want to set unique or multiple options, you can use the Format Picture pane (**New!**). The Size & Properties options allow you to make sure your pictures keep the same relative proportions as the original and lock size proportions.

Resize a Picture

1. Click the object you want to resize.

2. Drag one of the sizing handles to increase or decrease the object's size.

   ◆ Drag a middle handle to resize the object up, down, left, or right.

   ◆ Drag a corner handle to resize the object proportionally.

Resize a Picture Precisely

1. Click the object you want to resize.

2. Click the **Format** tab under Picture Tools.

3. Click the up and down arrows or enter a number (in inches) in the Height and Width boxes on the Ribbon and press Enter.

   If the **Lock aspect ratio** check box is selected in the Format Picture dialog box (under Size), height or width automatically changes when you change one of them. Click the **Size Dialog Box Launcher** to change the option.

Size Dialog Box Launcher

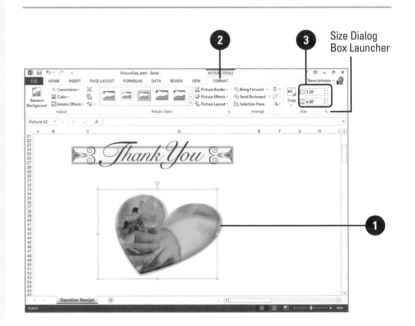

Precisely Scale a Picture

1. Click the object you want to resize.

2. Click the **Format** tab under Picture Tools.

3. Click the **Size Dialog Box Launcher**.

   The Format Picture pane opens, displaying format options (**New!**).

4. Do any of the following:

   ◆ **Keep the picture proportional.** Select the **Lock aspect ratio** check box.

   ◆ **Keep the picture the same relative size.** Select the **Relative to original picture size** check box.

5. Click the up and down arrows or enter a number in the Height and Width boxes in one of the following:

   ◆ **Size.** Enter a height and width size in inches.

   ◆ **Scale.** Enter a percentage size.

   If the Lock aspect ratio check box is selected, height or width automatically changes when you change one of them.

6. If you want to remove your changes, click **Reset**.

7. Click the **Close** button in the pane.

Did You Know?

Resizing bitmaps can cause distortion. Bitmap images are made up of dots, and do not lend themselves as easily to resizing because the dots can't expand and contract, which can lead to distortion. To avoid distortion, resize bitmaps proportionally and try to resize smaller instead of larger.

Compressing a Picture

Office allows you to compress pictures in order to minimize the file size of the image. In doing so, however, you may lose some visual quality, depending on the compression setting. You can pick the resolution that you want for the pictures in a document based on where or how they'll be viewed (for example, on the web or printed). You can also set other options, such as Delete cropped areas of picture, to get the best balance between picture quality and file size or automatically compress pictures when you save your document.

Compress a Picture

1. Click to select the pictures you want to compress.

2. Click the **Format** tab under Picture Tools.

3. Click the **Compress Pictures** button.

4. Select the **Apply only to this picture** check box to apply compression setting to only the selected picture. Otherwise, clear the check box to compress all pictures in your document.

5. Select or clear the **Delete cropped areas of pictures** check box to reduce file.

6. Click the **Print**, **Screen**, **E-mail**, or **Document** option to specify a target output.

7. Click **OK**.

Correcting a Picture

Once you have inserted a picture, you can control the image's colors, brightness, and contrast using Picture tools. The brightness and contrast controls let you make simple adjustments to the tonal range of a picture. The brightness and contrast controls change a picture by an overall lightening or darkening of the image pixels. In addition, you can sharpen and soften pictures by a specified percentage. If you want to set unique or multiple options, you can use the Format Picture pane (**New!**). You can experiment with the settings to get the look you want. If you don't like the look, you can use the Reset Picture button to return the picture back to its original starting point.

Change Brightness and Contrast or Sharpen and Soften

1. Click the picture you want to change.

2. Click the **Format** tab under Picture Tools.

3. Click the **Corrections** button, and then do one of the following:

   ◆ **Brightness and Contrast.** Click a brightness and contrast option.

   A positive brightness lightens the object colors by adding more white, while a negative brightness darkens the object colors by adding more black. A positive contrast increases intensity, resulting in less gray, while a negative contrast to decrease intensity, resulting in more gray.

   ◆ **Sharpen and Soften.** Click a sharpen and soften option.

4. To set custom correction percentages, click the **Corrections** button, click **Picture Corrections Options**, specify the options you want in the Format Picture pane (**New!**), and then click the **Close** button in the pane.

Recoloring a Picture

You can recolor clip art and other objects to match the color scheme of your document. For example, if you use a flower clip art as your business logo, you can change shades of pink in the spring to shades of orange in the autumn. The Color Picture Quick Style gallery provides a variety of different recolor formatting combinations. To quickly see if you like a Color Picture Quick Style, point to a thumbnail in the gallery to display a live preview of it in the selected shape. If you like it, you can apply it. You can also use a transparent background in your picture to avoid conflict between its background color and your document's background. With a transparent background, the picture takes on the same background as your document.

Recolor a Picture

1. Click the picture whose color you want to change.

2. Click the **Format** tab under Picture Tools.

3. Click the **Color** button.

4. Click one of the Color options.

   ◆ **Recolor.** Click an option to apply a color type:

   No Recolor. Click this option to remove a previous recolor.

   Grayscale. Converts colors into whites, blacks and shades of gray between black and white.

   Sepia. Converts colors into very light gold and yellow colors like a picture from the old west.

   Washout. Converts colors into whites and very light colors.

   Black and White. Converts colors into only white and black.

   ◆ **Color Saturation** or **Color Tone.** Click an option to apply a color saturation or tone based on the recolor selection.

   ◆ **More Variations.** Point to this option to select a specific color.

   ◆ **Picture Color Options.** Click this option to set custom recolor options by percentage.

No Recolor

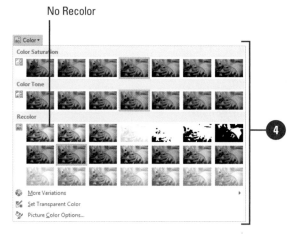

Set a Transparent Background

1. Click the picture you want to change.

2. Click the **Format** tab under Picture Tools.

3. Click the **Color** button, and then click **Set Transparent Color**.

4. Move the pointer over the object until the pointer changes shape.

5. Click the color you want to set as transparent.

6. Move the pointer over the picture where you want to apply the transparent color, and then click to apply it.

7. When you're done, click outside the image.

Did You Know?

Why is the Set Transparent Color command dimmed? Setting a color as transparent works only with bitmaps. If you are working with an object that is not a bitmap, you will not be able to use this feature.

You can't modify some pictures in Office. If the picture is a bitmap (.BMP, .JPG, .GIF, or .PNG), you need to edit its colors in an image editing program, such as Adobe Photoshop, Microsoft Paint, or Paint Shop Pro.

You can reset a picture back to its original state. Click the picture you want to reset, click the Format tab under Picture Tools, and then click the Reset Picture button.

Area made transparent

Cropping and Rotating a Picture

You can crop clip art to isolate just one portion of the picture. Because clip art uses vector image technology, you can crop even the smallest part of it and then enlarge it, and the clip art will still be recognizable. You can also crop bitmapped pictures, but if you enlarge the area you cropped, you lose picture detail. Use the Crop button to crop an image by hand. In addition, you can crop a picture while maintaining a selected resize aspect ratio or crop a picture based on a fill or fit. You can also rotate a picture by increments or freehand.

Crop a Picture Quickly

1. Click the picture you want to crop.

2. Click the **Format** tab under Picture Tools.

3. Click the **Crop** button.

4. Drag the sizing handles until the borders surround the area you want to crop.

5. Click outside the image when you are finished.

Crop a Picture with an Aspect Ratio

1. Click the picture you want to crop.

2. Click the **Format** tab under Picture Tools.

3. Click the **Crop** button arrow, point to **Aspect Ratio**, and then select an aspect ratio.

4. Drag the sizing handles until the borders surround the area you want to crop.

5. Click outside the image when you are finished.

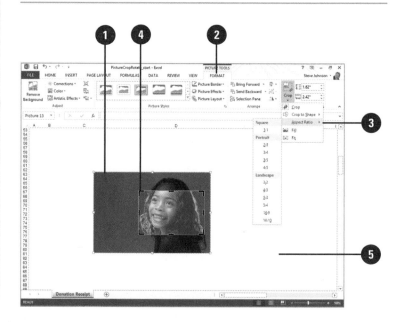

Crop a Picture with a Fill or Fit

① Click the picture you want to crop.

② Click the **Format** tab under Picture Tools.

③ Click the **Crop** button arrow, and then select an option:

   ◆ **Fill.** Resizes the picture so the entire picture area is filled while maintaining the aspect ratio. Any area outside of the picture area is cropped.

   ◆ **Fit.** Resizes the picture so the entire picture displays inside the picture area while maintaining the aspect ratio.

④ Drag the sizing handles until the borders surround the area you want to crop.

⑤ Click outside the image when you are finished.

Rotate a Picture

① Click the object you want to rotate.

② Position the pointer (which changes to the Free Rotate pointer) over the circle arrow rotate lever at the top of the object, and then drag to rotate it.

③ Click outside the object to set the rotation.

Did You Know?

You can rotate or flip a picture. Select the picture, click the Format tab, click the Rotate button, and then click Rotate Right 90, Rotate Left 90, Flip Vertical, Flip Horizontal, or click More Rotation Options.

Removing a Picture Background

Sometimes you want to use an element from a picture instead of the entire picture. With the Remove Background command, you can specify the element you want in a picture, and then remove the background. You can use automatic background removal or you can manually draw lines to specify which parts of the picture background you want to keep and which to remove.

Remove a Picture Background

1. Click the picture you want to change.

2. Click the **Format** tab under Picture Tools.

3. Click the **Remove Background** button.

4. Drag the handles on the marquee lines to specify the part of the picture you want to keep. The area outside the marquee gets removed.

5. To manually specify which areas to keep and which areas to remove, do the following:

   ◆ **Mark Areas to Keep.** Click the button, and then draw lines to specify which parts of the picture you do not want automatically removed.

   ◆ **Mark Areas to Remove.** Click the button, and then draw lines to specify which parts of the picture you do want removed in addition to those automatically marked.

   ◆ **Delete Mark.** Click the button, and then click marked lines to remove them.

6. Click the **Keep Changes** button to close and keep the removal or click the **Discard All Changes** button to close and cancel the automatic removal.

Background removed

Creating WordArt Text

The WordArt feature lets you create stylized text to draw attention to your most important words. Most users apply WordArt to a word or a short phrase, such as *Big Smiles*. You should apply WordArt to a document sparingly. Its visual appeal and unique look requires uncluttered space. When you use WordArt, you can choose from a variety of text styles that come with the WordArt Quick Style gallery, or you can create your own using tools in the WordArt Styles group. To quickly see if you like a WordArt Quick Style, point to a thumbnail in the gallery to display a live preview of it in the selected text. If you like it, you can apply it. You can also use the free angle handle (pink diamond) inside the selected text box to adjust your WordArt text angle.

Insert WordArt Text

1. Click the **Insert** tab.

2. Click the **WordArt** button, and then click one of the WordArt styles.

   A WordArt text box appears on the document with selected placeholder text.

3. Type the text you want WordArt to use.

   ◆ Drag a resize handle as needed to increase or decrease the size of the WordArt text box.

4. If applicable, use the Font and Paragraph options on the Home tab to modify the text you entered.

5. To edit WordArt text, click to place the insertion point where you want to edit, and then edit the text.

Did You Know?

You can convert text in a text box to WordArt. Select the text box, click the Format tab under Drawing Tools, and then click the WordArt text style you want from the Ribbon.

You can remove WordArt text. Select the WordArt text, click the Format tab, click the Quick Styles button, and then click Clear WordArt.

Formatting WordArt Text

In addition to applying one of the preformatted WordArt styles, you can also create your own style by shaping your text into a variety of shapes, curves, styles, and color patterns. The WordArt Styles group gives you tools for changing the fill and outline of your WordArt text. To quickly see if you like a WordArt Style, point to a thumbnail in the gallery to display a live preview of it in the selected text. If you like it, you can apply it.

Apply a Different WordArt Style to Existing WordArt Text

1. Click the WordArt object whose style you want to change.

2. Click the **Format** tab under Drawing or WordArt Tools.

3. Click the scroll up or down arrow, or click the **More** list arrow in the WordArt Styles group to see additional styles.

    The current style appears highlighted in the gallery.

4. Point to a style.

    A live preview of the style appears in the current shape text.

5. Click the style you want from the gallery to apply it to the selected shape.

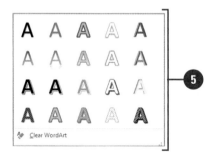

Did You Know?

You can add more formatting to WordArt text. Select the WordArt object, click the Home tab, and then use the formatting button in the Font and Paragraph groups.

You can change the WordArt fill color to match the background. Click the WordArt object, right-click the object, click Format Shape, click the Background option, and then click Close.

Apply a Fill to WordArt Text

1. Click the WordArt object you want to change.

2. Click the **Format** tab under Drawing or WordArt Tools.

3. Click the **Text Fill** or **Shape Fill** button arrow, and then click or point to one of the following:

   - **Color** to select a theme or standard color.

   - **No Fill** to remove a fill color.

   - **Picture** to select a picture file.

   - **Gradient** to select No Gradient, one of the shadow types, or More Gradients.

   - **Texture** to select one of the texture types, or More Textures.

Apply an Outline to WordArt Text

1. Click the WordArt object you want to change.

2. Click the **Format** tab under Drawing or WordArt Tools.

3. Click the **Text Outline** or **Shape Outline** button arrow.

4. Click a color, or point to **Weight** or **Dashes**, and then select a style.

Applying WordArt Text Effects

You can change the look of WordArt text by applying effects, such as shadows, reflections, glow, soft edges, 3-D rotations, and transformations. You can apply effects to a shape by using the Text Effects gallery for quick results. From the Text Effects gallery you can apply a built-in combination of 3-D effects or individual effects to WordArt text. To quickly see if you like the effect, point to a thumbnail in the Text Effects gallery to display a live preview of it. If you like it, you can apply it. If you no longer want to apply the effect, you can remove it. Simply, select the WordArt text, point to the effect type on the Text Effects gallery, and then select the No effect type option.

Apply an Effect to WordArt Text

1. Click the WordArt object you want to change.

2. Click the **Format** tab under Drawing or WordArt Tools.

3. Click the **Text Effects** button.

4. Point to one of the following:

   ◆ **Shadow** to select No Shadow, one of the shadow types, or Shadows Options.

   ◆ **Reflection** to select No Reflection, one of the Reflection Variations, or Reflection Options.

   ◆ **Glow** to select No Glow, one of the Glow Variations, More Glow Colors, or Glow Options.

   ◆ **Bevel** to select No Bevel, one of the bevel variations, or 3-D Options.

   ◆ **3-D Rotation** to select No Rotation, one of the rotation types, or 3-D Rotation Options.

   ◆ **Transform** to select No Transform, or one of the transform types (Follow Path or Warp).

5. Click the effect you want to apply to the selected shape.

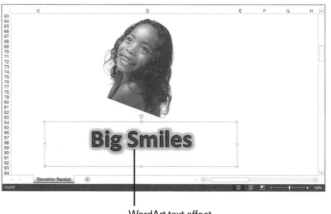

WordArt text effect

Modifying WordArt Text Position

You can apply a number of text effects to your WordArt objects that determine alignment and direction. The effects of some of the adjustments you make are more pronounced for certain WordArt styles than others. Some of these effects make the text unreadable for certain styles, so apply these effects carefully. You can apply effects to a shape by using the Format Shape pane (**New!**) for custom results. You can also use the free rotate handle (green circle) at the top of the selected text box to rotate your WordArt text.

Change WordArt Text Direction

1 Right-click the WordArt object you want to change, and then click **Format Shape** or **Format Object**.

2 Click **Text Options** in the Format Shape pane (**New!**).

3 Click **Text Box** (**New!**).

4 Click the **Vertical alignment** or **Horizontal alignment** list arrow, and then select an option: **Top**, **Middle**, **Bottom**, **Top Center**, **Middle Center**, or **Bottom Center**.

5 Click the **Text Direction** list arrow, and then select an option: **Horizontal**, **Rotate all text 90°**, **Rotate all text 270°**, or **Stacked**.

6 Click the **Close** button in the pane.

Rotate WordArt Text

1 Click the WordArt object you want to change.

2 Position the pointer (which changes to the Free Rotate pointer) over the circle arrow rotate lever at the top of the object, and then drag to rotate it.

3 When you're done, release the mouse button.

4 Click outside the object to deselect it.

Creating SmartArt Graphics

SmartArt graphics allow you to create diagrams that convey processes or relationships. Office provides a wide variety of built-in SmartArt graphic types, including graphical lists, process, cycle, hierarchy, relationship, matrix, pyramid, picture, and Office.com. Using built-in SmartArt graphics makes it easy to create and modify charts without having to create them from scratch. To quickly see if you like a SmartArt graphic layout, point to a thumbnail in the gallery to display a live preview of it in the selected shape. If you like it, you can apply it.

Create a SmartArt Graphic

1 Click the **Insert** tab.

2 Click the **SmartArt** button.

3 In the left pane, click a category, such as All, List, Process, Cycle, Hierarchy, Relationship, Matrix, Pyramid, Picture, or Office.com.

4 In the middle pane, click a SmartArt graphic style type.

5 Click **OK**.

The SmartArt graphic appears in the document.

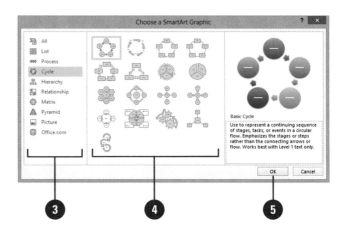

Did You Know?

You can change a SmartArt diagram type. Select the SmartArt graphic, click the Design tab under SmartArt Tools, click the More list arrow for Layouts, click More Layout, select a diagram type, and then click OK.

You cannot drag text into the Text pane. Although you can't drag text into the Text pane, you can copy and paste text.

SmartArt Graphic Purposes

Type	Purpose
List	Show non-sequential information
Process	Show steps in a process or timeline
Cycle	Show a continual process
Hierarchy	Show a decision tree or create an organization chart
Relationship	Illustrate connections
Matrix	Show how parts relate to a whole
Pyramid	Show proportional relationships up and down
Picture	Convert a picture to a SmartArt graphic
Office.com	Show SmartArt graphics from Office.com

6. Click the **Text Pane** button, or click the control with two arrows along the left side of the selection to show the Text pane.

7. Label the shapes by doing one of the following:

   ◆ Type text in the [Text] box.

   You can use the arrow keys to move around the Text pane, or use the Promote or Demote buttons to indent.

   ◆ At the end of a line, press Enter to insert a line (shape), or select line text, and then press Delete to remove a line (shape).

   ◆ Click a shape, and then type text directly into the shape.

8. When you're done, click outside of the SmartArt graphic.

Text Pane button

Did You Know?

You can change a SmartArt diagram type. Select the SmartArt graphic, click the Design tab under SmartArt Tools, click the More list arrow for Layouts, click More Layout, select a diagram type, and then click OK.

You cannot drag text into the Text pane. Although you can't drag text into the Text pane, you can copy and paste text.

You can create a blank SmartArt graphic. In the Text pane, press Ctrl+A to select all the placeholder text, and then press Delete.

Using the Text Pane with SmartArt Graphics

After you create a layout for a SmartArt graphic, a Text pane appears next to your selected SmartArt graphic. The bottom of the Text pane displays a description of the SmartArt graphic. The Text pane and SmartArt graphic contain placeholder text. You can change the placeholder text in the Text pane or directly in the SmartArt graphic. The Text pane works like an outline or a bulleted list and the text corresponds directly with the shape text in the SmartArt graphic. As you add and edit content, the SmartArt graphic automatically updates, adding or removing shapes as needed while maintaining the design. If you see a red "x" in the Text pane, it means that the SmartArt graphic contains a fixed number of shapes, such as Counterbalance Arrows (only two).

Show or Hide the Text Pane

1. Click the SmartArt graphic you want to modify.

2. Click the **Design** tab under SmartArt Tools.

3. Do any of the following:

   ◆ **Show**. Click the **Text Pane** button, or click the control with two arrows along the left side of the SmartArt graphic selection to show the Text pane.

   ◆ **Hide**. Click the **Text Pane** button, click the **Close** button on the Text pane, deselect the SmartArt graphic.

   The Text Pane button toggles to show or hide the Text pane.

Did You Know?

You can resize the Text pane. To resize the Text pane, point to any edge (pointer changes to double-headed arrow), and then drag to resize it.

You can move the Text pane. To move the Text pane, drag the top of the pane. The Text pane location resets when you exit Excel.

Work with Text in the Text Pane

1. Click the SmartArt graphic you want to modify.

2. Click the **Design** tab under SmartArt Tools.

3. If necessary, click the **Text Pane** button to show the Text pane.

4. Do any of the following tasks:

    ◆ **New line**. At the end of a line, press Enter.

    ◆ **Indent line right**. Press Tab, or click the **Promote** button.

    ◆ **Indent line left**. Press Shift+Tab, or click the **Demote** button.

    ◆ **Delete line**. Select the line text, and then press Delete.

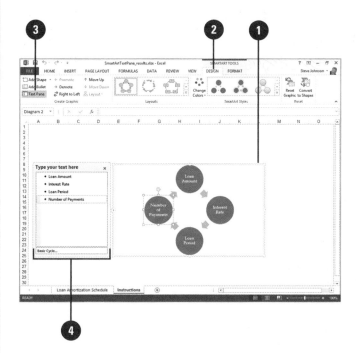

Did You Know?

You can format text in the Text pane. When you apply formatting to text in the Text pane, it doesn't display in the Text pane, but it does display in the SmartArt graphic.

You can remove a shape from a SmartArt graphic. Select the SmartArt graphic, click the shape you want to remove, and then press Delete.

Modifying a SmartArt Graphic

After you create a SmartArt graphic, you can add, remove, change, or rearrange shapes to create a custom look. For shapes within a SmartArt graphic, you can change the shape from the Shape gallery or use familiar commands, such as Bring to Front, Send to Back, Align, Group, and Rotate, to create your own custom SmartArt graphic. If you no longer want a shape you've added, simply select it, and then press Delete to remove it.

Add a Shape to a SmartArt Graphic

1. Select the shape in the SmartArt graphic you want to modify.

2. Click the **Design** tab under SmartArt Tools.

3. Click the **Add Shape** button to insert a shape at the end, or click the **Add Shape** button arrow, and then select the position where you want to insert a shape.

Change Shapes in a SmartArt Graphic

1. Select the shapes in the SmartArt graphic you want to modify.

2. Click the **Format** tab under SmartArt Tools.

3. Click the **Change Shape** button, and then click a shape.

Did You Know?

You can reset a SmartArt graphic back to its original state. Select the SmartArt graphic, click the Design tab under SmartArt Tools, and then click the Reset Graphic button.

Resizing a SmartArt Graphic

You can change the size of individual shapes within a SmartArt graphic or of an entire SmartArt graphic. If the size of an individual shape within a SmartArt graphic changes, the other shapes in the graphic may also change based on the type of layout. When you resize a shape with text or increase or decrease text size, the text may automatically resize to fit the shape depending on the space available in the SmartArt graphic. When you resize an entire SmartArt graphic, shapes within it scale proportionally or adjust to create the best look.

Resize a SmartArt Graphic

1. Select the shapes in the SmartArt graphic or the entire SmartArt graphic you want to modify.

2. Click the **Format** tab under SmartArt Tools.

3. Use one of the following methods:

   ◆ Drag a middle handle to resize the object up, down, left, or right.

   ◆ Drag a corner handle to resize the object proportionally.

   ◆ Click the **Size** button, and then specify the size you want.

   ◆ Click the **Larger** or **Smaller** button to increase or decrease the object in standard increments.

Larger and Smaller buttons   Size button

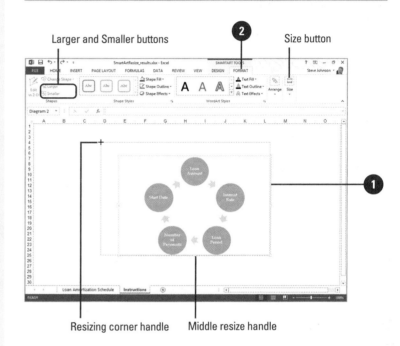

Resizing corner handle   Middle resize handle

Did You Know?

You can arrange shapes in a SmartArt graphic. Select the shape in the SmartArt graphic, click the Format tab under SmartArt Tools, click the Arrange button, and then use any of the arrange button options: Bring To Front, Send To Back, Align, Group, or Rotate.

You can edit a SmartArt graphic shape in 2-D. Select the SmartArt graphic with the 3-D style, click the Format tab under SmartArt Tools, and then click the Edit In 2-D button.

Formatting a SmartArt Graphic

If your current SmartArt graphics don't quite convey the message or look you want, use live preview to quickly preview layouts in the Quick Styles and Layout Styles groups and select the one you want. If you only want to change the color, you can choose different color schemes using theme colors by using the Change Color button. If the flow of a SmartArt graphic is not the direction you want, you can change the orientation.

Apply a Quick Style to a SmartArt Graphic

1. Click the SmartArt graphic you want to modify.

2. Click the **Design** tab under SmartArt Tools.

3. Click the scroll up or down arrow, or click the **More** list arrow in the Quick Styles group to see additional styles.

4. Point to a style.

   A live preview of the style appears in the current shape.

5. Click the layout for the SmartArt graphic you want from the gallery.

Change a Smart Graphic Orientation

1. Click the SmartArt graphic you want to modify.

2. Click the **Design** tab under SmartArt Tools.

3. Click the **Right to Left** button.

   The button toggles, so you can click it again to switch back.

Change a SmartArt Graphic Layout

1. Click the SmartArt graphic you want to modify.

2. Click the **Design** tab under SmartArt Tools.

3. Click the scroll up or down arrow, or click the **More** list arrow in the Layout Styles group to see additional styles.

   The gallery displays layouts designed for bulleted lists.

4. To view the entire list of diagram layouts, click **More Layouts**.

5. Point to a layout.

   A live preview of the style appears in the current shape.

6. Click the layout for the SmartArt graphic you want from the gallery.

7. If you opened the entire list of layouts, click **OK**.

Change a SmartArt Graphic Colors

1. Click the SmartArt graphic you want to modify.

2. Click the **Design** tab under SmartArt Tools.

3. Click the **Change Colors** button.

   The gallery displays the current layout with different theme colors.

4. Point to a style.

   A live preview of the style appears in the current shape.

5. Click the layout for the SmartArt graphic you want from the gallery.

Formatting a Shape in a SmartArt Graphic

In the same way you can apply shape fills, outlines, and effects to a shape, you can also apply them to shapes in a SmartArt graphic. You can modify all or part of the SmartArt graphic by using the Shape Fill, Shape Outline, and Shape Effects buttons. Shape Fill can be set to be a solid, gradient, texture or picture, or set the Shape Outline to be a solid or gradient. In addition, you can change the look of a SmartArt graphic by applying effects, such as glow and soft edges. If a shape in a SmartArt graphic contains text, you can use WordArt style galleries to modify shape text.

Apply a Shape Fill to a SmartArt Graphic

1. Select the shapes in the SmartArt graphic you want to modify.

    TIMESAVER *You can hold Ctrl while you click to select multiple shapes, or press Ctrl+A to select all the shapes.*

2. Click the **Format** tab under SmartArt Tools.

3. Click the **Shape Fill** button.

4. Click a color, **No Fill**, or **Picture** to select an image, or point to **Gradient**, or **Texture**, and then select a style.

Apply a Shape Outline to a SmartArt Graphic

1. Select the shapes in the SmartArt graphic you want to modify.

2. Click the **Format** tab under SmartArt Tools.

3. Click the **Shape Outline** button.

4. Click a color or **No Outline**, or point to **Weight** or **Dashes**, and then select a style.

Apply a Shape Effect to a SmartArt Graphic

1. Select the shapes in the SmartArt graphic you want to modify.

2. Click the **Format** tab under SmartArt Tools.

3. Click the **Shape Effects** button, and then point to one of the following:

   ◆ **Preset** to select No 3-D, one of the preset types, or More 3-D Settings.

   ◆ **Shadow** to select No Shadow, one of the shadow types, or More Shadows.

   ◆ **Reflection** to select No Reflection or one of the Reflection Variations.

   ◆ **Glow** to select No Glow, one of the Glow Variations, or More Glow Colors.

   ◆ **Soft Edges** to select No Soft Edges or a point size to determine the soft edge amount.

   ◆ **Bevel** to select No Bevel, one of the bevel types, or More 3-D Settings.

   ◆ **3-D Rotation** to select No Rotation, one of the rotation types, or More 3-D Settings.

   When you point to an effect, a live preview of the style appears in the current shape.

4. Click the effect you want from the gallery to apply it to the selected shape.

See Also

See "Formatting WordArt Text" on page 216 for information on applying WordArt styles to a SmartArt graphic.

Adding Pictures to a SmartArt Graphic

With SmartArt graphic layouts, you can insert pictures in the SmartArt shapes. In addition to the pictures, you can also add descriptive text using the Text pane or shape itself. The process is very simple. Insert a SmartArt picture layout, insert pictures, and then add descriptive text. If you already have pictures in your document, you can convert them to a SmartArt graphic.

Add a SmartArt Graphic to a Picture

1. Use either of the following to add pictures to a SmartArt graphic:

   ◆ **Create New.** Click the **Insert** tab, click the **SmartArt** button, click **Picture**, click a layout, and then click **OK**.

   ◆ **Convert Picture.** Select a picture, click the **Format** tab under Picture Tools, click the **Picture Layout** button, and then select a layout.

2. To add a shape, click the **Design** tab under SmartArt Tools, click the **Add Shape** button arrow, and then select the type of shape you want to add.

3. To add a picture, double-click a graphic placeholder, select a picture file, and then click **Insert**.

4. Label the shapes by doing one of the following:

   ◆ Type text in the [Text] box.

   ◆ Click a shape, and then type text directly into the shape.

Selected picture

Convert picture

Creating an Organization Chart

An organization chart shows the reporting relationships between individuals in an organization. For example, you can show the relationship between a manager and employees within a company. You can create an organization chart using a SmartArt graphic or using Microsoft Organization Chart. A SmartArt graphic organization chart makes it easy to add shapes using the graphic portion or the Text pane. Like any SmartArt graphic, you can add special effects—such as soft edges, glows, or 3-D effects, and animation—to an organization chart.

Create an Organization Chart Using a SmartArt Graphic

1. Click the **Insert** tab.

2. Click the **SmartArt** button.

3. In the left pane, click **Hierarchy**.

4. Click an organization chart type.

5. Click **OK**.

6. Label the shapes by doing one of the following:

    ◆ Type text in the [Text] box.

    ◆ Click a shape, and then type text directly into the shape.

7. To add shapes from the Text pane, place the insertion point at the beginning of the text where you want to add a shape, type the text you want, press Enter, and then to indent the new shape, press Tab or to promote, press Shift+Tab.

    You can also click the Add Shape button arrow on the Design tab under SmartArt Tools, and then select the type of shape you want to add.

8. When you're done, click outside of the SmartArt graphic.

Modifying an Organization Chart

Like any SmartArt graphic, you can add special effects—such as soft edges, glows, or 3-D effects, and animation—to an organization chart. If your organization chart doesn't quite look the way you want, live preview can help you preview layouts in the Quick Styles and Layout Styles groups and select the one you want. If you only want to change the color, you can choose different color schemes using theme colors by using the Change Color button.

Change the Layout or Apply a Quick Style to an Organization Chart

① Click the SmartArt graphic you want to modify.

② Click the **Design** tab under SmartArt Tools.

③ Click the scroll up or down arrow, or click the **More** list arrow in the Layouts group or Quick Styles group to see additional styles.

The gallery displays different layouts or the current layout with different theme colors.

④ Point to a style.

A live preview of the style appears in the current shape.

⑤ Click the layout or style for the SmartArt graphic you want from the gallery.

Did You Know?

You can change organization chart lines to dotted lines. Right-click the line you want to modify, click Format Object, click Line Style, click Dash type, click a style, and then click Close.

You can change the colors of an organization chart. Click the SmartArt graphic you want to modify, click the Design tab under SmartArt Tools, click the Change Colors button, and then click the color theme you want.

Drawing and Modifying Shapes

Introduction

When you want to add objects to a workbook, you can use Microsoft Excel as a drawing package. Excel offers a wide range of predesigned shapes, line options or freeform tools that allow you to draw, size, and format your own shapes and forms.

You can add several types of drawing objects to your Excel workbooks—shapes, text boxes, lines, and freeforms. **Shapes** are preset objects, such as stars, circles, or ovals. **Text boxes** are objects with text, a shape without a border. **Lines** are simply the straight or curved lines (arcs) that can connect two points or are used as arrows. **Freeforms** are irregular curves or polygons that you can create as a free-hand drawing.

Once you create a drawing object, you can move, resize, nudge, copy or delete it on your worksheets. You can also change its style, by adding color, creating a fill pattern, rotating it, and applying a shadow or 3-D effect. Take a simple shape and by the time you are done adding various effects, it could become an attractive piece of graphic art for your workbook.

Object placement on your worksheets is a key factor to all of your hard work. Multiple objects should be grouped if they are to be considered one larger object. Grouping helps you make changes later on, or copy your objects to another worksheet. Excel has the ability to line up your objects with precision—rulers and guides are part of the alignment process to help you. By grouping and aligning, you are assured that your drawing objects will be accurately placed.

What You'll Do

Draw and Resize Shapes

Insert Multiple Shapes

Add Text to a Shape

Draw Lines and Arrows

Create, Edit and Modify Freeforms

Copy and Move an Object

Add a Quick Style to a Shape and Shape Text

Apply Color Fills and Shape Effects

Apply Picture, Texture and Gradient Fills

Add 3-D and Rotation Effects to a Shape

Create Shadows

Align and Distribute Objects

Connect Shapes

Select Objects using the Selection Pane

Change Stacking Order

Rotate and Flip a Shape

Group and Ungroup Shapes

Drawing and Resizing Shapes

Excel supplies ready-made shapes, ranging from hearts to lightning bolts to stars. The ready-made shapes are available directly on the Shapes gallery on the Insert and Format tabs. Once you have placed a shape on a worksheet, you can resize it using the sizing handles. Many shapes have an **adjustment handle**, a small yellow or pink diamond located near a resize handle that you can drag to alter the shape. For precision when resizing, use the Size Dialog Box Launcher to specify the new size of the shape.

Draw a Shape

1. Click the **Insert** tab.

2. Click the **Shapes** button.

3. Click the shape you want to draw.

4. Drag the pointer on the worksheet where you want to place the shape until the drawing object is the shape and size that you want.

   The shape you draw uses the line and fill color defined by the workbook's theme.

   TIMESAVER *To draw a proportional shape, hold down Shift as you drag the pointer.*

Did You Know?

You can quickly delete a shape. Click the shape to select it, and then press Delete.

You can draw a perfect circle or square. To draw a perfect circle or square, click the Oval or Rectangle button on the Shapes gallery, and then press and hold Shift as you drag.

3 Shapes

Resize a Shape

1. Select the shape you want to resize.

2. Drag one of the sizing handles.

   ◆ To resize the object in the vertical or horizontal direction, drag a sizing handle on the side of the selection box.

   ◆ To resize the object in both the vertical and horizontal directions, drag a sizing handle on the corner of the selection box.

   ◆ To resize the object with precise measurements, click the **Format** tab under Drawing Tools, and then specify exact height and width settings in the Size group.

Adjust a Shape

1. Select the shape you want to adjust.

2. Click one of the adjustment handles (small yellow diamonds), and then drag the handle to alter the form of the shape.

Did You Know?

You can replace a shape. Replace one shape with another, while retaining the size, color, and orientation of the shape. Click the shape you want to replace, click the Format tab, click the Edit Shape button, point to Change Shape, and then click the new shape you want.

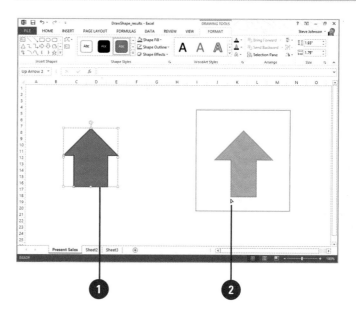

Inserting Multiple Shapes

If you need to draw the same shape several times on one or more worksheets in your workbook, you can use Excel's Lock Drawing Mode to draw as many of the same shapes as you want without having to reselect it from the Shapes gallery. This can be a timesaver and save you extra mouse clicks. Excel stays in Lock Drawing Mode until you press Esc. If a shape doesn't look the way you want, you can change the shape instead of redrawing it.

Insert Multiple Shapes

1. Click the **Insert** tab.

2. Click the **Shapes** button.

3. Right-click the shape you want to add, and then click **Lock Drawing Mode**.

4. Drag the pointer on the worksheet where you want to place the shape until the drawing object is the shape and size that you want. Continue to draw shapes as you want in your workbook.

5. When you're done, press Esc.

Change a Shape to Another Shape

1. Select the shape you want to modify.

2. Click the **Format** tab under Drawing Tools.

3. Click the **Edit Shape** button, point to **Change Shape**.

4. Click the shape you want to use from the Shapes gallery.

Adding Text to a Shape

You can add text to a shape in the same way you add text to a text box. Simply, select the shape object, and then start typing. Shapes range from rectangles and circles to arrows and stars. When you place text in a shape, the text becomes part of the object. If you rotate or flip the shape, the text rotates or flips too. You can use tools, such as an alignment button or Font Style, on the Mini-Toolbar and Home tab to format the text in a shape like the text in a text box.

Add Text to a Shape

1. Select the shape in which you want to add text.

2. Type the text you want.

3. To edit the text in a shape, click the text to place the insertion point, and then edit the text.

Create a Text Box

1. Click the **Insert** tab.

2. Click the **Text Box** button.

3. Perform one of the following:

   ◆ To add text that wraps, drag to create a box, and then start typing.

   ◆ To add text that doesn't wrap, click and then start typing.

4. To delete a text box, select it, and then press Delete.

5. Click outside the selection box to deselect the text box.

Drawing Lines and Arrows

The most basic drawing objects you can create on your worksheets are lines and arrows. Use the Line shape to create line segments or the Arrow shape to create arrows that emphasize key points in your workbook. You can quickly add multiple formatting to a line or arrow using Shape Quick Styles or change individual formatting—solid, dashed, or a combination—using the Shape Outline button and Format Shape pane (**New!**). The Shape Outline button lets you change the type of line or arrow. You can add arrowheads to any lines on your worksheet.

Draw a Straight Line or Arrow

1. Click the **Insert** tab.

2. Click the **Shapes** button, and then click a Line or Arrow shape in the Shapes gallery.

3. Drag the pointer to draw a line. The endpoints of the line or arrow are where you start and finish dragging.

4. Release the mouse button when the line or arrow is the correct length. Sizing handles appear at both ends of the line. Use these handles to resize your line or move an endpoint.

Add a Quick Style to a Line

1. Select the shape you want to modify.

2. Click the **Format** tab under Drawing Tools.

3. Click the scroll up or down arrow, or click the **More** list arrow in the Shapes Styles group to see additional styles.

4. Point to a style.

   A live preview of the style appears in the current shape.

5. Click the style you want from the gallery to apply it to the selected line.

Change a Line or Arrow

1. Select the line or arrow you want to edit.

2. Click the **Format** tab under Drawing Tools.

3. Click the **Shape Outline** button to select a line or arrow style or thickness.

4. Click a color, or point to **Weight**, **Dashes**, or **Arrows**, and then select a style.

5. Drag a sizing handle to change the size or angle of the line or arrow.

Modify a Line or Arrow

1. Select the line or arrow you want to edit.

2. Click the **Format** tab under Drawing Tools.

3. Click the **Shape Outline** button, point to **Weight**, **Dashes**, or **Arrows**, and then click **More Lines** or **More Arrows**.

4. In the Format Shape pane (**New!**) under Line & Fill, expand **Line**.

5. For line and arrow select a width, compound type (double or triple lines), dash type, cap type—end of line style (square, round, or flat end), or join type—style used to connect two lines together (round, bevel, or miter).

6. For an arrow, select a begin type, end type, begin size, and end size.

7. Click the **Close** button in the pane.

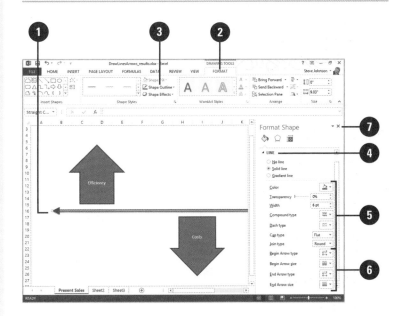

Creating and Editing Freeforms

When you need to create a customized shape, use the Excel freeform tools. Choose a freeform tool from the Lines category in the list of shapes. Freeforms are like the drawings you make with a pen and paper, except that you use a mouse for your pen and a document for your paper. A freeform shape can either be an open curve or a closed curve. You can edit a freeform by using the Edit Points command to alter the vertices that create the shape.

Draw a Freeform Polygon

1. Click the **Insert** tab.

2. Click the **Shapes** button and then click **Freeform** in the Shapes gallery under Lines.

3. Click the document where you want to place the first vertex of the polygon.

4. Move the pointer, and then click to place the second point of the polygon. A line joins the two points.

   ◆ To draw a line with curves, drag a line instead of clicking in steps 3 and 4.

5. Continue moving the mouse pointer and clicking to create additional sides of your polygon.

6. Finish the polygon. For a closed polygon, click near the starting point. For an open polygon, double-click the last point in the polygon.

Did You Know?

You can convert a shape to a freeform. Select the shape, click the Edit Shape button, and then click Convert To Freeform.

You can switch between a closed curve and an open curve. Right-click the freeform drawing, and then click Close Path or Open Path.

For Your Information

Modifying a Freeform

Each vertex indicated by a black dot (a corner in an irregular polygon and a bend in a curve) has two attributes: its position, and the angle at which the curve enters and leaves it. You can move the position of each vertex and control the corner or bend angles. You can also add or delete vertices as you like. When you delete a vertex, Excel recalculates the freeform and smooths it among the remaining points. Similarly, if you add a new vertex, Excel adds a corner or bend in your freeform. To edit a freeform, click the freeform object, click the Format tab under Drawing Tools, click the Edit Shape button, click Edit Points, modify any of the points (move or delete), and then click outside to set the new shape.

Copying and Moving Objects

After you create a drawing object, you can copy or move it. Use the mouse to quickly move objects, or if you want precise control over the object's new position, use Excel's Size and Position dialog box to specify the location of the drawing object. You can copy a selected one or more objects to the Office Clipboard and then paste them in other parts of the current workbook or another existing workbook, or Office document. You can paste these items, either individually or all at once.

Copy or Move an Object in One Step

1 Hold down the Ctrl key, and then drag the object to copy it, or simply drag the object to move it.

Make sure you aren't dragging a sizing handle or adjustment handle. If you are working with a freeform and you are in Edit Points mode, drag the interior of the object, not the border, or you will end up resizing or reshaping the object, not moving it.

Copy or Move an Object

1 Select the objects you want to copy or move.

2 Click the **Home** tab.

3 Click the **Copy** button (to copy) or click the **Cut** button (to move).

4 Display the worksheet on which you want to paste the object.

5 Use one of the following methods:

◆ Click the **Paste** button, or click the **Paste** button arrow, point to an option to display a live preview, and then click an option to paste it.

◆ Click the **Clipboard Dialog Box Launcher**, and then click an item to paste it.

Adding a Quick Style to a Shape

Instead of changing individual attributes of a shape—such as shape fill, shape outline, and shape effects—you can quickly add them all at once with the Shape Quick Style gallery. The Shape Quick Style gallery provides a variety of different formatting combinations. To quickly see if you like a Shape Quick Style, point to a thumbnail in the gallery to display a live preview of it in the selected shape. If you like it, you can apply it.

Add a Quick Style to a Shape

1. Select the shapes you want to modify.

2. Click the **Format** tab under Drawing Tools.

3. Click the scroll up or down arrow, or click the **More** list arrow in the Shapes Styles group to see additional styles.

   The current style appears highlighted in the gallery.

4. Point to a style.

   A live preview of the style appears in the current shape.

5. Click the style you want from the gallery to apply it to the selected shape.

Did You Know?

You can add a Quick Style to a text box. A shape is a text box without a fill and outline (border), so you can apply a Quick Style to a text box using the same steps.

You can use a Mini-Toolbar to apply styles, fills, and outlines. Right-click the object you want to modify, click the Style, Fill, or Outline button (**New!**), and then select an option.

Adding a Quick Style to Shape Text

Instead of changing individual attributes of text in a shape, such as text fill, text outline, and text effects, you can quickly add them all at once with the WordArt Quick Style gallery. The WordArt Quick Style gallery provides a variety of different formatting combinations. To quickly see if you like a WordArt Quick Style, point to a thumbnail in the gallery to display a live preview of it in the selected shape. If you like it, you can apply it.

Add a Quick Style to Shape Text

1 Select the shapes with the text you want to modify.

2 Click the **Format** tab under Drawing Tools.

3 Click the scroll up or down arrow, or click the **More** list arrow in the WordArt Styles group to see additional styles.

   The current style appears highlighted in the gallery.

4 Point to a style.

   A live preview of the style appears in the current shape text.

5 Click the style you want from the gallery to apply it to the selected shape.

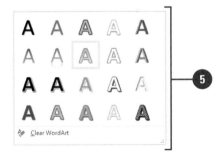

Did You Know?

You can arrange shapes in a SmartArt graphic. Select the shape in the SmartArt graphic, click the Format tab under SmartArt Tools, click the Arrange button, and then use any of the arrange button options: Bring To Front, Send To Back, Align, Group, or Rotate.

You can edit a SmartArt graphic shape in 2-D. Select the SmartArt graphic with the 3-D style, click the Format tab under SmartArt Tools, and then click the Edit In 2-D button.

Applying Color Fills

When you create a closed drawing object such as a square, it applies the Shape Fill color to the inside of the shape, and the Shape Outline color to the shape edge. A line drawing object uses the Shape Outline color. You can set the Shape Fill to be a solid, gradient, texture or picture, and the Shape Outline to be a solid or gradient. If you want to make multiple changes to a shape at the same time, the Format Shape pane (**New!**) can do it all in one place. If the solid color appears too dark, you can make the color fill more transparent. If you no longer want to apply a shape fill to an object, you can remove it.

Apply a Color Fill to a Shape

1. Select the shape you want to modify.

2. Click the **Format** tab under Drawing Tools.

3. Click the **Shape Fill** button.

4. Select a fill color option.

5. To remove a color fill, click the **Shape Fill** button, and then click **No Fill**.

   TIMESAVER *To apply a color fill, right-click the shape, click Fill button, and then click a color.*

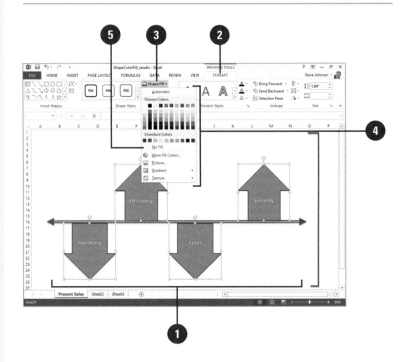

Did You Know?

You can set the color and line style for an object as the default. Right-click the object, and then click Set As Default Shape. Any new objects you create will use the same styles.

You can use the document background as the fill for a shape. Right-click the object, and then click Format Shape or Format Object. In the Format Shape pane (**New!**), click Line & Fill button, expand Fill, click the Fill icon, click the Background option, and then click the Close button in the pane.

Apply a Shape Color Fill with a Transparency

① Right-click the shape you want to modify, and then click **Format Shape** or **Format Object**.

② Click the **Fill & Line** button (**New!**), and then expand **Fill**.

③ Click the **Solid fill** option.

④ Click the **Color** button, and then select the fill color you want.

⑤ Drag the **Transparency** slider or enter a number from 0 (fully opaque) to 100 (fully transparent).

All your changes are instantly applied to the shape.

⑥ Click the **Close** button in the pane.

Apply a Color Outline to a Shape

① Select the shape you want to modify.

② Click the **Format** tab under Drawing Tools.

③ Click the **Shape Outline** button.

④ Select the outline color you want.

⑤ To remove an outline color, click the **Shape Outline** button, and then click **No Outline**.

Did You Know?

You can undo changes made in the Format Shape pane. Since changes made in the Shape Format pane are instantly applied, it's not possible to Cancel it. To remove changes, click the Undo button on the Quick Access Toolbar.

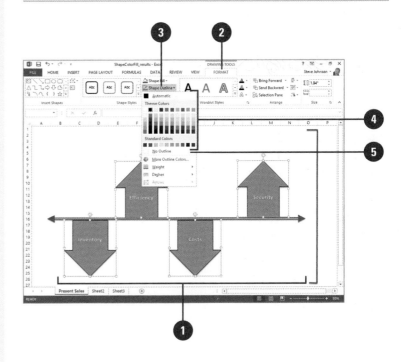

Applying Picture Fills

Applying a shape fill to a drawing object can add emphasis or create a point of interest in your document. You can insert a picture or clip art into a shape. You can insert a picture from a file, clip art on Office .com (**New!**), Bing Image Search (**New!**), online service (**New!**), such as Flickr, SkyDrive (**New!**), or Office 365 SharePoint (**New!**). Stretch a picture to fit across the selected shape or repeatedly tile it horizontally and vertically to fill the shape. When you stretch an image, you can also set offsets, which determine how much to scale an image to fit a shape relative to the edges. A positive offset number moves the image edge toward the center of the shape, while a negative offset number moves the image edge away from the shape. If the image appears too dark, you can make the picture more transparent.

Apply a Picture Fill to a Shape

1. Select the shape you want to modify.

2. Click the **Format** tab under Drawing Tools.

3. Click the **Shape Fill** button, and then click **Picture**.

   TIMESAVER *To apply a picture fill, right-click the shape, click Fill button, and then click Picture.*

4. Browse and select a picture file using any of the following:

   ◆ **From a file.** Click **Browse**, select a file on your computer or network.

   ◆ **Office.com Clip Art.** Search, and then select an online clip art image (**New!**).

   ◆ **Bing Image Search.** Search and then select an online image (**New!**).

   ◆ **SkyDrive or SharePoint.** Click **Browse**, and then select a file on your SkyDrive (**New!**) or SharePoint site (**New!**).

   ◆ **Online service.** Select a file from a service, such as Flickr (**New!**).

5. Click **Insert**.

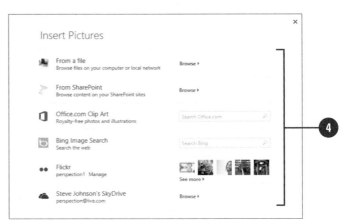

Applying Texture Fills

You can quickly apply a texture fill to a shape by using the Texture gallery or using the Format Shape pane (**New!**) to select custom options. Stretch a texture to fit across the selected shape or repeatedly tile the texture horizontally and vertically to fill the shape. If you tile a texture, you can also set offset, scale, alignment, and mirror options to determine the appearance of the texture in the selected shape. The offset x and y options determine how much to scale a texture to fit a shape relative to the edges, while scale x and y options determine horizontal and vertical scaling. If you want to play with the tile look, you can change the mirror type to determine whether the alternating tiles display a mirror or flip image with every other tile. If the texture doesn't provide enough contrast in the shape, you can make the texture more transparent.

Apply a Texture Fill to a Shape

1. Select the shape you want to modify.

2. Click the **Format** tab under Drawing Tools.

3. Click the **Shape Fill** button.

4. Point to **Texture**, and then select a texture from the gallery.

    TIMESAVER *To apply a texture fill, right-click the shape, click Fill button, and then click Texture.*

Did You Know?

You can apply a custom picture or texture fill. Right-click the object you want to modify, and then click Format Shape or Format Object. In the Format Picture pane (**New!**), click the Fill & Line button, expand Fill, click the Picture Or Texture Fill option, select a picture or texture, select the related options you want, and then click the Close button in the pane.

Applying Gradient Fills

Gradients are made up of two or more colors that gradually fade into each other. They can be used to give depth to a shape or create realistic shadows. Apply a gradient fill to a shape—now including lines—by using a gallery or presets for quick results, or by using the Format Shape pane (**New!**) for custom results. A gradient is made up of several gradient stops, which are used to create non-linear gradients. If you want to create a gradient that starts blue and goes to green, add two gradient stops, one for each color. Gradient stops consist of a position, a color, brightness, and a transparency percentage.

Apply a Gradient Fill to a Shape

1. Select the shape you want to modify.

2. Click the **Format** tab under Drawing Tools.

3. Click the **Shape Fill** button.

4. Point to **Gradient**, and then select a gradient from the gallery.

   Four gradient modes are available: linear (parallel bands), radial (radiate from center), rectangle (radiate from corners), and path (radiate along path).

Apply a Gradient Fill Preset

1. Right-click the shape you want to modify, and then click **Format Shape** or **Format Object**.

2. Click the **Fill & Lines** button under Shape Options (**New!**), and then expand **Fill**.

3. Click the **Gradient fill** option.

4. Click the **Preset colors** button arrow, and then select the built-in gradient fill you want.

   All your changes are instantly applied to the shape.

5. Click the **Close** button in the pane.

Apply a Custom Gradient Fill

1. Right-click the shape you want to modify, and then click **Format Shape** or **Format Object**.

2. Click the **Fill & Lines** button under Shape Options (**New!**), and then expand **Fill**.

3. Click the **Gradient fill** option.

4. Click the **Preset colors** button arrow, and then select the built-in gradient fill you want.

5. Click the **Type** list arrow, and then select a gradient direction.

6. Click the **Direction** list arrow, and then select a shading progression; options vary depending on the gradient type.

7. If you selected the Linear type, specify the angle (in degrees) the gradient is rotated in the shape.

8. Specify the following tiling options:

   ◆ **Add.** Click the **Add** button, and then set the gradient stop options you want.

   ◆ **Remove.** Select a gradient stop, and then click the **Remove** button.

   ◆ **Position.** Specify a location for the color and transparency change in the gradient fill.

   ◆ **Color.** Click the **Color** button, and then select a color for the gradient stop.

   ◆ **Brightness.** Drag the slider to adjust the brightness color contrast.

   ◆ **Transparency.** Drag the slider or enter a number from 0 (fully opaque) to 100 (full transparent) for the selected stop position.

9. Select the **Rotate with shape** check box to rotate the gradient with the shape's rotation.

10. Click **Close** button in the pane.

Custom gradient fill

Applying Shape Effects

You can change the look of a shape by applying effects, like shadows, reflections, glow, soft edges, bevels, and 3-D rotations. Apply effects to a shape by using the Shape Effects gallery for quick results, or by using the Format Shape pane (**New!**) for custom results. From the Shape Effects gallery you can apply a built-in combination of 3-D effects or individual effects to a shape. To quickly see if you like a shape effect, point to a thumbnail in the Shape Effects gallery to display a live preview of it in the selected shape. If you like it, you can apply it. If you no longer want to apply a shape effect to an object, you can remove it. Simply select the shape, point to the effect type in the Shape Effects gallery, and then select the No effect type option.

Add a Preset Effect to a Shape

1. Select the shape you want to modify.

2. Click the **Format** tab under Drawing Tools.

3. Click the **Shape Effects** button, and then point to **Preset**.

    The current effect appears highlighted in the gallery.

4. Point to an effect.

    A live preview of the style appears in the current shape.

5. Click the effect you want from the gallery to apply it to the selected shape.

6. To remove the preset effect, click the **Shape Effects** button, point to **Preset**, and then click **No Presets**.

Did You Know?

3-D effects take precedence. If you add a 3-D effect, such as a bevel or 3-D rotation, to a shape and then add soft edges, the soft edge effect doesn't appear in the shape until you delete the 3-D effect.

Add Individual Effects to a Shape

1 Select the shape you want to modify.

2 Click the **Format** tab under Drawing Tools.

3 Click the **Shape Effects** button, and then point to one of the following:

- ◆ **Shadow** to select No Shadow, one of the shadow types (Outer, Inner, or Perspective), or Shadows Options.

- ◆ **Reflection** to select No Reflection, one of the Reflection Variations, or Reflection Options.

- ◆ **Glow** to select No Glow, one of the Glow Variations, More Glow Colors, or Glow Options.

- ◆ **Soft Edges** to select No Soft Edges, a point size to determine the soft edge amount, or Soft Edges Options.

- ◆ **Bevel** to select No Bevel, one of the bevel variations, or 3-D Options.

- ◆ **3-D Rotation** to select No Rotation, one of the rotation types (Parallel, Perspective, or Oblique), or 3-D Rotation Options.

When you point to an effect, a live preview of the style appears in the current shape.

4 Click the effect you want from the gallery to apply it to the selected shape.

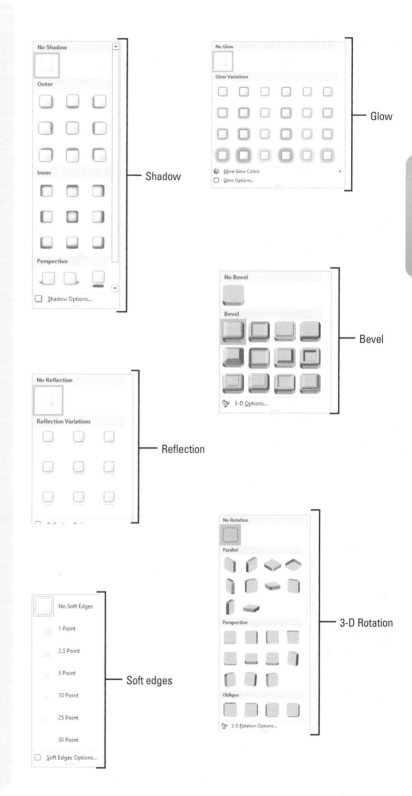

Adding 3-D Effects to a Shape

You can add the illusion of depth to your worksheets by adding a 3-D effect to a shape. Create a 3-D effect by using one of the preset 3-D styles, or use the 3-D format tools to customize your own 3-D style. The settings you can control with the customization tools include the bevel (a 3-D top or bottom edge effect), the shape depth (distance of shape from its surface), the contour (raised border), the surface material and lighting. You can apply interesting surfaces—matte, plastic, metal, wire frame, soft or dark edges, flat, translucent, and clear—to a 3-D shape. In addition, you can change the type of lighting—neutral, warm, cool, flat, glow, and bright room—applied to a 3-D shape. Each lighting type defines one or more lights that illuminate a 3-D scene, not just for the shape. Each light contains a position, intensity, and color.

Add a 3-D Effect to a Shape

1. Select the shape you want to modify.

2. Click the **Format** tab under Drawing Tools.

3. Click the **Shape Effects** button, and then point to **Preset** or **Bevel**.

    The current effect appears highlighted in the gallery.

4. Point to an effect.

    A live preview of the style appears in the current shape.

5. Click the effect you want from the gallery to apply it to the selected shape.

6. To remove the 3-D effect, click the **Shape Effects** button, point to **Preset** or **Bevel**, and then click **No Preset** or **No Bevel**.

Add a Custom 3-D Effect to a Shape

① Select the shape you want to modify.

② Click the **Format** tab under Drawing Tools.

③ Click the **Shape Effects** button, point to **Preset** or **Bevel**, and then click **3-D Options**.

④ Click the **Effects** button under Shape Options (**New!**), and then expand **3-D Format**.

⑤ Specify the following custom options:

◆ **Bevel.** Click **Top** or **Bottom** to apply a raised edge to the top or bottom of a shape. The corresponding width and height numbers appear.

◆ **Depth.** Click the **Color** button to select a depth color, and then enter a depth number.

◆ **Contour.** Click the **Color** button to select a contour color, and then enter a size.

◆ **Surface.** Click **Material** to select a surface, and then click **Lighting** to specify the way light illuminates the 3-D shape.

To rotate all of the lights around the front face of a shape, enter an angle.

All your changes are instantly applied to the shape.

⑥ To remove 3-D formatting and restore default setting, click **Reset**.

⑦ Click **Close** button in the pane.

Material

Lighting

Adding 3-D Rotation Effects to a Shape

After you create a 3-D or even a 2-D shape, you can use 3-D rotation options to change the orientation and perspective of the shape. You can also create a 3-D rotation effect using one of the preset 3-D rotation styles, or you can use the 3-D rotation tools to create your own 3-D effect. The settings control with the customization tools include the 3-D rotation (x, y, and z axis), text rotation, and object position (distance from ground).

Add a 3-D Rotation Effect to a Shape

1. Select the shape you want to modify.

2. Click the **Format** tab under Drawing Tools.

3. Click the **Shape Effects** button, and then point to **3-D Rotation**.

   The current effect appears highlighted in the gallery.

4. Point to an effect.

   A live preview of the style appears in the current shape.

5. Click the effect you want from the gallery to apply it to the selected shape.

6. To remove the 3-D rotation effect, click the **Shape Effects** button, point to **3-D Rotation**, and then click **No Rotation**.

Did You Know?

You can add a custom 3-D rotation effect to a shape. Click the shape you want to modify, click the Format tab, click the Shape Effects button, point to 3-D Rotation, click 3-D Rotation Options, select the rotation x and y, rotation z, rotation perspective, text and object position options you want, and then click Close.

Creating Shadows

You can give objects on your worksheets the illusion of depth by adding shadows. Excel provides several preset shadowing options, or you can create your own by specifying color, transparency, size, blur, angle, and distance. You can change all these shadow options at the same time in the Format Shape pane (**New!**). Instead of starting from scratch, you can select a preset shadow in the Format Shape pane (**New!**), and then customize it.

Add a Preset Shadow to a Shape

1. Select the shape you want to modify.

2. Click the **Format** tab under Drawing Tools.

3. Click the **Shape Effects** button, and then point to **Shadow**.

   The current effect appears highlighted in the gallery.

4. Point to an effect.

   A live preview of the style appears in the current shape.

5. Click the effect you want from the gallery to apply it to the selected shape.

6. To remove the shadow, click the **Shape Effects** button, point to **Shadow**, and then click **No Shadow**.

Did You Know?

You can add a custom shadow to a shape. Click the shape you want to modify, click the Format tab, click the Shape Effects button, point to Shadow, click More Shadows, click the Presets button, select a shadow, select the color, transparency, size, blur, angle, and distance options you want, and then click Close.

Aligning and Distributing Objects

In addition to using grids and guides to align objects to a specific point, you can align a group of objects to each other. The Align commands make it easy to align two or more objects relative to each other vertically to the left, center, or right, or horizontally from the top, middle, or bottom. To evenly align several objects to each other across the document, either horizontally or vertically, select them and then choose a distribution option. Before you select an align command, specify how you want Excel to align the objects. You can align the objects in relation to the document or to the selected objects.

Distribute Objects

1. Select the objects you want to distribute.

2. Click the **Format** tab under Drawing Tools.

3. Click the **Align** button.

4. On the Align menu, click the alignment method you want.

   ◆ Click **Snap to Grid** if you want the objects to align relative to the document grid.

   ◆ Click **Snap to Shape** if you want the objects to align relative to each other.

5. On the Align menu, click the distribution command you want.

   ◆ Click **Distribute Horizontally** to evenly distribute the objects horizontally.

   ◆ Click **Distribute Vertically** to evenly distribute the objects vertically.

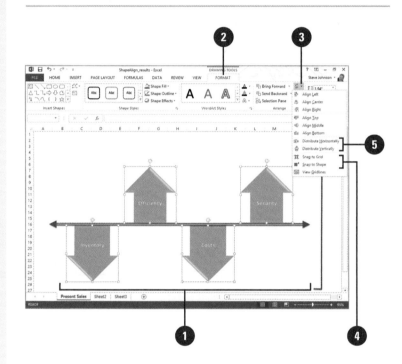

Align Objects with Other Objects

1. Select the objects you want to align.

2. Click the **Format** tab under Drawing Tools.

3. Click the **Align** button.

4. On the Align menu, click the alignment method you want.

   ◆ Click **Snap to Grid** if you want the objects to align relative to the document grid.

   ◆ Click **Snap to Shape** if you want the objects to align relative to each other.

5. On the Align menu, click the alignment command you want.

   ◆ Click **Align Left** to line up the objects with the left edge of the selection or document.

   ◆ Click **Align Center** to line up the objects with the center of the selection or document.

   ◆ Click **Align Right** to line up the objects with the right edge of the selection or document.

   ◆ Click **Align Top** to line up the objects with the top edge of the selection or document.

   ◆ Click **Align Middle** to line up the objects vertically with the middle of the selection or document.

   ◆ Click **Align Bottom** to line up the objects with the bottom of the selection or document.

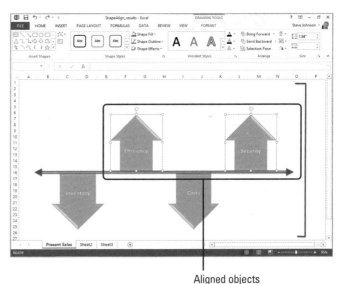

Aligned objects

Connecting Shapes

Excel makes it easy to draw and modify flow charts and diagrams. Flow charts and diagrams consist of shapes connected together to indicate a sequence of events. With Excel, you can join two objects with a connecting line. There are three types of connector lines: straight, elbow, and curved. Once two objects are joined, the connecting line moves when you move either object. The connecting line touches special connection points on the objects. When you position the pointer over an object, small red handles, known as **connection sites**, appear, and the pointer changes to a small box, called the connection pointer. You can drag a connection end point to another connection point to change the line or drag the adjustment handle (yellow diamond) to change the shape of the connection line. After you're done connecting shapes, you can format connector lines in the same way you format others lines in Excel, including the use of Shape Quick Styles.

Connect Two Objects

1 Click the **Insert** tab.

2 Click the **Shapes** button, and then click a connector (located in the Lines category) in the Shapes gallery.

◆ To draw multiple connector lines, right-click the connector in the Shapes gallery, and then click **Lock Drawing Mode**.

TIMESAVER *In the Shapes gallery, point to shapes in the Lines category to display ScreenTips to locate a connector.*

3 Position the pointer over an object handle (turns red).

4 Drag the connector to the object handle (turns red) on another object.

TIMESAVER *To constrain the line at 15-degree angles from its starting point, hold down Shift while you drag.*

An attached connector point appears as red circles, while an unattached connector point appears as light blue (almost transparent).

4 Drag to connect shapes

Selecting Objects Using the Selection Pane

Sometimes it's hard to select an object when it is behind another one. With the Selection task pane, you can now select individual objects and change their order and visibility. When you open the Selection task pane, Excel lists each shape on the current document by name (in terms of object type). You can click a shape title to select a "hard-to-select" object on the document, use the Re-order buttons to change the stacking order on the document, or click the eye icon next to a shape title to show or hide "hard-to-see" individual objects.

Select Objects Using the Selection Pane

1. Display the documents with the objects you want to select.

2. Click the **Format** tab under Drawing or Picture Tools.

3. Click the **Selection Pane** button.

    Titles for all the shapes on the current document appear in the task pane.

4. To select an object, click the title in the task pane.

    To select more than one object, hold down the Ctrl key while you click object titles.

5. To change the order of the objects, select an object, and then click the Re-order **Move Up** or **Move Down** buttons in the task pane.

6. To show or hide individual objects, click the eye icon in the task pane.

7. When you're done, click the **Close** button on the task pane.

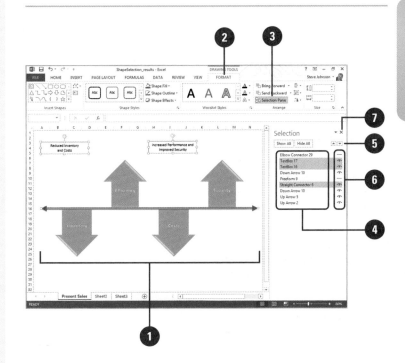

Changing Stacking Order

Multiple objects on a document appear in a stacking order, like layers of transparencies. Stacking is the placement of objects one on top of another. In other words, the first object that you draw is on the bottom and the last object that you draw is on top. You can change the order of this stack of objects by using Bring to Front, Send to Back, Bring Forward, and Send Backward commands on the Format tab under Drawing or Picture Tools.

Arrange a Stack of Objects

1 Select the objects you want to arrange.

2 Click the **Format** tab under Drawing or Picture Tools.

3 Click the stacking option you want.

◆ Click the **Bring to Front** button arrow, and then click **Bring to Front** or **Bring Forward** to move a drawing to the top of the stack or up one location in the stack.

◆ Click the **Send to Back** button arrow, and then click **Send to Back** or **Send Backward** to move a drawing to the bottom of the stack or back one location in the stack.

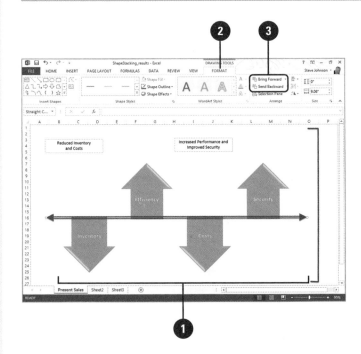

Did You Know?

You can view a hidden object in a stack. Press the Tab key or Shift+Tab to cycle forward or backward through the objects until you select the object you want.

Rotating and Flipping Objects

After you create an object, you can change its orientation on the document by rotating or flipping it. Rotating turns an object 90 degrees to the right or left; flipping turns an object 180 degrees horizontally or vertically. For a more freeform rotation, which you cannot achieve in 90 or 180 degree increments, drag the green rotate lever at the top of an object. You can also rotate and flip any type of picture–including bitmaps–in a document. This is useful when you want to change the orientation of an image, such as changing the direction of an arrow.

Rotate an Object to any Angle

1. Select the object you want to rotate.

2. Position the pointer (which changes to the Free Rotate pointer) over the green rotate lever at the top of the object, and then drag to rotate the object.

3. Click outside the object to set the rotation.

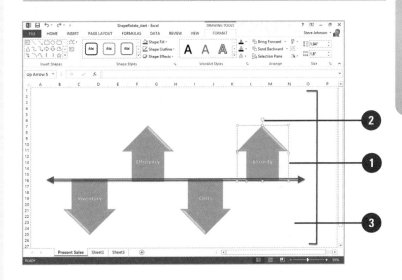

Rotate or Flip an Object Using Preset Increments

1. Select the object you want to rotate or flip.

2. Click the **Format** tab under Drawing or Picture Tools.

3. Click the **Rotate** button, and then click the option you want.

   ◆ Rotate. Click **Rotate Right 90°** or **Rotate Left 90°**.

   ◆ Flip. Click **Flip Vertical** or Flip **Horizontal**.

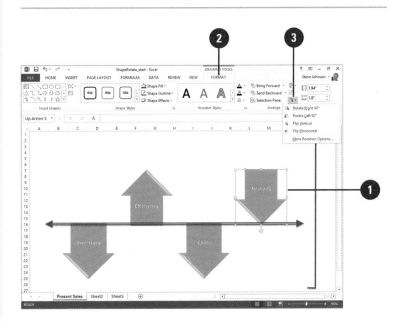

Grouping and Ungrouping Shapes

Objects can be grouped, ungrouped, and regrouped to make editing and moving them easier. Rather than moving several objects one at a time, you can group the objects and move them all together. Grouped objects appear as one object, but each object in the group maintains its individual attributes. You can change an individual object within a group without ungrouping. This is useful when you need to make only a small change to a group, such as changing the color of a single shape in the group. You can also format specific shapes, drawings, or pictures within a group without ungrouping. Simply select the object within the group, change the object or edit text within the object, and then deselect the object. However, if you need to move an object in a group, you need to first ungroup the objects, move it, and then group the objects together again. After you ungroup a set of objects, Excel remembers each object in the group and regroups those objects in one step when you use the Regroup command. Before you regroup a set of objects, make sure that at least one of the grouped objects is selected.

Group Objects Together

1. Select the objects you want to group together.

2. Click the **Format** tab under Drawing or Picture Tools.

3. Click the **Group** button, and then click **Group**.

Did You Know?

You can use the Tab key to select objects in order. Move between the drawing objects on your worksheet (even those hidden behind other objects) by pressing the Tab key.

You can use the shortcut menu to select Group related commands. Right-click the objects you want to group, point to Group, and then make your selections.

You can no longer ungroup tables. Due to the increased table size and theme functionality, tables can no longer be ungrouped.

Ungroup a Drawing

1. Select the grouped object you want to ungroup.

2. Click the **Format** tab under Drawing or Picture Tools.

3. Click the **Group** button, and then click **Ungroup**.

See Also

See "Selecting Objects Using the Selection Pane" on page 259 for information on selecting "hard-to-select" objects.

Regroup a Drawing

1. Select one of the objects in the group of objects you want to regroup.

2. Click the **Format** tab under Drawing or Picture Tools.

3. Click the **Group** button, and then click **Regroup**.

Did You Know?

You can troubleshoot the arrangement of objects. If you have trouble selecting an object because another object is in the way, you can use the Selection pane to help you select it.

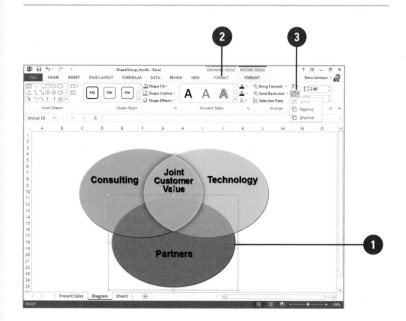

Creating and Modifying Charts

Introduction

When you're ready to share data with others, a worksheet might not be the most effective way to present the information. A page full of numbers, even if attractively formatted, can be hard to understand and perhaps a little boring. Microsoft Excel makes it easy to create and modify charts so that you can effectively present your information. A **chart** is a visual representation of selected data in your worksheet. Whether you turn numbers into a bar, line, pie, surface, or bubble chart, patterns become more apparent. For example, the trend of annual rising profits becomes powerful in a line chart. A second line showing diminishing annual expenses creates an instant map of the success of a business.

A well-designed chart draws the reader's attention to important data by illustrating trends and highlighting significant relationships between numbers. Excel generates charts based on data and chart type you select. If you're not sure which chart to use, you can use a chart recommended by Excel. Excel makes it easy to select the best chart type, design elements, and formatting enhancements for any type of information.

Once you create a chart, you may want to change your chart type to see how your data displays in a different style. You can move and resize your chart, and even draw on your chart to highlight achievements. Other formatting elements are available to assure a well-designed chart.

What You'll Do

Understand Chart Terminology

Choose the Right Type of Chart

Create and Edit a Chart

Move and Resize a Chart

Select and Change Chart Elements

Change a Chart Type

Change a Chart Layout and Style

Format Chart Elements

Change Chart Gridlines and Axes

Change Chart Titles and Labels

Pull Out a Pie Slice

Format Chart Data Series and Text

Format Line and Bar Charts

Change the Chart Background

Enhance a Chart

Edit Chart Data

Add and Delete a Data Series

Save a Chart Template

Manage Chart Templates

Understanding Chart Terminology

Handles
Small white circles that appear around the perimeter of a selected object, indicating that you can move, resize, copy, or delete the object

Title
Optional text that identifies the purpose of a chart

Chart buttons
Buttons that appear for a selected chart to quickly change the look and display of the chart (**New!**).

Data Marker
A chart object, such as a circle, dot, or square, that denotes a data point

Gridlines
Vertical and horizontal guidelines that appear behind a chart to make the chart easier to read

Legend
A key that explains the colors, patterns, or symbols in a chart

Y-axis
The vertical axis of a chart–default, a value axis

X-axis
The horizontal axis of a chart–by default, a value axis

Data series
A range of related data points in a chart, such as bars, columns, or pie slices

Choosing the Right Type of Chart

When you create a chart in Excel, you can choose from a variety of chart types. Each type interprets data in a slightly different way. For example, a pie chart is great for comparing parts of a whole, such as regional percentages of a sales total, while a column chart is better for showing how different sales regions performed throughout a year. Although there is some overlap, each chart type is best suited for conveying a different type of information.

When you generate a chart, you need to evaluate whether the chart type suits the data being plotted, and whether the formatting choices clarify or overshadow the information. Sometimes a colorful 3-D chart is just what you need to draw attention to an important shift; other times, special visual effects might be a distraction.

An **area chart** shows how value changes over time.

A **bar chart** contains data having different scales.

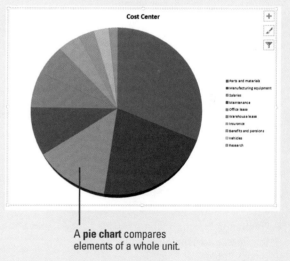

A **pie chart** compares elements of a whole unit.

Creating a Chart

A **chart** provides a visual, graphical representation of numerical data. Charts add visual interest and useful information represented by lines, bars, pie slices, or other markers. A group of data values from a row or column of data makes up a **data series**. Each data series has a unique color or pattern on the chart. Titles on the chart, horizontal (x-axis), and vertical (y-axis) identify the data. Gridlines are horizontal and vertical lines to make it easier to view data values. When you insert a chart, it's placed as an **embedded object**. Office programs use Excel to embed and display a chart. Start by selecting the data, and then choosing the chart type best suited for presenting your data using the Insert tab or Quick Analysis button (**New!**). If you're not sure which type to select, you can choose a recommended chart (**New!**) based on the data. There are a wide variety of chart types—2-D and 3-D— from which to choose.

Insert and Create a Chart

1. Select the data you want to use to create a chart.

2. To quickly create a chart, click the **Quick Analysis** button (**New!**), click **Chart**, and then click a chart button or click **More Charts**, and then click the chart type you want..

3. To create a chart with more control, click the **Insert** tab, and then continue.

4. Use one of the following methods:

   ◆ **Basic Chart Types.** Click a chart button (Column, Line, Pie, Bar, Area, Scatter, Other Charts) in the Charts group, and then click the chart type you want.

   ◆ **All Chart Types.** Click the **Charts Dialog Box Launcher**, click the **All Charts** tab, click a category in the left pane, click a chart, and then click **OK**.

5. To change the chart type, click the **Change Chart Type** button on the Design tab under Chart Tools.

Charts Dialog Box Launcher

Quick Analysis for charts

Basic chart types

Insert and Use a Recommended Chart

1. Select the data you want to use to create a chart.

2. Click the **Insert** tab.

3. Click the **Recommended Charts** button (**New!**).

4. Click the chart type you want from the recommended list.

5. Click **OK**.

Did You Know?

You can quickly create a default chart. Select the data you want to use for the chart, and then press F11 to create a chart on a new sheet, or press Alt+F1 to create an embedded chart on the active worksheet.

You can set the default chart. In the Insert Chart dialog box, click Templates, right-click the chart template you want to set as the default, and then click Set As Default Chart.

You can quickly select a recent chart template. If you want to use a recent chart template, you can quickly select a recently used chart. In the Chart Type dialog box, click Recent (**New!**) in the left pane, select the chart you want to use, and then click OK.

You can edit the contents of chart text. To edit the contents of a title, click the chart or axis title. To edit the contents of a data label, double-click the data label. Click to place the insertion, and then make changes.

Embedded charts are beneficial. A chart sheet is beneficial when you want to view or print a chart or PivotChart report separately from worksheet data or a PivotTable report.

Recently used chart templates

Editing a Chart

Editing a chart means altering any of its features, from data selection to formatting elements. For example, you might want to use more effective colors or patterns in a data series. To change a chart's type or any element within it, you must select the chart or element. When a chart is selected, handles are displayed around the window's perimeter, and chart tools become available on the Design and Format tabs and in the upper-right corner of the selected chart (three chart buttons). The chart buttons (**New!**) on the selected chart include Chart Elements, Chart Styles, and Chart Filters, which provide easy access to chart tools. The Chart Elements button (**New!**) allows you to show or hide chart elements. The Chart Styles button (**New!**) allows you to change the style and color of the chart. The Chart Filters button (**New!**) allows you to filter the data you want to display on the chart.

As the figure below illustrates, you can point to any object or area on a chart to see what it is called. When you select an object, its name appears in the Chart Objects list box on the Format tab, and you can then edit it. A chart consists of the following elements.

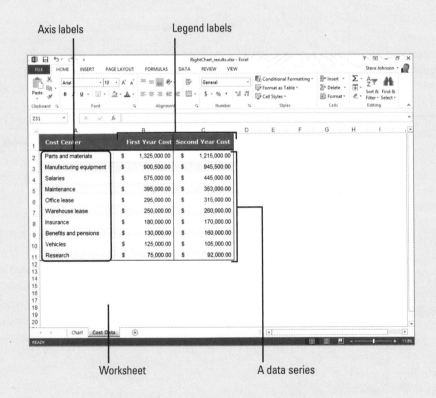

Axis labels

Legend labels

Worksheet

A data series

- **Data markers**. A graphical representation of a data point in a single cell. Typical data markers include bars, dots, or pie slices. Related data markers constitute a data series.

- **Legend**. A pattern or color that identifies each data series.

- **X-axis**. A reference line for the horizontal data values.

- **Y-axis**. A reference line for the vertical data values.

- **Tick marks**. Marks that identify data increments.

Editing a chart has no effect on the data used to create it. You don't need to worry about updating a chart. When you change worksheet data, Excel automatically updates and animates (**New!**) the change in data in the chart. The only chart element you might need to edit is a data range. If you decide you want to plot more or less data in a range, you can select the data series on the worksheet, as shown in the figure below, and then drag the outline to include the range you want in the chart.

Y-axis | Data marker

Chart buttons (**New!**)

Legend

Tick mark | Axis label | X-axis

Moving and Resizing a Chart

You can move or resize an embedded chart after you select it. If you've created a chart as a new sheet instead of an embedded object on an existing worksheet, the chart's size and location are fixed by the sheet's margins. You can change the margins to resize or reposition the chart. If you don't like the location, you can move the embedded chart off the original worksheet and onto another worksheet. When resizing a chart downward, be sure to watch out for legends and axis titles.

Move an Embedded Chart

1 Select a chart you want to move.

2 Position the mouse pointer over a blank area of the chart, and then drag the pointer to move the outline of the chart to a new location.

3 Release the mouse button.

Resize an Embedded Chart

1 Select a chart you want to resize.

2 Position the mouse pointer over one of the handles.

3 Drag the handle to the new chart size.

4 Release the mouse button.

See Also

See "Modifying Picture Size" on page 206 for information on how to size a chart using different methods.

Move a Chart to Another Worksheet

1. Click the chart you want to modify.

2. Click the **Design** tab under Chart Tools.

3. Click the **Move Chart** button.

4. Use one of the following methods:

   ◆ To move the chart to a chart sheet, click the **New sheet** option, and then type a new name for the chart tab.

   ◆ To move the chart to another worksheet as an embedded object, click the **Object in** option, and then select the worksheet you want.

5. Click **OK**.

Selecting Chart Elements

Chart elements are the individual objects that make up a chart, such as an axis, the legend, or a data series. The **plot area** is the bordered area where the data are plotted. The **chart area** is the area between the plot area and the chart elements selection box. Before you can change or format a chart element, you need to select it first. You can select a chart element directly on the chart or use the Chart Elements list arrow on the Ribbon. When you select a chart, handles (small white circles) display around the window's perimeter, and chart tools become available on the Design and Format tabs. When you select an element in a chart, the name of the object appears in the Chart Elements list, which indicates that you can now edit it.

Select a Chart Element

1. Select the chart you want to change.

2. Click the **Format** tab under Chart Tools.

3. Click the **Chart Elements** list arrow.

4. Click the chart element you want to select.

   When a chart object is selected, selection handles appear.

   TIMESAVER *To select a chart object, click a chart element directly in the chart.*

Did You Know?

You can enlarge a chart object to select it. Increase the zoom percentage to enlarge your view before using the mouse pointer to select chart objects.

Changing Chart Elements

The layout of a chart typically comes with a chart title, X and Y axes, axis titles, and a legend. However, you can also include other elements, such as data labels, a data table, and gridlines. A **legend** is a set of labels that helps the reader connect the colors and patterns in a chart with the data they represent. Legend text is derived from the data series plotted within a chart. You can rename an item in a legend by changing the text in the data series. If the legend location doesn't work with the chart, you can reposition it. **Data labels** show data values in the chart to make it easier for the reader to see, while a **Data table** shows the data values in a table next to the chart. To change elements, you can use the Add Chart Element button on the Design tab under Chart Tools or use the Chart Elements button (**New!**) (one of three) in the upper-right corner of the selected chart. If you want a customized look, you can double-click an element to set options using the Format pane (**New!**).

Change the Chart Elements

1. Select the chart you want to modify.

2. Click the **Design** tab under Chart Tools.

3. To quickly show or hide chart elements, click the **Chart Elements** button near the chart, and then select or clear the element check box (**New!**), or click an arrow, and then a command.

4. Click the **Add Chart Element** button (**New!**), and then point to one of the following options:

   - **Axes** to display the horizontal and vertical axes.
   - **Axis Titles** to display the horizontal and vertical axis titles.
   - **Chart Tile** to display or position the main chart title. Double-click the text box to modify text.
   - **Data Labels** to show or hide data labels.
   - **Data Table** to show or hide a data table along with the chart.
   - **Gridlines** to display different types of gridlines.
   - **Legend** to display or position the chart legend.

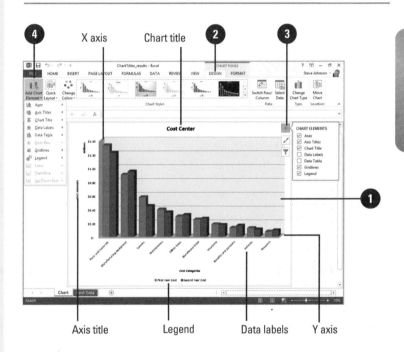

X axis Chart title

Axis title Legend Data labels Y axis

For Your Information

Linking a Chart or Axis Title to a Worksheet Cell

On the chart, click the chart or axis title you want to link, click in the formula bar, type equal sign (=), select the worksheet cell that contains the data or text you want to display in the chart, and then press Enter.

Changing a Chart Type

Your chart is what your audience sees, so make sure to take advantage of Excel's pre-built chart layouts and styles to make the chart appealing and visually informative. Start by choosing the chart type that is best suited for presenting your data. There are a wide variety chart types, available in 2-D and 3-D formats, from which to choose. For each chart type, you can select a predefined chart layout and style to apply the formatting you want. If you want to format your chart beyond the provided formats, you can customize a chart. Save your customized settings so that you can apply that chart formatting to any chart you create. You can change the chart type for the entire chart, or you can change the chart type for a selected data series to create a combination chart (**New!**).

Change a Chart Type for an Entire Chart

1. Select the chart you want to change.

2. Click the **Design** tab under Chart Tools.

3. Click the **Change Chart Type** button.

4. Click the chart type (2-D or 3-D) you want.

5. Click the chart type you want.

6. Click **OK**.

Did You Know?

You can reset chart formatting. Click the chart you want to reset, click the Format tab under Chart Tools, and then click the Reset To Match Style button.

You can delete a chart. Click the chart object, and then press Delete.

Change a Chart Type of a Single Data Series

① Select the data series in a chart you want to change.

You can only change the chart type of one data series at a time.

② Click the **Design** tab under Chart Tools.

③ Click the **Change Chart Type** button.

④ If the chart is 3-D, a dialog box appears, asking you to click **Change Chart** to change the chart to 2-D or click **Keep Chart** to cancel the change.

⑤ Click **Combo** in the left pane (**New!**).

⑥ Click the chart type you want.

⑦ Click the data series you want to change.

⑧ Click the **Chart Type** list arrow for the data series (**New!**), and then click a type.

⑨ To use as a secondary axis, select the **Secondary Axis** check box (**New!**).

⑩ Click **OK**.

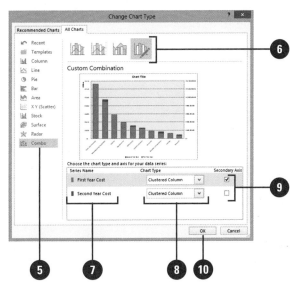

Did You Know?

You can create a pyramid and cone for a 3-D chart. Column and bar charts no longer show the pyramid and code chart types in the Insert and Change Chart Type dialog boxes. For a 3-D column or bar chart, right-click a data series in any 3-D column or bar chart, and then click Format Data Series. Under Column shape or Bar shape, select the shape you want (**New!**).

Changing a Chart Layout and Style

Excel's pre-built chart layouts and styles can make your chart more appealing and visually informative. Start by choosing the chart type that is best suited for presenting your data. There are a wide variety of chart types, available in 2-D and 3-D formats, from which to choose. For each chart type, you can select a predefined chart layout, style, and color to apply the formatting you want. If you want to format your chart beyond the provided formats, you can customize a chart. To change a chart design, you can use layout, style, and color options on the Design tab under Chart Tools or use the Chart Styles button (**New!**) (one of three) in the upper-right corner of the chart.

Change a Chart Layout

1. Select the chart you want to change.

2. Click the **Design** tab under Chart Tools.

3. To change the chart layout, click the **Quick Layout** button in the Chart Layouts group to see variations of the chart type.

4. Click the chart layout you want.

Did You Know?

You can record macros with chart elements. When you use the macro recorder with charts, it now records formatting changes to charts and other objects.

4 Layouts

Apply a Chart Style

1. Select the chart you want to change.

2. Click the **Design** tab under Chart Tools.

3. To quickly change the chart style and colors, click the **Chart Styles** button (**New!**) near the chart, click **STYLE** or **COLOR**, and then click a style or color.

   You can also use options on the Design tab:

   ◆ **Style.** Click the scroll up or down arrow, or click the **More** list arrow for Chart Styles, and then click the chart style you want.

   ◆ **Color.** Click the **Change Colors** button, and then click a color.

More list arrow for Chart Styles

Styles

Formatting Chart Elements

Before you can format a chart element, you need to select it first. You can select a chart element directly on the chart or use the Chart Elements list arrow on the Ribbon. After you select a chart element, you can use the Format Selection button to open the Format pane (**New!**), where you can change formatting options, including number, fill, border color and styles, shadow, 3-D format, and alignment. Formatting options vary depending on the selected chart element. In the same way you can apply shape fills, outlines, and effects to a shape, you can also apply them to elements and shapes in a chart.

Format a Chart Object

1. Select the chart element you want to modify.

2. Click the **Format** tab under Chart Tools.

3. Click the **Format Selection** button.

   ◆ You can also double-click a chart element.

4. In the Format pane (**New!**), click a button (Fill & Line, Effects, or Options), expand a category, and then select the options you want.

   Some common formatting option categories include the following:

   ◆ **Number** to change number formats.

   ◆ **Fill** to remove or change the fill color, either solid, gradient, picture, or texture.

   ◆ **Border** to remove or change the border color and styles, either solid or gradient line.

   ◆ **Shadow** to change shadow options, including color, transparency, size, blur, angle, and distance.

   ◆ **3-D Format** to change 3-D format options, including bevel, depth, contour, and surface.

   ◆ **Alignment** to change text alignment, direction, and angle.

5. Click the **Close** button in the pane.

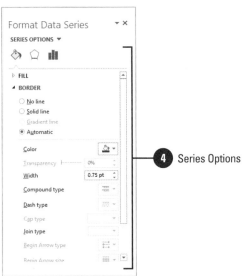

4. Series Options

Apply a Shape Style to a Chart Object

1 Select the chart element you want to modify.

2 Click the **Format** tab under Chart Tools.

3 Click the **Shape Fill**, **Shape Outline**, or **Shape Effects** button, and then click or point to an option.

◆ Fill. Click a color, No Fill, or Picture to select an image, or point to Gradient, or Texture, and then select a style.

◆ Outline. Click a color or No Outline, or point to Weight, or Dashes, and then select a style.

◆ Effects. Point to an effect category (Preset, Shadow, Reflection, Glow, Soft Edges, Bevel, or 3-D Rotations), and then select an option.

Did You Know?

You can quickly access chart formatting options. Double-click a chart element to open the Format pane (**New!**).

Changing Chart Gridlines and Axes

You can change the chart display by showing axis or gridlines with different measurements. An **axis** is a line bordering the chart plot area used as a reference for measurement. Chart axes are typically x (vertical or value), y (horizontal or category), and z (only for 3-D charts). If axis titles or scales are too long and unreadable, you might want to change the angle to make titles fit better in a small space, or change the interval between tick marks and axis labels to display with a better scale. **Tick marks** are small lines of measurement similar to divisions on a ruler on an axis. **Gridlines** are horizontal and vertical lines you can add to help the reader determine data point values in a chart. There are two types of gridlines: major and minor. Major gridlines occur at each value on an axis, while minor gridlines occur between values on an axis. Use gridlines sparingly and only when they improve the readability of a chart. You can select an Options command on th Add Chart Elements button or double-click an element to open the Format pane (**New!**), where you can customize chart settings.

Change Chart Gridlines

1. Select the chart element you want to modify.

2. Click the **Design** tab under Chart Tools.

3. Click the **Add Chart Elements** button, point to **Gridlines**, and then click to toggle on or off any of the following options:

   ◆ **Primary Major Horizontal**

   ◆ **Primary Major Vertical**

   ◆ **Primary Minor Horizontal**

   ◆ **Primary Minor Vertical**

4. To select custom chart gridlines options, click the **Add Chart Elements**, point to **Gridlines**, and then click **More Gridline Options**.

   ◆ In the Format pane (**New!**), click a button (Fill & Line or Effects), expand a category, and then select the gridline options you want.

   ◆ Click the **Close** button in the pane.

Change Chart Axes

1. Select the chart element you want to modify.

2. Click the **Design** tab under Chart Tools.

3. Click the **Add Chart Elements** button, point to **Axes**, and then click to toggle on or off any of the following options:

   ◆ **Primary Horizontal**

   ◆ **Primary Vertical**

4. To select custom chart axes options, click the **Add Chart Elements**, point to **Axes**, and then click **More Axis Options**.

   ◆ In the Format pane (**New!**) under Axis Options, expand a category (Axis Options, Tick Marks, Labels, and Number), and then select the axis options you want.

   ◆ Click the **Close** button in the pane.

Format pane

Close button

Custom axis options in the Format pane

Changing Chart Titles

The layout of a chart typically comes with a chart title, axis titles, and a legend. However, you can also include other elements, such as data labels, and a data table. You can show, hide, or change the positions of these elements to achieve the look you want. The chart title typically appears at the top of the chart. However, you can change the title position to appear as an overlap text object on top of the chart. When you position the chart title as an overlay, the chart is resized to the maximum allowable size. In the same way, you can also reposition horizontal and vertical axis titles to achieve the best fit in a chart. If you want a more custom look, you can set individual options using the Format pane (**New!**).

Change Chart Title

1. Select the chart you want to modify.

2. Click the **Design** tab under Chart Tools.

3. Click the **Add Chart Elements** button, point to **Chart Titles**, and then click one of the following:

   ◆ **None** to hide the chart title.

   ◆ **Above Chart** to position the chart title at the top of the chart and resize it.

   ◆ **Centered Overlay Title** to insert a title on the chart without resizing it.

   ◆ **More Title Options** to set custom chart title options.

4. Double-click the text box to place the insertion point, and then modify the text.

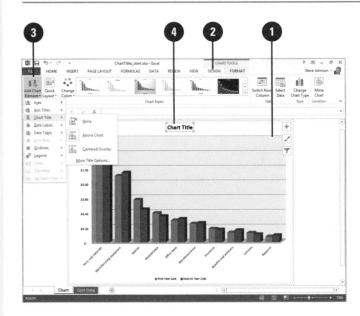

Did You Know?

You can link a chart or axis title to a worksheet cell. On the chart, click the chart or axis title you want to link, click in the formula bar, type an equal sign (=), select the worksheet cell that contains the data or text you want to display in the chart, and then press Enter.

Change Chart Axis Titles

1. Select the chart you want to modify.

2. Click the **Design** tab under Chart Tools.

3. Click the **Add Chart Elements** button, point to **Axis Titles**, and then click to toggle on or off any of the following options:

   ◆ **Primary Horizontal**

   ◆ **Primary Vertical**

4. To select custom chart axes options, click the **Add Chart Elements**, point to **Axes**, and then click **More Axis Title Options**.

   ◆ In the Format pane (**New!**), click a button (Fill & Line, Effects, or Size & Properties), expand a category , and then select the axis title options you want.

   ◆ Click the **Close** button in the pane.

5. To change title text, double-click the text box to place the insertion point, and then modify the text.

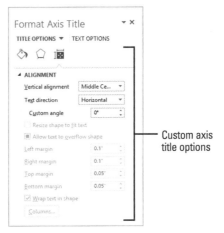

Custom axis title options

Changing Chart Labels

A **legend** is a set of text labels that helps the reader connect the colors and patterns in a chart with the data they represent. Legend text is derived from the data series plotted within a chart. You can rename an item within a legend by changing the text in the data series. If the legend chart location doesn't work with the chart type, you can reposition the legend at the right, left, top or bottom of the chart or overlay the legend on top of the chart on the right or left side. **Data labels** show data values in the chart to make it easier for the reader to see, while a Data table shows the data values in an associated table next to the chart. You can have data labels appears as callouts (**New!**) or just about any shape (**New!**), and even add leader lines (**New!**) to them. You can use the Format tab under Chart Tools to change and format data labels. If you want a customized look, you can set individual options using the Format pane (**New!**).

Change the Chart Legend

1. Select the chart you want to modify.

2. Click the **Design** tab under Chart Tools.

3. Click the **Add Chart Elements** button, point to **Legend**, and then click one of the following:

   ◆ **None** to hide the legend.

   ◆ **Right** to display and align the legend on the right.

   ◆ **Top** to display and align the legend at the top.

   ◆ **Left** to display and align the legend on the left.

   ◆ **Bottom** to display and align the legend at the bottom.

   ◆ **More Legend Options** to set custom legend options.

Change Chart Data Labels

1. Select the chart you want to modify.

2. Click the **Design** tab under Chart Tools.

3. Click the **Add Chart Elements** button, point to **Data Labels**, and then click one of the following:

   ◆ **None** to hide data labels.

   ◆ **Data Callout** to display data labels on the data points using callouts or shapes (**New!**).

   ◆ **More Data Label Options** to set custom data label options. Common options include Series Name, Category Name, Value, and Show Leader Lines (**New!**).

4. To change data callout shapes, select the shapes (**New!**), click the **Format** tab under Chart Tools, and then use the **Change Shape** button or other formatting buttons.

More Data Label Options

Callout shapes (**New!**)

Show or Hide a Chart Data Table

1. Select the chart you want to modify.

2. Click the **Design** tab under Chart Tools.

3. Click the **Add Chart Elements** button, point to **Data Table**, and then click one of the following:

   ◆ **None** to hide a data table.

   ◆ **No Legend Keys** to show the data table below the chart without legend keys.

   ◆ **With Legend Keys** to show the data table below the chart with legend keys.

   ◆ **More Data Table Options** to set custom data table options.

More Data Table Options

Pulling Out a Pie Slice

A pie chart is an effective and easily understood chart type for comparing parts that make up a whole entity, such as departmental percentages of a company budget. You can call attention to individual pie slices that are particularly significant by moving them away from the other pieces, or **exploding** the pie. Not only will this make a visual impact, it will also restate the values you are graphing.

Explode a Pie Slice

1. Select a pie chart.

2. To explode a single slice, click to select the pie slice you want to explode.

3. Drag the slice away from the pie.

4. Release the mouse button.

Did You Know?

You can select a pie slice to make it stand out. Because a pie chart has only one data series, clicking any slice selects the entire data series. Click a second time to select a specific slice.

Undo a Pie Explosion

1. Select a pie chart.

2. Drag a slice toward the center of the pie.

3. Release the mouse button.

Formatting Chart Data Series

If you want to further enhance a chart, you can insert a picture in a chart so that its image occupies a bar or column. You can use the Format Selection button to open the Format pane (**New!**) and change column and 3-D gap depth and width and shape (**New!**), including box, pyramid, cylinder, or cone. Fill options to format a chart data series with a solid, gradient, picture, or texture fill. In addition, you can also change a chart data series with a border color, border style, shadow, glow, soft edges, and 3-D formats, which include bevel, depth, contour, and surface styles.

Format a Chart Data Series

1️⃣ Select the chart series you want to modify.

2️⃣ Click the **Format** tab under Chart Tools.

3️⃣ Click the **Format Selection** button.

◆ You can also double-click a chart element.

4️⃣ In the Format pane (**New!**), click a button (Fill & Line, Effects, or Series Options), expand a category, and then select the options you want:

◆ **Series Options** to change the gap width and depth (for 3-D charts), or series overlap (for 2-D charts), and change the shape to a box, pyramid, cone, or cylinder (for 3-D charts).

◆ **Fill** to remove or change the fill, either solid color, gradient, picture, or texture.

◆ **Border** to remove or change the border color and styles, either solid or gradient line.

◆ **Shadow, Glow, and Soft Edges** to change options, including presets, color, transparency, size, blur, angle, and distance.

◆ **3-D Format** to change 3-D format options, including bevel, depth, contour, and surface.

5️⃣ Click the **Close** button in the pane.

Formatting Chart Text

Objects such as chart and axis titles, data labels, and annotated text are referred to as chart text. To make chart text more readable, you can use formatting tools on the Home or Format tabs to change the text font, style, and size. For example, you might decide to change your chart title size and alignment, or change your axis text color. If you want to change the way text appears, you can also rotate text to a diagonal angle or vertical orientation. On the Format tab under Chart Tools, you can apply WordArt and Shape Styles to chart text.

Format Chart Text

1 Select the chart that contains the text you want to change.

2 Select the text object in the chart you want to format.

If you want to select only a portion of the text, click the text object again to place the insertion point, and then select the part of the text you want to format.

3 Click the **Format** tab under Chart Tools, and then click the WordArt or Shape Style you want.

4 Click the **Home** tab.

5 In the Font group, select any combination of options: Font, Font Size, Increase Font Size, Decrease Font Size, Bold, Italic, Underline, Fill Color, or Font Color.

6 In the Alignment group, select any combination of alignment options.

TIMESAVER *To quickly format chart text, right-click the text, and then click a formatting button on the Mini-Toolbar.*

7 To set custom text formatting options, click the **Font** or **Alignment Dialog Box Launcher**.

Selection for axis label change

Selection for WordArt change

Formatting Line and Bar Charts

If you're using a line or bar chart, you can add trendlines, series lines, drop lines, high-low lines, up/down bars, or error bars with different options to make the chart easier to read. **Trendlines** are graphical representations of trends in data that you can use to analyze problems of prediction. For example, you can add a trendline to forecast a trend toward rising revenue. **Series lines** connect data series in 2-D stacked bar and column charts. **Drop lines** extend a data point to a category in a line or area chart, which makes it easy to see where data markers begin and end. **High-low lines** display the highest to the lowest value in each category in 2-D charts. Stock charts are examples of high-low lines and up/down bars. **Error bars** show potential error amounts graphically relative to each data marker in a data series. Error bars are usually used in statistical or scientific data. To format these charts, you can use the Add Chart Element button (**New!**) on the Design tab under Chart Tools.

Format Line and Bar Charts

1. Select the line or bar chart you want to modify.

2. Click the **Design** tab under Chart Tools.

3. Click the **Add Chart Element** button (**New!**), and then point to one of the following options:

   ◆ **Trendline** to remove or add different types of trendlines: Linear, Exponential, Linear Forecast, and Two Period Moving Average.

   ◆ **Lines** to hide Drop Lines, High-Low Lines or Series Lines, or show series lines on a 2-D stacked Bar/Column Pie or Pie or Bar of Pie chart.

   ◆ **Up/Down Bars** to hide Up/Down Bars, or show Up/Down Bars on a line chart.

   ◆ **Error Bars** to hide error bars or show error bars with using Standard Error, Percentage, or Standard Deviation.

Trend line

Changing the Chart Background

Format the background of a chart by showing or hiding the chart wall or floor with a default color fill, or by changing the 3-D view of a chart. The **chart area** is the entire chart, while the **plot area** is bounded by the axes, which includes all data series. The **chart wall** is the background (all, back or side), and the **chart floor** is the bottom in a 3-D chart. The 3-D view allows you to change the rotation of a 3-D chart using the x-, y-, or z-axis, and apply a 3-D perspective to the chart.

Change the Chart Background

1. Select the chart element you want to modify.

2. Click the **Format** tab under Chart Tools.

3. Click the **Chart Elements** list arrow, and then click the chart element you want to select.

   ◆ **Chart Area** to format the chart background.

   ◆ **Plot Area** to format the area bounded by axes.

   ◆ **Walls, Back Wall, or Side Wall** to format the background (all walls, back wall or side wall).

   ◆ **Floor** to format the bottom in a 3-D chart.

4. Click the **Format Selection** button.

   ◆ You can also double-click a chart element.

5. In the Format pane (**New!**), click a button (Fill & Line, Effects, or Size & Properties), expand a category, and then select the options you want.

   For 3-D charts, you can set the following:

   ◆ **3_D Rotation** under Effects to change the 3-D viewpoint of the chart.

   ◆ **3-D Format** under Effects to change 3-D format options, including bevel, depth, contour, and surface.

6. Click the **Close** button in the pane.

Plot area

Chart wall

Chart floor

Enhancing a Chart

If you want to further enhance a chart, you can insert a picture, shape or text annotation to add visual appeal. In the same way you insert a picture, shape, or text box into a worksheet, you can insert them into a chart. The Picture, Shapes, and Text Box options are available on the Format tab under Chart Tools.

Insert a Picture, Shape, or Text

1. Select the chart element you want to modify.

2. Click the **Format** tab under Chart Tools.

3. Use any of the following:

   - ◆ **Picture.** Click the **Shape Fill** button, click **Picture**, select a picture, and then click **Insert**.

   - ◆ **Shapes.** Click the **More** list arrow for Insert Shapes, click a shape, and then drag to draw the shape.

   - ◆ **Text Box.** Click the **More** list arrow for Insert Shapes, click the Text Box button, drag to create a text box, and then type the text you want.

4. Click the **Format** tab under Drawing Tools, and then format the shape or text box.

Arrow shape   Text box

Did You Know?

You can edit shape text. Right-click the shape or text object, click Edit Text, modify the text, and then click outside the object to deselect it.

You can convert a chart to a picture. Select the chart, click the Home tab, click the Copy button, click the Paste button arrow, point to As Picture, and then click Paste As Picture. Instead of using Paste As Picture, you can use Paste Special to paste a chart as a picture with a specific graphic format, such as PNG, JPEG, GIF, Enhanced Metafile, or Bitmap.

Editing Chart Data

You can edit chart data in a worksheet one cell at a time, or you can manipulate a range of data. If you're not sure what data to change to get the results you want, use the Edit Data Source dialog box to help you. In previous versions, you were limited to 32,000 data points in a data series for 2-D charts. Now you can have as much as your memory to store. You can work with data ranges by series, either Legend or Horizontal. The Legend series is the data range displayed on the axis with the legend, while the Horizontal series is the data range displayed on the other axis. Use the Collapse Dialog button to temporarily minimize the dialog to select the data range you want. After you select your data, click the Expand Dialog button to return back to the dialog box.

Edit Data in the Worksheet

1. In the worksheet, use any of the following methods to edit cell contents:

   ◆ To replace the cell contents, click the cell, type the data you want to enter in the cell. It replaces the previous entry.

   ◆ To edit the cell content, double-click the selected cell where you want to edit.

   Press Delete or Backspace to delete one character at a time, and then type the new data.

2. Press Enter to move the insertion point down one row or press Tab to move the insertion point right to the next cell.

Did You Know?

You can plot data series from rows or columns. Select the chart, click the Design tab under Chart Tools, and then click the Switch Row/Column button. This switches between plotting the data series in a chart from worksheet rows or from columns.

Edit the Data Source

1. Click the chart you want to modify.

2. Click the **Design** tab under Chart Tools.

3. Click the **Select Data** button on the Design tab under Chart Tools.

4. In the Select Data Source dialog box, use any of the following:

   IMPORTANT *Click the **Collapse Dialog** button to minimize the dialog, so you can select a range in the worksheet. Click the **Expand Dialog** button to maximize it again.*

   ◆ **Chart data range.** Displays the data range of the plotted chart.

   ◆ **Switch Row/Column.** Click to switch plotting the data series from rows or columns.

   ◆ **Add.** Click to add a new Legend data series to the chart.

   ◆ **Edit.** Click to make changes to a Legend or Horizontal series.

   ◆ **Remove.** Click to remove the selected Legend data series.

   ◆ **Move Up and Move Down.** Click to move a Legend data series up or down in the list.

   ◆ **Show or Hide.** Click to select or deselect check boxes (**New!**) to show or hide data.

   ◆ **Hidden and Empty Cells.** Click to plot hidden data and determine what to do with empty cells.

5. Click **OK**.

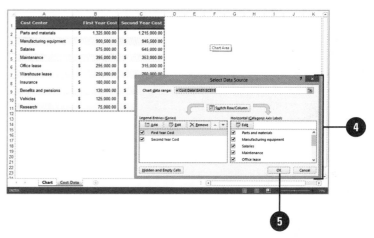

For Your Information

Displaying Hidden Data and Empty Cells in Charts

Hidden data in rows and columns of a worksheet is not displayed in a chart and empty cells are displayed as gaps. In the Select Data Source dialog box, you can click the Hidden and Empty Cells button to change the way Excel displays hidden data and empty cells in a chart. You can set options to show data in hidden rows and columns and show empty cells as a zero or connect data points with a line.

Adding and Deleting a Data Series

Many components make up a chart. Each range of data that comprises a bar, column, or pie slice is called a **data series**; each value in a data series is called a **data point**. The data series is defined when you select a range on a worksheet and then open the Chart Wizard. But what if you want to add a data series once a chart is complete? You can add a data series by using the Design tab under Chart Tools, or using the mouse. As you create and modify more charts, you might also find it necessary to show or hide data (**New!**), or delete or change the order of one or more data series. You can delete a data series without re-creating the chart.

Add a Data Series Quickly

1. Click the chart you want to modify.

2. Click the **Design** tab under Chart Tools, and then click the **Select Data** button.

3. Click **Add**.

4. Enter a data series name, specify the data series range, and then click **OK**.

5. To show or hide data, select or deselect a check box (**New!**).

6. Click **OK**.

Delete a Data Series

1. Click the chart you want to modify.

2. Click the **Design** tab under Chart Tools, and then click the **Select Data** button.

3. Click the data series you want to delete.

4. Click **Remove**.

5. To show or hide data, select or deselect a check box (**New!**).

6. Click **OK**.

Change a Data Series

1. Click the chart you want to modify.

2. Click the **Design** tab under Chart Tools, and then click the **Select Data** button.

3. Click the series name you want to change.

4. Click **Edit**.

5. Click the **Collapse Dialog** button to change the series name or values, make the change, and then click the **Expand Dialog** button.

6. Click **OK**.

7. Click **OK**.

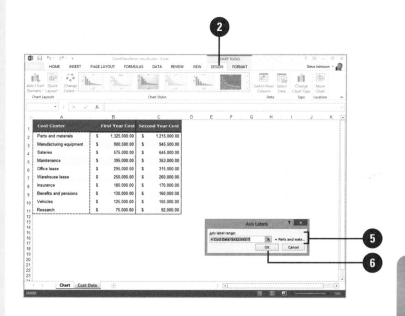

Change Data Series Order

1. Click the chart you want to modify.

2. Click the **Design** tab under Chart Tools, and then click the **Select Data** button.

3. Click the series name you want to change.

4. To switch data series position, click the **Switch Row/Column** button.

5. To reorder the data series, click the **Move Up** or **Move Down** button.

6. Click **OK**.

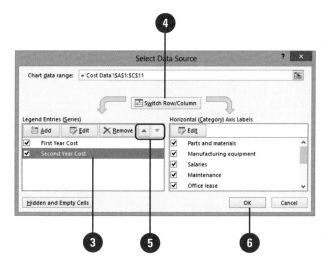

Saving a Chart Template

A chart template file (.crtx) saves all the customization you made to a chart for use in other workbooks. You can save any chart in a workbook as a chart template file and use it to form the basis of your next workbook chart, which is useful for standard company financial reporting. Although you can store your template anywhere you want, you may find it handy to store it in the Templates/Charts folder that Excel and Microsoft Office uses to store its templates. If you store your design templates in the Templates/Charts folder, those templates appear as options when you insert or change a chart type using My Templates. When you create a new chart or want to change the chart type of an existing chart, you can apply a chart template instead of re-creating it.

Create a Custom Chart Template

1. Click the chart you want to save as a template.

2. Right-click the chart, and then click **Save As Template**.

   ◆ The Save As Template button on the Design tab under Chart Tools is no longer available in Excel 2013 (**New!**).

3. Make sure the Charts folder appears in the Save in box.

   Microsoft Office templates are typically stored in the following location:

   Windows 8 or 7. C:/Users/*your name*/AppData/Roaming/Microsoft/Templates/Charts

4. Type a name for the chart template.

5. Click **Save**.

Chart template file format

Apply a Chart Template

1. Use one of the following methods:

   ◆ **New chart.** Click the **Insert** tab, and then click the **Charts Dialog Box Launcher**.

   ◆ **Change chart.** Select the chart you want to change, click the **Design** tab under Chart Tools, and then click the **Change Chart Type** button.

2. In the left pane, click **Templates**.

   ◆ **Recent chart.** Click **Recent** (**New!**) in the left pane.

3. Click the custom chart type you want.

4. Click **OK**.

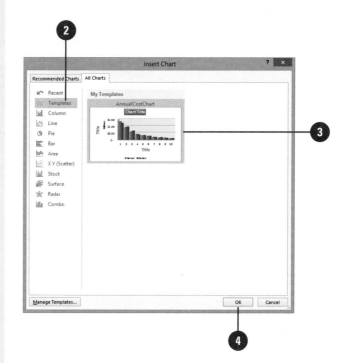

Did You Know?

You can quickly select a recent chart template. If you want to use a recent chart template, you can quickly select a recently used chart. In the Chart Type dialog box, click Recent (**New!**) in the left pane, select the chart you want to use, and then click OK.

You can set a chart template as the default. If you use the same chart template over and over again, you can set a chart as the default when creating a new chart. In the Chart Type dialog box, click Templates in the left pane, right-click the chart you want to use, and then click Set As Default Chart, and then click Cancel.

Managing Chart Templates

If you no longer need a chart template, you can use the Chart Type dialog box to access and manage chart templates files (.crtx). You can click the Manage Templates button to open the Charts folder and move, copy, or delete chart templates. Microsoft Office stores chart template files in the Charts folder, so all Office programs can use them. When you store templates in the Charts folder, those templates appear as options when you insert or change a chart type using My Templates. So, if you no longer need a chart template, you can move it from the Charts template folder for later use or you can permanently delete it from your computer.

Move or Delete a Custom Chart Template

1. Select a chart.

2. Click the **Design** tab under Chart Tools.

3. Click the **Change Chart Type** button.

   TIMESAVER *To open the Chart Types dialog box, you can click the Charts Dialog Box Launcher on the Insert tab.*

4. Click **Templates** in the left pane.

5. Click **Manage Templates**.

   The Charts folder opens.

   Windows 8 or 7. C:/Users/*your name*/AppData/Roaming/Microsoft/Templates/Charts

6. To move a chart template file from the Charts folder, drag it to the folder where you want to store it, or right-click the file and use the Cut and Paste commands.

7. To delete a chart template file, right-click it, and then click **Delete**.

8. When you're done, click the **Close** button.

9. Click **Cancel** in the Change Chart Type dialog box.

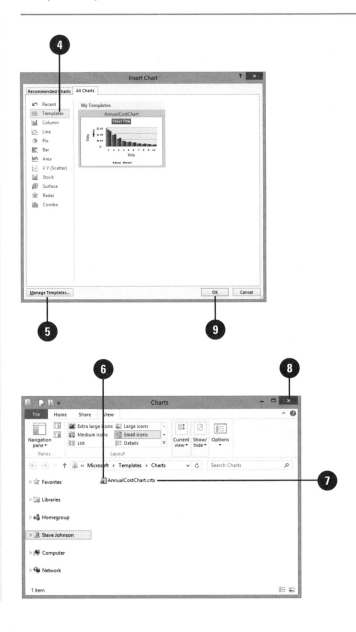

Analyzing Worksheet Data

Introduction

In addition to using a worksheet to calculate values, you can also use it to manage and analyze a table of information. For example, you can create an inventory list, a school grade book, or a customer database. You can quickly turn a range of cells into a table (previously referred to as an Excel list), and then format the data using Quick Styles. Additionally, you can insert and delete rows and columns, create a calculation column, display and calculate data totals, and reference a table by name instead of by cells.

Controlling how data is entered decreases errors and makes a worksheet more reliable. Data entry in a table is enhanced by features such as a pick list to ensure restricted field entry, and adding data validation rules which will restrict the entry of data into certain fields. You can also create a drop-down list of entries you define to help provide consistent, accurate data entry.

Sorting data in your list can be accomplished a few ways: one with the sort ascending or descending buttons, the other by using Excel's AutoFilter option. By typing in a set field to sort by, you can pull all the records in your list that contain a matching field. PivotTables are also available to pull your data together for easier viewing, filtering, and reporting. Excel has some designed reports that contain layout formatting to give that extra touch to your reports. You can also use Power View to visually interact with PivotTable data. You can create and interact with charts and maps, slicers, and other data visualizations and filter out the data you want. In addition, you can use PowerPivot to build simple data models directly in Excel. PowerPivot is helpful when you want to import, filter out, and quickly process millions of rows of data from multiple data sources.

What You'll Do

Understand Tables

Create and Format a Table

Create or Modify a Table Style

Format Table Elements

Create Calculations in a Table

Work with Tables

Remove Table Rows and Columns

Enter Data in a Table Using a Drop-Down List

Sort Data in a Table

Display Parts of a Table with AutoFilter

Create Custom Searches

Use Slicers to Filter a Table

Export a Table to a SharePoint List

Analyze Data Using a PivotTable or PivotChart

Modify a PivotTable and PivotChart

Use Slicers to Filter a PivotTable

Display a Timeline to Filter a PivotTable

Chart a PivotTable

Use Power View and PowerPivot

Create Groups and Outlines

Convert Text to Columns

Add Data Validation to a Worksheet

Create a Drop-Down List

Understanding Tables

A **table** is a series of rows and columns with data you manage separately from other data in a worksheet. Examples of tables are an address book, a list of customers or products, and a telephone directory. In Excel 2007, you can turn a range of cells into a table (previously referred to as an Excel list) to make it easier to manage and analyze a group of data. You can create more than one table in the same worksheet. However, you cannot create a table in a shared workbook.

When you create a table, Excel adds filtering in the header row where you can sort data by order or color, and filter data by criteria. After you create a table, you can easily format table data using Quick Styles. Additionally, you can insert and delete table rows and columns, create a calculation column, display and calculate data totals, reference the table by name instead of by cells, use built-in data validation to ensure data integrity, and export a table to a SharePoint list.

Record
One set of related fields, such as all the fields pertaining to one customer or product. In a worksheet, each row represents a unique record.

List range
The block of cell that contains some or all of the list you want to analyze. The list range cannot occupy more than one worksheet.

Field name
The title of a field. In an Excel list, the first row contains the names of each field. Each field name can have up to 255 characters, including uppercase and lowercase letters and spaces.

Field
One piece of information, such as customer's last name or an item's code number. On a worksheet, each cell represents a field.

Creating a Table

To create a table in Excel, you can enter data on worksheet cells, just as you do on any other worksheet data, but the placement of the field names and range must follow these rules: (1) Enter field names in a single row that is the first row in the list (2) Enter each record in a single row (3) Do not include any blank rows within the range (4) Do not use more than one worksheet for a single range. You can enter data directly in the table. Don't worry about entering records in any particular order; Excel tools can organize an existing list alphabetically, by date, or in almost any order you can imagine. You can create a table in a snap with the Quick Analysis tool (**New!**) or use the Table button to have a little more control over the results.

Create a Table

1. Open a blank worksheet, or use a worksheet that has enough empty columns and rows for your table.

2. Enter a label for each field in adjacent columns across the first row of the table.

3. Enter field content for each record in its own row; start with the row directly below the field names.

4. Select the range of cells for the table, including labels.

5. Do any of the following:

   - **Quick Analysis Tool.** Click the **Quick Analysis** button (**New!**), click **Tables**, and then click the **Table** button.

   - **Table Button.** Click the **Insert** tab, and then click the **Table** button. Adjust the table size, and select the **My table has headers** check box. Click **OK**.

Did You Know?

You can delete or clear a data table. Select the table, and then press Delete to delete the entire table. Select the table, click the Home tab, click the Clear button, and then click Clear Contents.

Table button

Insert Table dialog box

Quick Analysis tool

Table

Formatting a Table

Formatting worksheet table data can be quick and easy with Table Quick Styles. To make formatting data more efficient, Excel has a gallery of table styles based on the current theme. A table style includes preset combinations of fill colors and patterns, font attributes, borders, and font colors that are professionally designed to enhance your worksheets. You can apply a Table Quick Style using the Home (Format as Table button) or Design tab (Quick Styles button (**New!**)) under Table Tools.

Apply a Quick Style to a Table

1. Select a cell or range in the table to which you want to apply a Quick Style.

2. Do any of the following:

   ◆ Click the **Design** tab under Table Tools, and then click the **Quick Styles** button (**New!**).

   ◆ Click the **Home** tab, and then click the **Format as Table** button.

3. Select a table style.

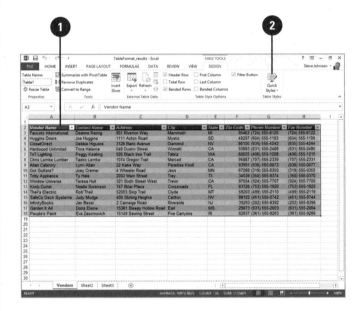

Did You Know?

You can copy cell formats with Format Painter. Select the cell or range whose formatting you want to copy, double-click the Format Painter button on the Home tab, select the cells you want to format, and then click the Format Painter button.

You can remove or clear a table style. Click a cell in the table, click the Design tab under Table Tools, click the More list arrow under Table Styles, and then click Clear.

You can print an Excel table. Click a cell within the table, click the File tab, click Print, click the Print What list arrow, click Print Selected Table, and then click Print.

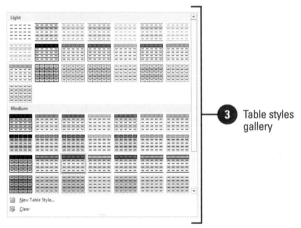

Table styles gallery

Creating or Modifying a Table Style

Excel Table Quick Styles give any worksheet a professional look, but you may need to modify a Quick Style to better suit the needs of a particular project. For example, the Quick Style you applied might be perfect except that the font or color used should be different—to match the rest of your report. You can modify an existing Table Quick Style or create a new one from scratch. When you create or modify a Table Quick Style, you have the option to set the table style as the default when you create a new table.

Create or Modify a Table Style

① Click the **Home** tab.

② Click the **Format as Table** button.

③ Do any of the following:

   ◆ **Create.** Click **New Table Style**.

   ◆ **Modify.** Right-click the style you want to change, and then click **Modify**.

④ Type a name for the Quick Style.

⑤ Select a table element.

⑥ Click **Format**.

⑦ Use the Font, Border, and Fill tabs to set formatting options you want, and then click **OK**.

⑧ Repeat steps 5 through 7 to complete the formatting you want.

⑨ Select or clear the **Set as default table quick style for this document** check box.

⑩ When you're done, click **OK**.

Did You Know?

You can delete a custom table style. Click the Home tab, click the Format As Table button, right-click the custom style you want to delete, and then click Delete.

Formatting Table Elements

When you create a table in a worksheet, Excel displays a standard set of elements, including headings, columns, and rows. You can select options on the Design tab under Table Tools to quickly format a table. These options allow you to format the header row, and first and last column as special. You can also format even columns or rows differently than odd columns or rows. If you want to total numbers in a column, you can format the bottom row of a table for column totals. If you want to customize a list to certain items, you can set AutoFilters, which you access using a Filter button (**New!**) (drop-down list arrow). If you no longer want these formatting elements, you can hide them. If you hide the header row, the table header AutoFilters and any applied filters are removed from the table.

Show or Hide Table Formatting Elements

1. Select a cell or range in the table you want to modify.

2. Click the **Design** tab under Table Tools.

3. Select or clear the check box for the element you want to show or hide:

   ◆ **Header Row** to format the top row of the table as special.

   ◆ **Total Row** to format the bottom row of the table for column totals.

   ◆ **First Column** to format the first column of the table as special.

   ◆ **Last Column** to format the last column of the table as special.

   ◆ **Banded Columns** to format even columns differently than odd columns.

   ◆ **Banded Rows** to format even rows differently than odd rows.

   ◆ **Filter Button** (**New!**) (drop-down list arrow) to filter elements in a list.

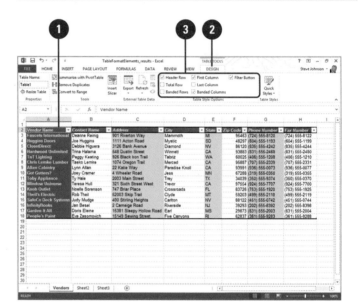

Creating Calculations in a Table

You can quickly total data in a table using the Total Row option. When you display a total row at the end of the table, a drop-down list appears for each total cell along with the word *Total* in the leftmost cell. The drop-down list allows you to select a function to perform a calculation. If the function you want is not available in the drop-down list, you can enter any formula you want in a total row cell. If you're not using a total function, you can delete the word *Total*.

Total the Data in a Table

1. Click a cell in a table.

2. Click the **Design** tab under Table Tools.

3. Select the **Total Row** check box.

   The total row appears as the last row in the table and displays the word *Total* in the leftmost cell.

4. Click the cell in the column for which you want to calculate a total, and then click the drop-down list arrow.

5. From the drop-down list, select the function you want to use to calculate the total.

   TIMESAVER *Enter a formula in the row directly below a table without a total row to create a total row without the word Total.*

Did You Know?

You can create a calculated column. A calculated column uses a single formula that adjusts for each row in a table. To create a calculated column, click a cell in a blank table column, and then type a formula. The formula is automatically filled into all cells of the column. Not every cell in a calculated column needs to be the same. You can enter a different formula or data to create an exception.

Working with Tables

After you create a table, you can sort the entries, add new entries, and display totals. You can insert rows anywhere in a table or add rows at the bottom of the table. To add a blank row at the end of the table, select any cell in the last row of the table, and then press Enter, or press Tab in the last cell of the last row. If you no longer need the data in table form, you can convert the list back to normal Excel data. Selecting table rows and columns is different than selecting worksheet rows and columns. Selecting cells is the same.

Insert a Row or Column

1. Click a cell in the table where you want to insert a row or column. To insert multiple rows or columns, select more than one row or column.

2. Click the **Home** tab.

3. Click the **Insert** button arrow, and then do one of the following:

   ◆ **Rows.** Click **Insert Table Rows Above** or **Insert Table Rows Below**.

   ◆ **Columns.** Click **Insert Table Columns to the Left** or **Insert Table Columns to the Right**.

Select Rows and Columns

◆ **Column**. Click the top edge of the column header or the column in the table to select column data (press Ctrl+Spacebar). Double-click the top edge to select the entire column (press Ctrl+Spacebar twice).

◆ **Row**. Click the left border of the row.

◆ **Entire Table**. Click the upper-left corner of the table to select table data (press Ctrl+A). Double-click the upper-left corner to select the entire table (press Ctrl+A twice).

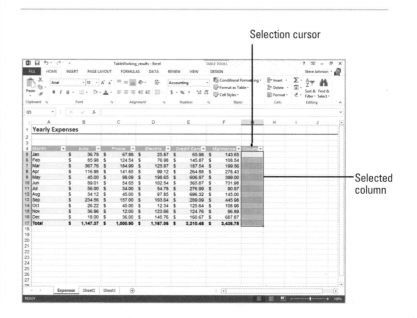

Selection cursor

Selected column

Resize a Table

1. Click a cell in the table.

2. Click the **Design** tab under Table Tools.

3. Click the **Resize Table** button.

4. Type the range you want to use for the table.

   You can click the **Collapse Dialog** button, select the range you want, and then click the **Expand Dialog** button.

   TIMESAVER *To resize the table using the mouse, drag the triangular resize handle at the lower-right corner of the table to select the range you want.*

5. Click **OK**.

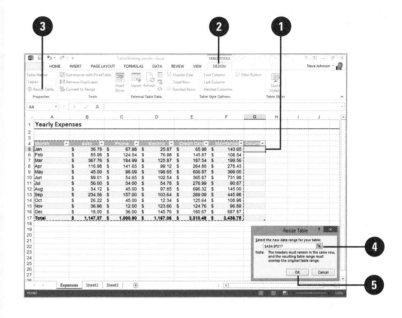

Convert a Table to a Range

1. Click a cell in the table.

2. Click the **Design** tab under Table Tools.

3. Click the **Convert to Range** button.

4. Click **Yes** to confirm the change.

Removing Table Rows and Columns

If you no longer need a row or column in a table, you can quickly remove it using Delete commands on the Home tab. You delete rows and columns in a table the same way you delete rows and columns in a worksheet. As you enter data in a table, sometimes you accidentally enter the same data more than once. Instead of searching for duplicates manually, Excel can search for duplicates and then remove them for you.

Delete Rows or Columns from a Table

1. Click a cell in the table where you want to delete a row or column.

2. Click the **Home** tab.

3. Click the **Delete** button arrow, and then click **Delete Table Rows** or **Delete Table Columns**.

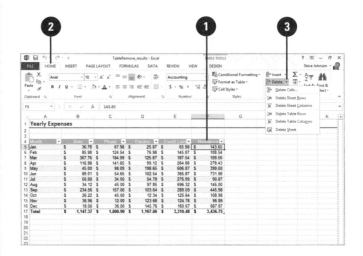

Remove Duplicate Rows from a Table

1. Click a cell in the table.

2. Click the **Design** tab under Table Tools.

3. Click the **Remove Duplicates** button.

4. Select the columns with duplicates you want to remove. You can click **Select All** or **Unselect All**.

5. Click **OK**.

6. Click **OK** to remove duplicates.

Entering Data in a Table Using a Drop-Down List

Entering data in a list can be tedious and repetitive. You can enter data using the PickList or List AutoFill feature to make the job easier. **PickList** is activated once you have entered at least one record in the list; it uses your previous entries to save you the trouble of typing repetitive information. PickList displays previous entries made in the current field in a list format. **List AutoFill** automatically extends the list's formatting and formulas to adjacent cells. As data is added to a list, AutoFill looks at the preceding cells to determine what formatting and formulas should be extended.

Enter Data in a List Using Pick From Drop-Down List

1. Right-click the cell in which you want to use PickList, and then click **Pick From Drop-Down List**.

2. Click a selection in the list.

3. Press Enter or Tab to accept the entry, or press Esc to cancel the entry.

See Also

See "Creating a Drop-Down List" on page 338 for information on creating a drop-down list using data validation.

Sorting Data in a Table

After you enter records in a list, you can reorganize the information by sorting the records. For example, you might want to sort records in a client list alphabetically by last name or numerically by their last invoice date. **Ascending order** lists records from A to Z, earliest to latest, or lowest to highest. **Descending order** lists records from Z to A, latest to earliest, or highest to lowest. You can sort the entire list or use AutoFilter to select the part of the list you want to display in the column. You can also sort a list based on one or more **sort fields**—fields you select to sort the list. A sort, for example, might be the telephone directory numerically by area code and then alphabetically by last name. If you have manually or conditionally formatted a range or table column by cell or font color or by an icon set, you can sort by these cell attributes using the Sort button.

Sort Data Quickly

1. Click the table cell with the field name by which you want to sort.

   ◆ You can also click a column header list arrow, and then click **Sort A to Z** or **Sort Z to A**.

2. Click the **Data** tab.

3. Click the **Sort Ascending** or the **Sort Descending** button.

   The list arrow displays an icon indicating the field is sorted.

4. To clear or reapply a data sort, do the following:

   ◆ To clear all filters in a worksheet and redisplay all rows, click the **Clear** button.

   ◆ To reapply a filter, click the **Reapply** button.

Column header list arrow

Did You Know?

You can sort data in rows. If the data you want to sort is listed across a row instead of down a column, click the table cell you want to sort by, click the Data tab, click the Sort button, click the Sort Left To Right option, and then click OK.

Sort a Table Using Multiple Fields and Attributes

1. Click anywhere within the table range.

2. Click the **Data** tab.

3. Click the **Sort** button.

4. Click the **Column** list arrow, and then select a sort field.

5. Click the **Sort on** list arrow, and then select a sort field: **Values**, **Cell Color**, **Font Color**, or **Cell Icon**.

   ◆ You can also click a column header list arrow, point to **Sort by Color**, click **Custom Sort**, and then use **Font Color** or **Cell Color** option for Sort On.

6. Click the **Order** list arrow, and then select a sort field: **A to Z**, **Z to A**, or **Custom List**.

7. To add another level of sorting, click **Add Level**, and then repeat steps 4 through 6.

8. To change the sort order, select a sort, and then click the **Move Up** or **Move Down** buttons.

9. To delete or copy a sort level, select a sort, and then click the **Delete Level** or **Copy Level**.

10. Click **OK**.

    The list arrow displays an icon indicating the field is sorted.

Sort results

Did You Know?

You can sort data with the case sensitive option. Click the table cell you want to sort by, click the Data tab, click the Sort button, click Options, select the Case Sensitive check box, and then click OK.

Displaying Parts of a Table with AutoFilter

Working with a list that contains numerous records can be difficult—unless you can narrow your view of the list. For example, rather than looking through an entire inventory list, you might want to see records that come from one distributor. The **AutoFilter** feature creates a list of the items found in each field, which is useful in tables and PivotTables. You select the items that you want to display in the column field by using the column header list arrow and AutoFilter menu. The column headers in a table now remain visible in long lists for ease of use. In the AutoFilter menu, you can use the Search box to quickly find what you want in a long list. Then you can work with the filtered list.

Display Specific Records Using AutoFilter

1. Click anywhere within the table.

2. Click the **Data** tab.

3. If necessary, click the **Filter** button to highlight and turn it on.

4. Click the column header list arrow where you want to set filter criteria.

5. Select the filter criteria you want:

   ◆ **Select Items.** Select the items that records must match to be included in the table.

   ◆ **Search.** Enter search criteria, and then press Enter.

   ◆ **Built-in Filters.** Point to **<Column Name> Filters**, and then select a filter option.

6. Repeat steps 4 and 5 to filter out more records using other fields.

   The list arrow displays an icon indicating the field is filtered.

7. To clear a filter, click the list arrow of the field, and then click **Clear Filter From <Column Name>**.

   ◆ To clear all filters and redisplay all rows, click the **Clear** button.

   ◆ To reapply a filter, click the **Reapply** button.

8. To turn off AutoFilter, click the **Filter** button to deselect it.

Creating Custom Searches

There are many times you'll want to search for records that meet multiple criteria. For example, you might want to see out-of-stock records of those orders purchased from a particular distributor. Using the AutoFilter feature and the Custom command, you can create complex searches. You can use **logical operators** to measure whether an item in a record qualifies as a match with the selected criteria. You can also use the **logical conditions** AND and OR to join multiple criteria within a single search. The result of any search is either true or false; if a field matches the criteria, the result is true. The OR condition requires that only one criterion be true in order for a record to qualify. The AND condition, on the other hand, requires that both criteria in the statement be true in order for the record to qualify.

Create a Custom Search Using AutoFilter

1. Click anywhere within the table range.

2. Click the **Data** tab.

3. Click the list arrow next to the first field you want to include in the search.

4. Point to **<type> Filter**, and then click **Custom Filter** to enable the command (a check mark appears).

5. Click the **Field** list arrow (on the left), and then select a logical operator.

6. Click the list arrow (on the right), and then select a field choice.

7. If you want, click the **And** or **Or** option.

8. If you want, click the list arrow (on the left), and then select a logical operator.

9. If you want, click the list arrow (on the right), and then select a field choice.

10. Click **OK**.

The list arrow displays an icon indicating the field is filtered.

Using Slicers to Filter a Table

Instead of using the AutoFilter menu each time you want to filter data in a table, you can create a slicer (**New!**) button that enables you to quickly filter data in a table with a single click. Each slicer is shown on the screen with button labels that indicate the data being filtered. A slicer includes a header, filtering buttons, a Clear Filter button, a scroll bar, and move and resize controls. You can have more than one slicer and move them around on the worksheet. You can also format slicers with styles to match the look and feel of your worksheet and easily set options to customize slicer settings.

Create, Format, and Delete a Slicer

1. Click any data field in the table for which you want to create a slicer.

2. Click the **Design** tab under Table Tools.

3. Click the **Insert Slicer** button.

4. Select the check boxes with the table fields for which you want to create a slicer.

5. Click **OK**.

   A slicer appears for every checked field.

6. In each slicer, click the items you want to filter.

   ◆ To select more than one item, press and hold Ctrl, and then click the items.

7. To format a slicer, click the slicer you want to format, click the **Options** tab under Slicer Tools, and then click a style in the Slicer Styles group.

8. To delete a slicer, click the slicer, and then press Delete.

Clear Filter button

Exporting a Table to a SharePoint List

If you have access to a Microsoft SharePoint Services site, such as Office 365 SharePoint (**New!**), you can export table data to a SharePoint list, for others to view, edit, and update. A SharePoint Services site is a server application that uses web site templates to create, organize, and share information. To access a SharePoint Services site, you might need access privileges. See your network administrator for a user name and password. You can access a SharePoint Services site from Excel or a web browser. When others make changes to the table in the SharePoint list, you can synchronize the changes to keep your Excel table up-to-date.

Export a Table to a SharePoint List

1. Select a cell in the table.

2. Click the **Design** tab under Table Tools.

3. Click the **Export** button, and then click **Export Table to SharePoint List**.

4. Enter a SharePoint address.

5. Type a name and description.

6. Click **Next**.

   If asked, enter a user name and password, and then click **OK**.

7. Click **Finish**.

8. Click **OK** to the alert.

See Also

See "Working Online with SharePoint and SkyDrive" on page 486 for information on working with a SharePoint Services site from Excel.

Analyzing Data Using a PivotTable

When you want to summarize information in a lengthy list using complex criteria, use the **PivotTable** to simplify your task. Without the PivotTable, you would have to manually count or create a formula to calculate which records met certain criteria, and then create a table to display that information. You can use the PivotTable layout to determine what fields and criteria you want to use to summarize the data and how you want the resulting table to look. You can create a PivotTable in a snap with the Quick Analysis tool (**New!**) or use the PivotTable button to have a little more control over the results. With this control, you can add multiple tables—either imported from a relational database from an external source or individually—in a PivotTable using the Excel Data Model (**New!**). A **Data Model** is a collection of tables and their relationship between the data. If you're not sure which type of PivotTable to select, you can choose a recommended chart (**New!**) based on the data.

Create a Recommended PivotTable

1. Click anywhere within the table range or select a range of cells.

2. Click the **Insert** tab.

3. Click the **Recommended PivotTable** button (**New!**).

4. Select the PivotTable you want in the left pane.

5. Click **OK** to use the selected data or click **Blank PivotTable** (**New!**) to create a blank PivotTable with no data selected.

   The Analyze and Design tab under PivotTable Tools appears.

6. In the Fields pane, select or deselect the check boxes next to the fields to add or remove data in the PivotTable.

   ◆ **Add Multiple Tables.** Click **More Tables** (**New!**), and then click **Yes**, if asked, to use the Data Model.

Create a PivotTable

1. Click anywhere within the table range or select a range of cells.

2. To quickly create a PivotTable, click the **Quick Analysis** button (**New!**), click **Tables**, point to a **PivotTable** button to preview the data, and then click a **PivotTable** button.

   Each PivotTable button as you go right adds more data. The **More** button acts like the PivotTable button on the Insert tab.

3. To create a chart with more control, click the **Insert** tab, and then continue.

4. Click the **PivotTable** button.

5. Click the **Select a table or range** option, or click the **Use an external data source** option, click **Choose Connection**, and then select a connection/data source.

6. Click the **New worksheet** option or **Existing worksheet** option, and specify a cell range.

7. To use multiple tables in a PivotTable, select the **Add this data to the Data Model** check box (**New!**).

8. Click **OK**.

   The Analyze and Design tab under PivotTable Tools appears.

9. Select or deselect the check boxes next to the fields to add or remove data in the PivotTable.

Did You Know?

You can delete a PivotTable. Click the PivotTable , click the Analyze tab, click the Select button, click Entire PivotTable, and then press Delete.

Preview of PivotTable data

PivotTable · PivotTable tools · Tools button

Field list

Analyzing Data Using a PivotChart

To help you present PivotTable data, you can create a chart. A chart of a PivotTable is called a **PivotChart**. With the PivotChart button, you can create a PivotChart or a PivotChart and PivotTable at the same time with the control you need to get the results you want. With this control, you can use multiple tables in a PivotChart using the Excel Data Model (**New!**). A PivotChart is not longer associated with a PivotTable (**New!**). A standalone PivotChart allows you to use the Drill Down, Drill Up, and Cross Drill to view different levels of data details (**New!**).

Create a PivotChart

1. Click anywhere within the table range or select a range of cells.

2. Click the **Insert** tab.

3. Click the **PivotChart** button, and then click **PivotChart**, or **PivotChart & PivotTable**.

4. Click the **Select a table or range** option, or click the **Use an external data source** option, click **Choose Connection**, and then select a connection/data source.

5. Click the **New worksheet** option or **Existing worksheet** option, and specify a cell range.

6. To use multiple tables in a PivotTable, select the **Add this data to the Data Model** check box (**New!**).

7. Click **OK**.

   The Analyze, Design and Format tab under PivotChart Tools appears.

8. Select or deselect the check boxes next to the fields to add or remove data from the PivotChart.

PivotChart

PivotChart tools

Field list

Updating a PivotTable or PivotChart

You can quickly update a PivotTable report using the PivotTable Field List or the Analyze tab under PivotTable or PivotChart Tools, which appears whenever a PivotTable or PivotChart is active. When you do want to add or remove data to and from a PivotTable or PivotChart, Excel makes it easy by allowing you to select or clear field check boxes. After selecting fields, you can change the display for rows and columns, filter data, and display a summary. In addition, you can use multiple tables in a PivotChart using the Excel Data Model (**New!**).

Add or Remove a Field in a PivotTable or PivotChart

1. Click any field in the PivotTable or PivotChart report.

2. Select or clear the check boxes next to the fields you want to include or exclude from the PivotTable and PivotChart.

3. To add multiple tables, click **More Tables** (**New!**), and then click **Yes**, if asked, to use the Data Model.

4. To change a field position, drag the field in the Field list to another one of the following boxes:

   ◆ **Values.** Use to display summary numeric data.

   ◆ **Rows.** Use to display fields as rows on the side of the report. Axis field in a PivotChart.

   ◆ **Columns.** Use to display fields as columns at the top of the report. Legend field in a PivotChart.

   ◆ **Filters.** Use to filter the entire report based on the selected item in the report filter.

   TIMESAVER *Right-click a field in the Field list to access move and other related field commands.*

   Each time you make a change, the layout is automatically updated.

5. To enable manual layout updating, select the **Defer layout update** check box. Click **Update** to manually update the report layout.

Add more tables

For Your Information

Changing the Data Source in a PivotTable

You can select a different data source for a PivotTable. For example, you can connect to data feeds (**New!**) like OData, Windows Azure DataMarket, and SharePoint. Click the PivotTable report, click the Analyze tab, click the Change Data Source button, click Change Data Source, click the Select A Table Or Range option and specify a range, or click the Use An External Data Source option and specify a connection, and then click OK. You can refresh PivotTable or PivotChart data. Click the PivotTable report, click the Analyze tab, and then click the Refresh button. Click the PivotChart report, click the Analyze tab, and then click the Refresh button.

Modifying a PivotTable

You can use the Analyze tab under PivotTable Tools to modify a PivotTable to summarize, organize, and display the information you want to present. Many of the options—Group, Clear, Select, or Move—are similar to the ones available for Excel tables and charts. You can use the Options button to change PivotTable layout, format, totals, filter, display, printing and data settings. Use the Field Setting button to change field layout, print, subtotals, and filter settings. Use the Drill buttons to view different levels of details in complex data (**New!**).

Modify a PivotTable

1. Click any field in the PivotTable report.

2. Click the **Analyze** tab under PivotTable Tools.

3. To change PivotTable options, click the **Options** button, make the changes you want, and then click **OK**.

4. To change field settings, select the field you want to change, click the **Field Settings** button, make changes, and then click **OK**.

5. Use any of the following options to change the PivotTable:

   ◆ **Drill Down, Drill Up,** or **Drill Cross.** Use to view levels of detail in complex data (**New!**).

   ◆ **Group Selection, Ungroup,** or **Group Field.** Use to group, ungroup PivotTable elements or fields.

   ◆ **Clear.** Use to clear filters, labels, values, and formatting.

   ◆ **Select.** Use to select PivotTable elements.

   ◆ **Fields, Items, & Sets.** Use to insert calculated fields and items, change solve order, and list formulas.

   ◆ **Field List.** Show or hide the Field List.

   ◆ **Buttons.** Show or hide group +/- buttons.

   ◆ **Field Headers.** Show or hide field headers for columns and rows.

PivotTable options

Field Settings

Formatting a PivotTable

After you create a PivotTable, you can use formatting tools on the Design tab under PivotTable Tools to modify the look and feel of a PivotTable. Formatting a PivotTable can be quick and easy with PivotTable Quick Styles. When you create a PivotTable, Excel displays a standard set of elements, including headings, columns, and rows. You can select or clear options on the Design tab to quickly format a PivotTable the way you want. Layout buttons, such as Subtotals, Grand Totals, Report Layout, and Blank Row, give you additional options to show or hide PivotTable elements.

Format a PivotTable Report

1. Click any field in the PivotTable report.

2. Click the **Design** tab under PivotTable Tools.

3. Click the **More** list arrow for PivotTable Styles, and then click the PivotTable style you want.

4. Select or clear the PivotTable format options you want to turn on or off:

   ◆ **Row Headers.**

   ◆ **Column Headers.**

   ◆ **Banded Rows.**

   ◆ **Banded Columns.**

5. Click any of the following layout buttons to select options to show or hide PivotTable elements:

   ◆ **Subtotals.** Show or hide subtotals.

   ◆ **Grand Totals.** Turn on or off grand totals for columns or rows.

   ◆ **Report Layout.** Set to compact, outline, or tabular form.

   ◆ **Blank Row.** Insert or remove a blank line after each item.

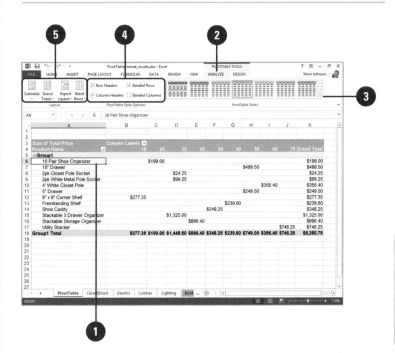

Working with PivotTable Data

After you create a PivotTable, you can use several features to enhance the display of the information you want. You can fill down and repeat labels to make viewing data easier, use the Search box to find data in fields and columns, use the AutoFilter menu to filter data in fields and columns, and use options to display data in different ways. When you sort and filter large amounts of data in a PivotTable, Excel uses multi-threading to improve performance. Excel also provides support for the Undo command in large PivotTables.

Work with Values in a PivotTable

1. Click the data field in the PivotTable you want to change.

2. Click the **Analyze** tab under PivotTable Tools.

3. To change the display values, select from the available options:

   ◆ **Summarize Values By.** Right-click a field, point to **Summarize Values By**, and then select one of the summarize options (Sum, Count, Average, Max, Min, or Product), or click **More Options**.

   ◆ **Show Values As.** Right-click a field, point to **Show Values As**, and then select one of the show options, or click **More Options**.

4. To work with fields, items and sets, click the **Fields, Items & Sets** button, and then select one of the options:

   ◆ **Calculated Field** or **Calculated Item**

   ◆ **Solve Order**

   ◆ **List Formulas**

   ◆ **Create Set Based on Row Items**

   ◆ **Create Set Based on Column Items**

   ◆ **Manage Sets**

For Your Information

Creating a Relationship Between Tables

When you have more than one table and a common column in a Data Model, you can create a relationship (**New!**) between them that lets you build PivotTables and other reports using fields from each table. Table relationships can be one-to-one (each student has one seat) or one-to-many (each class has many students), but not many-to-many, which would create dependency errors. Click the Data or Analyze (under PivotTable Tools) tab, click the Relationships button (if grayed out, it only contains one table), click New, specify the main table and common column (Foreign), specify the related table and related column, and then click OK.

Search, Sort, or Filter in a PivotTable

1. Click in the PivotTable, and then click the column header list arrow where you want to search, sort, or set filter criteria.

2. Select the search, sort or filter criteria you want:

   ◆ **Sort.** Select a sort option, or click **More Sort Options**.

   ◆ **Select Items.** Select the items that records must match to be included in the table.

   ◆ **Search.** Enter search criteria, and then press Enter.

   ◆ **Built-in Filters.** Point to **<Column Name> Filters**, and then select a filter option.

3. Click **OK**.

Repeat Labels in a PivotTable

1. Click the row or column label you want to repeat.

2. Click the **Analyze** tab under PivotTable Tools.

3. Click the **Field Settings** button.

4. Click the **Layout & Print** tab.

5. Select the **Repeat item labels** check box.

6. To show the repeated items in the PivotTable, select the **Show item labels in tabular form** option.

7. Click **OK**.

   When you edit or change the format for any of the repeated labels, the changes are applied to other cells with the same label.

Using Slicers to Filter a PivotTable

Instead of using the AutoFilter menu each time you want to filter data in a PivotTable, you can create a slicer button that enables you to quickly filter data in a PivotTable with a single click. Each slicer is shown on the screen with button labels that indicate the data being filtered. A slicer includes a header, filtering buttons, a Clear Filter button, a scroll bar, and move and resize controls. You can have more than one slicer and move them around on the worksheet. You can also format slicers with styles to match the look and feel of your worksheet and easily reuse them in other PivotTables, PivotCharts, and Online Analytical Professing (OLAP) Cube functions. If you have multiple PivotTables, you can share a slicer between them as needed. When you share a slicer, you create a connection to another PivotTable, which is called a shared slicer. A slicer only used by one PivotTable is called a local slicer.

Create, Format, and Delete a Slicer

1. Click any data field in the PivotTable for which you want to create a slicer.

2. Click the **Analyze** tab under PivotTable Tools.

3. Click the **Insert Slicer** button.

4. Select the check boxes with the PivotTable fields for which you want to create a slicer.

5. Click **OK**.

   A slicer appears for every checked field.

6. In each slicer, click the items you want to filter.

   ◆ To select more than one item, press and hold Ctrl, and then click the items.

7. To format a slicer, click the slicer you want to format, click the **Options** tab under Slicer Tools, and then click a style in the Slicer Styles group.

8. To delete a slicer, click the slicer, and then press Delete.

Share and Use a Slicer

1. Click the slicer you want to share in another PivotTable.

2. Click the **Options** tab under Slicer Tools.

3. Click the **Report Connections** button.

4. Select the check boxes with the PivotTables to which you want to connect.

5. Click **OK**.

6. Click the **Data** tab.

7. Click the **Existing Connections** button.

8. Click the **Show** list arrow, and then click **All Connections**.

9. Select the connection you want, and then click **Open**.

   ◆ If you don't see a connection, click **Browse for More**, click **New Source** to use the Data Connection Wizard.

10. Click **PivotTable Report**, and then click **OK**.

11. Click anywhere in the PivotTable where you want to insert a slicer from another PivotTable.

12. Click the **Analyze** tab under PivotTable Tools.

13. Click the **Insert Slicer** button arrow, and then click **Slider Connections**.

14. Select the check boxes with the PivotTable fields for which you want to create a slicer.

   ◆ You clear the check boxes to disconnect a slicer.

15. Click **OK**.

For Your Information

Creating a Stand-alone Slicer

In addition to creating a slicer in a PivotTable, you can also create a stand-alone slicer that can be referenced by Online Analytical Processing (OLAP) Cube functions or that you can associate with any PivotTable. To create a stand-alone slicer, click the Insert tab, click Slicer, click the Show list arrow, click All Connections, select the connection you want (If you don't see a connection, click Browse For More, click New Source to use the Data Connection Wizard), click Open, click the check boxes with the fields for which you want to create a slicer, and then click OK.

Display a Timeline to Filter a PivotTable

Instead of grouping by dates in a PivotTable or PivotChart, you can use the Insert Timeline button (**New!**) to filter data based on dates to create a timeline over different time periods. In order to create a timeline, you need to have at least one field formatted as Date. Otherwise, you'll get an error dialog box. After you create a timeline, you can specify a date range and apply a filter range to display the data you want. You can also use the Options tab under Timeline Tools to format the timeline and show the display information you want.

Create a Timeline

1. Click any data field in the PivotTable or PivotChart for which you want to create a timeline.

2. Click the **Analyze** tab under PivotTable Tools.

3. Click the **Insert Timeline** button.

4. Select the check boxes with the date fields for which you want to create a timeline.

5. Click **OK**.

   A timeline appears as an object on the worksheet.

6. Click the **Date Range** list arrow, and then select an option: **Years**, **Quarters**, **Months**, or **Days**.

7. Point to the **Filter Range**, and then drag the end points to apply the filter to the data in the PivotTable or PivotChart.

8. To remove the filter, click the **Clear Filter** button.

9. To format the timeline, select the timeline object, and then use the buttons and options on the Options tab under Timeline Tools.

10. To resize the timeline, drag a resize handle.

11. To delete the timeline, select the timeline object, and then press Delete.

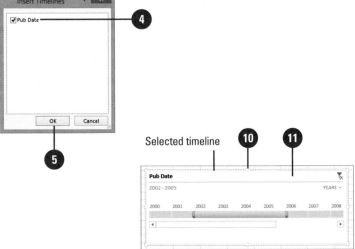

Selected timeline

Drilling into PivotTable Data

When you add multiple tables to a Data Model or use data from an Online Analytical Processing (OLAP) cube, you can use the Quick Explore button to quickly drill into large amounts of complex data to view different levels of details in a PivotTable. When you select data in a field, the Quick Explore button (**New!**) appears, where you can drill down one item at a time. When you click the Quick Explore button, a callout appears, where you can select the data field and then drill to or drill down to the data. After you drill, you can use the same technique to drill up or use the Undo button on the Quick Access Toolbar. In addition to PivotTables, you can also drill a PivotChart. When you select a chart element, the Quick Explore button appears. After you drill a PivotChart, the chart and table update. Drill buttons are also available on the Analyze tab under PivotTable Tools (**New!**).

Drill into PivotTable or PivotChart Data

1. Click the field in the PivotTable report or click an element in the PivotChart you want to drill.

2. Click the **Quick Explore** button.

   A callout appears, displaying fields and drill buttons.

3. If you want to change the field, click the field you want to drill.

4. Click **Drill To** or **Drill Down**.

   IMPORTANT *You cannot drill down in flat hierarchies.*

5. To drill up, click the field (previously drilled down), click the **Quick Explore** button, and then click **Drill Up**.

Did You Know?

You can drill multiple levels at once. Right-click the field you wan to drill, click Drill Down/Drill Up, and then select the level you want to drill to.

Drill buttons

Charting a PivotTable

Data summarized in a PivotTable is an ideal candidate for a chart, since the table itself represents an overwhelming amount of data. A chart of a PivotTable is called a **PivotChart**. Once you select data within the PivotTable or table (**New!**), you can chart it like any other worksheet data using similar tabs and buttons—PivotChart and Recommended PivotChart (**New!**)—under PivotChart Tools. You can also use the AutoFilter menu to filter data directly in the PivotChart report, just like in a table. The additional Analyze tab provides options to collapse or expand fields, insert a slicer, refresh or clear data, and show or hide the Field List and different Field Buttons on a PivotChart. To change chart elements, you can use the Add Chart Element button on the Design tab under Chart Tools or use the Chart Elements (**New!**) or Chart Styles button (**New!**) in the upper-right corner of the selected chart.

Create a PivotChart from a PivotTable

1. Click any data field in the PivotTable.

2. Click the **Analyze** tab under PivotTable Tools.

3. Click the **PivotChart** or **Recommended PivotChart** button (**New!**).

4. Click the chart type you want.

5. Click **OK**.

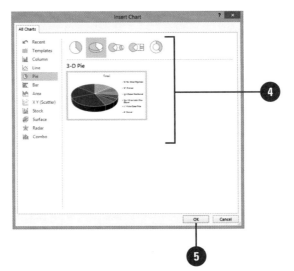

Did You Know?

You can delete a PivotChart. Click the PivotChart report, and then press Delete.

You can rename a PivotTable or PivotChart. Click the PivotTable or PivotChart report, click the Analyze tab, click the Name box, type a new name and then press Enter.

You can rename a field in a PivotTable or PivotChart. Click the PivotTable report, click the Analyze tab, click the Active Field Name box, type a new name and then press Enter. Click the PivotChart report, click the Analyze tab, click the Active Field Name box, type a new name and then press Enter.

PivotChart   PivotChart AutoFilter menu

Modify a PivotChart Report

① Click the PivotChart in the worksheet.

② Click the **Analyze** tab.

③ To show or hide field buttons, click the **Field Buttons** button, and then select an option (Report Filter, Legend, Axis, or Value) to toggle on or off.

◆ **Hide All.** Click to hide all field buttons on the PivotChart.

④ To filter fields, click the **AutoFilter** list arrow (name on list arrow varies based on data) on the PivotChart, and then select the filter options you want.

⑤ To show or hide the Field List, click the **Field List** button.

⑥ To modify the field display, select a field, and then click the **Expand Entire Field** or **Collapse Entire Field** button.

⑦ To quick format a PivotChart, click the **Chart Elements** or **Chart Styles** button (**New!**), and then select the options you want.

⑧ Use any of the tabs under PivotChart Tools to modify and format the PivotChart report:

◆ **Design.** Use to change chart styles, layouts, type, labels, axes, and background.

◆ **Format.** Use to format chart elements using Shape and WordArt styles.

Did You Know?

You can refresh PivotTable or PivotChart data. Click the PivotTable or PivotChart report, click the Analyze tab, and then click the Refresh button.

Chart styles

Presenting Data with Power View

If you're using Office Professional Plus, you can look at your data in different ways with Power View (**New!**) report. Power View allows you to visually interact with the data in a sheet so you can present it to others. You can create and interact with charts and Bing maps, slicers, and other visualizations and filter out the data you want. Power View analyzes the data and only enables the appropriate charts and options. On first use, you'll need to enable the Power View add-in (**New!**) for Excel, which also enables it for PowerPoint. If you don't have Microsoft Silverlight installed, you'll be prompted to install and reload it. If you use Office 365 SharePoint or SharePoint 2013 with Excel Services or Excel Web Apps, you can save a Power View sheet to the site, where you can view and interact with the data online in a web browser.

Present Data with Power View

1. Click the PivotTable or PivotChart with the data you want to view.

2. Click the **Insert** tab.

3. Click the **Power View** button (**New!**).

4. If prompted, on first use, do the following:

    ◆ Click **Enable** to install and use the Power View add-in.

    ◆ Click the **Install Silverlight** link, follow the install instructions, and then click **Reload**.

    Excel creates a Power View sheet tab.

5. In the Fields pane, select or deselect the check boxes next to the fields to add or remove data.

6. In the Fields pane, select a field, click the list arrow, and then select an option, or drag fields to the Title By or Fields boxes. To adjust field order, drag item in the Fields box.

7. To add filters, drag fields from the Fields pane to the Filters Area. To apply filters, expand fields, and then select or adjust filters.

8. To add a title, click *Click here to add a title*, and then type the text you want, and then use the Text tab to format it.

9   Click anywhere in the data.

10   Click the **Design** tab (**New!**).

11   Select from the following options (**New!**) on the Design tab:

◆ **Switch Visualization.** Change to view tables, charts, or maps.

◆ **Tiles.** View the data as a series of tiles.

◆ **Slicer.** Creates a slicer.

◆ **Card Style.** Changes the style of a table in card view.

◆ **Show Levels.** Changes the number of levels to display.

◆ **Totals.** Chooses totals and subtotals to display.

◆ **Number.** Formats numbers.

◆ **Text.** Changes the size of text.

◆ **Arrange.** Changes the stacking of objects.

12   To resize the display, drag a corner or click **Pop out** or **Pop in**.

Pop out/Pop in button; point to display options

Format View in Power View

1   Click the PivotTable or PivotChart with the data you want to view.

2   Click the **Power View** tab (**New!**).

3   Click **Field List** or **Filters Area** button to show or hide them.

4   Use the buttons on the tab to do any of the following:

◆ **Apply Themes.**

◆ **Insert Background Image.**

◆ **Refresh Data or Create Data Relationships.**

◆ **Insert Another Power View.**

◆ **Insert Text Box.**

◆ **Insert Picture.**

◆ **Arrange Objects.**

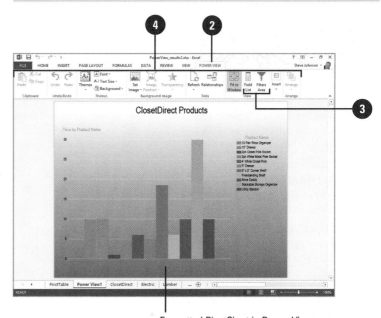

Formatted PivotChart in Power View

Working with PowerPivot

If you're using Office Professional Plus, you can also use the built-in PowerPivot add-in (**New!**), which allows you to build simple data models directly in Excel. PowerPivot is helpful when you want to import, filter out, and quickly process millions of rows of data from multiple data sources. You can use PowerPivot to define data hierarchies, calculation fields, and Key Performance Indicators (KPIs), and use the Data Analysis Expressions (DAX) language to create advanced formulas.

Build Data Models with PowerPivot

1. Click anywhere within the table range or select a range of cells.

2. Click the **PowerPivot** tab (**New!**).

   ◆ **Enable Add-in.** Click the **File** tab, click **Options**, click Add-Ins, select **Com Add-ins** in the Manage box, and then click **Go**.

3. Select from the following options (**New!**) on the PowerPivot tab:

   ◆ **Manage.** Manage or import data in the Data Model.

   ◆ **Calculated Fields.** Creates a new or manages existing fields with calculation formulas.

   ◆ **KPIs.** Creates a new or manages existing Key Performance Indicators.

   ◆ **Align Vertically or Align Horizontally.** Aligns slicers vertically or horizontally.

   ◆ **Add to Data Model.** Adds and links the current table to the Data Model, which creates a live link between them that automatically updates.

   ◆ **Update All.** Updates all the PowerPivot tables linked to the tables in Excel.

   ◆ **Detect.** Automatically detects and creates relationships between tables used on the selected PivotTable.

   ◆ **Settings.** Set options for support & diagnostics, language, and data categorization.

Use to work with the Data Model

Data in the Data Model

Creating Groups and Outlines

A sales report that displays daily, weekly, and monthly totals in a hierarchical format, such as an outline, helps your reader to sift through and interpret the pertinent information. In outline format, a single item can have several topics or levels of information within it. An outline in Excel indicates multiple layers of content by displaying a plus sign (+) on its left side. A minus sign (-) indicates that the item has no contents, is fully expanded, or both.

Create an Outline or Group

1. Organize data in a hierarchical fashion—place summary rows below detail rows and summary columns to the right of detail columns.

2. Select the data that you want to outline.

3. To create an outline, click the **Data** tab, click the **Group** button arrow, and then click **Auto Outline**.

4. To create a group, click the **Data** tab, click the **Group** button arrow, and then click **Group**. Click the **Rows** or **Columns** option, and then click **OK**.

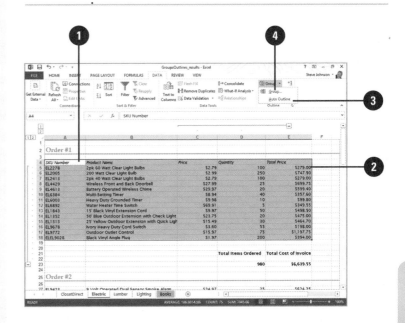

Work an Outline or Group

◆ Click a plus sign (+) to expand an outline level; click a minus sign (-) to collapse an outline level.

Did You Know?

You can ungroup outline data. Select the data group, click the Data tab, click the Ungroup button arrow, click Ungroup, click the Rows or Columns option, and then click OK.

You can clear an outline. Select the outline, click the Data tab, click the Group button arrow, and then click Clear Outline.

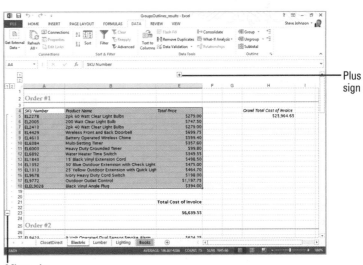

Plus sign

Minus sign

Converting Text to Columns

The Convert to Columns Wizard helps you separate simple cell contents into different columns. For example, if a cell contains first and last names, you can use the Convert to Columns Wizard to separate first and last name into different columns. The wizard uses the delimiter—such as a tab, semicolon, comma, space, or custom—to determine where to separate the cell contents into different columns; the wizard options vary depending on the delimiter type. For example, the cell contents *Julie, Kenney* uses the comma delimiter.

Convert Text to Columns

1. Select the range you want to convert to columns.

2. Click the **Data** tab.

3. Click the **Text to Columns** button.

4. In Step 1, click **Delimited**.

5. Click **Next**.

6. In Step 2, select the delimiter type you want to use, and then clear the other check boxes.

   The wizard options vary depending on the selected delimiter.

7. Click **Next**.

8. In Step 3, click a column in the Data preview box, click the **Text** option, and then repeat this for each column you want. .

9. Click the **Collapse Dialog** button, select a new destination for the separated data, and then click the **Expand Dialog** button.

10. Click **Finish**.

Two column results

Adding Data Validation to a Worksheet

Worksheet cells can be adjusted so that only certain values can be entered. Controlling how data is entered decreases errors and makes a worksheet more reliable. You might, for example, want it to be possible to enter only specific dates in a range of cells. You can use **logical operators** (such as equal to, not equal to, less than, or greater than) to set validation rules. When invalid entries are made, a message—developed and written by you—appears indicating that the entry is in violation of the validation rules. The rule set will not allow data to flow into the cell.

Create Validation Rules

1. Select the range you want covered in the validation rules.

2. Click the **Data** tab.

3. Click the **Data Validation** button.

4. Click the **Settings** tab.

5. Click the **Allow** list arrow, and then select a value type.

   Options vary depending on the Allow value type you select.

6. Click the **Data** list arrow, and then select a logical operator.

7. Enter values or use the **Collapse Dialog** button to select a range for the minimum and maximum criteria.

8. Click the **Input Message** tab, and then type a title and the input message that should be displayed when invalid entries are made.

9. Click the **Error Alert** tab, and then select an alert style, type a title, and error message.

10. Click **OK**.

11. To view invalid data, click the **Data Validation** button arrow, and then click **Circle Invalid Data**. To clear the circles, click the **Data Validation** button arrow, and then click **Clear Validation Circles**.

Data validation

Creating a Drop-Down List

Entering data in a table can be tedious and repetitive. To make the job easier, you can create a drop-down list of entries you define. This way you get consistent, accurate data. To create a drop-down list, create a list of valid entries in a single column or row without blanks, define a name, and then use the List option in the Data Validation dialog box. To enter data using a drop-down list, click the cell with the defined drop-down list, click the list arrow, and then click the entry you want.

Create a Drop-Down List

1. Type entries in a single column or row without blanks in the order you want.

2. Select the cell range, click the **Name** box, type a name, and then press Enter.

3. Select the cell where you want the drop-down list.

4. Click the **Data** tab.

5. Click the **Data Validation** button.

6. Click the **Settings** tab.

7. Click the **Allow** list arrow, and then click **List**.

8. Enter values or use the **Collapse Dialog** button to select a range of valid entries.

9. Click the **Input Message** tab, and then type a title and the input message that should be displayed when invalid entries are made.

10. Click the **Error Alert** tab, and then select an alert style, type a title, and error message.

11. Click **OK**.

Drop-Down list

Building More Powerful Worksheets

Introduction

Excel also includes a variety of add-ins—programs that provide added functionality—to increase your efficiency. Some of these supplemental programs—including Analysis ToolPak, Analysis ToolPak VBA, Euro Currency Tools, Solver, Inquire, Power View, and PowerPivot—are useful to almost anyone using Excel. Each one extends the functionality of Excel For example, the Analysis ToolPak adds customized features, functions, or commands specific to use in financial, statistical, and other highly specialized fields. The purpose of each of these customization features is the same—to make Excel even easier to use and to enable you to accomplish more with less effort.

Before you can use an Excel or a third-party add-in, you need to load it first. When you load an add-in, the feature may also add a command to a Ribbon tab or an entire tab. You can load one or more add-ins. If you no longer need an add-in, you should unload it to save memory and reduce the number of commands on a Ribbon tab. When you unload an add-in, you may also need to restart Excel to remove an add-in command from a Ribbon tab or add-in tab.

If your worksheet or workbook needs to go beyond simple calculations, Microsoft Excel offers several tools to help you create more specialized projects. With Excel, you can perform "what if" analysis using several different methods to get the results you want.

Functions are predesigned formulas that save you the time and trouble of creating them. Excel provides functions related to specific professions or tasks, such as Financial, Math & Trig, Engineering, Web, Logical, Text, Date & Time, and Lookup & Reference, to help you build more power worksheets.

What You'll Do

Use Data Analysis Tools

Use the Euro Conversion

Look at Alternatives with Data Tables

Ask "What If" with Goal Seek

Create Scenarios

Use Solver

Use Inquire Tools

Use Lookup and Reference Functions

Use Text Functions

Summarize Data Using Subtotals

Summarize Data Using Functions

Use Date & Time Functions

Use Logical Functions

Use Financial Functions

Use Math Functions

Use Statisti

Using Data Analysis Tools

Excel provides a collection of statistical functions and macros to analyze data in the **Analysis ToolPak**. The Analysis Toolpak is an Excel add-in program, which may need to be loaded using the Add-In pane in Excel Options. The tools can be used for a variety of scientific and engineering purposes and for general statistical analysis. You provide the data, and the tools use the appropriate functions to determine the result. To effectively use these tools, you need to be familiar with the area of statistics or engineering for which you want to develop an analysis. You can view a list of all the tools in the Data Analysis dialog box. For additional information about each tool, see the online Help.

Use Data Analysis Tools

① Click the **Data** tab.

② Click the **Data Analysis** button. If not available, load the Excel add-in.

③ Click the analysis tool you want to use.

④ To get help about each tool, click **Help**.

⑤ Click **OK**.

⑥ Select or enter the input range (a single row or column). You can use the **Collapse Dialog** button to select a range and the **Expand Dialog** button to return.

⑦ Select or enter the output range. You can use the **Collapse Dialog** button to select a range and the **Expand Dialog** button to return.

⑧ Specify any additional tool-specific options you want.

⑨ Click **OK**.

Using the Euro Conversion

The Euro Conversion Wizard helps you convert data from one european currency to another. Excel provides this feature as an Excel add-in program, which may need to be loaded using the Add-In pane in Excel Options. The wizard guides you through the process to convert specified data from one european currency to another. All you need to do is specify the source and destination range, currency conversion from and to, and an output format.

Use the Euro Conversion

① Click the **Formulas** tab.

② Select the data you want to convert.

③ Click the **Euro Conversion** button. If not available, load the Excel add-in.

④ Specify a source and destination range for the conversion.

You can use the **Collapse Dialog** button to select a range and the **Expand Dialog** button to return.

⑤ Click the **From** list arrow, select a From currency, click the **To** list arrow, and then select a To currency.

⑥ Click the **Output format** list arrow, and then select an output format.

⑦ Click **OK**.

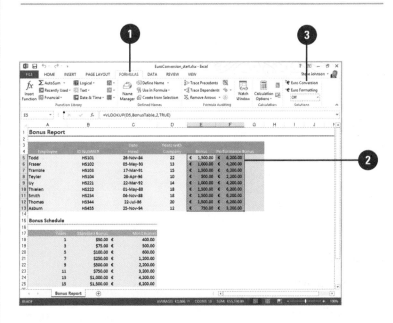

Did You Know?

You can quickly convert data. Select the data you want to convert, click the Formulas tab, click the Euro Formatting list arrow, and then click a conversion option.

Looking at Alternatives with Data Tables

Data tables provide a shortcut by calculating all of the values in one operation. A **data table** is a range of cells that shows the results of substituting different values in one or more formulas. For example, you can compare loan payments for different interest rates. There are two types of data tables: one-input and two-input. With a **one-input table**, you enter different values for one variable and see the effect on one or more formulas. With a **two-input table**, you enter values for two variables and see the effect on one formula.

Create a One-Input Data Table

1. Enter the formula you want to use.

   If the input values are listed down a column, specify the new formula in a blank cell to the right of an existing formula in the top row of the table. If the input values are listed across a row, enter the new formula in a blank cell below an existing formula in the first column of the table.

2. Select the data table, including the column or row that contains the new formula.

3. Click the **Data** tab.

4. Click the **What-If Analysis** button, and then click **Data Table**.

5. Enter the input cell.

   If the input values are in a column, enter the reference for the input cell in the Column Input Cell box. If the input values are in a row, enter the reference for the input cell in the Row Input Cell box.

6. Click **OK**.

Asking "What If" with Goal Seek

Excel functions make it easy to create powerful formulas, such as calculating payments over time. Sometimes, however, being able to make these calculations is only half the battle. Your formula might tell you that a monthly payment amount is $2,000, while you might only be able to manage a $1,750 payment. **Goal Seek** enables you to work backwards to a desired result, or goal, by adjusting the input values.

Create a "What-If" Scenario with Goal Seek

1. Click any cell within the list range.

2. Click the **Data** tab.

3. Click the **What-If Analysis** button, and then click **Goal Seek**.

4. Click the **Set Cell** box, and then type the cell address you want to change.

   You can also click the **Collapse Dialog** button, use your mouse to select the cells, and then click the **Expand Dialog** button.

5. Click the **To Value** box, and then type the result value.

6. Click the **By Changing Cell** box, and then type the cell address you want Excel to change.

   You can also click the **Collapse Dialog** button, use your mouse to select the cells, and then click the **Expand Dialog** button.

7. Click **OK**.

   The Goal Seek Status dialog box, opens displaying the goal seek results.

8. Click **OK**.

results

Creating Scenarios

Because some worksheet data is constantly evolving, the ability to create multiple scenarios lets you speculate on a variety of outcomes. For example, the marketing department might want to see how its budget would be affected if sales decreased by 25 percent. Although it's easy enough to plug in different numbers in formulas, Excel allows you to save these values and then recall them at a later time.

Create and Show a Scenario

1. Click the **Data** tab.

2. Click the **What-If Analysis** button, and then click **Scenario Manager**.

3. Click **Add**.

4. Type a name that identifies the scenario.

5. Type the cells you want to modify in the scenario, or click the **Collapse Dialog** button, use your mouse to select the cells, and then click the **Expand Dialog** button.

6. If you want, type a comment.

7. If you want, select the **Prevent changes** check box to protect the cell.

8. Click **OK**.

9. Type values for each of the displayed changing cells.

10. Click **OK**.

11. Click **Close**.

Show a Scenario

1. Click the **Data** tab.

2. Click the **What-If Analysis** button, and then click **Scenario Manager**.

3. Select the scenario you want to see.

4. Click **Show**.

5. Click **Close**.

Create a Scenario Summary or PivotTable Report

1. Click the **Data** tab.

2. Click the **What-If Analysis** button, and then click **Scenario Manager**.

3. Select the scenario you want to see.

4. Click **Summary**.

5. Click the **Scenario summary** or **Scenario PivotTable report** option.

6. Click **OK**.

   A scenario summary worksheet tab appears with the report.

Using Solver

The Solver is similar to Goal Seek and scenarios, but provides more options to restrict the allowable range of values for different cells that can affect the goal. The Solver is an Excel add-in program, which may need to be loaded using the Add-In pane in Excel Options. The Solver is useful for predicting how results might change over time based on different assumptions. For example, suppose you have sales goals and quotas for the next three months. The Solver can take the expectations and the current quotas for each month, and determine how sales quotas for all three amounts be adjusted to achieve the goal.

Use Solver

1. Click the **Data** tab.

2. Click the **Solver** button. If not available, load the Excel add-in.

3. Select the target cell.

4. Click an Equal To option, and then, if necessary, enter a value.

5. Select the range of cells the solver uses to compare against the target cell.

6. Click **Add**.

7. Enter specific cell reference and constraint, and then click **Add**. You can specify several cell constraints.

8. Click **OK**.

9. To modify the constraints, click any of the following:

   ◆ **Change.** Select a constraint, and then click **Change** to modify it.

   ◆ **Delete.** Select a constraint, and then click **Delete** to remove it.

   ◆ **Reset All.** Click **Reset All** to rest all Solver options and cell selection.

   ◆ **Load/Save.** Click **Load/Save** to select a range holding a saved model (to load) or select an empty range with a specified number of cells (to save).

Target cell

Constraints

10 Click the **Solving Method** list arrow, and then select a method:

- ◆ **GRG Nonlinear.** Select for smooth nonlinear problems.

- ◆ **Simplex LP.** Select for linear problems.

- ◆ **Evolutionary.** Select for non-smooth problems.

11 To set options for each of the solving methods, click Options, click the tab you want (**All Methods**, **GRG NonLinear**, or **Evolutionary**), select the options you want, and then click **OK**.

12 Click **Solve**.

If the Solver finds a solution, the Solver Results dialog box opens.

13 Click the **Keep Solver Solution** option.

14 Click a report type.

15 Click **OK**.

Did You Know?

The solver add-in is improved. The Solver has an improved user interface, a new Evolutionary Solver, based on genetic algorithms, that handles models with any Excel functions, new global optimization options, better linear programming and nonlinear optimization methods, and new linearity and feasibility reports.

Answer report with the solver solution

Using Inquire Tools

If you're using Office Professional Plus, you can also use the Inquire tab (**New!**) to analyze, review, and compare workbooks in Excel. The Inquire is a COM add-in program, which may need to be loaded using the Add-In pane in Excel Options. The Inquire tab is a collection of tools that allows you to analyze and interactively report workbook problems or inconsistencies, view relationship diagrams—a graphical map of connection links—for workbooks, worksheets, or cells, and compare the content for multiple workbooks. You can also clean excess cell formatting to optimize and reduce the file size. If a workbook is password protected, you need to add it to the password list in Workbook Passwords, so Inquire can open saved copies for processing and analysis.

Analyze a Workbook to Create a Report

1. Click the **Inquire** tab (**New!**). If not available, load the COM add-in.

2. Click the **Workbook Analysis Report** button (**New!**).

3. Select the check boxes for the workbook elements (**Summary**, **Workbook**, **Formulas**, **Cells**, **Ranges**, or **Warnings**) you want to include in your results.

4. Click the **Refresh** button.

5. To export the results, click **Excel Export**, specify a location, enter a file name, and then click **Save**.

   ◆ **Item detail limit.** The number indicates the limit for the maximum number of results you can export.

6. Click the **Close** button to exit the window.

Did You Know?

You can add passwords to use Inquire tools. Click the Inquire tab, click the Workbook Password button, click Add, specify a password and description, and then click OK. Select a password, and then use Edit to modify or Delete to remove, and then click OK to exit.

View a Workbook, Worksheet, or Cell Relationship Diagram

1. Click the **Inquire** tab (**New!**). If not available, load the COM add-in.

2. Select the button for the type of relationship diagram you want:

   ◆ **Workbook Relationship.** Manage or import data in the Data Model. (**New!**)

   ◆ **Worksheet Relationship.** Creates a new or manages existing fields with calculation. (**New!**)

   ◆ **Cell Relationship.** Creates a new or manages existing fields with calculation formulas. (**New!**)

3. To display more information about the diagram in a ScreenTip, point to a node.

4. Use toolbar buttons to change the diagram view, print the diagram, or refresh the diagram.

5. Click the **Close** button to exit the window.

Did You Know?

You can compare two workbooks.
Open the two workbooks to compare, click the Inquire tab, click the Compare Files button, and then use the Spreadsheet Compare window.

See "Working with Office Tools" on page 456 for details on comparing multiple workbooks in Excel.

You can clean excess cell formatting.
Click the Inquire tab, click the Clean Excess Cell Formatting button, click the Apply to list arrow, click All Sheets or Active Sheet, click OK, and then click Yes to save your changes.

Node ScreenTip

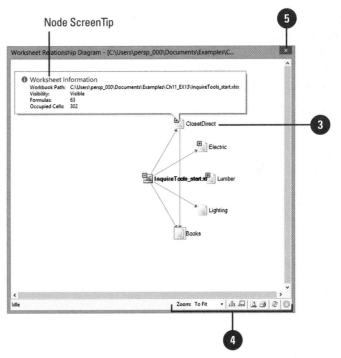

Using Lookup and Reference Functions

You can use lookup and reference functions in Excel to easily retrieve information from a data list. The lookup functions (VLOOKUP and HLOOKUP) allow you to search for and insert a value in a cell that is stored in another place in the worksheet. The HLOOKUP function looks in rows (a horizontal lookup) and the VLOOKUP function looks in columns (a vertical lookup). Each function uses four arguments (pieces of data) as shown in the following definition: =VLOOKUP (lookup_value, table_array, col_index_num, range_lookup). The VLOOKUP function finds a value in the left-most column of a named range and returns the value from the specified cell to the right of the cell with the found value, while the HLOOKUP function does the same to rows. In the example, =VLOOKUP(12,Salary,2,TRUE), the function looks for the value 12 in the named range Salary and finds the closest (next lower) value, and returns the value in column 2 of the same row and places the value in the active cell. In the example, =HLOOKUP ("Years",Salary,4,FALSE), the function looks for the value "Years" in the named range Salary and finds the exact text string value, and then returns the value in row 4 of the column.

Use the VLOOKUP Function

① Create a data range in which the left-most column contains a unique value in each row.

② Click the cell where you want to place the function.

③ Type **=VLOOKUP(***value, named range, column,* **TRUE** or **FALSE),** and then press Enter.

Or click the **Formulas** tab, click the **Look & Reference** button, click **VLOOKUP**, specify the function arguments, and then click **OK**.

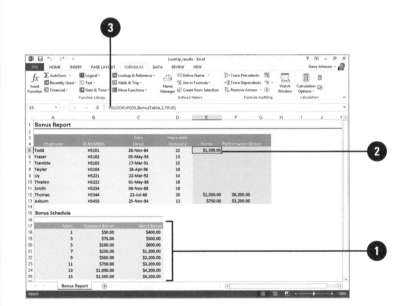

Did You Know?

You can use Paste Special to copy only formulas. Select the cells containing the formulas you want to copy, click the Copy button on the Home tab, click where you want to paste the data, click the Paste button arrow, click Paste Special, click the Formulas button, and then click OK.

Use the HLOOKUP Function

1. Create a data range in which the uppermost row contains a unique value in each row.

2. Click the cell where you want to place the function.

3. Type **=HLOOKUP(**value, named range, row, **TRUE** or **FALSE**), and then press Enter.

   Or click the **Formulas** tab, click the **Look & Reference** button, click **HLOOKUP**, specify the function arguments, and then click **OK**.

Did You Know?

You can display a formula using a function. With the function FORMULA-TEXT (**New!**), you can display a formula for a specified cell. For example, =FORMULATEXT(A1).

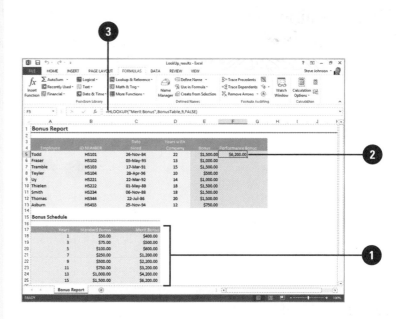

Lookup Function Arguments

Argument	Description
lookup_value	The value found in the row or the column of the named range. You can use a value, cell reference or a text string (enclosed in quotation marks).
table_array	The named range of information in which Excel looks up data.
col_index_num	The numeric position of the column in the named range (counting from the left) for the value to be returned (use only for VLOOKUP).
row_index_num	The numeric position of the row in the named range (counting from the top) for the value to be returned (use only for HLOOKUP).
range_lookup	The value returned when the function is to find the nearest value (TRUE) or an exact match (FALSE) for the lookup_value. The default value is TRUE.

Using Text Functions

You can use text functions to help you work with text in a workbook. If you need to count the number of characters in a cell or the number of occurrences of a specific text string in a cell, you can use the LEN and SUBSTITUTE functions. If you want to narrow the count to only upper or lower case text, you can use the UPPER and LOWER functions. If you need to capitalize a list of names or titles, you can use the PROPER function. The function capitalizes the first letter in a text string and converts all other letters to lowercase.

Use Text Functions

1. Create a data range in which the left-most column contains a unique value in each row.

2. Click the cell where you want to place the function.

3. Type = (equal sign), type a text function, specify the argument for the selected function, and then press Enter.

   Some examples include:

   ◆ =LEFT(A4,FIND(" ",A4)-1)

   ◆ =RIGHT(A4,LEN(A4-
     FIND("*",SUBSTITUTE(A4,"
     "," *",LEN(A4)-
     LEN(SUBSTITUTE(A4," ",""))))))

   ◆ =UPPER(A4)

   ◆ =LOWER(A4)

   ◆ =PROPER(A4)

   Or click the **Formulas** tab, click the **Text** button, click text function, specify the function arguments, and then click **OK**.

Did You Know?

You can use wildcard characters in a criteria. A question mark (?) matches any single character. An asterisk (*) matches any sequence of characters. If you want to find an actual question mark or asterisk, type a tilde (~) before the character.

Other Text Functions

Function	Description
NUMBERVALUE (**New!**)	Converts text to number in a locale-independent manner
UNICHAR (**New!**)	Returns the unicode character referenced by the given numeric value
UNICODE (**New!**)	Returns the number (code point) corresponding to the first character of the text

Summarizing Data Using Subtotals

If you have a column list with similar [t...] matically calculate subtotals and gran[...] calculated with a summary function, su[...] AGE, while Grand totals are created fro[...] subtotal values. **Detailed data** is typicall[...] or below or to the left of the summary da[...] using subtotals, the data list is also outlin[...] detailed rows for each subtotal.

Summarizin
Using F

Subtotal Data in a List

1. Organize data in a hierarchical fashion—place summary rows below detail rows and summary columns to the right of detail columns.

2. Select the data that you want to subtotal.

3. Click the **Data** tab.

4. Use sort buttons to sort the column.

5. Click the **Subtotal** button.

6. Click the column to subtotal.

7. Click the summary function you want to use to calculate the subtotals.

8. Select the check box for each column that contains values you want to subtotal.

9. To set automatic page breaks following each subtotal, select the **Page break between groups** check box.

10. To show or hide a summary row above the detail row, select or clear the **Summary below data** check box.

11. To remove subtotals, click **Remove All**.

12. Click **OK**.

13. To add more subtotals, use the **Subtotal** button again.

Subtotal results

Use +/- button to expand/collapse subtotals.

...g Data
...nctions

You can use conditional functions, such as SUMIF, COUNTIF, and AVERAGEIF to summarize data in a workbook. These functions allow you to calculate a total, count the number of items, and average a set of numbers based on a specific criteria. You can use the SUMIF function to add up interest payment for accounts over $100, or use the COUNTIF function to find the number of people who live in CA from an address list. If you need to perform these functions based on multiple criteria, you can use the SUMIFS, COUNTIFS, and AVERAGEIFS functions. If you need to find the minimum or maximum in a range, you can use the summarizing functions MIN and MAX.

Use Summarize Data Functions

1. Click the cell where you want to place the function.

2. Type = (equal sign), type a text function, specify the argument for the selected function, and then press Enter.

   Some examples include:

   ◆ =AVERAGE(D6:D19)

   ◆ ={=SUM(1/COUNTIF(C6:C19, C6:19))}

   ◆ =SUMIF(C6:C19,"Todd", Quantity_Order1)

   ◆ =SUM(Quantity_Order1)

   Or click the **Formulas** tab, click the **More Functions** button, point to **Statistical**, click a data function, specify the function arguments, and then click **OK**.

Average   Sum   SUM and COUNTIF

Did You Know?

You can use several functions to count items in a range. The COUNT function counts the number of cells that contain numbers within the list of arguments, while the COUNTA function counts the number of cells that are not empty and the values within the list of arguments.

Summarize Data Function Examples

Formula	Result	Descriptions
SUM(num1,num2,...)	SUM(A1:A10)	Add the cells within a range.
SUMIF(range, criteria,sum_range)	SUMIF(A1:A10,">100",B1:B10)	Add the cells within a range that meets specific criteria. The sum_range are the cells to add that corresponds to cells in the range that match the criteria. Blanks and text values are ignored. Criteria is 10, "10", "<10", or B3.
COUNT(value1,value2,...)	COUNT(A1:A10)	Counts the number of cells that contain numbers within the list of arguments.
COUNTA(value1,value2,...)	COUNTA(A1:A10)	Counts the number of cells that are not empty and the values within the list of arguments.
SUMIFS(sum_range,criteria_range1, criteria1, criteria_range2, criteria2...)	SUMIF(B1:B10,">100",A1:A10, "<1000,C1:C10)	Add the cells within a range that meets multiple criteria. The sum_range are the cells to add that corresponds to cells in the range that match the criteria. Blanks and text values are ignored. Criteria is 10, "10", "<10", or B3.
COUNTIF (range, criteria)	COUNTIF(A1:A10,"CA")	Counts the number of cells within a range that meets specific criteria. Blanks and text values are ignored. Criteria is 10, "10", "<10", or B3.
COUNTIFS(range1, criteria1, range2, criteria2...)	COUNTIFS(A1:A10,"CA", B1:B10,"94588")	Counts the number of cells within a range that meets multiple criteria. Blanks and text values are ignored. Criteria is 10, "10", "<10", or B3.
AVERAGE(range)	AVERAGE(A1:A10)	Adds a group of numbers and then divides by the count of those numbers.
AVERAGEIF(range, criteria, average_range)	AVERAGE(A1:A10,"<1000" B1:B10)	Returns the average of all the cell in a range that meets specific criteria. TRUE or FALSE are ignored. Criteria is 10, "10", "<10", or B3.
AVERAGEIFS(average_range, range1, criteria1,range2, criteria2...)	AVERAGE(B1:B10,"<1000" A1:A10,">500")	Returns the average of all the cell in a range that meets multiple criteria. TRUE or FALSE are ignored. Criteria is 10, "10", "<10", or B3.
MIN(num1,num2,...)	MIN(A1:A10)	Returns the smallest number in a set of values.
MAX(num1,num2,...)	MAX(A1:A10)	Returns the largest number in a set of values.

Using Date & Time Functions

Calculating Dates

You can use different formulas to return a specific date. Here are some common examples you can use.

Calculate a Specific Day

You can use the DATE function to quickly calculate a specific day, such as New Year's (January 1st) or Christmas (December 25th).

=DATE(A1,1,1)

=DATE(A1,12,25)

Calculate a Changing Day

You can use the DATE and WEEKDAY function to calculate a holiday that changes each year, such as Thanksgiving, which is celebrated on the fourth Thursday in November.

=DATE(A1,11,1)+IF(5<WEEKDAY (DATE(A1,11,1)), 7-WEEKDAY(DATE(A1,11,1))+5, 5-WEEKDAY(DATE(A1,11,1)))+((4-1)*7)

Calculate the Day of the Year

You can calculate the day of the year for a specific date in the A1 cell. This function

returns an integer between 1 and 365.

=A1-DATE(YEAR(A1),1,0)

Calculate the Day of the Week

You can use the WEEKDAY function to calculate the day of the week for a specific date in a cell. The function returns an integer between 1 and 7. This example returns 1 for Sunday, October 7, 2013.

=WEEKDAY(DATE(2013, 10,7))

Calculate a Person's Age

You can use the DATEIF function to calculate the age of a person. The function returns an integer. For this example, A1 is birth date, A2 is the current date, and "y" indicates years ("md" indicates days and "ym" indicates months). If you loaded the Analysis ToolPak, you can also use the INT function.

=DATEIF(A1, A2,"y") or INT(YEARFRAC(A1,A2))

Excel stores dates as sequential serial numbers so that they can be used in calculations. By default, January 1, 1900 is serial number 1 and each day counts up from there.

Date function

Date examples

Calculate Number Between Days

You can use the DAYS function (**New!**) to calculate the number of days between the start and end date.

=DAYS(TODAY(), "12/25/2014")

Working with Time

You can use different formulas to work with time. Here are some common examples you can use.

Display the Current Date and Time

You can use the NOW function to quickly display the current date and time. To display the current date and time, use the function:

=NOW()

Add Times

You can use the TIME function to quickly add different times together. To add 1 hour, 35 minutes, 10 seconds to a time in A1, use the function:

=A1 + TIME(1, 35, 10)

Subtract Times

You can use the TIME function to subtract one time from another. To subtract 1 hour, 35 minutes, 10 seconds from a time in A1, use the function:

=A1 - TIME(1, 35, 10)

Rounding Times

You can use the TIME function along with the HOUR and MINUTE functions to round time up or down to the nearest time interval. To round to the previous interval (always going earlier or staying the same), use the function:

=TIME(HOUR(A1),FLOOR(MINUTE(A1),B1,0)

To round to the next interval (always going later or staying the same), use the function:

=TIME(HOUR(A1),CEILING(MINUTE(A1),B1,0)

The FLOOR and CEILING functions are Math & Trig functions for rounding numbers.

Time function

Time examples

Using Logical Functions

You can use logical functions to help you test whether conditions are true or false or make comparisons between expressions. The logical functions in Excel include: AND, FALSE, IF, IFERROR, NOT, OR, and TRUE. The structure of the IF function is IF(logical_test, value_if_false, value_if_false). For example, IF(E6<31,F6,""). If E6 is less than 31, then display the contents of F6; if not, then display nothing. You can also nest logical functions within a logical function. For example, IF(AND(E7>=61, E7<=90),F7,""). If E7 is greater than or equal to 61 and less than or equal to 61, then display the contents of F7; if not, then display nothing.

Use Logical Functions

1. Click the cell where you want to place the function.

2. Type = (equal sign), type a text function, specify the argument for the selected function, and then press Enter.

Some syntax examples include:

◆ =IF(logical_test, value_if_false, value_if_false)

Some examples include:

◆ =IF(E6<31,F6,"")

◆ =IF(AND(E7>=61, E7<=90),F7,"")

◆ =IF(NOT(A2<=15),"Goal","Not Goal")

Or click the **Formulas** tab, click the **Logical** button, click a function, specify the function arguments, and then click **OK**.

Logical Functions

Function	Description
AND	Returns TRUE if all of its arguments are TRUE
FALSE	Returns the logical value FALSE
IF	Specifies a logical test to perform
IFERROR	Returns a value you specify if a formula evaluates to an error, otherwise returns the result of the formula
IFNA (**New!**)	Returns the value if expression resolves to #NA
NOT	Reverses the logic of its argument
OR	Returns TRUE if any argument is TRUE
XOR (**New!**)	Returns a logical exclusive OR of all arguments
TRUE	Returns the logical value TRUE

Using Financial Functions

You can use financial functions to help you work with formulas related to business, accounting, and investment. You can use formulas for depreciation, such as SLN (Straight-Line Depreciation) and SYD (Sum-of-Years' Digits), or formulas for interest and investments, such as FV (Future Value of an investment), EFFECT (Effective annual interest rate) IPMT (Interest Payment for an investment or loan), PDURATION (number of periods needed to reach a value) (**New!**) and RRI (equivalent interest rate for investment growth) (**New!**). Many of the investment functions use the following arguments: rate, nominal_rate, per, nper, pv, fv, pmt, and type. Rate is the interest rate per period; Nominal_rate is the nominal interest rate; Per is the period for which you want to find the interest (between 1 and nper); Nper is the total number of payments periods; Pv is the present value; Fv is the future value; Pmt is the payment made each period; and Type is the number 0 or 1 to indicate when payments are due (0 at the end of the period or 1 at the beginning of the period). Many of the depreciation functions use the following arguments: cost, salvage, and life. Cost is the initial cost of the asset; Salvage is the value at the end of the depreciation; Life is the number of periods the asset is depreciated.

Use Financial Functions

1. Click the cell where you want to place the function.

2. Type = (equal sign), type a text function, specify the argument for the selected function, and then press Enter.

    Some syntax examples include:

    ◆ =FV(rate, nper, pmt, pv, type)

    ◆ =EFFECT(nominal_rate, npery)

    ◆ =IPMT(rate, per, nper, pv, fv, type)

    ◆ =SLN(cost, salvage, life)

    ◆ =SYD(cost, salvage, life, per)

    Or click the **Formulas** tab, click the **Financial** button, click a function, specify the function arguments, and then click **OK**.

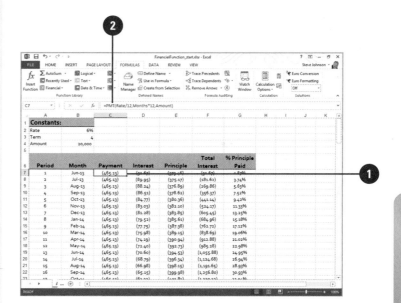

Using Math Functions

You can use math & trigonometry functions to help you perform mathematical calculations. You can use formulas for calculations, such as SQRT (Square root) or TAN (Tangent); formulas for conversion, such as DEGREES (radians to Degrees), or RADIANS (degrees to Radians); or formulas for rounding, such as FLOOR (number down, toward zero), CEILING (number up, towards nearest integer), INT (number down to nearest integer), or ROUND (number to a specific number of digits). You can also use the RAND function to generate random real numbers between 0 and 1, which you can use in an equation to create other random numbers, such as =RAND()*100—creates random numbers between 0 and 100. Many of the math functions use the following arguments: number, significance, and angle. Significance is the multiple to which you want to round. Other (**New!**) math functions include ACOT, ACOTH, ARABIC, BASE, CEILING.MATH, COMBINA, COT, COTH, CSC, CSCH, DECIMAL, FLOOR.MATH, ISO.CEILING, MUNIT, AND SEC.

Use Math & Trig Functions

1. Click the cell where you want to place the function.

2. Type = (equal sign), type a text function, specify the argument for the selected function, and then press Enter.

    Some syntax examples include:

    ◆ =FLOOR(number, significance)

    ◆ =CEILING(number, significance)

    ◆ =INT(number)

    ◆ =INT(number, num_digits)

    ◆ =DEGREES(angle)

    ◆ =RADIANS(angle)

    ◆ =SQRT(number)

    ◆ =TAN(number)

    ◆ =RAND()

    Or click the **Formulas** tab, click the **Math & Trig** button, click a function, specify the function arguments, and then click **OK**.

Using Statistical Functions

You can use statistical functions to help you perform analysis on a group of numbers. You can use formulas to find information, such as MAX or MIN (maximum or minimum value in a list), MEDIAN (median of given numbers), COUNT (number of items in a list), STDEV.S (standard deviation based on a sample), STDEV.P (standard deviation based on the entire population), SKEW (skewness of the distribution), or KURT (kurtosis of a data set). Other (**New!**) statistical functions include GAMMA, GAUSS (0.5 when less than standard normal cumulative distribution), BIN.DIST.RANGE (probability of a trial result using a binomial distribution), PERMUTATIONA (number of permutation for a given number of objects with repetitions), PHI (density for, and SKEW.P (skewness of the distribution based on a population).

Use Statistical Functions

1. Click the cell where you want to place the function.

2. Type = (equal sign), type a text function, specify the argument for the selected function, and then press Enter.

   Some syntax examples include:

   ◆ =MAX(number1, number2, ...)

   ◆ =MIN(number1, number2, ...)

   ◆ =MEDIAN(number1, number2, ...)

   ◆ =COUNT(value1, value2, ...)

   ◆ =STDEV.S(number1, number2, ...)

   ◆ =STDEV.P(number1, number2, ...)

   ◆ =SKEW(number1, number2, ...)

   ◆ =KURT(number1, number2, ...)

   Or click the **Formulas** tab, click the **More Functions** button, point to **Statistical**, click a function, specify the function arguments, and then click **OK**.

Using Information Functions

You can use information functions to help you determine the type of information in a cell or display information about formatting, location, or contents of a cell. The following information functions return TRUE when the function is valid: ISBLANK, ISERR, ISERROR, ISFORMULA (**New!**), ISEVEN, ISLOGICAL, ISNA, ISNONTEXT, ISNUMBER, ISODD, ISREF, and ISTEXT. The other main information functions are CELL, INFO, TYPE, and ERROR.TYPE, which display information about the cell contents. The SHEET function (**New!**) returns the sheet number of the referenced sheet, while the SHEETS function (**New!**) returns the number of sheets in a reference.

Use Information Functions

1. Click the cell where you want to place the function.

2. Type = (equal sign), type a text function, specify the argument for the selected function, and then press Enter.

   Some syntax examples include:

   ◆ =CELL("contents",cell)

   ◆ =INFO("directory")

   ◆ =TYPE(cell)

   ◆ =ERROR.TYPE (error_val)

   ◆ =IF(ISERROR(A1, "an error occurred.", A1 * 2)

   Or click the **Formulas** tab, click the **More Functions** button, point to **Information**, click a function, specify the function arguments, and then click **OK**.

Using Compatibility Functions

Excel has replaced several functions with new functions that provide improved accuracy and whose names better reflect their usage. For example, STDEVP has been replaced with STDEV.P. If you want to use an older version of a function for backwards compatibility in order to share your worksheets with those who do not have Excel 2013, you can use the Compatibility menu on the Formulas tab or the Compatibility option in the Insert Function dialog box to display and select the old function you want. When you enter a function, Formula AutoComplete lists both renamed and compatibility functions. If compatibility is not an issue, you can use the new functions, which are available in the different function categories. Before you save a workbook in an earlier version of Excel, you should use the Compatibility Checker to determine whether new functions are used, so you can change them.

Use Compatibility Functions

1. Click the cell where you want to place the function.

2. Type = (equal sign), type a text function, specify the argument for the selected function, and then press Enter.

   Some syntax examples include:

   ◆ =STDEV.S(number1, number2, ...)

   ◆ =STDEV.P(number1, number2, ...)

   Or click the **Formulas** tab, click the **More Functions** button, point to **Compatibility**, click a function, specify the function arguments, and then click **OK**.

   Or click the **Formulas** tab, click the **Insert Function** button, click the **Category** list arrow, click **Compatibility**, click a function, click **OK**, specify the function arguments, and then click **OK**.

Compatibility functions

See Also

See "Checking Compatibility" on page 28 for more information on using the Compatibility Checker.

Using Web Functions

With Excel, you can retrieve data from a web service directly into a worksheet. The web functions include: ENCODEURL, WEBSERVICE, and FILTERXML. ENCODEURL (**New!**) is a function that allows you to retrieve an URL-encoded string. It takes out all illegal characters in a URL and changes them to a % equivalent. WEBSERVICE (**New!**) is a function that allows you to retrieve XML data from a web service that doesn't require user name and password authentication, such as a Twitter feed or RSS feed. The WEBSERVICE function doesn't support all protocols, such as ftp:// or file://. FILTERXML (**New!**) is a function that allows you to retrieve specific data from the XML code by using the specific XPath. This function allows you to get specific data from the WEBSERVICE function.

Use Web Functions

1. Click the cell where you want to place the function.

2. Type = (equal sign), type a text function, specify the argument for the selected function, and then press Enter.

   Some syntax examples include:

   ◆ =WEBSERVICE(url)

   ◆ =FILTERXML(xml, xpath)

   ◆ =ENCODEURL(text)

   Or click the **Formulas** tab, click the **More Functions** button, point to **Web**, click a function, specify the function arguments, and then click **OK**.

   Or click the **Formulas** tab, click the **Insert Function** button, click the **Category** list arrow, click **Web**, click a function, click **OK**, specify the function arguments, and then click **OK**.

Array of formulas

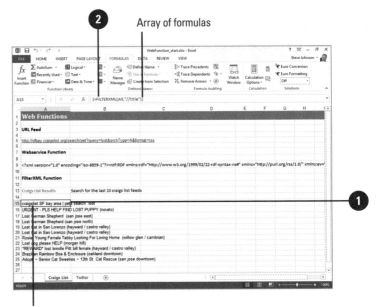

FILTERXML function

Protecting and Securing a Workbook

Introduction

When you've developed content in your workbook and want feedback, you can electronically send an Excel workbook to reviewers so that they can read, revise, and comment on the workbook without having to print it. Instead of reading hand-written text or sticky notes on your printout, you can get clear and concise feedback.

Adding a password to protect your workbook is not only a good idea for security purposes, it's an added feature to make sure that changes to your workbook aren't made by unauthorized people. You can protect all or part of a work-sheet or an entire workbook. In each case, you'll be asked to supply a password, and then enter it again when you want to work on the file. Not only can you guard who sees your workbook, you can set rights on who can add changes and comments to your workbook. If you need to validate the authenticity of a workbook, you can add an invisible digital signature, an electronic secure stamp of authentication on a workbook, or a visible signature line. A signature line allows you to create a paperless signature process for workbooks, such as contracts.

The Trust Center is a place where you set security options and find the latest technology information as it relates to workbook privacy, safety, and security from Microsoft. The Trust Center allows you to set security and privacy settings and provides links to Microsoft privacy statements, a customer improvement program, and trustworthy computing practices.

What You'll Do

Inspect Workbooks

Protect a Worksheet

Lock or Unlock Worksheet Cells

Add Password Protection to a Workbook

Add a Digital Signature

Add a Signature Line

Avoid Harmful Attacks

Use the Trust Center

Select Trusted Publishers and Locations

Set Document Related Security Options

Set App Catalog Security Options

Set Add-In, ActiveX and Macro Security Options

Change Message Bar Security Options

Set Privacy Options

Set External Content Security Options

Work with Office Safe Modes

Mark a Workbook as Read-Only

Inspecting Workbooks

While you work on your workbook, Excel automatically saves and manages personal information and hidden data to enable you to create and develop a workbook with other people. The personal information and hidden data includes comments, revision marks, versions, ink annotations, document properties, invisible content, header and footer information, rows and columns, worksheets, document server properties, custom XML data, and Office apps (**New!**), either content and task pane. The **Document Inspector** uses inspector modules to find and remove any hidden data and personal information specific to each of these modules that you might not want to share with others. If you remove hidden content from your workbook, you might not be able to restore it by using the Undo command, so it's important to make a copy of your workbook before you remove any information.

Inspect a Workbook

1. Click the **File** tab, click **Save As**, type a name to save a copy of the original, specify a folder location, and then click **Save**.

2. Click the **File** tab, and then click **Info**.

3. Click the **Check for Issues** button, and then click **Inspect Document**.

4. Select the check boxes with the content you want to find and remove:

   ◆ **Comments and Annotations.** Includes comments and ink annotations.

   ◆ **Document Properties and Personal Information.** Includes metadata document properties (Summary, Statistics, and Custom tabs), the file path for publishing web pages, document server properties, and content type information.

Did You Know?

What is metadata? Metadata is data that describes other data. For example, text in a workbook is data, while the number of worksheets is metadata.

- **Data Model.** Includes Data Model for embedded data (**New!**) that may not be visible on the sheets.

- **Content Apps.** Includes any content apps (**New!**) saved in the document body.

- **Task Pane Apps.** Includes any task pane apps (**New!**) saved in the document.

- **Custom XML Data.** Includes any custom XML data.

- **Headers and Footers.** Includes information in headers and footers.

- **Hidden Rows and Columns.** Includes information in hidden rows and columns.

- **Hidden Worksheets.** Includes information in hidden worksheets.

- **Invisible Content.** Includes objects formatted as invisible. Doesn't include objects covered by other objects.

5 Click **Inspect**.

6 Review the results of the inspection.

7 Click **Remove All** for each inspector module in which you want to remove hidden data and personal information.

TROUBLE? *Before you click Remove All, be sure you want to remove the information. You might not be able to restore it.*

8 Click **Close**.

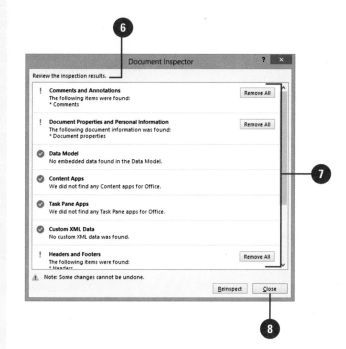

Protecting a Worksheet

To preserve all your hard work—particularly if others use your files—protect it with a password. You can protect a sheet or an entire document. In each case, you'll be asked to supply a password, and then enter it again when you want to work on the file. Passwords are case sensitive, so be sure to supply your password as it was first entered. If you forget a password, there is no way to open the file, so it's very important to remember or write down your password(s). Keep your password in a safe place. Avoid obvious passwords such as your name, your company, or your favorite pet.

Apply a Password to a Worksheet

1. Click the **Review** tab.

2. Click the **Protect Sheet** button.

3. Select the check boxes for the options you want protected in the worksheet.

4. Type a password.

5. Click **OK**.

6. Retype the password.

7. Click **OK**.

Did You Know?

You can protect document elements. Click the Review tab, click the Protect Document button, and then select or clear the Structure or Windows check boxes. Select the Structure check box to prevent users from viewing, copying, moving, or inserting worksheets. It also prevents users from recording new macros, displaying data from PivotTable reports, using analysis tools, or creating scenario summary reports. Select the Windows check box to prevent users from moving, resizing, or closing windows.

Apply a Password to Edit Parts of a Worksheet

1. Select the range in which you want to apply a password.

2. Click the **Review** tab.

3. Click the **Allow Users to Edit Ranges** button.

4. Click **New**.

5. If you want, type a range title.

6. Type a range password.

7. Click **OK**.

8. Retype the password.

9. Click **OK**.

10. To modify or delete a range, click a range, and then click **Modify** or **Delete**.

11. Click **OK**.

Did You Know?

You can quickly unprotect a worksheet or workbook. Click the Review tab, click the Unprotect Worksheet or Unprotect Workbook button, type the password, and then click OK.

See Also

See "Hiding and Unhiding Worksheets and Workbooks" on page 120 for information on hiding data in selected worksheets or workbooks without deleting it.

Locking or Unlocking Worksheet Cells

To prevent accidental changes to your data, you can lock worksheet cells. When you lock selected cells, you cannot make changes to them until you unlock them. When you lock cells, users can unlock the data and make changes unless you add password protection to the worksheet. For security or confidentiality reasons, you might want to hide formulas from view. If so, you can hide or unhide them using the Protection tab in the Format Cells dialog box.

Lock or Unlock Worksheet Cells

1. Select the cell or range you want to lock or unlock.

2. Click the **Home** tab.

3. Click the **Format** button, and then click **Lock Cell** to lock or unlock the current selection.

   This toggle command turns on or off the Locked check box on the Protection tab in the Format Cells dialog box.

Lock Cell command

Hide or Show Formulas

1. Select the cell or range with the formulas you want to hide or show.

2. Click the **Home** tab.

3. Click the **Format** button, and then click **Format Cells**.

4. Click the **Protection** tab.

5. Select the **Hidden** check box to hide formulas or clear it to show formulas.

6. Click **OK**.

Adding Security Encryption to a Workbook

File encryption is additional security you can apply to a workbook. File encryption scrambles your password to protect your workbook from unauthorized people from breaking into the file. You don't have to worry about the encryption, Excel handles everything. All you need to do is remember the password. If you forget it, you can't open the file. Password protection takes effect the next time you open the workbook. To set password protection using file encryption, use the Encrypt with Password command on the Info screen, enter a password, write it down for safekeeping, and then reenter the password again.

Apply File Encryption

1. Click the **File** tab, and then click **Info**.

2. Click the **Protect Workbook** button, and then click **Encrypt with Password**.

3. Type a password.

4. Click **OK**.

5. Retype the password.

6. Click **OK**.

Did You Know?

You can remove file encryption. Click the File tab, click Info, click the Protect Workbook button, click Encrypt With Password, delete the file encryption password, and then click OK.

Adding Password Protection to a Workbook

You can assign a password and other security options so that only those who know the password can open the workbook, or to protect the integrity of your workbook as it moves from person to person. At times, you will want the information to be used but not changed; at other times, you will want only specific people to be able to view the workbook. Setting a workbook as read-only is useful when you want a workbook, such as a company-wide bulletin, to be distributed and read, but not changed. Password protection takes effect the next time you open the workbook.

Add Password Protection to a Workbook

① Open the workbook you want to protect.

② Click the **File** tab, and then click **Save As**.

③ Click **Tools**, and then click **General Options**.

④ Type a password in the Password to open box or the Password to modify box.

> **IMPORTANT** *It's critical that you remember your password. If you forget your password, Microsoft can't retrieve it.*

⑤ Select or clear the **Remove automatically created personal information from this file on save** check box.

⑥ To set macro security options in the Trust center, click **Macro Security**.

⑦ Click **OK**.

⑧ Type your password again.

⑨ Click **OK**.

⑩ If you entered passwords for Open and Modify, type your password again, and then click **OK**.

⑪ Click **Save**, and then click **Yes** to replace existing workbook.

For Your Information

Using a Strong Password

Hackers identify passwords as strong or weak. A strong password is a combination of uppercase and lowercase letters, numbers, and symbols, such as Grea8t!, while a weak one doesn't use different character types, such as Hannah1. Be sure to write down your passwords and place them in a secure location.

Open a Workbook with Password Protection

1. Click the **File** tab, click **Open**, navigate to a workbook with password protection, and then click **Open**.

2. Click **Read Only** if you do not wish to modify the workbook, or type the password in the Password dialog box.

3. Click **OK**.

Change or Remove the Password Protection

1. Click the **File** tab, click **Open**, navigate to a workbook with password protection, and then click **Open**.

2. Type the password in the Password dialog box.

3. Click **OK**.

4. Click the **File** tab, click **Save As**, click **Tools**, and then click **General Options**.

5. Select the contents in the Password to modify box or the Password to open box, and then choose the option you want:

   ◆ **Change password.** Type a new password, click **OK**, and then retype your password.

   ◆ **Delete password.** Press Delete.

6. Click **OK**.

7. Click **Save**, and then click **Yes** to replace existing workbook.

Adding a Digital Signature

After you've finished a workbook, you might consider adding an invisible digital signature—an electronic, secure stamp of authentication on a workbook. Before you can add a digital signature, you need to get a **digital ID**, or **digital certificate**, which provides an electronic way to prove your identity. A digital certificate checks a public key to validate a private key associated with a digital signature. To assure a digital signature is authentic, it must have a valid (non expired or revoked) certificate issued by a reputable certification authority (CA), and the signing person must be from a trusted publisher. However, a verified certified digital ID is not always needed. If you don't need a verified digital certificate, you can create one of your own. If someone modifies the file, the digital signature is removed and revoked. If you're not sure if a document is digitally signed, you can use the Signatures task pane to view or remove valid signatures.

Create an Digital ID

1. Click the **File** tab, click **Info**, click the **Protect Workbook** button, and then click **Add a Digital Signature**.

2. Click the **Commitment Type** list arrow, and then select an option: **None, Created and approved this document, Approved this document**, or **Created this document**.

3. Enter a purpose for signing this document.

4. Click **Details**.

5. Enter your name or role/title and address.

6. Click **OK**.

7. To change the digital signature, click **Change**, select the one you want, and then click **OK**.

8. Click **Sign**.

View or Remove Signatures

1. Click the **Signature** icon on the Status bar, or click the **File** tab, click **Info**, and then click the **View Signatures** button.

   The Signatures task pane appears, displaying valid signatures in the document. Invalid signatures are no longer automatically removed.

2. Point to a signature, and then click the list arrow.

3. To see signature details, click **Signature Details**, select a signature, click **View**, click **OK** when you're done, and then click **Close**.

4. To remove a signature, point to a signature, click the list arrow, click **Remove Signature**, click **Yes**, and then if necessary click **OK**.

5. Click the **Close** button on the task pane.

Signature icon

Adding a Signature Line

If you prefer a visible signature line instead of an invisible digital signature, you can insert a visible signature line along with a digital certificate of authenticity. Signature lines allow you to create a paperless signature process for workbooks, such as contracts. A visible signature line looks like a typical signature line with a name, a date and a line for a signature. When you send a workbook out with a signature request, the signer sees a signature line and a notification request with instructions. The signer can type—or ink with a Tablet PC—a signature next to the *X*, or select a signature image. To add a signature line and digital signature at the same time, first you insert a signature line into your workbook, and then you sign it.

Add a Signature Line

1. Click the **Insert** tab.

2. Click the **Signature Line** button arrow, and then click **Microsoft Office Signature Line**.

3. If an alert message appears, click **Signature Services from the Office Marketplace** to open an informational web site where you can sign up for a digital certificate, or click **OK** to create your own.

4. Type information about the person who will be signing on this signature line.

5. If you want, type any instructions for the signer.

6. To show the signature date, select the **Allow the signer to add comments in the Sign dialog** check box.

7. To show the signature date, select the **Show sign date in signature line** check box.

8. Click **OK**.

Sign the Signature Line

① Double-click the signature line that needs a signature.

② To add a printed version of your signature, type your name.

If you have a Tablet PC, you can sign your name.

③ To select an image of your written signature, click **Select Image**, navigate to the signature image, and then click **Select**.

④ Click **Sign**.

Digital signature

Signature line

Avoiding Harmful Attacks

Many viruses and other harmful attacks spread through file downloads, attachments in e-mail messages, and data files that have macros, ActiveX controls, add-ins, or Visual Basic for Applications (VBA) code attached to them. Virus writers capitalize on people's curiosity and willingness to accept files from people they know or work with, in order to transmit malicious files disguised as or attached to benign files. When you start downloading files to your computer, you must be aware of the potential for catching a computer virus, worm, or Trojan Horse. Typically, you can't catch one from just reading a mail message or downloading a file, but you can catch one from installing, opening, or running an infected program or attached code.

Understanding Harmful Attacks

Phishing is a scam that tries to steal your identity by sending deceptive e-mail asking you for bank and credit card information online. Phishers spoof the domain names of banks and other companies in order to deceive consumers into thinking that they are visiting a familiar web site.

Phishers create a web address that looks like a familiar web address but is actually altered. This is known as a **homograph**. The domain name is created using alphabet characters from different languages, not just English. For example, the web site address "www.microsoft.com" looks legitimate, but what you can't see is that the "i" is a Cyrillic character from the Russian alphabet.

Don't be fooled by spoofed web sites that looks like the official site. Never respond to requests for personal information via e-mail; most companies have policies that do not ask for your personal information through e-mail. If you get a suspicious e-mail, call the institution to investigate and report it.

Spam is unsolicited e-mail, which is often annoying and time-consuming to get rid of. Spammers harvest e-mail addresses from web pages and unsolicited e-mail. To avoid spam, use multiple e-mail addresses (one for web forms and another for private e-mail), opt-out and remove yourself from e-mail lists. See the Microsoft Windows and Microsoft Outlook Help system for specific details.

Spyware is software that collects personal information without your knowledge or permission. Typically, spyware is downloaded and installed on your computer along with free software, such as freeware, games, or music file-sharing programs. Spyware is often associated with **Adware** software that displays advertisements, such as a pop-up ad. Examples of spyware and unauthorized adware include programs that change your home page or search page without your permission. To avoid spyware and adware, read the fine print in license agreements when you install software, scan your computer for spyware and adware with detection and removal software (such as Ad-aware from Lavasoft), and turn on Pop-up Blocker. See the Microsoft Windows Help system for specific details.

There are a few things you can do within any Office 2013 program to keep your system safe from the infiltration of harmful attacks.

1) Make sure you activate macro, ActiveX, add-in, and VBA code detection and notification. You can use the Trust Center to help protect you from attached code attacks. The Trust Center checks for trusted publisher and code locations on your computer and provides security options for add-ins, ActiveX controls, and macros to ensure the best possible protection. The Trust Center displays a security alert in the Message Bar when it detects a potentially harmful attack.

2) Make sure you activate web site spoofing detection and notification. You can use the Trust Center to help protect you from homograph attacks. The *Check Office documents that are from or link to suspicious web sites* check box under Privacy Options in the Trust Center is on by default and continually checks for potentially spoofed domain names. The Trust Center displays a security alert in the Message Bar when you have a document open and click a link to a web site with an address that has a potentially spoofed domain name, or you open a file from a web site with an address that has a potentially spoofed domain name.

3) Be very careful of file attachments in e-mail you open. As you receive e-mail, don't open or run an attached file unless you know who sent it and what it contains. If you're not sure, you should delete it. The Attachment Manager provides security information to help you understand more about the file you're opening. See the Microsoft Outlook Help system for specific details.

Avoiding Harmful Attacks Using Windows

There are a few things you can do within Microsoft Windows to keep your system safe from the infiltration of harmful attacks.

1) Make sure Windows Firewall is turned on. Windows Firewall helps block viruses and worms from reaching your computer, but it doesn't detect or disable them if they are already on your computer or come through e-mail. Windows Firewall doesn't block unsolicited e-mail or stop you from opening e-mail with harmful attachments.

2) Make sure Automatic Updates is turned on. Windows Automatic Updates regularly checks the Windows Update web site for important updates that your computer needs, such as security updates, critical updates, and service packs. Each file that you download using Automatic Update has a digital signature from Microsoft to ensure its authenticity and security.

3) Make sure you are using the most up-to-date antivirus software. New viruses and more virulent strains of existing viruses are discovered every day. Unless you update your virus-checking software, new viruses can easily bypass outdated virus checking software. Companies such as McAfee and Symantec offer shareware virus checking programs available for download directly from their web sites. These programs monitor your system, checking each time a file is added to your computer to make sure it's not in some way trying to change or damage valuable system files.

4) Be very careful of the sites from which you download files. Major file repository sites, such as FileZ, Download.com, or TuCows, regularly check the files they receive for viruses before posting them to their web sites. Don't download files from web sites unless you are certain that the sites check their files for viruses. Internet Explorer monitors downloads and warns you about potentially harmful files and gives you the option to block them.

Using the Trust Center

The **Trust Center** is a place where you set security options and find the latest technology information as it relates to workbook privacy, safety, and security from Microsoft. The Trust Center allows you to set security and privacy settings—Trusted Publishers, Trusted Locations, Trusted Documents, Trusted App Catalogs (**New!**), Add-ins, ActiveX Settings, Macro Settings, Protected view, Message Bar, External Content, File Block Setting, and Privacy Options —and provides links to Microsoft privacy statements, a customer improvement program, and trustworthy computing practices.

View the Trust Center

1. Click the **File** tab, and then click **Options**.

2. In the left pane, click **Trust Center**.

3. Click the links in which you want online information at the Microsoft Online web site.

   ◆ **Show the Microsoft Excel privacy statement.** Opens a Microsoft web site detailing privacy practices.

   ◆ **Office.com privacy statement.** Opens a Microsoft Office web site detailing privacy practices.

   ◆ **Customer Experience Improvement Program.** Opens the Microsoft Customer Experience Improvement Program (CEIP) web site.

   ◆ **Microsoft Office Feedback "Send a Smile" Privacy Statement.** Opens a Microsoft web site with information about Microsoft's privacy statement (**New!**).

   ◆ **Microsoft Trustworthy Computing.** Opens a Microsoft web site detailing security and reliability practices.

4. When you're done, close your web browser or dialog box, and return to Excel.

5. Click **OK**.

Selecting Trusted Publishers and Locations

The Trust Center security system continually checks for external potentially unsafe content in your workbooks. Hackers can hide web beacons in external content—images, linked media, data connections and templates—to gather information about you or cause problems. When the Trust Center detects potentially harmful external content, the Message Bar appears with a security alert and options to enable or block the content. Trusted publishers are reputable developers who create application extensions, such as a macro, ActiveX control, or add-in. The Trust Center uses a set of criteria—valid and current digital signature, and reputable certificate—to make sure publishers' code and source locations are safe and secure. If you are sure that the external content is trustworthy, you can add the content publisher and location to your trusted lists, which allows it to run without being checked by the Trust Center.

Modify Trusted Publishers and Locations

1. Click the **File** tab, and then click **Options**.

2. In the left pane, click **Trust Center**.

3. Click **Trust Center Settings**.

4. In the left pane, click **Trusted Publishers**.

5. Select a publisher, and then use the **View** and **Remove** buttons to make the changes you want.

6. In the left pane, click **Trusted Locations**.

7. Select a location, and then use the **Add new location**, **Remove**, and **Modify** buttons to make the changes you want.

8. Select or clear the **Allow Trusted Locations on my network (not recommended)** check box.

9. Select or clear the **Disable all Trusted Locations** check box.

10. Click **OK**.

11. Click **OK**.

Setting Document Related Security Options

The Trust Center security system allows you to set file-related options to check for potentially unsafe content in your documents. In Trusted Documents, you can set options to open trusted documents without any security prompts for macros, ActiveX controls and other types of active content in the document. For a trusted document, you won't be prompted the next time you open the document even if new active content was added to the document or changes were made to existing active content. You should only trust documents if you trust the source. Protected view provides a place to open potentially dangerous files, without any security prompts, in a restricted mode to help minimize harm to your computer. If you disable Protected view, you could expose your computer to possible harmful threats. In File Block Settings, you can select the Open and Save check boxes to prevent each file type from opening, or just opening in Protected view, and from saving.

Set Options for Trusted Documents

1. Click the **File** tab, and then click **Options**.

2. In the left pane, click **Trust Center**.

3. Click **Trust Center Settings**.

4. In the left pane, click **Trusted Documents**.

5. Select or clear the check boxes you do or don't want.

   ◆ **Allow documents on a network to be trusted.**

   ◆ **Disable Trusted Documents.**

6. To clear all trusted documents so they are no longer trusted, click **Clear**.

7. Click **OK**.

8. Click **OK**.

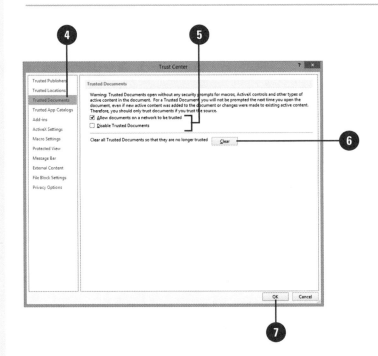

Set Options for Protected View

1. Click the **File** tab, and then click **Options**.

2. In the left pane, click **Trust Center**.

3. Click **Trust Center Settings**.

4. In the left pane, click **Protected View**.

5. Select or clear the check boxes you do or don't want.

   ◆ **Enable Protected View for files originating from the Internet.**

   ◆ **Enable Protected View for files located in potentially unsafe locations.**

   ◆ **Enable Protected View for Outlook attachments.**

6. Click **OK**.

7. Click **OK**.

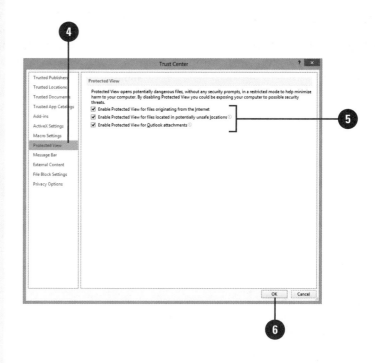

Set Options for File Block Settings

1. Click the **File** tab, and then click **Options**.

2. In the left pane, click **Trust Center**.

3. Click **Trust Center Settings**.

4. In the left pane, click **File Block Settings**.

5. Select the **Open** and **Save** check boxes you want to block for the different file types from opening or saving or clear the ones you don't want.

6. Select the open behavior option you want.

7. Click **OK**.

8. Click **OK**.

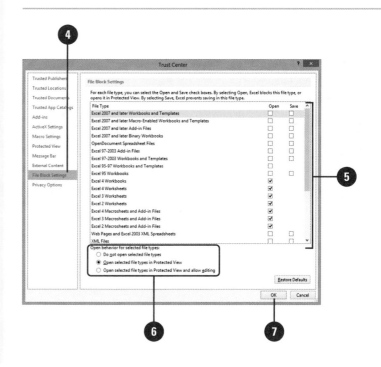

Setting App Catalog Security Options

You can store apps for SharePoint and Office apps for your organization's internal use in an App Catalog site (**New!**). The App Catalog site is a special site collection on a web application. When you create an App Catalog site, you get two libraries for apps: Apps for SharePoint and Apps for Office. App Catalog security options in the Trust Center allow you to set security settings that allow you to specify the trusted app catalogs you want to use.

Set App Catalog Security Options

1. Click the **File** tab, and then click **Options**.

2. In the left pane, click **Trust Center**.

3. Click **Trust Center Settings**.

4. In the left pane, click **Trusted App Catalogs**.

5. Select or clear the check boxes you do or don't want.

   ◆ **Don't allow any apps to start.** Select to not let any apps start.

   ◆ **Don't allow apps from the Office Store to start.** Select to not allow apps from the Office Store to start.

6. Enter a URL for the app catalog, and then click **Add catalog**.

7. To remove or clear a URL, select the URL, and then click **Remove** or **Clear**.

8. Click **OK**, and then click **OK** to save your settings.

   The settings will be applied the next time you start Office.

9. Click **OK**.

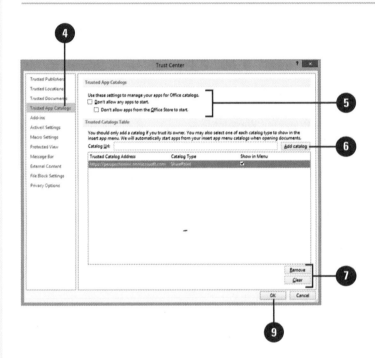

For Your Information

Creating an App Catalog on Office 365

If you have an Office 365 Enterprise team site, you can create an App Catalog site. In your browser, sign-in to your Office 365 Enterprise team site, click Admin, and then click SharePoint. In SharePoint admin center, click App on the left menu, click App Catalog to create a new App Catalog site, and then specify the details you want for your App Catalog site. After you create an App Catalog site, you can add apps to it, such as the ones you create and package from Access 2013.

Setting Add-in Security Options

An add-in, such as smart tags, extends functionality to Microsoft Office programs. An add-in can add buttons and custom commands to the Ribbon. When an add-in is installed, it appears on the Add-Ins tab of an Office program and includes a special ScreenTip that identifies the developer. Since add-ins are software code added to Microsoft Office programs, hackers can use them to do malicious harm, such as spreading a virus. The Trust Center uses a set of criteria—valid and current digital signature, reputable certificate and a trusted publisher—to make sure add-ins are safe and secure. If it discovers a potentially unsafe add-in, it disables the code and notifies you in the Message Bar. If the add-in security options are not set to the level you need, you can change them in the Trust Center.

Set Add-in Security Options

1. Click the **File** tab, and then click **Options**.

2. In the left pane, click **Trust Center**.

3. Click **Trust Center Settings**.

4. In the left pane, click **Add-ins**.

5. Select or clear the check boxes you do or don't want.

   ◆ **Require Application Add-ins to be signed by Trusted Publisher.** Select to check for a digital signature on the .dll file.

   ◆ **Disable notification for unsigned add-ins (code will remain disabled).** Only available if the above check box is selected. Select to disable unsigned add-ins without notification.

   ◆ **Disable all Application Add-ins (may impair functionality).** Select to disable all add-ins without any notifications.

6. Click **OK**.

7. Click **OK**.

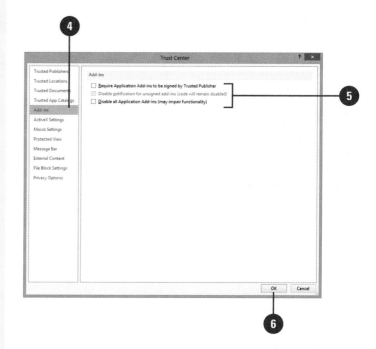

Setting ActiveX Security Options

An ActiveX control provides additional functionality, such as a text box, button, dialog box, or small utility program. ActiveX controls are software code, so hackers can use them to do malicious harm, such as spreading a virus. You can use the Trust Center to prevent ActiveX controls from harming your computer. If the ActiveX security options are not set to the level you want, you can change them in the Trust Center. If you change ActiveX control settings in Excel, it effects all Microsoft Office programs. The Trust Center uses a set of criteria—checks the kill bit and Safe for Initialization (SFI) settings—to make sure ActiveX controls run safely.

Change ActiveX Security Settings

1. Click the **File** tab, and then click **Options**.

2. In the left pane, click **Trust Center**.

3. Click **Trust Center Settings**.

4. In the left pane, click **ActiveX Settings**.

5. Click the option you want for ActiveX in documents not in a trusted location.

   ◆ Disable all controls without notification.

   ◆ Prompt me before enabling Unsafe for Initialization (UFI) controls with additional restrictions and Safe for Initialization (SFI) controls with minimal restrictions (default).

   ◆ Prompt me before enabling all controls with minimal restrictions.

   ◆ Enable all controls without restrictions and without prompting (not recommended; potentially dangerous controls can run).

6. Click **OK**.

7. Click **OK**.

Setting Macro Security Options

A macro allows you to automate frequently used steps or tasks to save time and work more efficiently. Macros are written using VBA (Visual Basic for Applications) code, which opens the door to hackers to do malicious harm, such as spreading a virus. The Trust Center uses a set of criteria—valid and current digital signature, reputable certificate and a trusted publisher—to make sure macros are safe and secure. If the Trust Center discovers a potentially unsafe macro, it disables the code and notifies you in the Message Bar. You can click Options on the Message Bar to enable it or set other security options. If the macro security options are not set to the level you need, you can change them in the Trust Center.

Change Macro Security Settings

1. Click the **File** tab, and then click **Options**.

2. In the left pane, click **Trust Center**.

3. Click **Trust Center Settings**.

4. In the left pane, click **Macro Settings**.

5. Click the option you want for macros in documents not in a trusted location.

   - Disable all macros without notification.

   - Disable all macros with notification (default).

   - Disable all macros except digitally signed macros.

   - Enable all macros (not recommended; potentially dangerous code can run).

6. If you're a developer, select the **Trust access to the VBA project object model** check box.

7. Click **OK**.

8. Click **OK**.

Changing Message Bar Security Options

The Message Bar displays security alerts when Office detects potentially unsafe content in an open document. The Message Bar appears below the Ribbon when a potential problem arises. The Message Bar provides a security warning and options to enable external content or leave it blocked. If you don't want to receive alerts about security issues, you can disable the Message Bar.

Modify Message Bar Security Options

1. Click the **File** tab, and then click **Options**.

2. In the left pane, click **Trust Center**.

3. Click **Trust Center Settings**.

4. In the left pane, click **Message Bar**.

5. Click the option you want for showing the Message bar.

    ◆ Show the Message Bar in all applications when active content, such as ActiveX controls and macros, has been blocked (default).

      This option is not selected if you selected the Disable all macros without notification check box in the Macros pane of the Trust Center.

    ◆ Never show information about blocked content.

6. Click **OK**.

7. Click **OK**.

Setting Privacy Options

Privacy options in the Trust Center allow you to set security settings that protect your personal privacy online. For example, the *Check Office documents that are from or link to suspicious web sites* option checks for spoofed web sites and protects you from phishing schemes. If your kids are doing research online using the Research task pane, you can set Privacy Options to enable parental controls and a password to block sites with offensive content.

Set Privacy Options

1. Click the **File** tab, and then click **Options**.

2. In the left pane, click **Trust Center**.

3. Click **Trust Center Settings**.

4. In the left pane, click **Privacy Options**.

5. Select or clear the privacy check boxes you do or don't want.

   The options allow or prevent Office connections to the Internet and suspicious web sites, or install new services for the Research task pane.

6. Click **Research Options**.

7. Click **Parental Control**.

8. Select the **Turn on content filtering to make services block offensive results** check box.

9. Select the **Allow users to search only the services that can block offensive results** check box, if necessary.

10. Enter a password, so users cannot change these settings.

11. Click **OK**, retype the password, and then click **OK**.

12. Click **OK**.

13. Click **OK**.

Setting External Content Security Options

External content is any content that is connected or linked to a document from a potentially unsafe external source, such as images, linked media, hyperlinks, data connections, or templates. Excel allows you to connect to external data from databases and other documents. Blocking external content prevents hackers from hiding malicious code in it that might do harm to your files and computer. You can set security options for data connections and document links to enable or disable the external content or display a security warning.

Set Security Settings for Data Connections

1. Click the **File** tab, and then click **Options**.

2. In the left pane, click **Trust Center**.

3. Click **Trust Center Settings**.

4. In the left pane, click **External Content**.

5. Click the option you want for data connections security.

   ◆ **Enable all Data Connections (not recommended).** Select to open documents with external data connections or to create external data connections without security warnings.

   ◆ **Prompt user about Data Connections.** Select to receive a security warning when you open or create documents with external data connections.

   ◆ **Disable all Data Connections.** Select to not allow any external data connections.

6. Click **OK**.

7. Click **OK**.

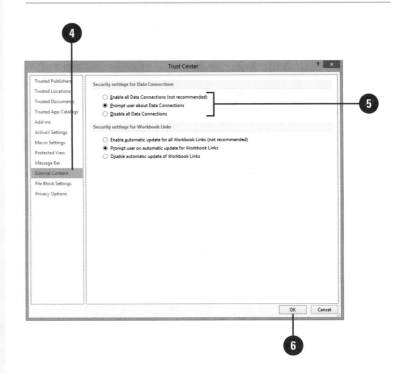

Set Security Settings for Document Links

1. Click the **File** tab, and then click **Options**.

2. In the left pane, click **Trust Center**.

3. Click **Trust Center Settings**.

4. In the left pane, click **External Content**.

5. Click the option you want for document links security.

   ◆ **Enable automatic update for all <Document> Links (not recommended).** Select to automatically update links to data in another document without security warnings.

   ◆ **Prompt user on automatic update for <Document> Links.** Select to receive a security warning when you run automatic updates for links to data in another document.

   ◆ **Disable automatic update of <Document> Links.** Select to not allow any automatic updates for links to data in another document.

6. Click **OK**.

7. Click **OK**.

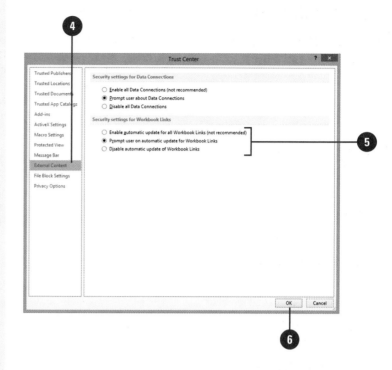

Working with Office Safe Modes

Microsoft Office uses two types of safe modes—Automated and User-Initiated—when it encounters a program problem. When you start an Office program, it automatically checks for problems, such as an extension not properly loading. If the program is not able to start the next time you try, the programs starts in **Automated Safe mode**, which disables extensions—macros, ActiveX controls, and add-ins—and other possible problem areas. If you're having problems and the Office program doesn't start in Automated Safe mode, you can start the program in **User-Initiated Safe mode**. When you start an Office program in Office Safe mode, not all features are available. For instance, templates can't be saved, AutoCorrect list is not loaded, preferences cannot be saved, and all command-line options are ignored except /a and /n. Before you can use Office Safe mode, you need to enable it in the Trust Center. When you're in safe mode, you can use the Trust Center to find out the disabled items and enable them one at a time to help you pin point the problem.

Enable Safe Mode

1. Click the **File** tab, and then click **Options**.

2. In the left pane, click **Trust Center**.

3. Click **Trust Center Settings**.

4. In the left pane, click **ActiveX Settings**.

5. Select the **Safe Mode (helps limit the control's access to your computer)** check box.

6. Click **OK**.

7. Click **OK**.

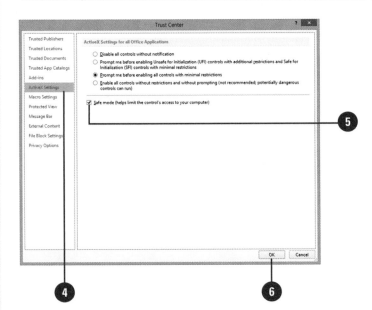

See Also

See "Maintaining and Repairing Office" on page 458 for information on fixing problems with a Microsoft Office 2013 program.

View Disabled Items

1. Click the **File** tab, and then click **Options**.

2. In the left pane, click **Add-Ins**.

3. Click the **Manage** list arrow, and then click **Disabled Items**.

4. Click **Go**.

5. In the dialog box, you can select an item, click **Enable** to activate and reload the add-in, and then click **Close**.

6. Click **OK**.

Did You Know?

You can use the Run dialog box to work in Safe mode. At the command prompt, you can use the */safe* parameter at the end of the command-line to start the program.

You can start an Office app in safe mode. In Windows 7, click the Start button on the taskbar, point to All Programs, and then click Microsoft Office. Press and hold Ctrl, and then click Microsoft <Program> 2013.

Marking a Workbook as Read-Only

As a precaution to prevent readers and reviews from making accidental changes, you can use the Mark as Final command to make an Excel workbook read-only. The Mark as Final command disables or turns off typing, editing commands, and proofing marks, and sets the *Status property* field in the Document Information Panel to Final. The Mark as Final command is not a security option; it only prevents changes to the workbook while it's turned on and it can be turned off by anyone at any time.

Mark a Workbook as Final

1. Click the **File** tab, click **Info**, click the **Protect Workbook** button, and then click **Mark as Final**.

2. Click **OK**.

   The workbook is marked as final and then saved.

3. If necessary, click **OK**.

   The Mark as Final icon appears in the Status bar to indicate the workbook is currently marked as final.

   IMPORTANT *An Excel 2013 workbook marked as final is not read-only when opened in an earlier version of Microsoft Excel.*

Did You Know?

You can enable editing for a workbook marked as final. Click the Edit Anyway button in the Message Bar or click the File tab, click Info, click the Protect Workbook button, and then click Mark As Final again to toggle off the Mark As Final feature.

Reviewing and Sharing Workbook Data

Introduction

Creating successful workbooks is not always a solitary venture; you may need to share a workbook with others or get data from other programs before a project is complete. In Microsoft Excel, you have several methods that you can use to create a joint effort. In many offices, your co-workers (and their computers) are located across the country or the world. They are joined through networks that permit users to share information by opening each other's files and to simultaneously modify data.

Excel makes it easy for you to communicate with your teammates. Instead of writing on yellow sticky notes and attaching them to a printout, you can insert electronic comments within worksheet cells. You can also track changes within a workbook made by you and others. After you finish making changes to your workbook, you can quickly send it to another person for review using e-mail, an Internet Fax service, or instant message.

By using a variety of techniques, you can link, embed, hyperlink, export, or convert data to create one seamless workbook that is a group effort by many co-workers. You can also use Excel to create and edit connections to external data sources, such as Microsoft Access, to create more permanent links to data.

XML (Extensible Markup Language) is a universal language that enables you to create documents in which data is stored independently of the format so you can use the data more seamlessly in other forms. When you work with XML, you can attach an XML Schema—a set of rules that defines the elements and content used in an XML document. XML schemas are created by developers who understand XML.

What You'll Do

Share Workbooks

Create and Read a Cell Comment

Edit and Delete a Cell Comment

Track Changes

Send a Workbook Using E-Mail

Send a Workbook by Internet Fax

Send a Workbook by Instant Message

Present a Workbook Online

Share Information Between Programs

Link and Embed Data and Files

Export and Import Data

Consolidate Data

Get External Data

Get Text Data

Connect to External Data

Get Query Data from a Database

Get Data from Microsoft Access

Work with XML

Create an XML Data Map

Save or Export Data in XML

Sharing Workbooks

When you're working with others in a networked environment, you may want to share workbooks you have created. You may also want to share the responsibilities of entering and maintaining data. **Sharing** means users can add columns and rows, enter data, and change formatting, while allowing you to review their changes. When sharing is enabled, "[Shared]" appears in the title bar of the shared workbook. This type of work arrangement is particularly effective in team situations where multiple users have joint responsibility for data within a single workbook. In cases where multiple users modify the same cells, Excel can keep track of changes, and you can accept or reject them at a later date.

Enable Workbook Sharing

1. Open the workbook you want to share.

2. Click the **Review** tab.

3. Click the **Share Workbook** button.

4. Click the **Editing** tab.

5. Select the **Allow changes by more than one user at the same time** check box.

6. Click **OK**.

7. Click **OK** again to save your workbook.

Did You Know?

You can set file options to prompt to open as read-only. To prevent accidental changes to a workbook, you can display an alert requesting (not requiring) the user open the file as read-only. A read-only file can be read or copied. If the user makes changes to the file, the modifications can only be saved with a new name.

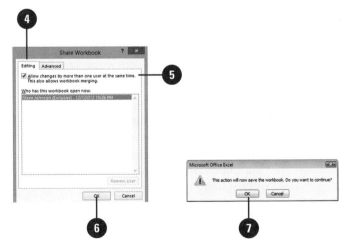

Change Sharing Options

1. Open the workbook you want to share.

2. Click the **Review** tab.

3. Click the **Share Workbook** button.

4. Click the **Advanced** tab.

5. To indicate how long to keep changes, select one of the Track changes options, and then set the number of days, if necessary.

6. To indicate when changes should be saved, select one of the Update changes options, and then set a time internal, if necessary.

7. To resolve conflicting changes, select one of the Conflicting Changes Between Users options.

8. Select one or both of the Include In Personal View check boxes.

9. Click **OK**.

Creating and Reading a Cell Comment

Any cell on a worksheet can contain a **comment**—information you might want to share with co-workers or include as a reminder to yourself without making it a part of the worksheet. (Think of a comment as a nonprinting sticky note attached to an individual cell.) A cell containing a comment displays a red triangle in the upper-right corner of the cell. By default, comments are hidden and are displayed only when the mouse pointer is held over a cell with a red triangle.

Add a Comment

1. Click the cell to which you want to add a comment.

2. Click the **Review** tab.

3. Click the **New Comment** button; the button changes to Edit Comment.

4. Type the comment in the comment box.

5. Click outside the comment box when you are finished, or press Esc twice to close the comment box.

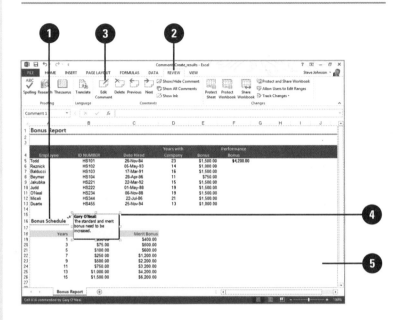

Read a Comment

1. Position the mouse pointer over a cell with a red triangle to read its comment.

2. Move the mouse pointer off the cell to hide the comment.

3. Click the **Review** tab.

4. Do any of the following navigation buttons:

   ◆ Click the **Previous Comment** or **Next Comment** button to move from comment to comment.

   ◆ Select a cell, and then click the **Show/Hide Comment** button to show or hide comments.

Editing and Deleting a Cell Comment

You can edit, delete, and even format cell comments just as you do other text on a worksheet. If you are working with others online, they may want to delete a comment after reading it. You might want to format certain comments to add emphasis. You can use formatting buttons—such as Bold, Italic, Underline, Font Style, Font Color, or Font Size—on the Home tab. When you no longer need a comment, you can quickly delete it.

Edit a Comment

1. Click the cell with the comment you want to edit.

2. Click the **Review** tab.

3. Click the **Edit Comment** button.

4. Make your changes using common editing tools, such as the Backspace and Delete keys, as well as the Format tab buttons.

5. Press Esc twice to close the comment box.

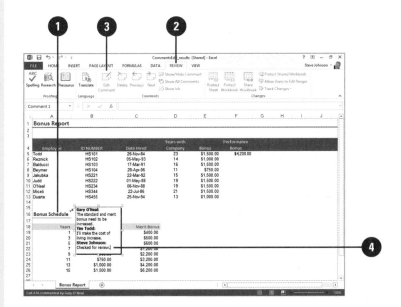

Delete a Comment

1. Click the cell with the comment you want to delete.

2. Click the **Review** tab.

3. Click the **Delete Comment** button.

Tracking Workbook Changes

As you build and fine-tune a workbook—particularly if you are sharing workbooks with co-workers—you can keep track of all the changes that are made at each stage in the process. The Track Changes feature makes it easy to see who made what changes and when, and to accept or reject each change, even if you are the only user of a worksheet. When you or another user applies the Track Changes command to a workbook, the message "[Shared]" appears in the title bar of the workbook to alert you that this feature is active. To take full advantage of this feature, turn it on the first time you or a co-worker edits a workbook. Then, when it's time to review the workbook, all the changes will be recorded. You can review tracked changes in a workbook at any point. Cells containing changes are surrounded by a blue border, and the changes made can be viewed instantly by moving your mouse pointer over any outlined cell. When you're ready to finalize the workbook, you can review each change and either accept or reject it.

Turn On Track Changes

1. Click the **Review** tab.

2. Click the **Track Changes** button, and then click **Highlight Changes.**

3. Select the **Track changes while editing** check box.

4. Select the **When**, **Who**, and/or **Where** check box. Click an associated list arrow, and then select the option you want.

5. Select or clear the **Highlight changes on screen** or **List changes on a new sheet** check boxes.

6. Click **OK**, and then click **OK** again, if necessary.

7. Make changes in worksheet cells.

   Column and row indicators for changed cells appear in red. The cell containing the changes has a blue outline.

8. To view tracked changes, position the mouse pointer over an edited cell.

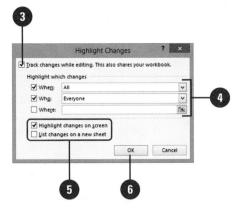

Accept or Reject Tracked Changes

1. Click the **Review** tab.

2. Click the **Track Changes** button, and then click **Accept/Reject Changes**. If necessary, click **OK** in the message box.

3. If you want, change tracking, and then click **OK** to begin reviewing changes.

4. If necessary, scroll to review all the changes, and then click one of the following buttons:

   ◆ Click **Accept** to make the selected change to the worksheet.

   ◆ Click **Reject** to remove the selected change from the worksheet.

   ◆ Click **Accept All** to make all of the changes to the worksheet after you have reviewed them.

   ◆ Click **Reject All** to remove all of the changes to the worksheet after you have reviewed them.

5. Click **Close**.

Did You Know?

You can protect a shared workbook. Open the shared workbook you want to protect. Click the Review tab, click the Protect Shared Workbook button, select the Shared With Track Changes check box, type a password if you want, and then click OK. You can only add a password if the workbook is unshared.

Sending a Workbook Using E-Mail

After you finish making changes to a workbook, you can quickly send it to another person for review using e-mail. Excel allows you to send workbooks out for review as an attachment, either a workbook, PDF, or XPS document, using e-mail from within the program so that you do not have to open your e-mail program. An e-mail program, such as Microsoft Outlook, needs to be installed on your computer before you begin. When you send your workbook out for review, reviewers can add comments and then send it back to you.

Send a Workbook for Review Using E-Mail

1. Click the **File** tab, click **Share**, and then click **Email**.

2. Click the **Send as Attachment**, **Send a Link**, **Send as PDF**, or **Send as XPS**.

3. If the Compatibility Checker appears, click **Continue** or **Cancel** to stop the operation.

   IMPORTANT *To complete the following steps, you need to have an e-mail program installed on your computer and an e-mail account set-up.*

   An e-mail message opens in Microsoft Outlook with your document attached. The subject line contains the file name of the document that you are sending.

4. Enter your recipients and subject (appears with document name by default).

   ◆ To add recipients from your address book or contacts list, click **To**, click the recipient names, click **To**, **Cc**, or **Bcc** until you're done, and then click **OK**.

5. Enter a message for your reviewer with instructions.

6. Click the **Send** button.

Sending a Workbook by Internet Fax

If you are a member of an online fax service—such as eFax, InterFAX, MyFax, or Send2Fax—you can use Excel to send and receive faxes over the Internet directly from within your Microsoft Office program. If you're not a member, a web site can help you sign up. You also need to have Microsoft Outlook and Word installed to use the fax service and Outlook must be open to send your fax. If Outlook is not open and you send the fax, it will be stored in your Outbox and not sent until you open Outlook again.

Send a Workbook by Internet Fax

1. Click the **File** tab, click **Share**, and then click **Email**.

2. Click the **Send as Internet Fax** button.

3. If you're not signed up with an Internet Fax service, click **OK** to open a web page and sign up for one. When you're done, return to Excel, and then repeat Step 1.

4. If the Compatibility Checker appears, click **Continue** or **Cancel** to stop the operation.

   An e-mail message opens in Microsoft Outlook with your document attached as a .tif (image) file.

5. Enter a Fax Recipient, Fax Number and Subject (appears with workbook name by default).

   ◆ You can enter a fax number from your address book. Country codes must begin with a plus sign (+).

   ◆ To send your fax to multiple recipients, click **Add More**, and then enter fax information.

6. In the Fax Service pane, choose the options you want.

7. Complete the cover sheet in the body of the e-mail message.

8. Click the **Send** button.

For Your Information

Using Fax Templates

If you want to use an Office fax template, you can download a template from Office.com (**New!**). Click the File tab, click New, type *fax* in the Search for online templates box, press Enter, click an Office app, click the fax template you want, and then click Create.

Sending a Workbook by Instant Message

Microsoft Lync is an instant messaging program that allows you to hold online meetings with an audio and video experience. Lync uses a SharePoint or Office 365 site as the host location for the online meeting. With Lync, you can send an Excel or Office document to a participant in an instant message. You can use the Send IM button (**New!**) on the Share screen to start an instant message conversation in Lync and transfer the currently opened document. After the files gets transferred, you can carry on with the instant message conversation by using the action buttons to work with messages, dial pad to call, add video, share presentation content, or work with audience.

Send a Workbook by Instant Message

1. Click the **File** tab, click **Share**, and then click **Send by Instant Message**.

2. Enter a contact name or click the Address Book button to select a contact, enter a subject and message for the instant message.

3. Click the **Send IM** button.

   Microsoft Lync opens and then transfers the document in the Conversation window.

4. In the Conversation window, you can continue the session.

5. Use the action buttons to work with messages, dial pad to call, add video, share presentation content, or work with audience.

6. To end the meeting, click the **More Options** button, and then click **End Meeting**.

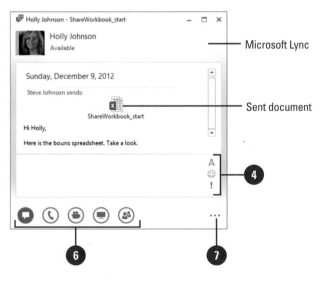

Microsoft Lync

Sent document

Presenting a Workbook Online

With Lync, you can present a workbook to an online meeting. With the Present Online command (**New!**), you can start a Lync meeting with the currently opened workbook. Microsoft Lync is an instant messaging program that allows you to hold online meetings with an audio and video experience. Lync uses a SharePoint or Office 365 site as the meeting or conversation host. During the meeting, a toolbar appears at the top of the Excel window, which appears with a yellow border, where you can control or stop the presentation. Lync opens behind the Excel window. You can switch to it in order to invited attendees to participate in the meeting and send instant messages. If not everyone is able to attend, you can also record the meeting (More Options) to play it back later.

Present a Workbook in a Lync Meeting or Conversation

1. Click the **File** tab, click **Share**, and then click **Present Online**.

2. Click the **Present Online** button.

3. Click **Start a new Lync Meeting**, and then click **OK**. If prompted, sign-in to the meeting with your SharePoint credentials.

4. Specify an audio and video option, and then click **OK**.

    A toolbar appears at the top of the Excel window, which now appears with a yellow border.

5. To switch to Lync, click the **Lync** icon on the taskbar.

6. Use the action buttons (**Messages**, **Dial Pad**, **Video**, **Content**, or **People**) to send instant messages, make a call, change audio settings, send content, or invite participants to join in.

7. To give or take control of the workbook, click the **Give Control** button on the toolbar, and then click **Give Control Automatically** or **Take Back Control**.

8. When you're done, click **Stop Presenting**.

9. To end the meeting, click the **More Options** button, click **End Meeting**, and then click **OK**.

More Options

Sharing Information Between Programs

Excel can convert data or text from one format to another using a technology known as **object linking and embedding (OLE)**. OLE allows you to move text or data between programs in much the same way as you move them within a program. The familiar cut and paste or drag and drop methods work between programs and documents just as they do within a document. In addition, Excel and all Office programs have special ways to move information from one program to another, including importing, exporting, embedding, linking, and hyperlinking.

Importing and Exporting

Importing and exporting information are two sides of the same coin. **Importing** copies a file created with the same or another program into your open file. The information becomes part of your open file, just as if you created it in that format. Some formatting and program-specific information such as formulas may be lost. **Exporting** converts a copy of your open file into the file type of another program. In other words, importing brings information into your open document, while exporting moves information from your open document into another program file.

Embedding

Embedding inserts a copy of a file created in one program into a file created in another program. Unlike imported files, you can edit the information in embedded files with the same commands and buttons used to create the original file. The original file is called the **source file**, while the file in which it is embedded is called the **destination file**. Any changes you make to an embedded object appear only in the destination file; the source file remains unchanged.

For example, if you place an Excel chart into a PowerPoint presentation, Excel is the source program, and PowerPoint is the destination program. The chart is the source file; the workbook is the destination file.

Linking

Linking displays information from one file (the source file) in a file created in another program (the destination file). You can view and edit the linked object from either the source file or the destination file. The changes are stored in the source file but also appear in the destination file. As you work, Excel updates the linked object to ensure you always have the most current information. Excel keeps track of all the drive, folder, and file name information for a source file. However, if you move or rename the source file, the link between files will break. Once the link is broken, the information in the destination file becomes embedded rather than linked. In other words, changes to a copy of the file will no longer affect the other.

Embedding and Linking	
Term	**Definition**
Source program	The program that created the original object
Source file	The file that contains the original object
Destination program	The program that created the document into which you are inserting the object
Destination file	The file into which you are inserting the object

Linking Data

A link can be as simple as a reference to a cell on another worksheet, or it can be part of a formula. You can link cells between sheets within one workbook or between different workbooks. Cell data to be linked is called the source data. The cell or range linked to the source data is called the destination cell or destination range. If you no longer want linked data to be updated, you can easily break a link. Create links instead of making multiple identical entries; it saves time and ensures your entries are correct.

Create a Link Between Worksheets or Workbooks

1. Select the cell or range that contains the source data.

2. Click the **Home** tab.

3. Click the **Copy** button.

4. Click the sheet tab where you want to link the data.

5. Select the destination cell or destination range.

6. Click the **Paste** button.

7. Click the **Paste Options** button, and then click **Paste Link**.

Did You Know?

You can include a link in a formula and treat the linked cell as one argument in a larger calculation. Enter the formula on the formula bar, and then select a cell in the worksheet or workbook you want to link. A cell address reference to a worksheet is =tab name!cell address (=Orders!A6). A cell reference to a workbook is ='[workbook name.xls]tab name'!cell address (='[Product Orders.xls]Orders'!A6).

You can arrange worksheet windows to make linking easier. To arrange open windows, click the View tab, and then click the Arrange All button.

Linking and Embedding Files

Information created using other Office programs can be shared among them. This means that data created in an Excel workbook, can be included in a Word document without being retyped. This makes projects such as annual or departmental reports simple to create. Information can be either **linked** or **embedded**. Data that is linked has the advantage of always being accurate because it is automatically updated when the linked document is modified.

Create a Link to Another File

1. Open the source file and any files containing information you want to link.

2. Select the information in the source file.

3. Click the **Home** tab.

4. Click the **Copy** button.

5. Click the insertion point in the file containing the link.

6. Click the **Paste** button arrow, and then click **Paste Link**.

   ◆ You can point to a paste option icon to display a ScreenTip with the function name, and display a preview of the data.

Did You Know?

You can edit an embedded object. Edit an embedded object only if the program that created it is installed on your computer.

You can manually update or break an object link. Right-click the linked object, and then click Update Link or point to Linked <Item> Object, click Links, click the link you want to update, and then click Manual Update. To break a link, click Break Link.

Embed a New Object

1. Click the **Insert** tab.

2. Click the **Insert Object** button.

3. Click the **Create New** tab.

4. Click the object type you want to insert.

5. Click **OK**.

6. Follow the necessary steps to insert the object.

   The steps will vary depending on the object type.

Embed or Link to an Existing Object

1. Click the **Insert** tab.

2. Click the **Insert Object** button.

3. Click the **Create from File** tab.

4. Click **Browse**, locate and select the file that you want to link, and then click **Open**.

5. To create a link to the object, select the **Link to file** check box.

6. Click **OK**.

Did You Know?

You can update links each time you open a linked workbook. When you open a workbook that contains links, a warning dialog box opens asking you if you want to update all linked information (click Yes) or to keep the existing information (click No).

Exporting and Importing Data

In cases where you don't need the data you are using from another source to be automatically updated if the source data changes, the most expedient way to get the data is to copy and paste it. In cases where you want to copy data from one program to another, you can convert the data to a format that the other program accepts. If you have text you want to include in your workbook, you can **import**, or open, a text file in a workbook.

Export Data Using Copy and Paste

1. Select the cell or range that you want to copy.

2. Click the **Home** tab.

3. Click the **Copy** button.

4. Open the destination file, or click the program's taskbar button if the program is already open.

5. Select the cell where you want the data to be copied.

6. Click the **Paste** button.

7. Click the **Paste Options** button, and then click the option icon you want.

   ◆ You can point to a paste option icon to display a ScreenTip with the function name, and display a preview of the data.

Did You Know?

Excel can save a file to a format only with an installed converter. If the format you want to save a file in does not appear in the Save As Type list, you'll need to install it by running Setup for Microsoft Excel 2013 or Office 2013.

Export a File to Another Program Format

1. Open the file from which you want to export data.

2. Click the **File** tab, click **Export**, and then click **Change File Type**.

3. Click the format type you want, and then click **Save As**.

   ◆ You can also click the **File** tab, click **Save As**, click **Computer**, and then click **Browse**.

4. Click the **Save in** list arrow, and then click the drive or folder where you want to save the file.

5. Click the **Save as type** list arrow, and then click the format you want.

6. If you want, change the file name.

7. Click **Save**.

Import a Text File

1. Click the **File** tab, click **Open**, click **Computer**, and then click **Browse**.

2. Click the **Files of type** list arrow, and then click **Text Files**.

3. Click the **Look in** list arrow, and then select the folder where the text file is located.

4. Click the text file you want to import.

5. Click **Open**.

6. If a wizard starts, follow the instructions to import the text the way you want.

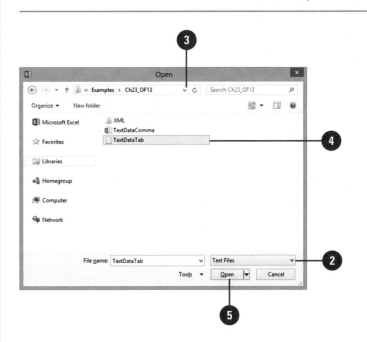

Consolidating Data

In some cases, you'll want to consolidate data from different worksheets or workbooks into one workbook, rather than simply linking the source data. For instance, if each division in your company creates a budget, you can pull together, or **consolidate**, the totals for each line item into one company-wide budget. If each divisional budget is laid out in the same way, with the budgeted amounts for each line item in the same cell addresses, then you can very easily consolidate the information without any retyping. If data in individual workbooks change, the consolidated worksheet or workbook will always be correct.

Consolidate Data from Other Worksheets or Workbooks

1. Open all the workbooks that contain the data you want to consolidate.

2. Open or create the workbook that will contain the consolidated data.

3. Select the destination range.

4. Click the **Data** tab.

5. Click the **Consolidate** button.

6. Click the **Function** list arrow, and then select the function you want to use to consolidate the data.

7. Type the location of the data to be consolidated, or click the **Collapse Dialog** button, and then select the cells to be consolidated.

Did You Know?

You can include all labels. Make sure you select enough cells to accommodate any labels that might be included in the data you are consolidating.

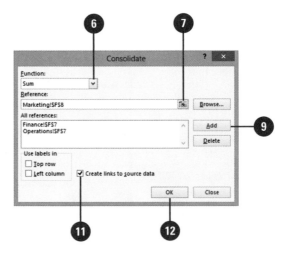

8 Click the **Expand Dialog** button.

9 Click **Add** to add the reference to the list of consolidated ranges.

10 Repeat steps 7 through 9 until you have listed all references to consolidate.

11 Select the **Create links to source data** check box.

12 Click **OK**.

Did You Know?

You can consolidate worksheets even if they are not laid out identically. If the worksheets you want to consolidate aren't laid out with exactly the same cell addresses, but they do contain identical types of information, select the Top Row and Left Column check boxes in the Consolidate dialog box so that Excel uses labels to match up the correct data.

You can arrange multiple workbooks. Use the Window group on the View tab to move between workbooks or to arrange them so they are visible at the same time.

Selected cell

Click to collapse the data   Data added up here

Getting External Data

Introduction

If you need to temporarily exchange data between programs, copying and pasting or linking works the best. However, if you need to permanently exchange data, creating a connection to the data source is the best solution. A **data source** is a stored set of information that allows Excel to connect to an external database. A cell range, table, PivotTable report, or PivotChart report in Excel can be connected to an external data source.

External Data Sources

Microsoft allows you to retrieve data from several types of databases, including Microsoft Access, Microsoft Excel, Microsoft SQL Server, Microsoft SQL Server OLAP services, dBASE, Microsoft FoxPro, Oracle, Paradox, and text file databases. You can also retrieve data from feeds like OData (**New!**), Windows Azure DataMarket (**New!**), and SharePoint (**New!**). In addition, you can use ODBC (Open Database Connectivity) drivers or data source drivers from other manufactures to retrieve information from other data sources. You can use the Data Connection

Wizard to connect to an external data source that has already been established. To open the Data Connection Wizard, click the Data tab, click the From Other Sources button, and then click From Data Connection Wizard. The Data tab also includes buttons to access Microsoft Access, Web, and Text data.

You retrieve data from a database by creating a query, which is data selection criteria to retrieve the data you want. Microsoft Query makes connections to external data sources and shows you what data is available. The **Query Wizard** helps you select data from different tables and fields in the data source, such as a database. During the wizard process you can sort and filter the data to retrieve only the information you want. After you create a query and import the data in a workbook, Microsoft Query provides Excel with query and data source information that you can use for other purposes.

After you connect to an external data source in an Excel workbook, all you need to do is refresh the data to update it from the source. You can refresh external data automatically when you open a workbook or at regular time intervals, or you can manually refresh external data using the Refresh button on the Data tab.

Security

When you open a workbook that connects to external data, the connection to the data source might be disabled if Excel detects a possible security risk. To connect to data when you open a workbook, you need to enable data connections by using the Trust Center, or by putting the workbook in a trusted location.

Getting Text Data

If you have data in a text file, you can either open the file using the Open command on the File tab, or you can import the text file as an external data range using the From Text button on the Data tab. There are two commonly used text file formats to store data that you can import in Excel: Tab delimited text (.txt) and Comma separated values text (.csv). When you open a .txt file, Excel starts the Import Text Wizard. When you open a .csv file, Excel opens the file using current default data format settings.

Import a Text File

1. Open the workbook in which you want to insert text data.

2. Click the **Data** tab.

3. Click the **From Text** button.

4. Click the **Files of type** list arrow, and then click **Text Files**.

5. Click the **Look in** list arrow, and then select the folder where the text file is located.

6. Click the text file you want to import.

7. Click **Import**.

8. If the file is a text file (.txt), Excel starts the Import Text Wizard. Step through the wizard (3 steps), and then click **Finish**.

9. Click the **Existing worksheet** option, and then specify a cell location, or click the **New worksheet** option.

10. Click **OK**.

Connecting to External Data

If you need to permanently exchange data, creating a connection to the data source is the best solution. A data source is a stored set of information that allows Excel to connect to an external database. A cell range, table, PivotTable report, or PivotChart report in Excel can be connected to an external data source. You can use Excel to create and edit connections to external data sources. When you create a connection, Excel stores the connection in the workbook or a connection file, such as Office Data Connection (ODC) file or a Universal Data Connection (UDC) file. A connection file is useful for sharing connections with other users. When you use a connection file, Excel copies the connection information into your Excel workbook. However, if you change connection information, the connection file is not updated. You can manage one or more connections to external data sources using the Workbook Connections dialog box. You can set options for connections to external data sources, and to use, reuse, or switch connection files.

Connect to External Data Using an Existing Connection

1. Click the **Data** tab.

2. Click the **Existing Connections** button.

3. Click the **Show** list arrow, and then click **All Connections** or the specific connection type you want to display.

4. Select the connection you want to use. If you don't see the connection you want, click **Browse for More**, and then click **New Source** to start the Data Connection Wizard.

5. Click **Open**.

6. If requested, click the table you want, and then click **OK**.

7. Click the **Table**, **PivotTable Report** or **PivotChart** option.

8. Click the **Existing worksheet** option, and then specify a cell location, or click the **New worksheet** option.

9. Click **OK**.

Change Connection Properties

1. Click the **Data** tab.

2. Click the **Connections** button.

3. To manage connections, do any of the following:

   ◆ **Add.** Click **Add**, click **OK** (if necessary for the security alert), and then connect to external data using the Existing Connections dialog box.

   ◆ **Remove.** Select the connection you want to remove, click **Remove**, and then click **OK**.

   ◆ **Properties.** Select the connection you want to change, click **Properties**, set refresh, formatting, and layout options, and then click **OK**.

   ◆ **Refresh.** Select a connection, click the **Refresh** button arrow, and then click a refresh option.

4. Click **Close**.

Refresh options

OLAP options

Did You Know?

You can refresh data in Excel from the data source. Click the Data tab, click the Refresh button arrow, and then click Refresh All to refresh multiple external data ranges. To refresh imported text, click the Refresh button arrow, click Refresh, select the text file, and then click Import.

You can remove the data connection from the external data range. Click the Name box arrow, click the name of the external data range you want to remove the data connection, click the Tools tab, and then click the Unlink button.

For Your Information

Retrieving Data from Different Sources

Microsoft allows you to retrieve data from several types of databases, including Microsoft Access, Microsoft Excel, Microsoft SQL Server, Microsoft SQL Server OLAP services, Azure, Oracle, and text file databases. You can also use ODBC (Open Database Connectivity) drivers or data source drivers from other manufactures to retrieve information from other data sources. You can use the Data Connection Wizard to connect to an external data source that has already been established. To open the Data Connection Wizard, click the Data tab, click the From Other Sources button, and then click From Data Connection Wizard.

Getting Query Data from a Database

If you have data in a database, you can use functions in Excel to retrieve data from a table in a database. To retrieve the data, you can select or create a data source, build a query to create a link to the data, and optionally, create a filter to limit the information. When you select or create a data source, you need to identify the database type and then connect to it. To build a query, you can use the Query wizard to step you through the process, or you can manually create a query the same way you do in Microsoft Access. You can also retrieve data from other sources. If you use the same table in a database for data, you can define and save the data source for use later.

Define a New Data Source

1. Click the **Data** tab.

2. Click the **From Other Sources** button, and then click **From Microsoft Query**.

3. Click the **Databases** tab.

4. Click **<New Data Source>**.

5. Click **OK**.

6. Type the name of the source.

7. Click the second box list arrow, and then select a driver for the type of database, such as Driver do Microsoft Access (*.mdb).

8. Click **Connect**.

9. Click **Select**.

10. Navigate to the folder with the database you want to use, and then click **OK**.

11. Click **OK** again.

12. Click the fourth box list arrow, and then click the default table for the data source.

13. Click **OK**.

    Follow the steps to create a query on the next page, starting with step 6.

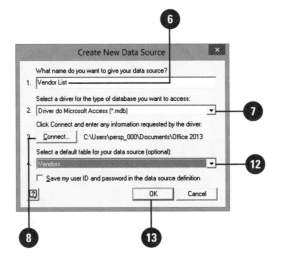

Create a Database Query

① Click the **Data** tab.

② Click the **From Other Sources** button, and then click **From Microsoft Query**.

③ Click the **Databases** tab.

④ Click the name of the data sources you want to use.

⑤ Click **OK**.

⑥ Click a table column name, and then click **Add** to add it to your query. Add the columns you want.

⑦ Click **Next** to continue.

⑧ Click the name of the column by which you want to filter the results.

⑨ Click the first comparison operator list arrow, and then click the operator you want to use.

⑩ Type the first value to use in the comparison.

⑪ If necessary, type a second value in the second value box.

⑫ Click **Next** to continue.

⑬ Click the **Sort by** list arrow, and then click the name of the column by which to sort the query results.

⑭ Click **Next** to continue.

⑮ Click **Save Query**, type a name for the query, and then click **Save**.

⑯ Click **Finish**.

⑰ Select the import options you want.

⑱ Click **OK**.

Getting Data from Microsoft Access

Information you want to analyze may not always exist in an Excel workbook; you might have to retrieve it from another Office program, such as Access. Access table data can be easily converted into Excel worksheet data. Before you can analyze Access data in a workbook, you must convert it to an Excel file. You can either use the Excel command in Access to export data as an Excel table file, or use the PivotTable or PivotChart and PivotTable Report option in Excel to use the Access data as a PivotTable, a table you can use to perform calculations with or rearrange large amounts of data.

Export an Access Database Table into an Excel Workbook

① In Access, open the database you want, and then display Tables in the task pane.

② Click the table you want to analyze.

③ Click the **External Data** tab.

④ Click the **Excel** button in the Export group.

⑤ Specify the destination file name and format.

⑥ Specify the export options you want.

⑦ Click **OK**, and then click **Close**.

⑧ Use Excel tools to edit and analyze the data.

Create an Excel Workbook PivotTable from an Access Database

1. Click the **Data** tab.

2. Click the **From Access** button.

3. Select the Access database file, and then click **Open**.

4. Click the table from Access you want to use.

5. Click **OK**.

6. Click the **PivotTable Report** or **PivotChart** option.

7. Click the **Existing worksheet** option, and then specify a cell location, or click the **New worksheet** option.

8. To set refresh, formatting, and layout options for the imported data, click **Properties**, make the changes you want, and then click **OK**.

9. Click **OK**.

10. Use tabs under PivotChart Tools to create and format the PivotChart.

Working with XML

XML (Extensible Markup Language) is a universal language that enables you to create documents in which data is stored independently of the format so you can use the data more seamlessly in other forms. XML is supported in Office 2013 through Word, Excel, and Access. XML allows you to work with the familiar Office interface and create and save documents as XML, without ever knowing the XML language. When you work with XML, you can attach an XML Schema—a set of rules that defines the elements and content used in an XML document. XML schemas are created by developers who understand XML. After you attach a schema, you should change XML map properties before you map schema elements to cells in your worksheet.

Attach a Schema

1. Click the **Developer** tab.

2. Click the **Source** button.

3. In the task pane, click **XML Maps**.

4. Click **Add**.

5. Locate and select the XML schema file you want to attach, and then click **Open**.

6. If necessary, click **OK** to create a schema based on the XML source data.

7. To rename or delete an XML schema, select the schema, and then click **Rename** or **Delete**.

8. Click **OK**.

9. When you're done, click the **Close** button on the task pane.

XML schema

Did You Know?

You can change XML view options. In the XML Source task pane, click Options to turn on or off options to preview data in the task pane, hide help text in the task pane, automatically merge elements when mapping, include data heading, and hide border of inactive lists.

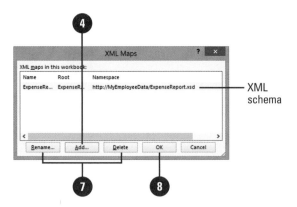

XML schema

Change XML Data Map Properties

1 Open the worksheet in which you want to map the XML data.

2 Click the **Developer** tab.

3 Click the **Source** button.

4 Click the **Map Properties** button.

5 If you want, change the name of the XML Map.

6 Select or clear the following options:

◆ **Validate data against schema for import and export.**

◆ **Save data source definition in workbook.**

◆ **Adjust column width.**

◆ **Preserve column filter.**

◆ **Preserve number formatting.**

7 Select the refreshing or importing data option you want.

8 Click **OK**.

For Your Information

Showing and Hiding the Developer Tab

If the Developer tab doesn't appear on the Ribbon, you can use the Customize Ribbon option in the Options dialog box to show it. Click the File tab, click Options, and then click Customize Ribbon in the left pane. In the right column, select the Developer check box to show the Developer tab, or clear the check box to hide it. When you're done, click OK.

Creating an XML Data Map

Using XML data in Excel follows the same basic process: (1) Add an XML schema file (.xsd) to a workbook, (2) map XML schema elements to individual cells, (3) Import an XML data file (.xml), (4) enter data, and (5) export revised data from mapped cells to an XML data file. You can use the XML Source task pane to create and manage XML maps. The task pane displays a hierarchical list of XML elements in the current XML map that you use to map to worksheet cells. After you create an XML data map, you can import XML data to fill in the information you want from a data source.

Create an XML Data Map

1. Open the worksheet in which you want to map the XML data.

2. Click the **Developer** tab.

3. Click the **Source** button.

4. Click the **Map name** list arrow, and then click the XML schema you want to use.

5. Drag the named elements from the XML Source task pane to the corresponding cells in the worksheet.

6. Click the **Header Options** button, and then click the header option you want.

7. When you're done, click the **Close** button on the task pane.

Drag XML element

Did You Know?

You can change the list of XML elements in the XML Source task pane. In the XML Source task pane, click the Options button, and then click the display option you want.

An XML data map is a potential security risk. From a security perspective, Excel saves an XML map and its data source with a workbook, which any user can view using VBA.

Import XML Data

1. Open the worksheet in which you want to map the XML data.

2. Click the **Developer** tab.

3. Click the **Import** button.

4. Click the **Files of type** list arrow, and then click **XML Files**.

5. Locate, and then select the XML data file you want to import.

6. Click **Import**.

Did You Know?

You can open an XML data file. Click the File tab, click Open, click Computer, click Browse, click the Files of type list arrow, click XML Files, select the XML data file, click Open, click the As An XML Table, As A Read-only Workbook, or Use The XML Source task pane option, and then click OK.

You can add XML expansion packs. Click the Developer tab, click the Expansion Packs button, click Add, locate and select an expansion pack, and then click Open. You can also attach, update, or delete XML expansion packs.

Imported data

Saving or Exporting Data in XML

After you finish working with your XML document, you can save or export the data for use in other XML compatible documents and applications. You can save the contents of a mapped range with the XML Data format or XML Spreadsheet format. The XML Data format is an independent XML industry standard that uses a separate XML schema, while the XML Spreadsheet format is a specialized Excel XML file that uses its own XML schema to store information, such as file properties.

Save XML Data

① Open the worksheet with the XML data.

② Click the **File** tab, click **Save As**, click **Computer**, and then click **Browse**.

③ Click the **Save as type** list arrow, and then click **XML Data** or **XML Spreadsheet 2003**.

④ Select a location where you want to save the XML data.

⑤ Type a name for the XML file.

⑥ Click **Save**.

⑦ If necessary, click **Continue**, select the XML map, and then click **OK**.

IMPORTANT *When you save with the XML Data format, the active worksheet is now the XML data. To work with the original worksheet, you need to re-open it.*

Did You Know?

You can quickly verify a data map before you export the data. Click the Developer tab, click the Source button, click the Verify Map For Export link in the task pane, and then click OK.

You can export XML data. Click the Developer tab, click the Export button, click the XML map you want to use, click OK, select the location where you want to export the XML data, type a file name, and then click Export.

Publishing Workbook Data as Web Pages

Introduction

Microsoft Excel provides you with the tools you need to create and save your workbook as a web page and to publish it on the web. The Save As command allows you to format your workbook in **Hypertext Markup Language (HTML)**, a simple coding system used to format documents for an intranet or the Internet. Saving your workbook in HTML format means you can use most web browsers to view your workbook. Any workbook can easily be saved as a web document and viewed in a web browser. By saving your Excel workbooks as web pages, you can share your data with others via the Internet.

Incorporating hyperlinks within your Excel worksheet adds an element of connectivity to your work. You can create a worksheet and then have a hyperlink with supporting research to add to the content of your data. Or, you can copy data from a web page and incorporate it into your Excel workbook. Either way, using the web to publish Excel data or incorporate research into your workbook, is a great resource.

What You'll Do

Open a Workbook as a Web Page

Preview a Web Page

Create a Hyperlink

Format a Hyperlink

Change Web Page Options

Save a Worksheet as a Web Page

Publish a Web Page

Copy a Web Table to a Worksheet

Create Refreshable Web Queries

Get Data from Web Queries

Get Documents from the Web

Opening a Workbook as a Web Page

After saving a workbook as a web page, you can open the web page, an HTML file, in Excel. This allows you to quickly and easily switch from HTML to the standard Excel format and back again without losing any formatting or functionality. For example, if you create a formatted chart in an Excel workbook, save the workbook file as a web page, and then reopen the web page in Excel, the chart will look the same as the original chart in Excel. Excel preserves the original formatting and functionality of the workbook.

Open a Workbook as a Web Page in Excel

1. Click the **File** tab, and then click **Open**.

2. Click **Computer**.

3. Click **Browse** or a recent folder.

4. Click the **Files of type** list arrow, and then click **All Web Pages**.

5. Navigate to the location where you want to open the web file, and then select the HTML file.

6. Click **Open**.

   ◆ To open the web page in your browser, click the **Open** button arrow, and then click **Open in Browser**.

Did You Know?

You can change the appearance of web pages and Help Viewer window. In the Internet Options dialog box for Windows, click Accessibility on the General tab, select the Ignore Colors Specified On Web Pages check box, and then click OK. In the Internet Properties dialog box, click Colors to select text and background colors or Fonts to change text style.

Recent folder locations

Previewing a Web Page

You can view any Excel worksheet as if it were already on the web by previewing the web page. By previewing a file you want to post to the web, you can see if there are any errors that need to be corrected, formatting that needs to be added, or additions that need to be made. Just as you should always preview a document before you print it, you should preview a web page before you post it. Previewing the web page in your browser shows you what the page will look like once it's posted on the Internet. You do not have to be connected to the Internet to preview a document as a web page.

View a Web Page

1. Open the web file you want to view as a web page.

2. Click the **Web Page Preview** button on the Quick Access Toolbar.

   ◆ To add the button to the toolbar, click the **Customize Quick Access Toolbar** list arrow on the Quick Access Toolbar, click **More Commands**, add the Web Page Preview button, and then click **OK**.

   Your default web browser starts and displays the web page.

3. Click the **Close** button to quit your web browser.

Customize Quick Access Toolbar list arrow

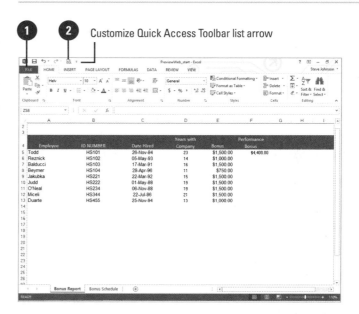

Did You Know?

Web addresses and URLs mean the same thing. Every web page has a Uniform Resource Locator (URL), or web address. Each URL contains specific parts that identify where a web page is located. For example, the URL for Perspection's web page is: *http://www.perspection.com/index.htm* where "http://" shows the address is on the web, "www.perspection.com" shows the computer that stores the web site, and "index.htm" is a web page on the web site.

Workbook web page

Creating a Hyperlink

With instant access to the Internet, your worksheet can contain links to specific sites so you and anyone else using your worksheet can access Web information. An Internet link that is embedded on a worksheet is called a **hyperlink**—because when it is clicked, you are instantly connected to the link's defined address on the web. If your worksheet contains a hyperlink, the link appears in a worksheet cell as blue text. When you point to hyperlinked text or an object, the cursor changes to a pointing hand to indicate it's a hyperlink. To connect to the linked location, such as a web site, just click the hyperlink.

Create or Edit a Hyperlink

1. Select a cell or object, such as a picture, where you want to create or edit a hyperlink.

2. Click the **Insert** tab.

3. Click the **Hyperlink** button.

   TIMESAVER *Press Ctrl+K.*

4. Click one of the icons on the Link To bar for quick access to frequently used files, web pages, and links.

   ◆ **Existing File or Web Page.** Click to link to a document or other file.

   ◆ **Place in This Document.** Click to link to another location in the current document. Select or type a cell reference, or select a defined name.

   ◆ **Create New Document.** Click to link to a new document.

   ◆ **E-mail Address.** Click to create a link to an e-mail address. When you click the e-mail address, your e-mail program automatically opens with the address.

5. Type or select the name and location of the file or web page you want to link to.

6. Click **OK**.

Jump to a Hyperlink

① Click the hyperlink on your worksheet.

Excel opens the linked location. For web addresses, Excel opens your web browser, displaying the web page associated with the hyperlink.

Did You Know?

You can create a custom ScreenTip for a hyperlink. Select the hyperlink you want to customize, click the Insert tab, click the Hyperlink button, click ScreenTip, type the ScreenTip text you want, and then click OK twice.

Remove a Hyperlink

① Right-click the cell containing the hyperlink you want to remove.

② Do one of the following:

◆ **Clear Contents** to delete a hyperlink and the text.

◆ **Remove Hyperlink** to remove the hyperlink and keep the text.

Did You Know?

You can select a hyperlink without activating the link. To select a hyperlink without activating the link. Click the cell that contains the hyperlink, hold down the mouse button until the pointer becomes a cross, and then release the mouse. If the hyperlink is a graphic, hold down Ctrl, and then click the graphic.

Formatting a Hyperlink

Excel comes with a set of predefined cell styles for various data types, including hyperlinks, in a worksheet. When you create a hyperlink, the default cell style is used to format the text. If you want to change the appearance of hyperlinks in your workbook, you need to change the cell style for hyperlinks.

Change the Hyperlink Cell Style

1. Click the **Home** tab.

2. Click the **Cell Styles** button.

3. Right-click the **Hyperlink** or **Followed Hyperlink**, and then click **Modify**.

4. Click **Format**.

5. Select the formatting options you want on the Font and Fill tabs, and then click **OK**.

6. Select the check boxes with the formatting you want to include in the modified cell style.

7. Click **OK**.

Did You Know?

You can change the text or graphic for a hyperlink. Select the cell with the hyperlink, click in the formula bar, and then edit the text. Right-click the graphic, and then click the option you need to change in the hyperlink.

You can copy or move a hyperlink. Right-click the hyperlink you want to copy or move, click Copy or Cut. Right-click the cell you want to copy or move the hyperlink to, and then click Paste.

Select format options

Changing Web Page Options

When you save or publish a workbook as a web page, you can change the appearance of the web page by changing Excel's web options. You can set web options to save any additional hidden data necessary to maintain formulas, allow PNG as a graphic format, rely on CSS for font formatting, reply on VML for displaying graphics in browser, and save new web pages as Single File Web Pages. Web pages are saved using the appropriate international text encoding so users on any language system are able to view the correct characters.

Change Web Page Options

1. Click the **File** tab, and then click **Options**.

2. In the left pane, click **Advanced**.

3. Click **Web Options**.

4. Click the **General** tab, and then select or clear the web pages options:

   ◆ **Save any additional hidden data necessary to maintain formulas.**

   ◆ **Load pictures from Web pages not created in Excel.**

5. Click the **Browsers** tab.

6. Click the **Target Browsers** list arrow, and then select the version you want to support.

7. Select or clear the web page options:

   ◆ **Allow PNG as a graphic format.**

   ◆ **Rely on CSS for font formatting.** Cascading Style Sheets for web page formatting.

   ◆ **Reply on VML for displaying graphics in browsers.** VML is Vector Markup Language, XML based graphics.

   ◆ **Save new web pages as Single File Web Pages.**

8. Click **OK**.

9. Click **OK**.

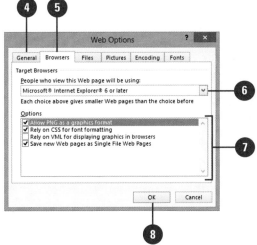

Saving a Worksheet as a Web Page

You can place an existing Excel worksheet on the Internet for others to use. In order for any document to be placed on the web, it must be in **HTML** (Hypertext Markup Language) format—a simple coding system that specifies the formats a web browser uses to display the document. This format enables you to post, or submit Excel data on a web site for others. You don't need any HTML knowledge to save an Excel worksheet as a web page. When you save a worksheet as a web page, you can save it using the Web Page or Single File Web Page format. The Web Page format saves the worksheet as an HTML file and a folder that stores supporting files, such as a file for each graphic, worksheet, and so on. Excel selects the appropriate graphic format for you based on the image's content. A single file web page saves all the elements of a web site, including text and graphics, into a single file in the MHTML format, which is supported by Internet Explorer 4.0.1 or later.

Save a Workbook or Worksheet as a Web Page

1. Click the **File** tab, and then click **Save As**.

2. Click **Computer**, and then click **Browser** or select a recent folder.

3. Click the **Save as type** list arrow, and then click **Web Page**.

4. Click the **Save in** list arrow, and then select a location for your web page.

5. Type the name for the web page.

6. Click the **Entire Workbook** or **Selection: Sheet** option.

7. To change the title of your web page, click **Change Title**, type the new title, and then click **OK**.

8. To save a thumbnail preview of the web page, select the **Save Thumbnail** check box.

9. Click **Save**.

10. If necessary, click **Yes** to keep formatting.

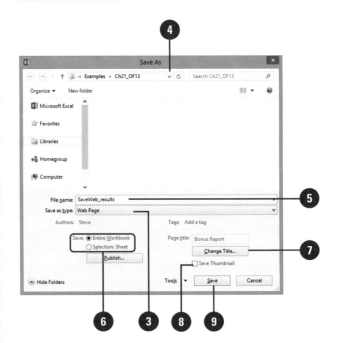

Save a Workbook or Worksheet as a Single File Web Page

1. Click the **File** tab, and then click **Save As**.

2. Click **Computer**, and then click **Browser** or select a recent folder.

3. Click the **Save as type** list arrow, and then click **Single File Web Page**.

4. Click the **Save in** list arrow, and then select a location for your web page.

5. Type the name for the web page.

6. Click the **Entire Workbook** or **Selection: Sheet** option.

7. To change the title of your web page, click **Change Title**, type the new title, and then click **OK**.

8. To save a thumbnail preview of the web page, select the **Save Thumbnail** check box.

9. Click **Save**.

10. If necessary, click **Yes** to keep formatting.

The web page is saved as a single file.

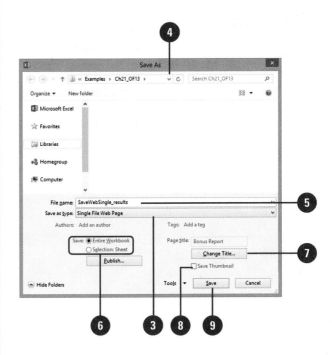

Publishing a Web Page

At times, you'll want to publish a copy of your current workbook in HTML format directly to a **web server** (a computer on the Internet or intranet that stores web pages) so others can view and manipulate your data. Publishing to a web server is as simple as saving a file. You can publish a complete workbook, a single worksheet, or a range of worksheets. A worksheet saved as a web page retains all its spreadsheet, charting, or PivotTable functionality and formatting properties. This interactivity means that while your worksheet is on the web, others can manipulate your data. You can elect to let anyone using Internet Explorer 4.01 or later interact with your data from Excel.

Save and Publish a Worksheet as an Interactive Web Page

1. To publish part of a worksheet, select the range you want saved as a web page.

2. Click the **File** tab, and then click **Save As**.

3. Click **Computer**, and then click **Browser** or select a recent folder.

4. Click the **Save as type** list arrow, and then click **Web Page**.

5. Click the **Save in** list arrow, and then select a publish location.

6. Click the **Selection: Sheet** or **Entire Worksheet** option.

7. Type the name for the web page or web address.

8. To change the title of your web page, click **Change Title**, type the new title, and then click **OK**.

9. Click **Publish**.

10. Click the **Choose** list arrow, and then select the items you want to publish in the web page.

11. Select or clear the **AutoRepublish every time this workbook is saved** check box.

12. Select or clear the **Open published web page in browser** check box.

13. Click **Publish**.

Copying a Web Table to a Worksheet

You can copy tabular information on a web page and paste or drag the information into an Excel worksheet. It's an easy way to transfer and manipulate web-based table data using Excel. Excel simplifies access to table data by making it available to anyone with a browser. If you need to make changes to the table, you can use normal editing techniques in Excel.

Copy a Web Table to a Worksheet

1. Open your web browser.

2. In the Address bar, type the location of the web page with the table data you want to copy, and then press Enter.

3. Select the table data in the web page you want to copy.

4. Open the Excel worksheet where you want to paste the table data.

5. Right-click the taskbar, and then click **Show Windows Side by Side**.

6. Drag the table data from the web browser window to the location on the worksheet where you want the table data, and then release the mouse button.

Did You Know?

You can use copy and paste to transfer table data to Excel. In your browser, select the table data you want, copy the data, switch to Excel, click the cell where you want to place the table data, and then click the Paste button on the Home tab.

Creating Refreshable Web Queries

If you need to analyze web data in a worksheet, you can use the copy and paste commands to bring the data from a web page into the worksheet. The Paste Options button allows you to specify whether you want the information to keep the data as it is right now or make it refreshable to the current data on the web. As the data changes on the web, you can use the Refresh button to quickly update the data in your worksheet. You don't need to copy the information again.

Copy and Paste Refreshable Data from the Web

1. Open the web page with the information you want to copy into an Excel worksheet, and then select the data.

2. Copy the data.

3. Switch to Excel, and then click the active cell where you want the data.

4. Click the **Paste** button on the Home tab.

5. Click the **Paste Options** button, and then click **Refreshable Web Query**.

   ◆ You can point to a paste option icon to display a ScreenTip with the function name, and display a preview of the data.

6. Click the arrow buttons to select the information you want.

7. Click **Import**.

Did You Know?

You can quickly refresh a web query. Click a cell in the worksheet with the query data, click the Data tab, and then click the Refresh button. A spinning refresh icon appears in the status bar to indicate that the query is running. You can double-click the icon to check the status of the query.

Getting Data from Web Queries

You can import data into Excel through database and web queries and analyze data with formulas and formatting. You can insert columns within query tables and apply formulas and formatting. When data is refreshed, the formatting and analysis are retained. Excel helps you through the process of bringing data from a web page to your worksheet. You can create a new web query as you choose the URL and parameters for how you want to import the web data. Once you save the query, you can run it again at any time.

Get Data from a New Web Query

1. Click the **Data** tab.

2. Click the **From Web** button.

3. Type the address for the web page that contains the data you want.

4. Click the arrow buttons to select the information you want.

5. Click **Options** to select the formatting you want your data to keep.

6. Click **Import**.

7. Click the **Existing worksheet** option and specify a starting cell, or click the **New worksheet** option.

8. Click **OK**.

Did You Know?

You can save a web query. Click the Data tab, click the From Web button, select the web data, click the Save Query button, specify a location and name (.iqy extension), click Save, and then click Cancel.

You can import a web query. Click the Data tab, click th Existing Connections, select the web query, click Open, select a worksheet option, and then click the Refresh All button arrow, and then click Refresh.

Getting Documents from the Web

File Transfer Protocol (FTP) is an inexpensive and efficient way to transfer files between your computer and others on the Internet. You can download or receive, from another computer, any kind of file, including text, graphics, sound, and video files. To download a file, you need an ID and password to identify who you are. Anonymous FTP sites are open to anyone; they usually use *anonymous* as an ID and your *e-mail address* as a password. You can also save the FTP site address to revisit the site later.

Add FTP Locations

1. Click the **File** tab, click **Open**, click **Computer**, and then click **Browse**.

2. Click **Computer** in the left pane.

3. Right-click a blank area, and then click **Add a network location**.

4. Follow the Add Network Location wizard to create a link to an FTP site or other network, and then click **Finish** to complete it.

   ◆ To complete the process, you need the complete address for a FTP site, and a user name and password.

Access a FTP Site

1. Click the **File** tab, click **Open**, click **Computer**, and then click **Browse**.

2. Click **Computer** in the left pane.

3. Double-click the FTP site to which you want to log in.

4. Enter a password (your E-mail address or personal password), and then select a log on option.

5. Click **Log On**.

6. Select a folder location, and then select a file.

7. Click **Open**.

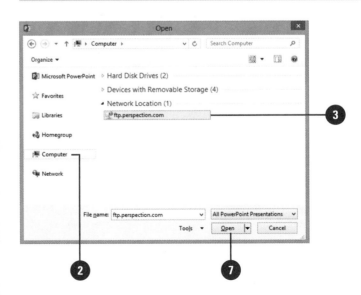

Tools for Working More Efficiently

Introduction

Once you've become familiar with Microsoft Excel and all its features, you might want to customize the way you work with Excel. You can change your view settings so that your Excel window looks the way you want it to. Excel comes with set defaults—such as opening all documents using a certain view, showing the vertical ruler, or how many files you've recently opened—which you can change to suit your needs.

Some of the other Excel customization features allow you to set a default font and related attributes to use when you are typing text in text boxes. Other defaults might be the color or line style of a shape object that you create. You can change the location of the Ribbon and the configuration of the Quick Access Toolbar to include commands not available on the Ribbon. You can changes these customization option by using the Excel Options dialog box.

In addition to Excel, Microsoft Office 2013 also comes with other helpful tools including Upload Center, Lync, Lync Recording Manager, SkyDrive Pro, Language Preferences, Spreadsheet or Database Compare, and Telemetry Log or Dashboard.

What You'll Do

Set General Excel Options

Set New Workbook and Start Up Options

Set Editing Options

Set Image Options

Set Chart Options

Set Workbook and Worksheet Display Options

Set Display View Options

Set Advanced Options

Set Formula Options

Change Advanced Document Properties

Customize the Way You Create Objects

Access Commands Not in the Ribbon

Work with Office Tools

Maintain and Repair Office

Setting General Excel Options

You can customize the performance of many Excel features including its editing, saving, spelling, viewing, printing and security procedures. Each person uses Excel in a different way. Excel Options allows you to change general options to personalize what appears in the Excel window including live previews, toolbars, buttons, ScreenTips, and an Office background or theme (**New!**). When you change these options, Excel uses them for all subsequent Excel sessions until you change them.

Change General Options

1. Click the **File** tab, and then click **Options**.

2. In the left pane, click **General**.

3. Select the Top options for working with Excel you want:

   ◆ **Show Mini Toolbar on Selection**. Select to show a miniature toolbar that helps you work with selected text.

   ◆ **Show Quick Analysis options on selection**. Select to show the Quick Analysis button (**New!**).

   ◆ **Enable Live Preview**. Select to show preview changes in a workbook.

   ◆ **ScreenTip style**. Select an option to show or hide ScreenTips.

4. Type your name as you want them to appear in Properties, and review comments.

5. Select Office related options for Excel you want:

   ◆ **Always use these values regardless of sign in to Office**. Select to always use the Office options (**New!**).

   ◆ **Office Background**. Select to apply a background at the top of the program window (**New!**).

   ◆ **Office Theme**. Select to apply a color scheme to the program window (**New!**).

6. Click **OK**.

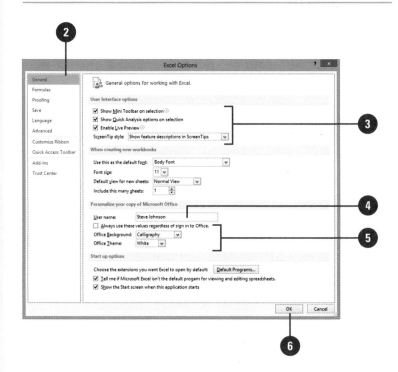

Setting New Workbook and Start Up Options

You can customize several settings in the Excel work environment to suit the way you like to work. You can make general changes, including the default font and the number of sheets in a new workbook. If your workbooks usually contain five sheets, you could make five the workbook default. In addition, you can set start up options (**New!**) for Excel including opening files with specified extensions, detecting if Excel isn't the default program for spreadsheets, and showing the Start screen when Excel starts. Taking a few minutes to change Excel's default setting saves time in the long run.

Change New Workbook and Start Up Options

1. Click the **File** tab, and then click **Options**.

2. In the left pane, click **General**.

3. Click the **Use this as the default font** list arrow, and then select a font.

4. Click the **Font size** list arrow, and then select a font size.

5. Click the **Default view for new sheets** list arrow, and then select a view, either Normal View, Page Break Preview, or Page Layout View.

6. Specify the number of sheets you want to include in this workbook.

7. Select the Start up options for Excel you want:

   ◆ **Default Programs**. Click to select the extensions you wan to open withe Excel (**New!**).

   ◆ **Tell me if Microsoft Excel isn't the default program for viewing and editing spreadsheets**. Select to detect if Excel isn't the default spreadsheet program (**New!**).

   ◆ **Show the Start screen when this application starts**. Select to show it or deselect to show a blank workbook (**New!**).

8. Click **OK**.

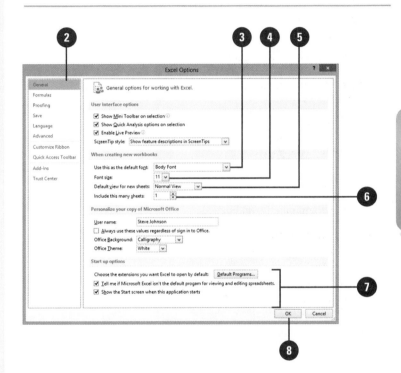

Setting Editing Options

If you spend a lot of time modifying worksheets, you can set editing options in Excel to customize the way you work. You can set options to specify the move direction after pressing Enter, allow editing directly in cells, use system number separators or ones you specify, automatically insert a decimal point, extend data range formats and formulas, or use AutoComplete or Flash Fill (**New!**).

Change Edit Options

1. Click the **File** tab, and then click **Options**.

2. In the left pane, click **Advanced**.

3. Select or clear any of the check boxes to change the options you want, some options include:

   ◆ **After pressing Enter, move selection Direction.** Specify a direction (Default Down).

   ◆ **Automatically insert a decimal point.** Specify number of decimal places.

   ◆ **Enable fill handle and cell drag-and-drop.** (Default on).

   ◆ **Allow editing directly in cells.** (Default on).

   ◆ **Extend data range formats and formulas.** (Default on).

   ◆ **Enable automatic percent entry.** (Default on).

   ◆ **Enable AutoComplete for cell values.** (Default on).

   ◆ **Automatically Flash Fill** (Default on). (**New!**)

   ◆ **Alert the user when a potentially time consuming operation occurs.** (Default on).

   ◆ **Use system separators.** Number format separators (Default on).

   ◆ **Cursor movement.** Select Logical (Default) or Visual.

   ◆ **Do not automatically hyperlink screen shot.** (Default off). (**New!**)

4. Click **OK**.

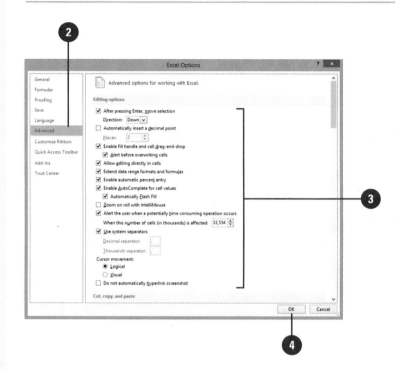

For Your Information

AutoFormatting While You Type

As you work in Excel, you can use AutoCorrect Options to automatically format certain types of text. You can set options to replace Internet and network paths with hyperlinks as you type, include new rows and columns in tables, and automatically fill in formulas in tables to create calculations in columns. To change AutoFormat options, click the File tab, click Options, click Proofing in the left pane, click AutoCorrect Options, click the AutoFormat As You Type tab, select or clear options, and then click OK.

Change Cut, Copy, and Paste Options

1. Click the **File** tab, and then click **Options**.

2. In the left pane, click **Advanced**.

3. Select or clear any of the check boxes to change the options you want, some options include:

   ◆ **Show Paste Options button when content is pasted.** Select to show the Paste Options button or clear to hide it.

   ◆ **Show Insert Options buttons.** Select to show the Insert Options button or clear to hide it.

   ◆ **Cut, copy, and sort inserted objects with their parent cells.** Select to maintain a link and a parent cell when you cut, copy, or sort inserted objects.

4. Click **OK**.

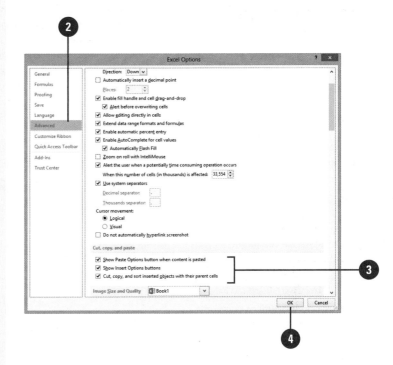

Setting Image Options

Excel Options allows you to set options for images in a workbook. When you insert images into a workbook, the size of the file increases. You can set image options to compress all images to reduce the file size, or don't compress all images to maintain image quality in a larger file size. If you edit an image and don't want to keep the original content for restore purposes, you can discard it. If you want to print high quality images, you can set a print option to do it.

Change Image Options

1. Click the **File** tab, and then click **Options**.

2. In the left pane, click **Advanced**.

3. Select or clear any of the check boxes to change the image size and quality options you want.

   ◆ **Image Size and Quality.** Click the list arrow, and then select the workbook where you want to apply display options.

   ◆ **Discard editing data.** Select to delete data which is used to restore edited pictures to their original state.

   ◆ **Do not compress images in file**. Select to don't compress all images in the file to maintain quality or clear to compress all images to reduce the file size.

   ◆ **Set default target output to.** Specify a resolution output size for graphics in the file.

4. Select the **High quality mode for graphics** check box to print images with a high quality output.

5. Click **OK**.

Setting Chart Options

Excel Options allows you to set options for charts in a workbook. When you insert charts into a workbook, you can set options to show data point values or chart element names when you point to (hover) the item on the chart. You can also set an option to have custom formatting and chart data labels follow data points as they move or change in the chart for the current workbook or for all new workbooks (**New!**).

Change Chart Options

1. Click the **File** tab, and then click **Options**.

2. In the left pane, click **Advanced**.

3. Select or clear any of the check boxes to change the chart options you want.

   ◆ **Show data point values on hover.** Select to show data point values when you point to them. (Default on).

   ◆ **Show chart element names on hover.** Select to show chart element names when you point to them. (Default on).

   ◆ **Properties follow chart data point for all new workbooks.** Select to have custom formatting and chart data labels follow data points as they move or change in the chart for all new workbooks. (Default on). (**New!**)

   ◆ **Current Workbook.** Select the workbook to which you want to apply property chart options. (**New!**)

   ◆ **Properties follow chart data point for current workbook.** Select to have custom formatting and chart data labels follow data points as they move or change in the chart. (Default on). (**New!**)

4. Click **OK**.

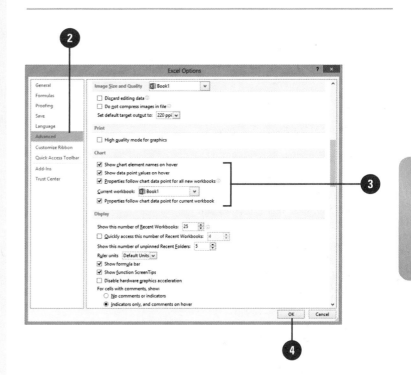

Setting Workbook and Worksheet Display Options

You can customize the way Excel appears when you work on a worksheet. If you don't use scroll bars or sheet tabs, you can hide them to display more data. If you are creating a custom spreadsheet, you can change the color of the gridlines or hide them all together. If you prefer not to see zeroes in cells, you can hide zero values until they change. The Advanced pane in the Excel Options dialog box allows you to change the way you view a worksheet or workbook in Excel to suit your needs. For example, if you prefer the sheet tabs on the right side of the workbook instead of the left, you can set an option to change it.

Change Workbook Display Options

1. Click the **File** tab, and then click **Options**.

2. In the left pane, click **Advanced**.

3. Click the **Display options for this workbook** list arrow, and then select the option where you want to apply display options.

4. Select the workbook display options you want:

    ◆ **Show horizontal scroll bar.** Select to display horizontal scroll bars.

    ◆ **Show vertical scroll bar.** Select to display vertical scroll bars.

    ◆ **Show sheet tabs.** Select to display worksheet tabs.

    ◆ **Group dates in the AutoFilter menu**. Select to group the list of dates at the bottom of the AutoFilter menu in a date filter. Clear to manually select dates from the list.

    ◆ **For objects, show.** Click All or Nothing (hide objects) option.

5. Click **OK**.

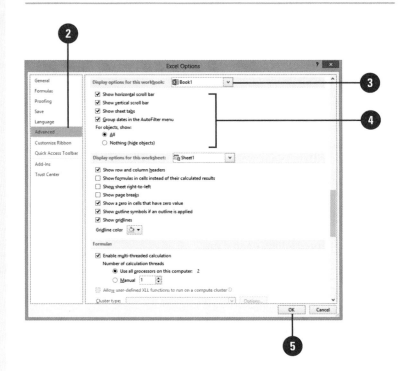

Change Worksheet Display Options

① Click the **File** tab, and then click **Options**.

② In the left pane, click **Advanced**.

③ Click the **Display options for this worksheet** list arrow, and then select the option where you want to apply display options.

④ Select the worksheet display options you want:

◆ **Show row and column headers**. Select to show row and column headers.

◆ **Show formulas in cells instead of their calculated results**. Select to show formulas instead of results.

◆ **Show sheet right-to-left**. Select to display worksheet tab on the right side of the window.

◆ **Show page breaks**. Select to show page breaks.

◆ **Show a zero in cells that have zero value.** Select to show 0 in cells with a zero value.

◆ **Show outline symbols if an outline is applied**. Click All or Nothing (hide objects) option.

◆ **Show gridlines**. Select to show gridlines. Click Gridline color button, and then select a color.

⑤ Click **OK**.

Setting Display View Options

Excel Options allows you to personalize what appears in the Excel window. You can customize the way Excel appears when you work on a worksheet. If you need more room to view another row of data, you can hide the Formula bar or Status bar. If you're working with functions to create a formula, you can show function ScreenTips to help decide which function to use and how to use it. For easy access to files, you can specify whether to show recent workbooks on the File tab (**New!**) and the number of recent workbooks or folder to show (**New!**).

Change Display View Options

① Click the **File** tab, and then click **Options**.

② In the left pane, click **Advanced**.

③ Select or clear any of the check boxes to change the display options you want.

◆ **Show this number of Recent Workbooks.** Set the number of recent workbooks (**New!**).

◆ **Quickly access this number of Recent Workbooks.** Select to access workbooks on the File tab (**New!**).

◆ **Show this number of unpinned Recent Folders.** Set the number of recent folders (**New!**).

◆ **Ruler units.** Set ruler units to Inches, Centimeters, or Millimeters in Page Layout view. (Default is Default Units).

◆ **Show formula bar.** (Default on).

◆ **Show function ScreenTips.** (Default on).

◆ **Disable hardware graphics acceleration.** (Default off).

◆ **For cells with comments, show: No comments or indicators, Indicators only, and comments on hover** (Default), or **Comments and indicators.**

◆ **Default direction.** Select the Right-to-left or Left-to-right (Default) option.

④ Click **OK**.

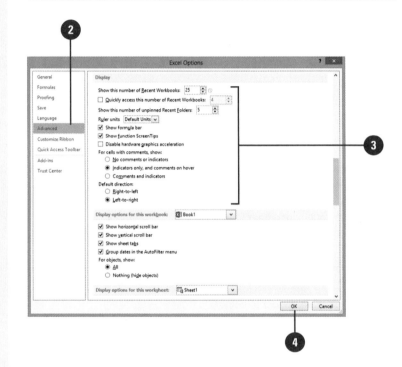

Setting Advanced Options

In addition to display options, the Advanced pane in Excel options also includes options when performing calculations in a workbook and when providing general user feedback. You can set the precision option to permanently change stored values in cells from full precision (15 digits) to the current format, or you can set the feedback options to play sound, show add-in user interface error, or display alerts to update links. If you want to open one or more specific files when you start Excel, you can specify a folder in Advanced options.

Change Advanced Options

1. Click the **File** tab, and then click **Options**.

2. In the left pane, click **Advanced**.

3. Click the **When calculating this workbook** list arrow, and then select the workbook where you want to apply display options.

4. Select the calculating options you want:
   - **Update links to other documents.** (Default on).
   - **Set precision as displayed.**
   - **Use 1904 date system.**
   - **Save external link values.**

5. Select the general options you want:
   - **Provide feedback with sound.** (Default off).
   - **Ignore other applications that use Dynamic Data Exchange (DDE).** Select to disable embedding and linking. (Default off).
   - **Ask to update automatic links.**
   - **Show add-in user interface errors.**
   - **Scale content for A4 or 8.5 x 11' paper sizes.**

6. To open one or more files when you start Excel, specify a folder.

7. Click **OK**.

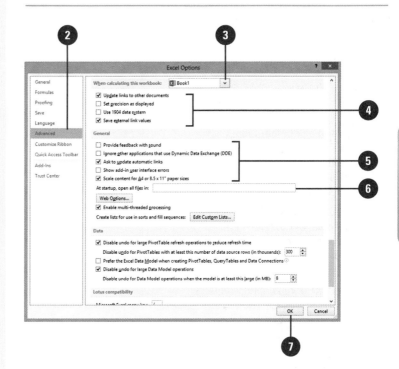

Setting Formula Options

Performing calculations is an important part of working with Excel. To customize the way you work with formulas, you can set options on the Formulas pane in the Excel Options dialog box. If you need to create a nested function (one that references itself), you can set a calculation option to enable iterative calculations. Instead of using the A1 cell reference style, you can use the R1C1 cell reference style, which labels columns and row numerically.

Change Formula Options

1. Click the **File** tab, and then click **Options**.

2. In the left pane, click **Formulas**.

3. Select the calculation options you want:

   ◆ **Workbook Calculation**. Click the Automatic (Default), Automatic except for data tables, or Manual option.

   ◆ **Enable iterative calculation**. Select to allow nested calculations. (Default off). Specify the maximum number of time, and the amount of change to stop it.

4. Select the formula options you want:

   ◆ **R1C1 reference style**. Select to label columns and rows numerically (Default off).

   ◆ **Formula AutoComplete**. (Default on).

   ◆ **Use table name in formulas**. (Default on).

   ◆ **Use GetPivotData functions for PivotTable references**. (Default on).

5. Click **OK**.

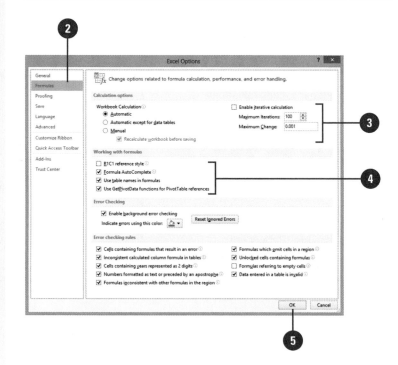

See Also

See "Correcting Formulas" on page 104 for information on setting error checking options.

Changing Advanced Document Properties

You can use document properties—also known as metadata—to help you manage and track files. Search tools can use the metadata to find a workbook based-on your search criteria, such as title, subject, author, category, keywords, or comments. You can create advanced custom properties to associate more specific criteria for search tools to use. If you associate a document property to an item in the document, the document property updates when you change the item.

Customize Advanced Properties

1. Click the **File** tab, and then click **Info**.

2. Click the **Properties** button, and then click **Advanced Properties**.

3. Click the tabs to view and add information:

   ◆ **General**. To find out file location or size.

   ◆ **Summary**. To add title and author information for the workbook.

   ◆ **Statistics**. To display the number of slides, paragraphs, words and other details about the workbook.

   ◆ **Contents**. To display a list of the workbook contents by sheet.

4. Click the **Custom** tab.

5. Type the name for the custom property or select a name from the list.

6. Select the data type for the property you want to add.

7. Type a value for the property.

8. Click **Add**.

9. Click **OK**.

For Your Information

Changing the Document Information Panel

The Document Information Panel helps you manage and track document property information—also known as metadata—such as title, author, subject, keywords, category, and status. The Document Information Panel displays an XML-based mini-form using an InfoPath Form Template (.xsn) file developed in Microsoft InfoPath. By using an XML InfoPath form, you can create your own form templates to edit the document property data and perform data validation. Click the Developer tab, click the Document Panel button, click Browse to select a custom template, select Display By Default properties, select the Always show Document Information Panel On Document Open And Initial Save check box, and then click OK.

Customizing the Way You Create Objects

When you create a text box, Excel applies a set of default text attributes. Some examples of Excel's font default settings include font style, size, and formatting options, such as bold, italic, and underline. When you draw an object, Excel applies a set of default object attributes. Examples of object default settings include fill color, shadow, and line style. To find out the current default settings for your workbook, you can draw an object, or create a text object and check the object's attributes. If you change a default setting, Excel will use the new setting for all subsequent Excel sessions until you change the setting again.

Customize the Way You Create Text Objects

1. Create a text box.

2. Change the text attributes, including font type, style, and size.

3. Right-click the shape, and then click **Set as Default Text Box**.

Customize the Way You Create Shape Objects

1. Create a shape.

2. Change the shape attributes, including fill color or effect, text color, outline color and style; and font type, style, and size.

3. Right-click the shape, and then click **Set as Default Shape**.

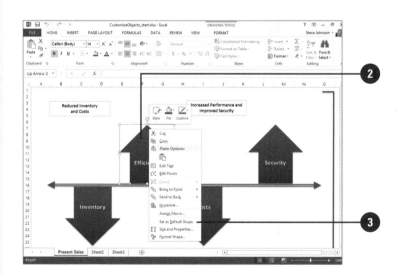

Accessing Commands Not in the Ribbon

If you don't see a command in the Ribbon that was available in an earlier version of Excel, you might think Microsoft removed it from the product. To see if a command is available, check out the Quick Access Toolbar or Customize Ribbon section in Excel Options. The Quick Access Toolbar or Customize Ribbon give access to commands not in the Ribbon, which you can add to the toolbar or ribbon. For example, you can add the following commands: Create Microsoft Outlook Task, Replace Fonts, Send to Microsoft Word, and Web Page Preview.

Add Commands Not in the Ribbon to the Quick Access Toolbar or Ribbon

1. Click the **File** tab, click **Options**, and then click **Quick Access Toolbar** or **Customize Ribbon**.

2. Click the **Choose commands from** list arrow, and then click **Commands Not in the Ribbon**.

3. Click the **Customize Quick Access Toolbar** and then click **For all documents (default)**, or click the **Customize the Ribbon** list arrow, and then click **For All Tabs**.

4. Click the command you want to add (left column).

   TIMESAVER *For the Quick Access Toolbar, click <Separator>, and then click Add to insert a separator line between buttons.*

5. Click **Add**.

6. Click the **Move Up** and **Move Down** arrow buttons to arrange the commands in the order you want them to appear.

7. To reset the Quick Access Toolbar to its original state, click **Reset**, click **Reset only Quick Access Toolbar** or **Reset only selected Ribbon tab**, and then click **Yes**.

8. Click **OK**.

Added button

Working with Office Tools

In addition to the main programs, Office 2013 includes some helpful tools including SkyDrive Pro (**New!**), Upload Center, Language Preferences, Spreadsheet or Database Compare (**New!**), and Telemetry Log or Dashboard (**New!**). With SkyDrive Pro, you can connect and synchronize your SkyDrive cloud storage on a SharePoint site with your desktop. As you upload files to a server, like a SharePoint site, you can use the Upload Center to view progress or issues on a transfer. The Upload Center shows you pending uploads, recently uploaded files and all cached files from a server. If you need to compare two Excel spreadsheets, you can use the Spreadsheet Compare tool, a stand-alone app or Excel option with the Inquire add-in. Telemetry Log records Office events in an Excel spreadsheet to help you troubleshoot problems. Telemetry Dashboard is an Excel spreadsheet that connects to an SQL database to collect client data from other sources in a shared folder.

Compare Spreadsheets

1. Start **Spreadsheet Compare 2013** or **Database Compare 2013**.

   ◆ **Windows 8.** Click the tile on the All Apps screen.

   ◆ **Windows 7.** Click **Start** on the taskbar, point to **All Programs**, point to **Microsoft Office**, and then point to **Office 2013 Tools**.

2. Click the **Browse** folder, and then select the two files you want to compare.

3. Click **OK**.

   The differences appears color coded in the two panes and list.

4. Select or clear option check boxes to show or hide results.

5. Use the Home tab buttons to show results, export results, or copy results to the Clipboard.

6. To exit, click the **Close** button.

See Also

See "Using Multiple Languages" on page 72 for information on using Language Preferences.

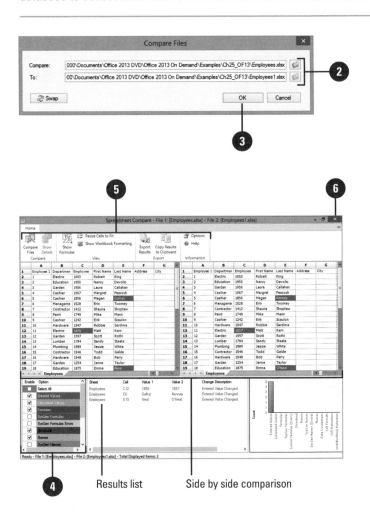

Results list   Side by side comparison

Work with the Upload Center

1. Start **Office 2013 Upload Center**.

   ◆ **Windows 8.** Click the tile on the All Apps screen.

   ◆ **Windows 7.** Click **Start** on the taskbar, point to **All Programs**, point to **Microsoft Office**, and then point to **Office 2013 Tools**.

   ◆ **Desktop taskbar.** Click the **Upload Center** icon on the desktop taskbar, and then click **Open Upload Center.**

2. To display pending uploads, click the **View** list arrow, and then click **Pending Uploads**.

3. Use any of the following options:

   ◆ **Actions.** Use options to open the selected file, open site with the file, save a copy, or discard changes.

   ◆ **Upload All.** Use to upload all files.

   ◆ **Pause Uploads.** Use to pause the selected file.

   ◆ **Settings.** Use to open settings dialog box.

   ◆ **Refresh.** Use to refresh the files in the Upload Center.

4. To resolve issues or take actions, click **Resolve** or **Actions**, and then select an option.

5. To display recent uploads, click the **View** list arrow, and then click **Recently Uploaded**.

6. To exit Upload Center, click the **Close** button.

See Also

See "Syncing Documents with SharePoint" on page 494 for information on using SkyDrive Pro.

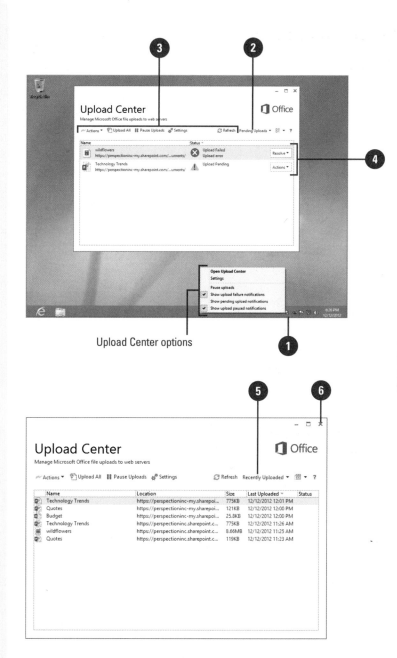

Upload Center options

Maintaining and Repairing Office

At times you may determine that an Office program is not working as efficiently as it once did. This sometimes happens when you install new software or move files into new folders. Office does the work for you with the Repair option, which locates, diagnoses, and fixes any errors in the program itself. Note that this feature does not repair personal files like documents, presentations, or workbooks. If the Repair option does not fix the problem, you might have to reinstall Office. If you need to add or remove features, reinstall Office, or remove it entirely, you can use Office Setup's maintenance feature.

Perform Maintenance on Office Programs

1. Insert the Office disc in your drive or navigate to the folder with the setup program.

2. In File or Windows Explorer, double-click the Setup icon.

3. Click one of the following maintenance buttons.

   ◆ **Add or Remove Features** to change which features are installed or remove specific features.

   ◆ **Remove** to uninstall Microsoft Office 2013 from this computer.

   ◆ **Repair** to repair Microsoft Office 2013 to its original state.

   ◆ **Enter a Product Key** to type the product registration key (located in the product packaging) for Office 2013.

4. Click **Continue**, and then follow the wizard instructions to complete the maintenance.

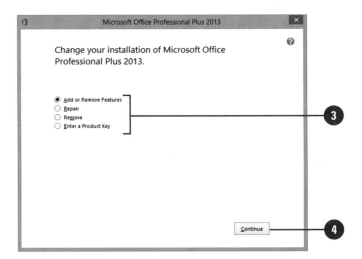

For Your Information

Updating Office 2013 along with Windows 8

Microsoft continually improves Office with updates that include bug fixes and feature improvements. With Windows 8, you can automatically get updates to Office 2013 along with the operating system. To set the update option, open the Desktop app, open the Control Panel, click System and Security, click Windows Update, click Change settings in the left pane, select the Give Me Updates For Other Microsoft Products When I Update Window check box, and then click OK. When Windows 8 scans your system and checks for updates, it also checks for Office 2013 updates as well as other Microsoft products.

Expanding Excel Functionality

Introduction

An Office App is a third-party software component that adds functionality or extends features in an Office document. For example, you can add an app called Radial Bar Chart to provide additional options for charting in Excel. You can quickly install, insert, and manage apps from the Office Store at Office.com directly from an Office program.

An add-in extends the functionality of Excel and other Microsoft Office programs. Excel includes a variety of add-ins—programs that are included with Excel but not essential to its functionality. Some of these supplemental programs—including Analysis ToolPak, Analysis ToolPak VBA, Euro Currency, and Solver—are useful to almost anyone using Excel. Before you can use an Excel or a third-party add-in, you need to load it first. When you load an add-in, the feature may add a command to a Ribbon tab.

If you want to customize Excel and create advanced workbooks, you'll need to learn how to work with the Microsoft Office programming language, **Microsoft Visual Basic for Applications (VBA)**. VBA is powerful and flexible, and you can use it in all major Office programs. To create a VBA application, you have to learn VBA conventions and syntax. Office makes VBA more user-friendly by providing the Visual Basic Editor, an application that includes several tools to help you write error-free VBA applications. The Visual Basic Editor provides extensive online Help to assist you in this task. A practical way to use VBA is to create macros. Macros can simplify common repetitive tasks that you regularly use in Excel.

An ActiveX control is a software component that adds functionality, such as a form, to an existing document. Excel includes several pre-built ActiveX controls—including a label, text box, command button, and check box—to help you create a user interface.

What You'll Do

Add and Insert Apps for Office

View and Manage Add-ins

Load and Unload Add-ins

Enhance a Workbook with VBA

View the Visual Basic Editor

Set Developer Options

Understand How Macros Automate Your Work

Record or Create a Macro

Run and Control a Macro

Add a Digital Signature to a Macro Project

Assign a Macro to a Toolbar or Ribbon

Save and Open a Workbook with Macros

Insert ActiveX Controls

Use ActiveX Controls

Set ActiveX Control Properties

Add VBA Code to an ActiveX Control

Adding and Inserting Apps for Office

With the Office Store at Office.com (**New!**), you can add functionality with a third-party app to an Office program, and then use the app to extend features in a document. For example, you can add an app called Radial Bar Chart to provide additional options for charting in Excel or an app called Dictionary - Merriam to use an enhanced dictionary. To use Office.com, you need to have a Microsoft account, and be signed in with your Office program. You can insert an app by using the Apps for Office button (**New!**) on the Insert tab. The apps you add to your Office programs are inserted and managed online using your web browser. Apps are designed for specific Office programs and only appear for them.

Manage or Add an Office App

1. Click the **Insert** tab.

2. Click the **Apps for Office** button (**New!**), and then click **See All**.

   A list of installed apps appears under MY APPS.

3. Click **FEATURED APPS**.

   A list of available apps appears under FEATURED APPS.

4. To locate an app, type your search text in the Search box, and then click the **Search** button or press Enter to open your browser to the Office Store.

   If you want to add an app, click the app, and then click **Add**. When you're done, click the **Close** button to exit your browser.

5. To add an app in the Apps for Office window, click the app title or the **Add** button.

6. To manage your apps, click **Manage My Apps**, and then wait for your browser to open. Sign-in to your account, if prompted. Use the available options, and then click the **Close** button to exit.

   ◆ To hide an app, click Visible, and then click the **Hide** link.

   ◆ To show an app, click Hidden, and then click the **Retrieve** link.

7. To exit, click the **Close** button.

MY APPS

Apps added to Excel

Insert an App for Office

① Click the **Insert** tab.

② To insert a recently used app object, click the **Apps for Office** button (**New!**), and then click the recently used app on the menu.

③ Click the **Apps for Office** button (**New!**), and then click **See All**.

A list of installed apps appears under MY APPS.

④ Click the app tile you want to insert.

⑤ Click **Insert**.

The app inserts an object with the specified functionality. Follow the on-screen instructions for the app object to use the app.

Did You Know?

You can delete an Office app. To delete an Office app, select the app object, and then press Delete.

Radial Bar Chart app in Excel

MY APPS

Viewing and Managing Add-ins

An add-in extends functionality to Excel and other Microsoft Office programs. An add-in can add buttons and custom commands to the Ribbon or menu items or buttons within the program. You can get add-ins for Excel on the Office.com web site in the Downloads area, or on third-party vendor web sites. When you download and install an add-in, it appears on the Add-Ins or other tabs depending on functionality, and includes a special ScreenTip that identifies the developer. You can view and manage add-ins from the Add-Ins pane in Options. In Options from the Ribbon page, you can also show or hide the Add-ins tab.

View Installed Add-ins

1. Click the **Add-Ins** tab, or click the **File** tab, click **Add-Ins**, point to an add-in menu option, and then select a command.

   Add-ins with buttons and controls appear on the Ribbon. To display a ScreenTip, point to a button or control.

2. Click the **File** tab, and then click **Options**.

3. In the left pane, click **Add-Ins**.

   The installed add-ins appear in the list by category.

   ◆ **Active Application Add-ins.** Lists the registered and running add-ins. A selected check box for a COM add-in appears here.

   ◆ **Inactive Application Add-ins.** Lists the installed add-ins, but not currently loaded. A cleared check box for a COM add-in appears here.

   ◆ **Document Related Add-ins.** Lists template files currently open in a document.

   ◆ **Disabled Application Add-ins.** Lists automatically disabled add-ins causing Office programs to crash.

4. Click an add-in to display information about it.

5. Click **OK**.

Add-in

Information about the selected add-in.

Manage Installed Add-ins

1 Click the **File** tab, and then click **Options**.

2 In the left pane, click **Add-Ins**.

3 Click the **Manage** list arrow, and then click the add-in list you want to display:

- ◆ **Excel Add-ins.** Opens the Add-Ins dialog box and lists the currently installed add-ins.

- ◆ **COM Add-ins.** Opens the COM Add-Ins dialog box and lists the Component Object Model (COM) add-ins.

- ◆ **Actions.** Opens the AutoCorrect dialog box with the Actions tab and list the installed actions.

- ◆ **XML Expansion Pack.** Opens XML Expansion Packs that provide additional XML functionality.

- ◆ **Disabled Items.** Opens the Disabled Items dialog box and lists the disabled items that prevent Office from working properly. If you want to try and enable an item, select it, click Enable, click Close, and then restart Office.

4 Click **Go**.

5 Click **OK**.

See Also

See "Inserting Apps in Office Programs" on page 460 for information on getting and inserting Office Apps, which you can use to add functionality to Office like an Add-in.

Add-ins Installed with Excel

Add-in	Descriptions
Analysis ToolPak	Provides data analysis tools for statistical and engineering analysis.
Analysis ToolPak VBA	VBA Functions for Analysis ToolPak.
Euro Currency Tools	Conversion and formatting for the euro currency.
Solver	Tool for optimization and equation solving.

Loading and Unloading Add-ins

Add-ins are additional programs, designed to run seamlessly within Excel or other Office programs. There are two main types of add-ins: Excel and **Component Object Model (COM)**. Excel add-ins are custom controls designed specifically for Excel, while COM add-ins are designed to run in one or more Office programs and use the file name extension .dll or .exe. Some add-ins are installed when you run the Setup program, while others can be downloaded from Microsoft Office Online (Office.com) or purchased from third-party vendors. To load or unload add-ins, Excel provides commands you can access from an added button on the Quick Access Toolbar or the Add-Ins pane in Excel Options. When you load an add-in, the feature may add a command to a tab or toolbar. You can load one or more add-ins. If you no longer need an add-in, you should unload it to save memory and reduce the number of commands on a tab. When you unload an add-in, you also may need to restart Excel to remove an add-in command from a tab.

Load or Unload an Add-in

1. Click the **Developer** tab.

   ◆ To display the Developer tab, use the Customize Ribbon pane in Options.

2. Click the **Add-Ins** button.

3. To add an add-in to the list, click **Browse**, locate and select the add-in you want, and then click **OK**.

4. Select a check box to load an add-in or clear a check box to unload an add-in.

5. Click **OK**.

Did You Know?

You can open the Add-Ins dialog box from Options. Click the File tab, click Options, click Add-ins, click the Manage list arrow, click Excel Add-ins, and then click Go.

Load or Unload a COM Add-in

① Click the **Developer** tab.

   ◆ To display the Developer tab, use the Customize Ribbon pane in Options.

② Click the **COM Add-Ins** button.

③ Select the check box next to the add-in you want to load, or clear the check box you want to unload.

   TROUBLE? *If the add-in is not available in the list, click Add, locate and select the add-in you want, and then click OK.*

④ To remove the selected add-in, click **Remove**.

⑤ Click **OK**.

Did You Know?

You can open the COM Add-Ins dialog box from Options. Click the File tab, click Options, click Add-ins, click the Manage list arrow, click COM Add-ins, and then click Go.

You can can get more information about COM online. Visit *www.microsoft.com/com.*

See Also

See "Using the Ribbon" on page 4 and "Working with the Ribbon and Toolbars" on page 6 for information on adding a button to the Quick Access Toolbar.

COM Add-ins Installed with Excel

Add-in	Descriptions
Inquire (**New!**)	Analyze workbooks, diagram workbook, worksheet, or cell relationships, compare workbooks, and clean excess formatting (Office Professional Plus)
Microsoft Office PowerPivot for Excel 2013 (**New!**)	Builds simple data models that let you filter data, calculate fields, and create key performance indicators (KPIs) (Office Professional Plus)
Office Telemetry Dashboard add-in (**New!**)	An Excel spreadsheet that connects to an SQL database to collect client data from other sources in a shared folder
Power View (**New!**)	Creates a presentation sheet that lets you visually interact with the data (Office Professional Plus)

For Your Information

Dealing with an Add-in Security Alert

When there is a problem with an add-in, Excel disables it to protect the program and your data. When a problem does occur, a security alert dialog box appears, displaying information about the problem and options you can choose to fix or ignore it. You can choose an option to help protect you from unknown content (recommended), enable this add-in for this session only, or enable all code published by this publisher. See "Setting Add-in Security Options" on page 368 for more information about setting options that trigger the Add-in security alert.

Enhancing a Workbook with VBA

Office programs like Excel, Access, Word, PowerPoint, and Visio share a common programming language: Visual Basic for Applications (VBA). With VBA, you can develop applications that combine tools from these Office products, as well as other programs that support VBA. Because of the language's power and flexibility, programmers often prefer to use VBA to customize their Office programs.

Introducing the Structure of VBA

VBA is an object-oriented programming language because, when you develop a VBA application, you manipulate objects. An object can be anything within your workbook, such as a shape, text box, picture, or table. Even Excel itself is considered an object. Objects can have properties that describe the object's characteristics. Text boxes, for example, have the Font property, which describes the font Excel uses to display the text. A text box also has properties that indicate whether the text is bold or italic.

Objects also have methods—actions that can be done to the object. Deleting and inserting are examples of methods available with a record object. Closely related to methods are events. An event is a specific action that occurs on or with an object. Clicking a button initiates the Click event for the button object. VBA also refers to an event associated with an object as an event property. The form button, for example, has the Click event property. You can use VBA to either respond to an event or to initiate an event.

Writing VBA Code

A VBA programmer types the statements, or **code**, that make up the VBA program. Those statements follow a set of rules, called **syntax**, that govern how commands are formulated. For example, to change the property of a particular object, the command follows the general form:

    Object.Property = Expression

Where **Object** is the name of a VBA object, **Property** is the name of a property that object has, and **Expression** is a value that will be assigned to the property. The following statement places text "Expense Report" in cells A1 and A5 on Sheet1:

    Worksheets("Sheet1").Range("A1, A5") =
        "Expense Report"

You can use Office and VBA's online Help to learn about specific object and property names. If you want to apply a method to an object, the syntax is:

    Object.Method arg1, arg2, ...

Where **Object** is the name of a VBA object, **Method** is the name of method that can be applied to that object, and **arg1**, **arg2**, ... are optional **arguments** that provide additional information for the method operation. For example, to set columns A and B on Sheet2 to AutoFit cell contents, you could use the AutoFit method as follows:

    Worksheets("Sheet2").Column(A:B).AutoFit

Working with Procedures

You don't run VBA commands individually. Instead they are organized into groups of commands called **procedures**. A procedure either performs an action or calculates a value. Procedures that perform actions are called **Sub procedures**. You can run a Sub procedure directly, or Office can run it for you in response to an event, such as clicking a button or opening a form. A Sub procedure initiated by an event is also called an **event procedure**. Office provides event procedure templates to help you easily create procedures for common events. Event procedures are displayed in each object's event properties list.

A procedure that calculates a value is called a **function procedure**. By creating function procedures you can create your own function library, supplementing the Office collection of built-in functions. You can access these functions from within the Expression Builder, making it easy for them to be used over and over again.

Working with Modules

Procedures are collected and organized within **modules**. Modules generally belong to two types: class modules and standard modules. A **class module** is associated with a specific object. In more advanced VBA programs, the class module can be associated with an object created by the user. **Standard modules** are not associated with specific objects, and they can be run from anywhere within a database. This is usually not the case with class modules. Standard modules are listed in the Database window on the Modules Object list.

Building VBA Projects

A collection of modules is further organized into a **project**. Usually a project has the same name as a workbook. You can create projects that are not tied into any specific workbook, saving them as Excel add-ins that provide extra functionality to Excel.

Using the Visual Basic Editor

You create VBA commands, procedures, and modules in Office's **Visual Basic Editor**. This is the same editor used by Excel, Word, and other Office programs. Thus, you can apply what you learn about creating programs in Excel to these other applications.

The Project Explorer

One of the fundamental tools in the Visual Basic Editor is the Project Explorer. The **Project Explorer** presents a hierarchical view of all of the projects and modules currently open in Excel, including standard and class modules.

The Modules Window

You write all of your VBA code in the **Modules** window. The Modules window acts as a basic text editor, but it includes several tools to help you write error-free codes. Excel also provides hints as you write your code to help you avoid syntax errors.

The Object Browser

There are hundreds of objects available to you. Each object has a myriad of properties, methods, and events. Trying to keep track of all of them is daunting, but the Visual Basic Editor supplies the **Object Browser**, which helps you examine the complete collection of objects, properties, and methods available for a given object.

Viewing the Visual Basic Editor

The Project Explorer displays a hierarchical list of all open projects and modules.

The Modules window allows you to enter VBA commands.

VBA projects

Currently selected module

The Properties window displays properties for selected objects.

A VBA statement

Method

The Object Browser displays a list of available objects, properties, methods, and events.

Objects

Properties

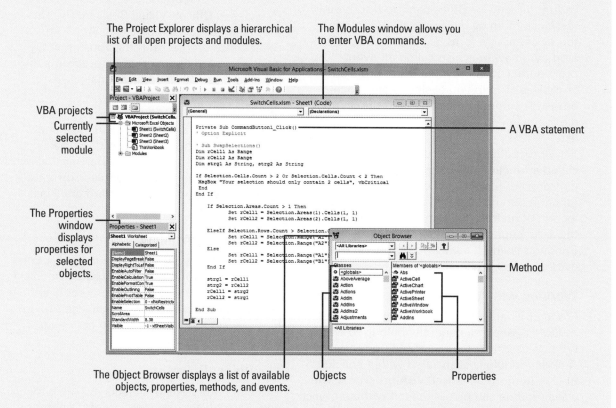

Setting Developer Options

The Developer tab is a specialized Ribbon that you can use to access developer controls, write code, or create macros. You can set an option in the Customize Ribbon pane in Options to show or hide the Developer tab. As a developer, you can also set an option to show errors in your user interface customization code.

Set Developer Options

1. Click the **File** tab, and then click **Options**.

2. In the left pane, click **Customize Ribbon**.

3. Select the **Developer** check box to display the Developer tab.

4. In the left pane, click **Advanced**.

5. Select the **Show add-in user interface errors** check box.

6. Click **OK**.

Understanding How Macros Automate Your Work

To complete many tasks in Excel, you need to execute a series of commands and actions. To print two copies of a selected range of Sheet2 of a worksheet, for example, you need to open the workbook, switch to Sheet2, select the print area, open the Print dialog box, and specify that you want to print two copies. If you often need to complete the same task, you'll find yourself repeatedly taking the same series of steps. It can be tiresome to continually repeat the same commands and actions when you can easily create a mini-program, or macro, that accomplishes all of them with a single command.

Creating a **macro** is easy and requires no programming knowledge on your part. Excel simply records the steps you want included in the macro while you use the keyboard and mouse. When you record a macro, Excel stores the list of commands with any name you choose. You can store your macros in the current workbook, in a new workbook, or in Excel's Personal Macro workbook.

Storing your macros in the Personal Macro workbook makes the macros available to you from any location in Excel, even when no workbook is open. When you select the Personal Macro Workbook option to store a macro, Excel creates a hidden personal macro workbook file (Personal.xlsb) and saves the macro in this workbook. The file is stored in the XLStart folder so it will load automatically when Excel starts. The XLSTART folder is typically located in the C:\Users*user name*\App Data\Roaming\Microsoft\Excel folder for Windows 8 or 7.

Once a macro is created, you can make modifications to it, add comments so other users will understand its purpose, and test it to make sure it runs correctly.

You can run a macro by choosing the Macro command on the View or Developer tab, or by using a shortcut key or clicking a Quick Access Toolbar button you've assigned to it. From the Macro dialog box, you can run, edit, test, or delete any Excel macro on your system, or create a new one.

If you have problems with a macro, you can step through the macro one command at a time, known as **debugging**. Once you identify any errors in the macro, you can edit it.

Indicates the workbook(s) from which you can access the selected macro.

When you create a macro, you can add a description of what the macro does.

Recording a Macro

If you find yourself repeating the same set of steps over and over, you can record a macro. Macros can run several tasks for you at the click of a button. When you turn on the macro recorder, Excel records every mouse click and keystroke action you execute until you turn off the recorder. You can even record formatting changes to charts and other objects. Then you can "play," or run, the macro whenever you want to repeat that series of actions—but Excel will execute them at a much faster rate. The macro recorder doesn't record in real time, so you can take your time to correctly complete each action.

Record a Macro

1. Click the **Developer** or **View** tab.

2. To record a macro with actions relative to the initially selected cell, click the **Use Relative References** button.

3. Click the **Record Macro** button.

   ◆ If you use the View tab, click **View Macros** on the menu.

   TIMESAVER *To quickly start or stop a macro recording, click the Record icon or Stop Record icon on the Status bar (left side).*

4. Type a name for the macro.

5. Assign a shortcut key to use a keystroke combination to run the macro.

6. Click the **Store macro in** list arrow, and then select a location.

   ◆ **Personal Macro Workbook**. The macro is available whenever you use Excel.

   ◆ **New Workbook**. The macro is available in new workbooks.

   ◆ **This Workbook**. The macro is available only in this workbook.

7. If you want, type a description.

8. Click **OK**.

9. Execute the commands or actions you want to complete the task.

10. Click the **Stop Recording** button.

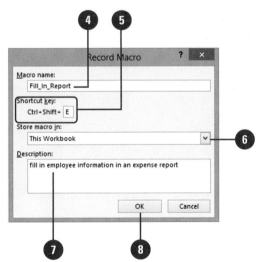

Creating a Macro

If you find yourself repeating the same set of steps over and over, or if you need to add new functionality to Excel, you could create a macro. If you find it difficult to record a macro, you can create one using a programming language called Microsoft Visual Basic for Applications (VBA). With VBA, you create a macro by writing a script to replay the actions you want. The macros for a particular workbook are stored in a macro module, which is a collection of Visual Basic codes.

Create a Macro

1. Click the **Developer** or **View** tab.

2. Click the **Macros** button.

   ◆ If you use the View tab, click **View Macros** on the menu.

3. Type a name for the macro.

4. Click the **Macros in** list arrow, and then click **All Open Workbooks** or the workbook to which you want the macro stored.

5. Click **Create**.

   The Microsoft Visual Basic window opens.

6. Click the Module window (if necessary), and then type new Visual Basic commands, or edit existing ones.

   To run the macro, press F5.

7. When you're done, click the **Save** button, and then click the program **Close** button.

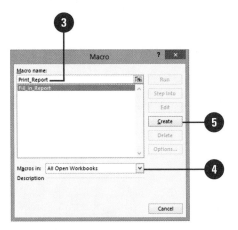

Did You Know?

You can record macros with chart elements. When you use the macro recorder with charts, it now records formatting changes to charts and other objects.

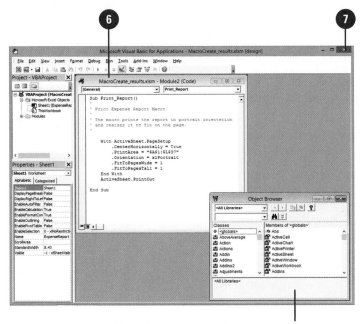

Object Browser helps you insert commands.

Running a Macro

Running a macro is similar to choosing a command in Excel. When you record or edit the macro, you have the choice of making it available through a menu command, a keyboard combination, or even a toolbar button. As with other options in Excel, your choice depends on your personal preferences—and you can choose to make more than one option available. Where you store a macro when you save it determines its availability later. Macros stored in the Personal Macro workbook are always available, and macros stored in any other workbooks are only available when the workbook is open.

Run a Macro

1. Click the **Developer** or **View** tab.

2. Click the **Macros** button.

    ◆ If you use the View tab, click **View Macros** on the menu.

    TIMESAVER *Click the Macros button on the Status bar.*

3. Click the macro you want to run.

4. Click **Run**.

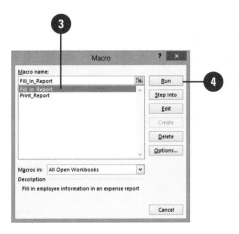

Delete a Macro

1. Click the **Developer** or **View** tab.

2. Click the **Macros** button.

    ◆ If you use the View tab, click **View Macros** on the menu.

3. Click the macro you want to delete.

4. Click **Delete**, and then click **Delete** again to confirm the deletion.

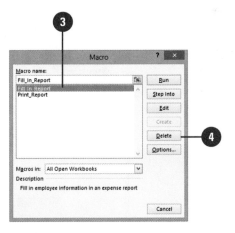

Did You Know?

You can stop a macro. Press Ctrl+Break to stop a macro before it completes its actions.

Controlling a Macro

If a macro doesn't work exactly the way you want it to, you can fix the problem using Microsoft Visual Basic for Applications (VBA). VBA allows you to **debug**, or repair, an existing macro so that you change only the actions that aren't working correctly. All macros for a particular workbook are stored in a macro module, a collection of Visual Basic programming codes that you can copy to other workbook files. You can view and edit your Visual Basic modules using the Visual Basic editor. By learning Visual Basic you can greatly increase the scope and power of your programs.

Debug a Macro Using Step Mode

1. Click the **Developer** or **View** tab.

2. Click the **Macros** button.

   ◆ If you use the View tab, click **View Macros** on the menu.

3. Click the macro you want to debug.

4. Click **Step Into**.

   The Microsoft Visual Basic window opens.

5. Click the **Debug** menu, and then click **Step Into** (or press F8) to proceed through each action.

   ◆ You can also use other commands like **Step Over** and **Step Out** to debug the code.

6. When you're done, click the **Save** button, and then click the program **Close** button.

7. Click **OK** to stop the debugger.

Step debugging

Debug toolbar

Did You Know?

You can display the Debug toolbar. In the Visual Basic editor, click the View menu, point to Toolbars, and then click Debug.

Edit a Macro

1. Click the **Developer** or **View** tab.

2. Click the **Macros** button.

   ◆ If you use the View tab, click **View Macros** on the menu.

3. To open a macro, click the macro you want to change, and then click the **View Code** button.

4. Click the Module window containing the Visual Basic code for your macro.

5. Type new Visual Basic commands, or edit the commands already present.

6. Click the **Save** button, and then click the program **Close** button.

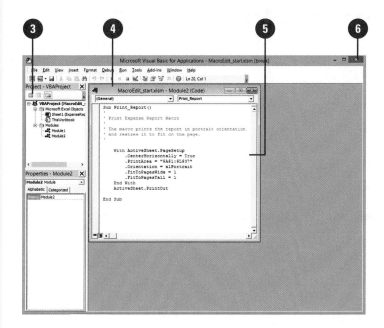

Copy a Macro Module to Another Workbook

1. Open the workbook files you want to copy the macro from and to.

2. Click the **Developer** tab.

3. Click the **Visual Basic** button.

4. Click the **View** menu, and then click **Project Explorer**.

5. Drag the module you want to copy from the source workbook to the destination workbook.

6. Click the **Save** button, and then click the program **Close** button.

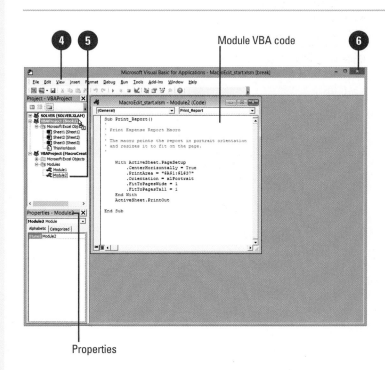

Module VBA code

Properties

Adding a Digital Signature to a Macro Project

If you want to add a digital signature to a workbook with a macro, you need to add it using the Visual Basic editor. If you open a workbook that contains a signed macro project with a problem, the macro is disabled by default and the Message Bar appears to notify you of the potential problem. You can click Enable Content in the Message Bar to use it. For more details, you can click Show Signature Details to view certificate and publisher information. If a digital signature has problems—it's expired, not issued by a trusted publisher, or the workbook has been altered—the certificate information image contains a red X. When there's a problem, contact the signer to have them fix it, or save the workbook to a trusted location, where you can run the macro without security checks.

Sign a Macro Project

1. Open the workbook that contains the macro project, and then click the **Developer** tab.

2. Click the **Visual Basic** button to open the Visual Basic window.

3. Click the **Tools** menu, and then click **Digital Signature**.

4. Click **Choose**.

5. Select a certificate in the list.

6. To view a certificate, click **View Certificate** or a link, and then click **OK**.

7. Click **OK**.

8. Click **OK** again.

9. Click the **Save** button, and then click the program **Close** button.

Assigning a Macro to a Toolbar or Ribbon

After you create a macro, you can add the macro to the Ribbon or Quick Access Toolbar for easy access. When you create a macro, the macro name appears in the list of available commands when you customize the Ribbon or Quick Access Toolbar in Options. When you point to a macro button on the Ribbon or Quick Access Toolbar, a ScreenTip appears, displaying Macro: *document name*!*macro name*.

Assign a Macro to a Toolbar or Ribbon

1. Click the **File** tab, click **Options**, and then click **Quick Access Toolbar** or **Customize Ribbon**.

2. Click the **Choose commands from** list arrow, and then click **Macros**.

3. Click the **Customize Quick Access Toolbar** and then click **For all documents (default)**, or click the **Customize the Ribbon** list arrow, and then click **For All Tabs**.

4. Click the macro you want to add (left column).

5. Click **Add**.

6. Click the **Move Up** and **Move Down** arrow buttons to arrange the commands in the order you want them to appear.

7. Click **Modify** or **Rename**.

8. Type a name for the button.

9. Click an icon in the symbol list.

10. Click **OK**.

11. Click **OK**.

See Also

See "Using the Ribbon" on page 4 and "Working with Toolbars" on page 6 for information on using the Quick Access Toolbar.

Macro button

Saving a Workbook with Macros

Macros are created using Visual Basic for Applications (VBA) code. If you add a macro to a workbook, you need to save it with a file name extension that ends with an "m", either Excel Macro-Enabled Workbook (.xlsm), or Excel Macro-Enabled Template (.xltm). If you try to save a workbook containing a macro with a file name extension that ends with an "x" (such as .xlsx or .xltx), Excel displays an alert message, restricting the operation. These Excel file types are designated to be VBA code-free.

Save a Workbook with Macros

1 Click the **File** tab, and then click **Save As**.

2 Click **Computer**, and then click **Browse** or a recent folder.

3 Click the **Save in** list arrow, and then click the drive or folder where you want to save the file.

4 Type a workbook file name.

5 If necessary, click the **Save as type** list arrow, and then select the macro format you want:

   ◆ **Excel Macro-Enabled Workbook.** A workbook (.xlsm) that contains VBA code.

   ◆ **Excel Macro-Enabled Template.** A template (.xltm) that includes preapproved macros.

6 Click **Save**.

Opening a Workbook with Macros

When you open a workbook with a macro, VBA, or other software code, Excel displays a security warning to let you know the workbook might contain potentially harmful code that may harm your computer. If you know and trust the author of the workbook, you can change security options to enable the macro content and use the workbook normally. If you don't trust the content, you can continue to block and disable the content and use the workbook with limited functionality in Protected view. If you don't want a security alert to appear, you can change security settings in the Trust Center in Excel Options.

Open a Workbook with Macros

1. Click the **File** tab, and then click **Open**.

2. Click **Computer**, and then click **Browse** or a recent folder.

3. If necessary, click the **File as type** list arrow, and then the workbook type that contains a macro.

4. If the file is located in another folder, click the **Look in** list arrow, and then navigate to the file.

5. Click the workbook with macros you want to open, and then click **Open**.

6. Click the **File** tab, click **Info**, click the **Enable Content** button, and then click **Advanced Options**. To enable all content (make trusted), click **Enable All Content** on the menu.

   ◆ You can also click **Enable Content** in the Message Bar with the Security Warning.

7. If you trust the document content, click the **Enable content for this session** option to use it. If you don't trust it, click the **Help protect me from unknown content (recommended)** option to block and disable the macros.

8. Click **OK**.

Options in the Message Bar

Inserting ActiveX Controls

An ActiveX control is a software component that adds functionality to an existing program. An ActiveX control is really just another term for an OLE (Object Linking and Embedding) object, known as a Component Object Model (COM) object. An ActiveX control supports a customizable, programmatic interface. Excel includes several pre-built ActiveX controls on the Developer tab, including a label, text box, command button, image, scroll bar, check box, option button, combo box, list box, and toggle button. To create an ActiveX control, click the Insert button on the Developer tab, and then click the ActiveX control you want, and then drag to insert it with the size you want. If there is a problem with an ActiveX control, Excel disables it to protect the program and your data. When a problem does occur, a security alert dialog box appears, displaying information about the problem and options you can choose to leave it disabled in Protected view or enable it.

Insert ActiveX Controls

1. Click the **Developer** tab.

2. Click the **Design Mode** button (highlighted).

3. Click the **Insert** button arrow, and then click the button with the ActiveX control you want to use.

    See the next page for a list and description of each ActiveX control.

4. Display the worksheet where you want to place the ActiveX control.

5. Drag (pointer changes to a plus sign) to draw the ActiveX control the size you want.

6. To resize the control, drag a resize handle (circles) to the size you want.

7. To add Visual Basic code to the ActiveX control, click the **View Code** button, or to change display properties, click the **Properties** button. To exit, click the **Save** and **Close** buttons.

8. Click the **Design Mode** button (not highlighted) to exit.

For Your Information

Using Form Controls

Form controls are objects that users can interact with to enter or manipulate data. For example, you can add a Check box control to your document so that users can turn an option on and off. You can select a control from the Developer tab and drag to create the control directly on your document just like an ActiveX control. For an example on using form controls, see project downloads for Excel 2013 On Demand available on the web at *www.perspection.com*.

Deal with an ActiveX Control Security Alert

1. Click the **File** tab, and then click **Open**.

2. Click **Computer**, and then click **Browse** or a recent folder.

3. Click the **File as type** list arrow, and then click the document type that contains the ActiveX control.

4. If the file is located in another folder, click the **Look in** list arrow, and then navigate to the file.

5. Click the document with the ActiveX control you want to open, and then click **Open**.

6. Click the **File** tab, click **Info**, click the **Enable Content** button, and then click **Advanced Options**. To enable all content (make trusted), click **Enable All Content** on the menu.

   ◆ You can also click **Enable Content** in the Message Bar with the Security Warning.

7. If you trust the document content, click the **Enable content for this session** option to use it. If you don't trust it, click the **Help protect me from unknown content (recommended)** option to block and disable the macros.

8. Click **OK**.

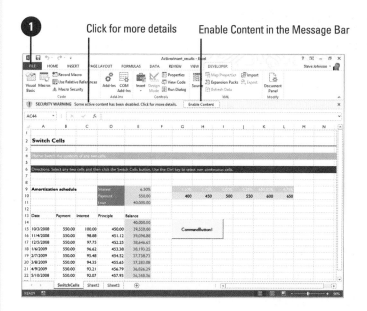

Click for more details   Enable Content in the Message Bar

See Also

See "Setting ActiveX Security Options" on page 369 for more information about setting options that trigger the ActiveX security alert.

See "Setting ActiveX Control Properties" on page 467 for more information about setting ActiveX display properties.

Using ActiveX Controls

ActiveX Controls

Button	Name	Description
A	Label	This button creates a text label. Because the other controls already include a corresponding label, use this button to create labels that are independent of other controls.
abl	Text Box	This button creates a text box in which the user can enter text (or numbers). Use this control for objects assigned to a text or number data type.
(spin)	Spin Button	This button creates a box in which the user can click arrows to increase or decrease numbers in a box. Use this control assigned to a number data type.
(button)	Command Button	This button creates a button that runs a macro or Microsoft Visual Basic function when the user clicks the button in the form.
(image)	Image	This button inserts a frame, in which you can insert a graphic in your form. Use this control when you want to insert a graphic, such as clip art or a logo.
(scroll)	Scroll Bar	This button creates a scroll bar pane in which the user can enter text (or numbers) in a scrollable text box. Use this control or objects assigned to a text or number data type.
☑	Check Box	This button creates a check box that allows a user to make multiple yes or no selections. Use this control for fields assigned to the yes/no data type.
◉	Option Button	This button creates an option button (also known as a radio button) that allows the user to make a single selection from at least two choices. Use this control for fields assigned to the yes/no data type.
(combo)	Combo Box	This button creates a combo box in which the user has the option to enter text or select from a list of options. You can enter your own options in the list, or you can display options stored in another table.
(list)	List Box	This button creates a list box that allows a user to select from a list of options. You can enter your own options in the list, or can have another table provide a list of options.
(toggle)	Toggle Button	This button creates a button that allows the user to make a yes or no selection by clicking the toggle button. Use this control for fields assigned to the yes/no data type.
(more)	More Controls	Click to display other controls, such as Adobe Acrobat Control for ActiveX, Microsoft Forms 2.0, Microsoft InfoPath controls, and Microsoft web Browser.

Setting ActiveX Control Properties

Every ActiveX control has properties, or settings, that determine its appearance and function. You can open a property sheet that displays all the settings for that control in alphabetic or category order directly from Excel. The ActiveX controls appear in the Properties window in two columns: the left column displays the name of the control, and the right column displays the current value or setting for the control. When you select either column, a list arrow appears in the right column, allowing you to select the setting you want. After you set properties, you can add VBA code to a module to make it perform.

Set ActiveX Control Properties

1. Click the **Developer** tab.

2. Click the **Design Mode** button (highlighted).

3. Select the control whose properties you want to modify.

4. Click the **Properties** button.

5. To switch controls, click the **Controls** list arrow (at the top), and then select the one you want.

6. Click the **Alphabetic** or **Categorized** tab to display the control properties so you can find the ones you want.

7. Click the property box for the property you want to modify, and then do one of the following.

   ◆ Type the value or information you want to use, such as the control name.

   ◆ If the property box contains a list arrow, click the arrow and then click a value in the list.

   ◆ If a property box contains a dialog button (...), click it to open a dialog box to select options or insert an object, such as a picture.

8. When you're done, click the **Close** button on the Properties window.

9. Click the **Design Mode** button (not highlighted) to exit.

For Your Information

Playing a Movie Using an ActiveX Control

Although you cannot insert a Flash movie into an Excel workbook, you can play one using an ActiveX control and the Flash player. Before you can use the control, the ActiveX control and Flash player need to be installed on your computer. You can get the ActiveX control at *http://activex.microsoft.com/activex/activex/*. To play the Flash (.swf) movie, you add the Shockwave Flash Object ActiveX control to the worksheet and create a link to the file. If a movie doesn't play, check ActiveX security options in the Trust Center in Excel Options.

Adding VBA Code to an ActiveX Control

After you add controls and set properties, you can add VBA code to a module to determine how the controls respond to user actions. All controls have a predefined set of events. For example, a command button has a Click event that occurs when the user clicks the button. When you select a control in Design Mode and then click the View Code button, the Visual Basic Editor opens with a Code window, displaying the start of a procedure that runs when the event occurs. The top of the Code window displays the active object and event procedure. The Object list displays the ActiveX control, such as *CommandButton1*, and the Procedure list displays the trigger event, such as *Click*.

Add VBA Code to an ActiveX Control

1. Click the **Developer** tab.

2. Click the **Design Mode** button (highlighted).

3. Select the control to which you want to add VBA code.

4. Click the **View Code** button.

   The Visual Basic Editor window opens.

5. To show the Properties window, click the **Properties window** button.

6. To help with scripting commands, click the **Object Browser** button on the toolbar.

7. Click in the Code window between the beginning and ending line of the procedure, and then type VBA code to perform the task you want.

   The Object list is set to *CommandButton1*, and the Procedure list is set to *Click*.

8. When you're done, click the **Save** button on the toolbar.

9. Click the **Close** button or click the **File** menu, and then click **Close and Return to Microsoft Excel**.

10. Click the **Design Mode** button (not highlighted) to exit.

Module — Object list — Procedure list

Properties for the ActiveX Control

Working Online with Office Documents

Introduction

Instead of storing and working on Office documents on your desktop, you can store them on the web and work on them with an Office Web App. An Office Web App allows you to work with an Office document in a web browser. The process of using the web instead of a desktop as a base of operation is known as **cloud computing**. SkyDrive and SharePoint are two types of cloud computing sites, where you can store and share information. SkyDrive is a free service provided by Microsoft, which is available at *www.skydrive.com* with a Microsoft account, while SharePoint is web server software created by Microsoft.

When you store an Office document on SkyDrive or on a Microsoft SharePoint server configured with Office Web Apps, such as Office 365 SharePoint, a subscription-based service provided by Microsoft, you can view or edit the document in a web browser using the same look and feel as an Office 2013 program. To make storing files on SkyDrive or SharePoint quick and easy, Office 2013 programs provide command on the Save As screen on the File tab for you to save Office documents directly to a SkyDrive or SharePoint folder.

If you have a Windows Phone, Apple iOS (iPhone and iPad), BlackBerry, or Android, you can use your web browser or Office Web Apps to work with your Office documents from anywhere. You can view and edit Office documents stored on your phone, sent to you as e-mail attachments, or stored on a SkyDrive or SharePoint site. Since the files are synced online, the changes you make on your mobile device are available on your desktop too.

What You'll Do

Work Online with SharePoint and SkyDrive

Sign in to SharePoint or SkyDrive

Save and Open on SharePoint or SkyDrive

Access Documents on SharePoint

Sync Documents on SharePoint

Share Documents on SkyDrive

Access Documents on SkyDrive

Manage Documents on SkyDrive

Download or Upload Documents on SkyDrive

Create Office Documents on SkyDrive

Send Links to Documents on SkyDrive

Compare the Office Desktop App to the Web App

Work with Office Web Apps

Save or Print Documents in Office Web Apps

Co-author Documents with Office Web Apps

Working Online with SharePoint and SkyDrive

Office 2013 is integrated to work with online services (**New!**) to make it easier for you to save and open Office documents on other devices and share Office documents with others. Office provides two main online services: SkyDrive and SharePoint. **SkyDrive** is a personal cloud storage and sharing system on the web provided as a free service by Microsoft at *www.skydrive.com* with a Microsoft account. You can store and share information, such as contacts, e-mail (using hotmail), photos, and files. Microsoft **SharePoint** server is an organizational cloud storage, sharing, and tracking system with customizable apps hosted on the web by an organization. Instead of setting up your own SharePoint site, you can use **Office 365**, a subscription-based Microsoft web site with SharePoint services that allows you to take advantage of expanded cloud capabilities.

Connecting to a SkyDrive or SharePoint Site

You can access and connect to a SkyDrive and SharePoint site by using your web browser or any Office 2013 program. For SkyDrive, you can also use a stand-alone app, such as SkyDrive (Win 8) or SkyDrive for Windows (Win 7 or 8)—an app downloaded from the SkyDrive site that allows you to access files from Windows Explorer.

In order to connect to SkyDrive or SharePoint from Office, you need to sign in and connect with your account. When you set up Office 2013, it requests a Microsoft account to work with SkyDrive and other online services. However, you can add other accounts for Office 365 SharePoint and other online services, such as Facebook, Twitter, Linkedin, and Flickr. To access account settings in Office, click the user name (upper-

right corner of any Office program), and then click an account option, or click the File tab, and then click Accounts. You can add, switch, or modify accounts or sign out entirely.

SkyDrive or SkyDrive Pro?

When you install Office 2013, you also get a helpful tool called SkyDrive Pro (**New!**). The name is similar to SkyDrive, however it works with SharePoint, not SkyDrive personal. A SharePoint site includes its own SkyDrive as well as other Document Libraries. With SkyDrive Pro, you can connect to and synchronize the contents of a SkyDrive or Document Library on a SharePoint or Office 365 site with a folder on your desktop. SkyDrive Pro performs the same function for SharePoint sites as the stand-alone SkyDrive apps—SkyDrive (Win 8) or SkyDrive for Windows (Win 7 or 8)—do for a personal SkyDrive.

Using a SkyDrive or SharePoint Site from Office

In Office 2013, you can save and open documents directly to a SkyDrive or SharePoint site. With your Office documents on a SkyDrive or SharePoint site, you can do a lot of things. You can sync the files from the SkyDrive or SharePoint site to your desktop or other devices, such as a tablet or mobile phone for easy access from anywhere. You can view or edit Office documents online from an Office program or Office Web App, and get access to files even when you're offline. You can share a document with other people using e-mail or social networks (**New!**) and even work on the same Office document at the same time with more than one person (**New!**).

Using Office 365

Office 365 is a subscription-based Microsoft web site with SharePoint services that provides cloud-based storage and sync capabilities to keep your Office content up-to-date everywhere. Office 365 provides web-based collaboration and sharing that allows you to work with Outlook mail, calendar, people, newsfeed, SkyDrive, and SharePoint Team sites and public web sites. Newsfeed lets you follow documents, sites and people to track what they are doing. You can also collaborate with instant messaging, video/audio conferencing and online meetings with Lync. In Outlook, you can access Site Mailboxes (**New!**) with e-mail and documents in the same place. You can access Office 365 at *www.office365.com*, where you can sign up for a subscription or trial.

Using Office Web Apps

An Office Web App allows you to work with an Office document in a web browser. When you store an Office document on a SkyDrive or SharePoint site, you can view or edit the document in a web browser using the same look and feel as an Office 2013 program, although some what limited in functionality. Office Web Apps provide a web-based version of Word, Excel, PowerPoint, and OneNote (**New!**). For a SharePoint site, Access and Lync are also available. You can view Office documents in a web browser using a Web App or edit the document in the desktop Office program.

Using Office on Mobile Devices

If you have a Windows Phone, Apple iOS (iPhone and iPad), BlackBerry, or Android, you can use your web browser or Office Web Apps to work with your Office documents from any-where. You can view and edit Office documents stored on your phone, sent to you as e-mail attachments, or stored on a SkyDrive or SharePoint site. Since the files are synced online, the changes you make on your mobile device are available on your desktop too.

Using Office Co-authoring

If you're working on a SharePoint site, you can have multiple authors work on the same Office document from a Document Library at the same time without intruding on one another's work or locking out other users. When multiple authors are working on the same document, you can see who is editing the document and where they are working in the Status bar or on the File tab Info screen. Any changes made by other authors get merged into the main document where you can review and modify them. You can co-author Office documents using Word, Excel, PowerPoint, and Visio Professional (**New!**) as well as Word Web App (**New!**) and PowerPoint App (**New!**), which include support for comments and revision marks (**New!**).

Excel Web App in a web browser

Signing in to SharePoint or SkyDrive

Office provides access to two main online services: SkyDrive and SharePoint. SkyDrive personal is a free storage and sharing service provided by Microsoft. SharePoint is a web-hosted server for storage, sharing, and tracking documents. Instead of setting up your own SharePoint site, you can use Office 365 SharePoint, a subscription-based service provided by Microsoft. Before you can work with Office documents on SkyDrive or SharePoint, you need to create a Microsoft account for SkyDrive or a site account for SharePoint. When you set up Office 2013, it requests a Microsoft account to work with online services, such as SkyDrive. If you already have a Hotmail, Messenger, Windows Live, or Xbox Live account, you can use it as your Microsoft account. To get a SharePoint account, you need to contact your site administrator or sign up for Office 365. After you establish accounts, you need to add them to Office in order to work seamlessly with the online services (**New!**).

Sign in to Office 365 SharePoint

1. Open your web browser, and go to *www.office365.com*.

2. If you don't have an account, click the link to get a free trial. Follow the online instructions to create the account.

3. Click the **Sign in** link.

4. Enter your User ID and Password for your Office 365 account.

5. Select the **Remember me** and/or **Keep me signed in** check boxes to speed up sign in process in the future. However, it allows others who have access to your computer to sign in.

6. Click **Sign in**.

   Your Office 365 SharePoint site appears in your web browser.

7. To sign out, click the Account Name on the toolbar, and then click **Sign out**.

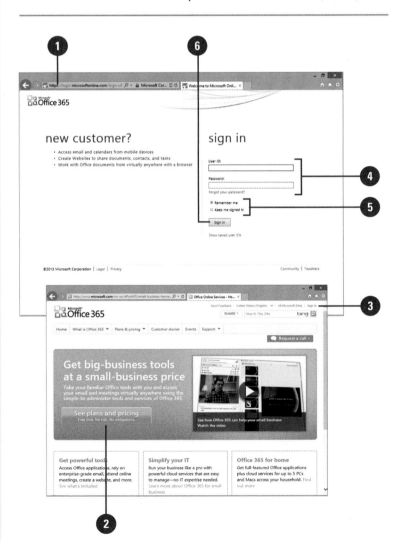

Sign in to SkyDrive

1. Open your web browser, and go to *www.skydrive.com*.

2. If you don't have a Microsoft account, click the link to get a free account. Follow the online instructions to create the account.

3. Enter you Microsoft account user name and password.

4. Select the **Keep me signed in** check box to speed up sign in process in the future. However, it allows others who have access to your computer to sign in.

5. Click **Sign in**.

   Your SkyDrive site appears in your web browser.

6. To sign out, click the Account Name on the toolbar, and then click **Sign out**.

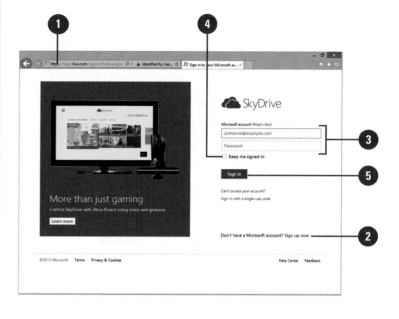

Add Online Storage Services

1. Click the **File** tab, and then click **Account (New!)**.

2. Click **Add a service (New!)**, and then point to **Storage**.

3. Click **Office 365 SharePoint** or **SkyDrive**, and then follow the on-screen connection instructions to sign in and add the service.

4. Click the **Back** button to exit the File tab.

Saving and Opening on SharePoint or SkyDrive

Office is integrated to work with online services (**New!**) to make it easier for you to save and open Office documents on other devices and share Office documents with others. With your Microsoft or SharePoint account, you can save Office documents directly to a SkyDrive (**New!**), a cloud-based online storage system, or Office 365, a Microsoft web site with SharePoint services. When you save documents online, you can have multiple authors work on the same Office document from the server at the same time (**New!**). Before you can use these online services, you need to add (connect) them to Office 2013. During the process, you'll need to provide a user name and password to establish a connection.

Save an Office Document to SharePoint or SkyDrive

1. Create or open an Office document.

2. Click the **File** tab, and then click **Save As**.

3. Click the SkyDrive or SharePoint name.

   ◆ **Sign in.** If prompted, sign-in to your account.

4. Click **Browse** or a recent folder.

5. Navigate to the location where you want to save the file.

6. Type a document file name.

7. Click the **Save as type** list arrow, and then click **<Program> <Document>**, such as Word Document, or Excel Workbook.

8. To change browser view options in Excel, click **Browser View Options**, select the elements to show in a browser and add parameters to named single cells for editing in a browser, and then click **OK**.

9. Click **Save**.

Open an Office Document from SharePoint or SkyDrive

1. Click the **File** tab, and then click **Open**.

2. Click the SkyDrive or SharePoint name.

3. Click **Browse** or a recent folder.

4. Navigate to the location where you want to open the file, and then select the Office file.

5. Click **Open**.

Did You Know?

You can add a place for easy access later. In the Open or Save As screen, click Add a Place, click Office 365 SharePoint or SkyDrive, and then follow the on-screen connection instructions.

Set Browser View Options

1. In Excel, click the **File** tab, and then click **Info**.

2. Click the list arrow, and then select **Entire Workbook**, **Sheets**, or **Items in the Workbook**.

3. Select the check boxes for the elements to show in a browser.

4. Click the **Parameters** tab.

   A parameter is a named single cell for editing in a browser.

5. To add parameters, click **Add**, select the check boxes you want, and then click **OK**.

6. To delete parameters, click **Delete All**, or select a parameter, click **Delete**, and then click **OK**.

7. Click **OK**.

Office 365 SharePoint

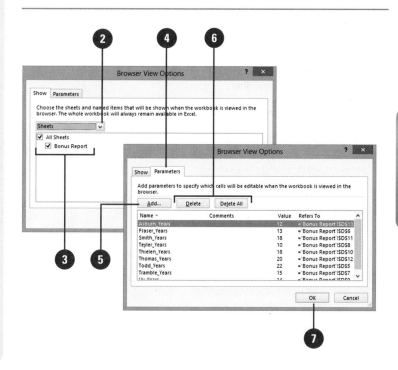

Accessing Documents on SharePoint

Any Office document that resides on SharePoint (**New!**) can be accessed from any computer or device that has an Internet connection. You can access Office documents on SharePoint using your web browser or File Explorer on your desktop. In your web browser, you can navigate to a document and then open it in an Office Web App. An Office Web App provides a subset of the features in the desktop version. In your desktop, you can open File Explorer, navigate to a document in a SharePoint Document Library or SkyDrive Pro (**New!**), and then open it in the Office Desktop App. SkyDrive Pro is SkyDrive on SharePoint, which is separate and different from SkyDrive personal.

Access SharePoint in a Web Browser

1. Open your web browser, go to SharePoint Team Site web address or *www.office365.com*, and then sign in.

2. Navigate to the SharePoint or SkyDrive folders:

   ◆ **SharePoint.** Click **Sites**, click **Team Site**, and then click a library.

   ◆ **SkyDrive.** Click **SkyDrive**.

3. Click a folder icon to navigate to the folder with the Office document.

4. To navigate back to a previous location, click a navigation or Home link, or click the Back button.

5. To manage files, select the files or folders you want to work with, click the **Files** tab, and then use the toolbar buttons, such as Create Folder, Delete, Upload Document, Download Copy, or Share.

6. To open an Office document in the Office Web App, click the document name link.

   ◆ To edit the document, click the **Edit <document>** menu, and then click **Edit in <program>** or **Edit in <program> Web App**.

   ◆ To exit and return, click the **File** tab, and then click **Exit**.

Files tab

Access SharePoint from a Desktop

1. In the Start screen, click the Desktop tile (Win 8).

2. Click the **File Explorer** icon on the taskbar.

3. In the Navigate pane under Favorites, click either of the following:

   ◆ **SharePoint.** Opens the Document Library folders on the SharePoint Team Site.

   ◆ **SkyDrive Pro.** Opens the Documents folder on the SharePoint SkyDrive.

4. Click a folder icon to navigate to the folder with the Office document.

5. To add or remove files, use the following:

   ◆ Add. Copy and paste or drag files to the folder.

   ◆ Remove. Select the files, and then click the **Delete** button on the Home tab.

   The folders are synchronized for both locations, desktop and site.

6. To open an Office document in the Office Desktop App, double-click the document icon.

   ◆ To exit, click the **Close** button.

File Explorer in Windows 8

Office 365 SharePoint Document Library

Syncing Documents on SharePoint

With SkyDrive Pro (**New!**), you can connect to and sync the contents of a SkyDrive or Document Library on a SharePoint (Team Site) or Office 365 site with a folder on your desktop. You can set up the sync by entering a site address to the SkyDrive or Document Library or using the SYNC button on the SharePoint or Office 365 site for the open SkyDrive or Document Library. After creating a connection, you'll notice a SkyDrive Pro cloud icon on the notification tray in the taskbar, which you can use to access the desktop folder or modify syncing options. SkyDrive Pro syncs to your user folder by default, though you can change the location. In the Open and Save As dialog boxes in Office programs or in an Explorer window in Windows, you can select the site —SharePoint or SkyDrive Pro—from the Favorites list to access your files.

Set Up or Change SkyDrive Pro for a SharePoint Site

1. Start **SkyDrive Pro 2013**.

   ◆ Windows 8. Click the tile on the Start screen.

   ◆ Windows 7. Click **Start** on the taskbar, point to **All Programs**, and then point to **Microsoft Office**.

   ◆ Office 365 Site. Click **SkyDrive** or **Sites**, display the library to sync, and then click **SYNC** on the toolbar.

   The site is connected to your system or a dialog box opens.

2. Enter the URL address to the SkyDrive or Document library on the SharePoint or Office 365 site.

3. To change the desktop folder, click the **Change** link.

4. Click **Sync Now**.

   After you setup SkyDrive Pro, starting the program opens the folder on your desktop.

Office 365 SharePoint SkyDrive

Click to select a SkyDrive or SharePoint site (Libraries)

Work with SkyDrive Pro on SharePoint

1. In the desktop, click the **SkyDrive Pro** icon on the desktop taskbar, and then click **Open your SkyDrive Pro folder**.

2. Click **SkyDrive Pro** or **SharePoint** in the Navigate pane under Favorites, and then navigate to the folder you want to use.

3. To add or remove files, use the following:

   ◆ **Add.** Copy and paste or drag files to the folder.

   ◆ **Remove.** Select the files, and then click the **Delete** button on the Home tab.

   The folders are synchronized for both locations, desktop and site.

4. To change syncing options, click the **SkyDrive Pro** icon on the desktop taskbar, and then click any of the following:

   ◆ **Sync a new library.** Use to add a new SharePoint site library.

   ◆ **Sync now.** Use to manually sync files.

   ◆ **Pause syncing.** Use to pause syncing.

   ◆ **View sync programs.** Use to open Office Upload Center.

   ◆ **Stop syncing a folder.** Use to select a folder to stop syncing.

5. To exit SkyDrive Pro, click the **SkyDrive Pro** icon on the desktop taskbar, and then click **Exit**.

See Also

See "Working with Office Tools" on page 456 for information on using Office 2013 Upload Center.

File Explorer in Windows 8

Office 365 SharePoint SkyDrive

Sharing Documents on SkyDrive

After you save an Office document to a SkyDrive (**New!**), you can share it with others. On the Share screen under the File tab, you can use three related options—Invite People (**New!**), Get a Sharing Link (**New!**), and Post to Social Networks (**New!**)—to allow others to access to a SkyDrive document. The Invite People option allows you to send an invitation for other to access the SkyDrive document. The Get a Sharing Link option lets you create links to the document you can share with others. And finally, the Post to Social Networks option lets you make blog posts on your connected social networks, such as Facebook, Linkedin, Twitter, Flickr, or Google.

Invite People to Share a SkyDrive Document

1. Open the Office document you want to share.

2. Click the **File** tab, click **Share**, and then click **Invite People**.

3. If the document is not saved to a SkyDrive, click the **Save To Cloud** button, and then save it to your SkyDrive. If prompted, sign-in to your account.

4. Enter a contact name or click the Address Book button to select a contact.

5. Click the **Access** list arrow, and then click **Can edit** or **Can view**.

6. Enter a message for the invitation.

7. Select or clear the **Require user to sign in before accessing document** check box.

8. Click **Share**.

   An email is sent to the contact with a link to access the SkyDrive document, and contact status appears at the bottom of the Share screen.

   You can click the contacts to send mail or instant messages.

Get a Sharing Link to a SkyDrive Document

① Open the Office document you want to share.

② Click the **File** tab, click **Share**, and then click **Get a Sharing Link**.

③ Click the **Create Link** button for View Link or Edit Link.

A link to the SkyDrive document appears and a status icon appears at the bottom of the Share screen.

④ Select and copy (Ctrl+C) the link, where you can paste it in a place, such as a network, where others can access it.

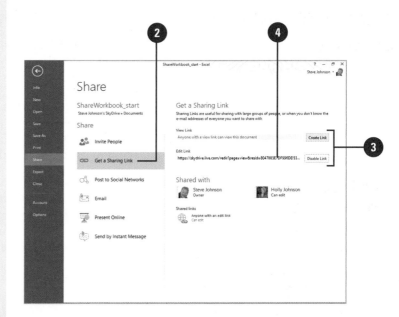

Post a SkyDrive Document Link to a Social Network

① Open the Office document you want to share.

② Click the **File** tab, click **Share**, and then click **Post to Social Networks**.

If you're not connected to your social networks, click the **Click here to connect social networks** link to make the connections you want, and then click **Refresh** button.

③ Select the check boxes for the connected social networks you want to post.

④ Click the **Access** list arrow, and then click **Can edit** or **Can view**.

⑤ Enter a message for the post.

⑥ Click the **Post** button.

Accessing Documents on SkyDrive

Any Office document that resides on SkyDrive (**New!**) can be accessed from any computer or device that has an Internet connection. You can access Office documents on SkyDrive using your web browser or a SkyDrive app on your desktop or device, including smartphones and tablets. In your web browser, you can navigate to a document and then open it in an Office Web App. An Office Web App provides a subset of the features in the desktop version. In your desktop or device, you can open the SkyDrive app, navigate to a document, and then open it in the Office Desktop App or Office Web App. If you don't have the app on your desktop or device, you can download it at *http://apps.live.com/skydrive*.

Access a SkyDrive in a Web Browser

1 Open your web browser, go to *www.skydrive.com*, and then sign in.

◆ You can also go to Windows Live, *www.live.com*, and then click the **SkyDrive** link.

2 Click a folder icon to navigate to the folder with the Office document.

3 To navigate back to a previous location, click a navigation link.

4 To change the view in the current folder, click a view button: **List** or **Tiles**.

5 To sort the documents in the current folder, click the **Sort by:** link, and then click **Name**, **Date modified**, **Date created**, or **Size**.

6 To open an Office document in the Office Web App, click the document icon.

◆ To open an Office document in the Office Desktop App, right-click the document, and then click **Open in <program>**.

◆ To exit and return, click the **File** tab, and then click **Exit**.

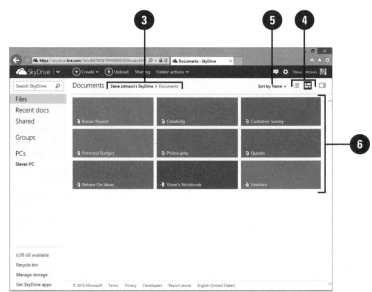

Access a SkyDrive from a Desktop or Device

1 In the Start screen, click the **SkyDrive** tile.

◆ **Download.** You can download the SkyDrive app for devices at *http://apps.live.com/skydrive*.

2 Click a folder icon to navigate to the folder with the Office document.

3 To navigate back to a previous location, click the **Back** button.

4 To change the view in the current folder, click the **Thumbnails** or **Details** button on the App bar.

5 To open an Office document in the Office Desktop App (desktop) or Web App (device), click the document icon.

◆ To exit, click the **Close** button (Desktop App or click the **File** tab, and then click **Exit** (Web App).

Did You Know?

You can manage storage space on a SkyDrive. SkyDrive comes with 7 GB of free space that you can use with your Microsoft account. You can view your storage usage and purchase more space if you want under options. In the SkyDrive app (Win 8), click Settings on the Charm bar, and then click Options. In your web browser, click the Settings button, and then click Options.

SkyDrive app on Windows 8

App bar

Managing Documents on SkyDrive

SkyDrive comes with four default folders: Documents, Favorites, Shared Favorites, and Public. The Documents and Favorites folders are private for your eyes only, while the Shared Favorites and Public folders are viewable by everyone in your SkyDrive (Windows Live) network. If you want to share your documents with others, then you need to add, move, or copy them to the Public folder. Instead of using the default folders, you can create and use your own. If you no longer need a file or folder, you can delete it. You cannot rename a default folder, however, you can rename the ones you create.

Work with SkyDrive Files or Folders in a Web browser

1. Open your web browser, go to *www.skydrive.com*, and then sign in.

2. Navigate to the folder where you want to manage files or folders.

3. To create a folder, click the **Create** list arrow, click **Folder**, type a name for the folder, and then press Enter or click outside the box.

4. Point to a file or folder to display a check box, and then click the check box to select it.

   ◆ You can select multiple files or folders to delete, move, or copy them.

5. To manage the selected file(s) or folder(s), click the **Manage** list arrow, and then click any of the following commands:

   ◆ **Rename.** Type a new name for the folder, and then press Enter or click outside the box.

   ◆ **Delete.** Click **Undo** to cancel it or click the **Close** button.

   ◆ **Move to.** Select the destination folder, and then click **Move**.

   ◆ **Copy to.** Select the destination folder, and then click **Copy**.

New folder

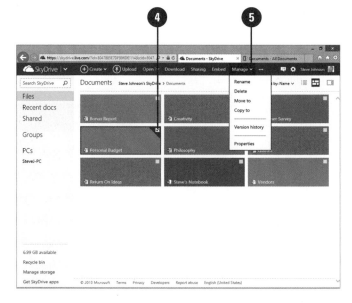

Work with SkyDrive Files or Folders from a Desktop

1. In the Start screen, click the **SkyDrive** tile.

   ◆ **Download.** You can download the SkyDrive app for devices at *http://apps.live.com/skydrive*.

2. Navigate to the folder where you want to manage files or folders.

3. To create a folder, click the **New Folder** on the App bar, type a name for the folder, and then click **Create folder**.

4. Right-click a file or folder to select it.

   ◆ You can select multiple files or folders to delete or move them.

5. To manage the selected file(s) or folder(s), click the **Manage** button on the App bar, and then click any of the following commands:

   ◆ **Rename.** Type a new name for the folder, and then click **Rename**.

   ◆ **Delete.** Click **Delete** to confirm the deletion.

   ◆ **Move.** Select the destination folder, and then click **Move here** on the Apps bar.

SkyDrive app on Windows 8

App bar

Downloading or Uploading Documents on SkyDrive

When you no longer want a document or folder of documents on SkyDrive or you want to share them with others, you can download them to your local drive on your computer. You can download individual files one at a time in their native Office file format, such as .xlsx, or a multiple selection of documents or an entire folder of documents as a zipped file. The .zip file format compresses all the files in the folder into a single file. You can open a zipped file on Microsoft Windows by double-clicking it and then using an Extract button or by using the Winzip.exe software, which you can download for free from the web at one of many download sites, such as *www.download.com*. If you have one or more documents or entire folder of documents on a local drive, and want to include on your SkyDrive, you can upload them to the cloud site, so you can access them from other computers and devices.

Download or Upload a File or Folder on SkyDrive

1. Open your web browser, go to *www.skydrive.com*, and then sign in.

2. Navigate to the folder where you want to download or upload files or folders.

3. To Upload files or folders to the SkyDrive, click the **Upload** button, select the files or folders you want, and then click **Open**.

4. Point to a file or folder to display a check box, and then click the check box to select it. You can select multiple files or folders.

5. To download the selected file(s) or folder(s), click the **Download** button.

6. Click **Save**, navigate to the location where you want to download the file, and then click **Save**.

   The document is downloaded to the specified folder.

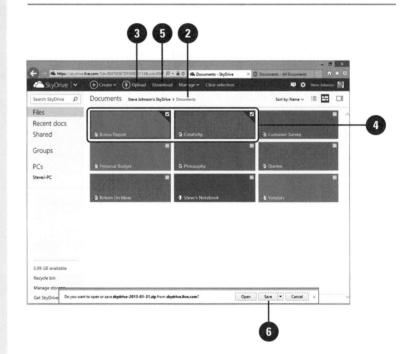

Creating Office Documents on SkyDrive

When you're working on SkyDrive, you create a new Office document. You can create an Excel workbook, a PowerPoint presentation, a Word document, or an OneNote notebook. This option allows you to create a new Office document on a computer that doesn't have the Microsoft Office software. So, if you're working on a different computer while you're on the road that doesn't have the Office programs installed and you need to create a new document to get some work done, you can do it online on SkyDrive.

Create Office Documents on SkyDrive

1. Open your web browser, go to *www.skydrive.com*, and then sign in.

2. Navigate to the folder where you want to create a new Office document.

3. Click the **Create** list arrow, and then click a document option:

   ◆ **Word document.**

   ◆ **Excel workbook.**

   ◆ **PowerPoint presentation.**

   ◆ **OneNote notebook.**

4. Type a name for the document.

5. Click **Create**.

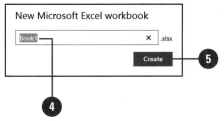

Sending Links to Documents on SkyDrive

After you upload your Office documents to a folder on SkyDrive, you can share access to them with others for review with Office Web Apps. You can share access to individual Office documents or an entire folder on SkyDrive by sending a link in e-mail, posting a link in Twitter, Facebook, LinkedIn or other online services (**New!**), or creating a link (**New!**) and sending it to those you want to access it. In addition, you can also embed a link in a blog or web page, so others can access the folder. The recipients of the link can click it to access the documents on SkyDrive.

Send a Link to a File or Folder

1 Open your web browser, go to *www.skydrive.com*, and then sign in.

2 Navigate to the folder with the documents you want to share.

3 Point to a file or folder to display a check box, and then click the check box to select it. You can select multiple files or folders.

4 Click the **Sharing** button.

5 For a folder, click **Share this folder**. To cancel, click **Don't share this folder**.

6 Click **Send email**, **Post to <service>** (**New!**), or **Get a link** (**New!**) to select a send method.

7 Specify the following for the selected method:

◆ **Send email.** Specify recipients, select or clear options to edit or require sign in, and then click **Share**.

◆ **Post to <service>.** Select the check boxes for the services you want, enter a message, select or clear the option to edit, and then click **Post**.

◆ **Get a Link.** Click **Create** for View only or View and edit, or click **Make public** for everyone to access. Press Ctrl+C to copy the link, and then click **Done**. You can paste the link for others to use.

Post to   Twitter   Add more services

Get a link

Embed a Link to a File or Folder in a Blog or Web Page

1. Open your web browser, go to *www.skydrive.com*, and then sign in.

2. Navigate to the folder with the documents you want to share.

3. Point to a file or folder to display a check box, and then click the check box to select it. You can select multiple files or folders.

4. Click the **Embed** button (**New!**).

5. Click **Generate**.

6. Click the **Copy** link to copy the embed code to the Clipboard.

7. To customize an Excel workbook, click the **Customize how this embedded workbook will appear to others** link (**New!**).

   A new worksheet opens in a new browser tab, where you can specify the options you want. Click the **Copy** link to copy the embed code to the Clipboard, and then close the web browser tab.

8. Click **Done**.

9. Paste the code into a blog post or web page.

   ◆ **Blog.** Create a blog post in a blogger, such as Windows Live Writer, and then paste the code.

   ◆ **Web Page.** Open a web page in an HTML editor, and then paste the code.

10. Open your web browser, display the blog post or web page, and then click the link to the shared folder or document on SkyDrive.

Creates a custom browser view for an Excel workbook

Comparing the Office Desktop App to the Web App

An Office Web App provides a subset of the features in the desktop version. Each Office Web App comes with a scaled-down version of the desktop Ribbon and Quick Access Toolbar. The Web Apps Ribbon typically comes with a File tab, Home tab, Insert tab, and View tab. Within each tab, you get a sub-set of commands on the desktop Ribbon. There are no contextual tabs in the Office Web Apps. The Quick Access Toolbar appears above the Ribbon and contains just the Undo and Redo buttons. The content area for each of the Office Web Apps is similar to the desktop version.

Desktop App

File tab
Click to access Office file commands.

Quick Access Toolbar
Click to access commands on this customizable toolbar.

Tabs
Click to access tools and commands.

Dialog Box Launcher
Click to open dialog boxes or task panes.

Program window
Enter text and data here.

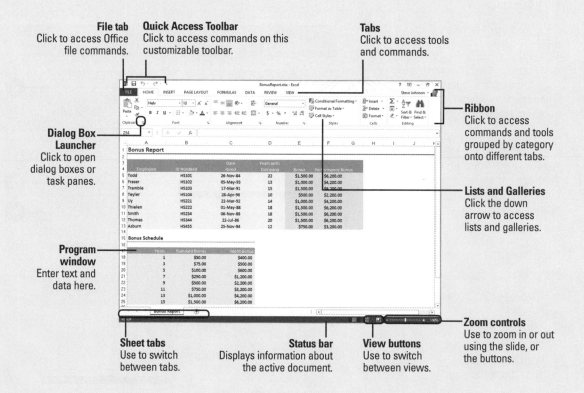

Ribbon
Click to access commands and tools grouped by category onto different tabs.

Lists and Galleries
Click the down arrow to access lists and galleries.

Sheet tabs
Use to switch between tabs.

Status bar
Displays information about the active document.

View buttons
Use to switch between views.

Zoom controls
Use to zoom in or out using the slide, or the buttons.

Web App (Edit in Browser)

Quick Access Toolbar
Click to access commands
on a toolbar.

Tabs
Click to access tools
and commands.

File tab
Click to access
file commands.

Ribbon
Click to access
commands and tools
grouped by category
onto different tabs.

Program window
Enter text and data
here.

Sheet tabs
Use to switch
between tabs.

Web App (View in Browser)

File tab
Click to access
file commands.

Menus
Click to access menus
and commands.

Program window
Enter text and data
here.

Sheet tabs
Use to switch
between tabs.

Working with Office Web Apps

An Office Web App allows you to work with an Office document stored on a SkyDrive (**New!**) or SharePoint site in a web browser and on different mobile devices—such as Windows Phones, Apple iOS (iPhones, and iPads), BlackBerry, and Android. Office Web Apps provide a web-based version of Word, Excel, PowerPoint, and OneNote (**New!**). For a SharePoint site, Access and Lync are also available. You can view or edit Office documents in a web browser using a Web App or in the Desktop App. An Office Web App provides a subset of the features in the desktop version. However, in some Web Apps, such as Excel, it adds options, such as the ability to create an online survey (**New!**).

View an Office Document Using Office Web Apps

1 Open your web browser, and then go to *www.skydrive.com* or SharePoint Team Site web address.

◆ **From E-mail or Posts.** If you received an e-mail or a post with a sharing link, click the link to access the document.

2 Navigate to the folder with the document you want to open.

3 Click the Office document you want to view.

The Web App opens, displaying the document.

4 Use the menus and tools to navigate and view the document.

◆ **File management.** You can use the File tab to edit, save as, print, or share the document.

◆ **Parameters.** If you added parameters (**New!**) when you saved the workbook in Excel, you can enter data in the Parameters pane, and then click **Apply**.

◆ **Edit document.** Click the **Edit <document>** menu, and then click **Edit in <program>** or **Edit in <program> Web App**.

5 To exit, click the **File** tab, and then click **Exit** (Web App) or click the **Close** button (desktop program).

SkyDrive

Collapse/Expand pane

Enter data

Edit an Office Document Using Office Web Apps

1. Open your web browser, and then go to *www.skydrive.com* or SharePoint Team Site web address.

   ◆ **From E-mail or Posts.** If you received an e-mail or a post with a sharing link, click the link to access the document.

2. Navigate to the folder with the document you want to open.

3. Click the Office document you want to edit.

   The Web App opens, displaying the document.

4. Click the **Edit <document>** menu, and then click **Edit in <program> Web App**.

   ◆ **Edit in Desktop App.** Click the **Edit <document>** menu, and then click **Edit in <program>**.

5. Use the Ribbon tabs to make changes to the Office document; any changes in a Web App are automatically saved.

   ◆ To create an online survey in Excel, click the **Survey** button on the Home tab, click **New Survey**, enter a title and description, add questions, and then click **Save and View** or **Share Survey**.

6. To close the document and switch to work local in the Desktop App, click the **Open in <program>** button.

7. To exit, click the **File** tab, and then click **Exit** (Web App) or click the **Close** button (desktop program).

1 SkyDrive

2

3

7 **5** **6**

Creates an online survey in Excel

Saving or Printing Documents in Office Web Apps

As you work in an Office document in a web browser, an Office Web App automatically saves your work, so you don't have to do it. However, you might want to download a version to your local computer or network location as a backup or save a copy (in the Excel Web App) of a document in the original location with a different name. Besides saving an Office document, you can also print it to a printer (in the Excel Web App) or create a printable PDF (in the Word Web App and PowerPoint Web App).

Save or Download an Office Document in an Office Web App

1. Open your web browser, and then go to *www.skydrive.com* or SharePoint Team Site web address.

2. Navigate to the folder with the document you want to open.

3. Click the Office document you want to edit.

   The Web App opens, displaying the document.

4. Click the **Edit <document>** menu, and then click **Edit in <program> Web App.**

5. Click the **File** tab, click **Save As**, and then click an option (options vary depending on the Office Web App):

   ◆ **Download.** Downloads the entire document to your computer.

   ◆ **Save a Copy.** In Excel, saves a copy of the workbook in the same online folder as the original.

6. Click **Save**.

7. Navigate to the location where you want to download the file, and then click **Save**.

Save as options

Print or PDF an Office Document in an Office Web App

1 Open your web browser, and then go to *www.skydrive.com* or SharePoint Team Site web address.

2 Navigate to the folder with the document you want to open.

3 Click the Office document you want to edit.

The Web App opens, displaying the document.

4 Click the **Edit <document>** menu, and then click **Edit in <program> Web App**.

5 Click the **File** tab, click **Print**, and then click an option (options vary depending on the Office Web App):

◆ **Print.** In Excel, select an option to print the current selection or entire sheet, click **Print**, and then click **Print** again in the web browser window.

◆ **Print to PDF.** In Word and PowerPoint, creates saves a copy of the workbook in the same online folder as the original. Click a link to view the PDF or click **Close**.

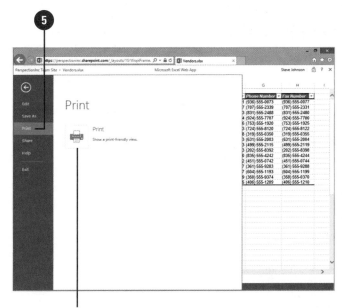

Print to a printer in Excel

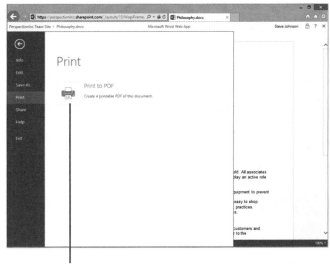

Print to PDF in Word

Co-authoring Documents with Office Web Apps

If you're working with an Office document stored on a SharePoint site, multiple authors can collaborate on the same document at the same time (**New!**), known as co-authoring. Co-authoring allows you to see who is editing the document and where they are working in the Status bar or on the File tab Info screen. With Office Web Apps you can simultaneously edit documents, known as co-authoring. Co-authoring allows two or more people to work on a document at the same time in real-time without the need to save and reject or accept changes. If two people edit the same thing, each Office Web App deals with differently. Before you can co-author a document, you need to send a link in e-mail, online service post, such as Twitter, Facebook, or LinkedIn, to those you want to share the Office document or embed a link in a blog or web page, so others can access it.

Co-author an Office Document on SharePoint

1. Have each author open the Office document from the library on the SharePoint site.

   ◆ **From Office.** Click the **File** tab, click **Open**, click the SharePoint site, click **Browse**, and then open the document.

   ◆ **From Web browser.** Start your web browser, go to the SharePoint site address, and then open the document.

   ◆ **From E-mail or Posts.** If you received an e-mail or a post with a sharing link, click the link to access the document.

2. If prompted, sign in to the SharePoint site.

   The Web App opens, displaying the document.

3. For a Web App, click the **Edit <document>** menu, and then click **Edit in <program>** or **Edit in <program> Web App.**

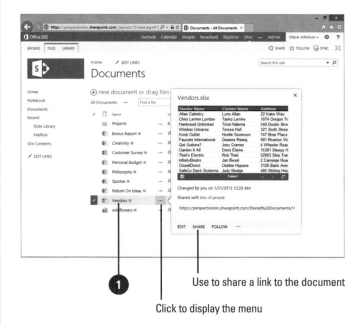

Click to display the menu

Use to share a link to the document

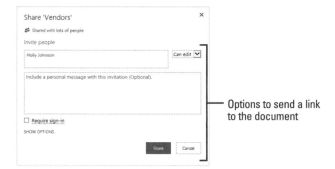

Options to send a link to the document

4 To view who is editing the documents, click the **Authors** button on the Status bar or click the **File** tab, and then click **Info**.

◆ On the Share screen, you can use the **Share with People** button to send a message.

5 Each author can edit the document using the program tools.

◆ **Comments and Track Changes.** In Word, PowerPoint, and Excel (desktop), each author can insert and show comments and enable track changes during editing so all the authors can see the changes being made.

6 To exit, click the **File** tab, and then click **Exit** (Web App) or click the **Close** button (desktop program).

See Also

See "Working with Office Web Apps" on page 508 for more information on using Office Web Apps.

For Your Information

Roundtripping with Office Web Apps

When you edit or view an Office document with an Office Web App, the file format doesn't change or affect the content of the file. In other words, you can upload an Office file to the web, make changes using an Office Web App, download the file back to your desktop, and then make changes to it using your desktop Office App without any problems. This is called **roundtripping**. Any unsupported features in the Office Web App doesn't affect the Office file during a roundtrip.

New! Features

Microsoft Excel 2013

Microsoft Excel 2013 is a spreadsheet program that you can use to track and analyze sales, create budgets, and organize finances—both business and personal. With enhancements to the user interface, including the Start and New screens, online pictures, and SkyDrive and SharePoint direct access, and the addition of advanced data tools, including Flash Fill, recommended tables, Power View and PowerPivot, and apps for Office, you can accomplish a variety of business or personal tasks more efficiently in Excel 2013.

Only New Features

If you're already familiar with Excel 2010, you can access and download all the tasks in this book with Microsoft Excel 2013 New Features to help make your transition to the new version simple and smooth. The Excel 2013 New Features as well as other 2010 to 2013 transition helpers are available on the web at *www.perspection.com.*

What's New

If you're searching for what's new in Excel 2013, just look for the icon: **New!**. The new icon appears in the table of contents and throughout this book so you can quickly and easily identify a new or improved feature in Excel 2013. The following is a brief description of each new feature and its location in this book.

Office 2013

◆ **Start Screen (p. 2, 10-11, 135, 443)**   Office programs open to a Start Screen where you have options to open an existing document or create a new blank document or one from a template.

◆ **User Account (p. 3, 196)**   Office integrates a user account that lets you connect to online services, such as SkyDrive, Office 365 SharePoint, YouTube, Facebook, Linkedin, Twitter, and Flickr. Within any Office 2013 program, you can add, modify or switch accounts or sign out entirely.

◆ **Ribbon Display Options (p. 4)**   Office includes a Ribbon Display Options button that lets you change the way the Ribbon works. The options include Auto-hide Ribbon, Show Tabs, or Show Tabs and Commands.

◆ **Back Button (p. 5)**   The File tab includes a Back button that lets you return back to the main screen for the Office program.

◆ **New Screen (p. 10-11)**   The New command on the File tab opens to the New Screen where you have options to create a new blank document or one from a template.

◆ **Pin Recent Files or Folders (p. 11)**   If you frequently open a specific file or folder, you can pin the recently used file or folder to the Start, Open, or Save As screens. If you frequently use a template, you can pin the template to the Start or New screens.

◆ **Strict Open XML (p. 12)**   You can open documents in the Strict Open XML format to resolve leap year issues with 1900.

◆ **SkyDrive (p. 12, 22, 26, 196-198, 246, 486-491, 496-505)**   SkyDrive is a cloud-based online storage system that requires a Microsoft account to access. You can open and save files from a SkyDrive directly from Office, and share them with others. In addition, you can use three related options—Invite People, Get a Sharing Link, and Post to Social Networks—to allow others to access to a SkyDrive document.

◆ **Document Windows (p. 18-19, 34)**   Office documents open in their own program window instead of one program window and a collection of individual windows to make it easier to display several windows at once.

◆ **Windows Help (p. 20-21)**   The web browser-like Help Viewer allows you to browse a catalog of topics to locate information, use popular searches, or enter your own phrases to search for information.

◆ **Save Options (p. 22-23)**   Office adds new save options, which include Don't Show the Backstage when opening or saving files, Show additional places for saving, even if sign-in may be required, and Save to Computer by default.

◆ **Office 365 and SharePoint (p. 26, 196-198, 246, 317, 486-495)**   SharePoint server is an organizational cloud storage, sharing, and tracking system with customizable apps on the web. Office 365 is a subscription-based Microsoft web site with SharePoint services that allows you to take advantage of expanded cloud and sharing capabilities.

◆ **Online Services (p. 26-27, 196-198, 246)**   You can connect to and integrate online services into Office programs. The online services include SkyDrive and Office 365 SharePoint for storage, Flickr and YouTube for images and video, and Facebook, LinkedIn, and Twitter for sharing and messaging.

◆ **Touch/Mouse Mode (p. 73)**   To make Office easier to use with a touch screen, each Office program provides Touch/Mouse Mode, which adds or removes more space between commands on the Ribbon.

◆ **Personal Templates (p. 133-135)**   You can specify a default folder, such as My Templates, in Save Options for your own custom personal templates, which you can access from the Start and New screens.

◆ **Online Pictures (p. 160, 194-197, 246)**   If you need a picture to insert into a document and don't have one, you can search for and insert clip art from Office.com, a picture from the web using Bing Image Search, a picture from your SkyDrive, or a picture from an online service, such as Flickr.

◆ **Options Pane (p. 205-207, 209, 238-239, 244-245, 247-250, 253-255, 280-284)**
Office changes the Format Shape, Format Picture, Format Text, and Format
Background dialog boxes to panes that appear on the right side of the screen.

◆ **Enhanced Mini-Toolbar (p. 242)**   You can use a Mini-Toolbar to apply styles,
fills, and outlines. Right-click the object you want to modify, click the Style, Fill,
or Outline button, and then select an option.

◆ **Trusted Apps Catalog (p. 380, 384)**   An App Catalog site is a special site
collection on a web application. You can store apps for SharePoint and Office
apps for your organization's internal use in an App Catalog site.

◆ **Lync (p. 304-305)**   Microsoft Lync is an instant messaging program that allows
you to send and receive instant messages, hold video chats, meetings, and
share files.

◆ **Send Documents by Instant Message (p. 304)**   With Lync, you can send an
Office document to a participant in an instant message.

◆ **Office Presentation Service (p. 305)**   The Office Presentation Service (OPS)
allows you to deliver an Office document as a presentation over the Internet.
OPS is a free public service provided by Microsoft for use with your Microsoft
account ID.

◆ **Apps for Office (p. 366-367, 460-461)**   With Office.com, you can add
functionality with a third-party app to an Office program, and then use the app
to extend features in a document. You can also use Document Inspector to find
any app problems.

◆ **Office Background and Theme (p. 442)**   You can select an Office program
background and theme in Excel General Options.

◆ **Office Web Apps (p. 486-487, 492-493, 498-499, 504-513)**   An Office Web App
allows you to work with an Office document stored on a SkyDrive or SharePoint
site in a web browser or on different mobile devices. Office Web Apps provide a
web-based version of Word, Excel, PowerPoint, and OneNote.

Office Tools

◆ **Spreadsheet or Database Compare (p. 348-349, 456-457)**   If you need to
compare two Excel spreadsheets or Access databases, you can use the
Spreadsheet Compare or Database Compare tools.

◆ **Upload Center (p. 456-457)**   The Upload Center shows you pending uploads,
recently uploaded files and all cached files from a server in one location, which
includes working with SkyDrive and SharePoint sites.

◆ **Lync Recording Manager (p. 456-457)**   If not everyone is able to attend an
online Lync meeting, you can record the session to play it back later. You can
manage the recording with the Lync Recording Manager tool.

◆ **Telemetry Log or Dashboard (p. 456-457)**   Telemetry Log records Office events
in an Excel spreadsheet to help you troubleshoot problems. Telemetry Database
is an Excel spreadsheet that connects to an SQL database to collect client data
from other sources in a shared folder.

- **SkyDrive Pro (p. 456-457, 486-487, 492-495)** With SkyDrive Pro, you can connect and synchronize your SkyDrive cloud storage on a SharePoint site with your desktop.

- **Update Office (p. 458)** With Windows 8, you can automatically get updates to Office 2013 along with the operating system.

Excel 2013

- **Navigate with Touch (p. 16)** You can move around a worksheet using your finger on a tablet or touch screen.

- **Save Formats (p. 25)** Excel adds save options for the following file formats:?Strict Open XML Spreadsheet (.xlsx) and OpenDocument Spreadsheet (.ods).

- **Flash Fill (p. 46, 444)** Flash Fill allows you to automatically fill in data based on the content it recognizes in other cells.

- **Quick Analysis Tool (p. 98, 142-145, 150, 269, 303, 318-318, 442)** When you select a range of cells, you can use the Quick Analysis tool to calculate totals for the data, format data, and create charts and tables.

- **New Functions (p. 110, 351, 352, 356-364)** Here are some new functions available in Excel. In Logical, IFNA and XOR; in Text, NUMBERVALUE, UNICHAR, and UNICODE; in Date & Time, DAYS and ISOWEEKNUM; in Financial, PDURATION and RRI; in Information, ISFORMULA, SHEET, and SHEETS; in Lookup, FORMULATEXT; in Trig & Math, ACOT, ACOTH, ARABIC, BASE, and COMBINA; and in Web, ENCODEURL, FILTERXML, and WEBSERVICE.

- **Chart Buttons (p. 266, 270-271, 275, 278-279, 291, 330-331)** When you create or select a chart, buttons—Chart Styles, Chart Elements, and Chart Filters—appear on the workbook for easy access to format the chart, modify chart elements, and filter chart data.

- **Recommended Charts (p. 268-269, 318-319, 330)** You can choose a recommended chart based on the selected data in the worksheet.

- **Animation in Charts (p. 270-271)** When you change worksheet data, Excel automatically updates and animates the change in data in the chart.

- **Combo Charts (p. 276-277)** You can use the Combo chart type to create and modify a chart with multiple data series.

- **Chart Labels (p. 286-287)** You can have data labels appears as callouts or just about any shape, and even add leader lines to them.

- **Show or Hide Data Series (p. 276-277)** When you select a data source, you can show or hide individual data series instead of reselecting the range.

- **Recently Used Charts (p. 299)** In the Insert Chart dialog box, you can quickly select a recently used chart.

- **Quick Styles Button (p. 304)** With the Quick Styles button, you can apply a preset style to a table style. The Quick Styles include preset combinations of fill colors and patterns, font attributes, borders, and font colors that are professionally designed to enhance your worksheets.

◆ **AutoFilters (p. 306)**   If you want to customize a list to certain items, you can set AutoFilters, which you access using a Filter button (drop-down list arrow).

◆ **Slicer (p. 316)**   Instead of using the AutoFilter menu each time you want to filter data in a table, you can create a slicer button that enables you to quickly filter data in a table with a single click.

◆ **Excel Data Model (p. 318-321, 324, 366-367)**   You can add multiple tables in a PivotTable using the Excel Data Model. A Data Model is a collection of tables and their relationship between the data. When you have more than one table and a common column in a Data Model, you can create a relationship between them that lets you build PivotTables and other reports using fields from each table.

◆ **Drill Down to Data (p. 320, 322, 329)**   Use the Drill buttons to view different levels of details in complex data. When you select data in a field, the Quick Explore button appears, where you can drill down one item at a time.

◆ **Data Sources (p. 321, 414)**   You can connect to data feeds like OData, Windows Azure DataMarket, and SharePoint.

◆ **Timeline (p. 321)**   Instead of grouping by dates in a PivotTable or PivotChart, you can use the Insert Timeline button to filter data based on dates to create a timeline over different time periods.

◆ **Power View (p. 332-333)**   With the Power View add-in, you can create and visually interact with charts and Bing maps, slicers, and other visualizations with the data in a sheet, so you can present it to others.

◆ **PowerPivot (p. 334)**   With the PowerPivot add-in, you can build simple data models directly in Excel. PowerPivot is helpful when you want to import, filter out, and quickly process millions of rows of data from multiple data sources.

◆ **Inquire (p. 348-349)**   With the Inquire add-in, you can use tools to analyze and interactively report workbook problems or inconsistencies, view relationship diagrams—a graphical map of connection links—for workbooks, worksheets, or cells, and compare the content for multiple workbooks.

◆ **Excel as the Default (p. 443)**   In Excel General Options, you can set the option to tell me if Microsoft Excel isn't the default program for viewing and editing spreadsheets.

◆ **Excel Extension Associations (p. 443)**   In Excel General Options, you can select the extensions you want to open withe Excel.

◆ **Chart Options (p. 447)**   In Excel Chart Options, you can set custom formatting and chart data labels to follow data points as they move or change in the chart for all new workbooks or the current workbook.

◆ **File Tab Options (p. 450)**   In Excel Advanced Options, you can set File tab options to set the number of recent workbooks and set the number of unpinned recent folders to show on Start, New, Open, and Save As screens.

◆ **COM Add-ins (p. 465)**   Office Professional Plus includes several COM?add-ins, including Inquire, PowerPivot, and Power View.

◆ **Browser View Options (p. 490-491)** You can select the elements (entire workbook, sheets, or cells) you want to show in a browser and add parameters to named single cells for editing in a browser.

What Happened To . . .

◆ **Blank Workbook (p. 10)** In previous versions of Excel, when you saved workbook settings you used in the blank workbook template called Book.xltx that is stored in the XLStart folder (typically C:\Users*user name*\AppData\Local\ Microsoft\ Excel\XLStart), the template automatically opened when you created a blank template. In Excel 2013, the blank workbook is not automatically created with Book.xltx when you start. If you want to still use Book.xltx as a custom blank workbook, click the File tab, click Options, click General, deselect the Show the Start screen when this application starts check box, and then click OK.

◆ **Exit Command (p. 34)** The command has been removed from the File tab. Since each document opens in its own program window, it's not needed. To exit, you click the Close button on the program window.

◆ **Split box (p. 129)** The Split box control on the worksheet to split the window into panes has been removed. However, you can still split the window into panes using the Split button on the Ribbon. Click the View tab, then click Split.

◆ **Pyramid and Cone Chart Types (p. 289)** The chart types have been changed to column and bar chart shapes. Instead you can apply pyramid and cone shapes to any 3-D column or bar chart. Right-click a data series in any 3-D column or bar chart, click Format Data Series, and then click a shape.

◆ **Fax Templates (p. 403)** Fax templates are not included in the Office 2013 installation to reduce the size of the installation. However, you can still download them. Click the File tab, click New, and then type fax in the Search for online templates.

◆ **Save Workspace** The command has been removed. However, you can still open a workspace file (*.xlw) that was created in an earlier version of Excel.

◆ **Save as Template** The command has been removed from the Chart Tools tab on the Ribbon. To save a chart template, right-click the chart, and then click Save as Template.

◆ **Microsoft Office Picture Manager** Picture Manager has been replaced by Windows Photo Gallery.

◆ **Microsoft Clip Organizer** Clip Organizer has been replaced by Online Pictures, which allows you to insert content from the Office.com Clip Art collection and other resources, such as Bing Image/Video search, Flickr, and your SkyDrive or Facebook page.

Microsoft Office Specialist

About the MOS Program

The Microsoft Office Specialist (MOS) certification is the globally recognized standard for validating expertise with the Microsoft Office suite of business productivity programs. Earning an MOS certificate acknowledges you have the expertise to work with Microsoft Office programs. To earn the MOS certification, you must pass a certification exam for the Microsoft Office desktop applications of Microsoft Word, Excel, PowerPoint, Outlook, Access, OneNote, SharePoint, or Office 365. (The availability of Microsoft Office Specialist certification exams varies by program, program version, and language. Visit *www.microsoft.com* and search on *MOS* or *Microsoft Office Specialist* for exam availability and more information about the program.) The Microsoft Office Specialist program is the only Microsoft-approved program in the world for certifying proficiency with Microsoft Office programs.

What Does This Logo Mean?

It means this book has been approved by the Microsoft Office Specialist program to be certified courseware for learning Microsoft Excel 2013 and preparing for the certification exam. This book will prepare you for the Microsoft Office Specialist exam for Microsoft Excel 2013. Each certification level, either Core or Expert, has a set of objectives, which are organized into broader skill sets. Content that pertains to a Microsoft Office Specialist objective is identified with the following objective number and the specific pages throughout this book:

EX13C-1.1
EX13C-2.2

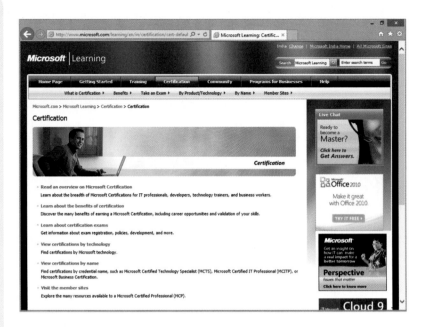

Preparing for a MOS Exam

Every Microsoft Office Specialist certification exam is developed from a list of objectives based on how Microsoft Office programs are actually used in the workplace. The list of objectives determine the scope of each exam, so they provide you with the information you need to prepare for MOS certification. Microsoft Office Specialist Approved Courseware, including the On Demand series, is reviewed and approved on the basis of its coverage of the objectives. To prepare for the certification exam, you should review and perform each task identified with a MOS objective to confirm that you can meet the requirements for the exam.

Taking a MOS Exam

The Microsoft Office Specialist certification exams are not written exams. Instead, the exams are performance-based examinations that allow you to interact with a "live"

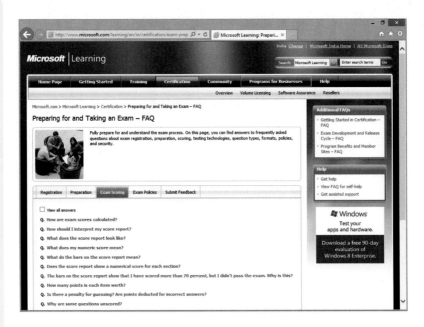

Office program as you complete a series of objective-based tasks. All the standard ribbons, tabs, toolbars, and keyboard shortcuts are available during the exam. Microsoft Office Specialist exams for Office 2013 programs consist of 25 to 35 questions, each of which requires you to complete one or more tasks using the Office program for which you are seeking certification. A typical exam takes from 45 to 60 minutes. Passing percentages range from 70 to 80 percent correct.

The Exam Experience

After you fill out a series of information screens, the testing software starts the exam and the Office program. The test questions appear in the exam dialog box in the lower right corner of the screen.

◆ The timer starts when the first question appears and displays the remaining exam time at the top of the exam dialog box. If the timer and the counter are distracting, you can click the timer to remove the display.

◆ The counter at the top of the exam dialog box tracks how many questions you have completed and how many remain.

◆ If you think you have made a mistake, you can click the Reset button to restart the question. The Reset button does not restart the entire exam or extend the exam time limit.

◆ When you complete a question, click the Next button to move to the next question. It is not possible to move back to a previous question on the exam.

◆ If the exam dialog box gets in your way, you can click the Minimize button in the upper right corner of the exam dialog box to hide it, or you can drag the title bar to another part of the screen to move it.

Tips for Taking an Exam

◆ Carefully read and follow all instructions provided in each question.

◆ Make sure all steps in a task are completed before proceeding to the next exam question.

◆ Enter requested information as it appears in the instructions without formatting unless you are explicitly requested otherwise.

- Close all dialog boxes before proceeding to the next exam question unless you are specifically instructed otherwise.

- Do not leave tables, boxes, or cells "active" unless instructed otherwise.

- Do not cut and paste information from the exam interface into the program.

- When you print a document from an Office program during the exam, nothing actually gets printed.

- Errant keystrokes or mouse clicks do not count against your score as long as you achieve the correct end result. You are scored based on the end result, not the method you use to achieve it. However, if a specific method is explicitly requested, you need to use it to get credit for the results.

- The overall exam is timed, so taking too long on individual questions may leave you without enough time to complete the entire exam.

- If you experience computer problems during the exam, immediately notify a testing center administrator to restart your exam where you were interrupted.

Exam Results

At the end of the exam, a score report appears indicating whether you passed or failed the exam. An official certificate is mailed to successful candidates in approximately two to three weeks.

Getting More Information

To learn more about the Microsoft Office Specialist program, read a list of frequently asked questions, and locate the nearest testing center, visit:

www.microsoft.com

For a more detailed list of Microsoft Office Specialist program objectives, visit:

www.perspection.com

Index

ruler units, setting, 450
Run dialog box in safe mode, 393

S

Safe for Initialization (SFI) controls, 386
safe modes
  automated safe mode, 392-393
  enabling, 392
  user-initiated safe mode, 392-393
saturation of color, defined, 165
Save as type
  list, 410
  macros, saving, 478
Save button, 22
Save dialog box, 22-23
saving. *See also* workbooks; XML
      (Extensible Markup Language)
  SharePoint, workbooks to, 490-491
  SkyDrive, workbooks to, 490-491
  in HTML (Hypertext Markup Language),
      428
  older version workbooks, 23
  PDF documents, workbooks as, 191
  setting options, 23
  shapes as pictures, 202
  Web queries, 439
Scale to Fit Dialog Box Launcher, 187
scaling
  paper sizes, 451
  pictures, 206-207
  print scaling, changing, 178-179
scenarios
  creating, 344
  showing, 345
  summaries, creating, 345
scientific format, 43
scope, names for, 88
Screen shot, inserting, 200
ScreenTips
  for add-in security options, 385
  for dialog box options, 8
  for functions, 450
  for hyperlinks, 431
  for macros, 477
  style, selecting, 442
  for themes, 163
  turning on/off, 6

scroll bars
  for ActiveX controls, 482
  showing, 448
  synchronizing scrolling of documents, 19
searching. *See also* clip art; finding and
      replacing
  for cell values, 129
  conditional formatting, cells with, 149
  for help, 21
  tables, custom searches of, 315
  for themes, 162
security, 365. *See also* digital signatures;
      passwords; Trust Center
  ActiveX controls security settings, 386
  add-in security options, 385, 465
  App Catalog security settings, 384
  for cell styles, 173
  data connections, security settings for,
      390
  external content security options,
      390-391
  for external data, 414
  file encryption, adding, 371
  formulas, showing/hiding, 370
  harmful attacks, avoiding, 378-379
  locking/unlocking cells, 370
  of macros, 368, 387
  Message Bar security options, changing,
      388
  safe modes, 392-393
  for shared workbooks, 401
  XML data maps, 424
Select All button, 159
selecting
  borders, 159
  cells, 37
  columns and rows, 38, 122
  contiguous cells, 37
  hyperlinks, 431
  multisheet ranges, 39
  noncontiguous cells, 37
  ranges, 39
  special ranges, 39
  tables, columns and rows in, 308
  worksheets, 116
Selection Mode Status bar, 9
Selection pane for objects, 259
Send to Back

31901051906123